Teaching for Doctrin

Tradition i. ___ ___ Mormonism

Robert Smith

Table of Contents

Preface

I can't think of anything I'd want to do less than write this book. The idea first came into my mind as a result of a conversation I had with a family member. I was making a poor attempt at summarizing dozens of hours of research on a gospel subject, trying to persuade him to arrive at the same conclusion I had come to. He said to me, in effect, "You can't just refer me to books I will never read. I don't have time to study these things just because you say I should." In that conversation and in subsequent others, I realized that people's beliefs are not some simply binary switch, but a complex, multi-layered web, a mixture of facts, faded recollections, and highly charged emotions. Injecting new evidence—particularly conflicting evidence—into this web is like knocking a perfectly balanced, fast rotating drum. It's really going to mess things up. It is not a light thing to wrestle with well-established belief systems. My relative was right, I could not expect people to consider significant changes to their belief systems without an exceptionally well crafted and succinct argument. Such an argument is very difficult to achieve in conversation. A book would be required both for the length of the content and also the degree of organization needed. I knew from the onset that I would need to revisit years of notes from gospel study—originally written for myself—to add the missing detail necessary for others. I knew I would have to reread a shelf worth of books and spend countless days googling topics that I hadn't taken complete notes on. I knew I would need to spend significant efforts developing my ability to phrase things in a way that would allow honest evaluation without outright dismissal, tactfully dodging emotive landmines to permit rational thought to occur in a sea of trained predisposition.

I was and am completely inadequate to the task of writing this book. I was and am as equipped to write this book as I would be to design and build a rocket capable of reaching the moon. When the dual realization that this book was both necessary and as yet unwritten occurred to me, I half-heartedly began the effort, hoping that someone else was working on a similar volume and would publish it before I accomplished any significant writing. As desperately as I wished someone else would do it, no one did.

I began writing without any idea what these pages would contain or how they would be structured. Signs followed that convinced me that this work was commissioned by heaven. That being said, I am very well aware of my own deficiencies, and am positive that these have translated into more than a few typos, grammatical mistakes, and perhaps even a few inadvertent inaccuracies. I claim full credit for these. Notwithstanding, there is no doubt in my mind that the Lord wanted me to write this book, and that those to whom it is directed will be held accountable for what it contains. As this book came together, I pled with the Lord to spare me from having to publish it. I was shown what the outcome would be, and at the time it was a bitter cup for me to drink. I questioned whether it was worth it, when I did not expect any sizeable number of people to come closer to him as a result of reading it. He told me plainly that the purpose of this book was not to convert, although great pains had to be taken to make it suitable for that purpose. Instead, it was to lay the case out so plainly as to leave those to whom it is directed without excuse when the judgments he has foretold occur.

My simple desire is that it may be pleasing to God.

Introduction

I have learned that there are only ever two things that are worth preaching over. The first and greatest is to turn to God. This is commonly called repentance, as in "preach nothing but repentance unto the people." Unfortunately, repentance has often been reduced to convincing individuals to commit or abstain from a list of things. This is wresting of the principle in more ways than can briefly be summarized, and for the sake of the length of the book, I will refrain from elaborating. The second topic worth preaching about is the tearing down of false traditions that prevent people from turning to God. Just as the second great commandment is the way we live the first great commandment (as we love God through loving our neighbor), most are prevented from turning to God through a misunderstanding of what God is like (and what he is not like), what he is saying (and what he is not saying), and what his will is for us (and what it is not). One can only repent to the degree that they are free from false traditions. Therefore, one cannot preach repentance without preaching against false traditions.

Helping others see and overcome false traditions has been the task of messengers of God from the beginning of time. Joseph Smith taught that "to become a joint heir of the heirship of the Son, one must put away all his false traditions." (TPJS, p 321.) Jesus himself spent the majority of his ministry doing just that. Truth is a plant that doesn't compete well with the weeds of false tradition. We are told in the Book of Mormon that one cannot come to a knowledge of the truth without the prerequisite removal of false traditions:

> And behold, ye do know of yourselves, for ye have witnessed it, that as many of them as are brought to the knowledge of the truth, and to know of the wicked and abominable traditions of their fathers, and are led to believe the holy scriptures, yea, the prophecies of the holy prophets, which are written, which leadeth them to faith on the Lord, and unto repentance, which faith and repentance bringeth a change of heart unto them-- (Helaman 15:5-7.)

Questioning traditions is exceedingly taboo in Modern Mormonism. It generates an immediate emotive reaction that prevents us from achieving many facets of spiritual growth. Self-judgment is the key to finding greater light and truth. It is the key to seeing our sins in scriptural warnings.

The task of identifying false traditions has been taken up by prophets throughout history. Ezekiel was charged,

> Wilt thou judge them, son of man, wilt thou judge them? cause them to know the abominations of their fathers: (Ezekiel 20:4.)

God made clear that the purpose of pointing out false tradition was always to obtain the closer relationship with God that comes through repentance:

> "Now let them put away their whoredom, and the carcases of their kings, far from me, and I will dwell in the midst of them for ever. (Ezekiel 43:9.)

Conversely, remaining in false tradition causes the loss of light and truth:

> And that wicked one cometh and taketh away light and truth, through disobedience, from the children of men, and because of the tradition of their fathers. (D&C 93:39.)

False tradition is introduced when a people gradually becoming less in tune with God than their predecessors through disobedience and/or sloth. Eventually, all that remains of their chosen status are memories of the fruits of closeness to God that are no longer apparent. Through time, God's continuous living word is replaced by static recordings of past revelations. What God is saying is replaced by what God has said. At this key time, sometimes well-meaning individuals misinterpret, modify, or replace his sayings, all the while in an environment that, witnessed by the lack of continuous revelation, is devoid of the spirit making it difficult to discern the unauthorized changes. This is how false tradition and commandments of men are born.

Tradition is sclerotic. Tradition has a way of being promoted to something more than it is; it becomes calcified and entrenched into the culture. When it hardens in our cultural/collective memory, it becomes something more than it was originally intended. Tradition almost always becomes policy, and policies almost always become commandments.

> Sometimes traditions, customs, social practices, and personal preferences of individual Church members may, through repeated or common usage be misconstrued as Church procedures or policies. Occasionally, such traditions, customs and practices may even be regarded by some as eternal principles. (Elder Ronald Poelman, 1984 General Conference.)

In the church today, we are seeing the result of over 150 years of tradition creation. Increasingly—particularly among the tech-aware youth of the church—traditions are uncovered as false. The outcome is predictable. As B.H. Roberts sagely predicted long ago, the youth throw out both church tradition and gospel truth (having associated them as one) as soon as cracks in the traditional narrative appear:

> Suppose your youth receive their impressions of church history from "pictures and stories" and build their faith upon these alleged miracles [and] shall someday come face to face with the fact that their belief rests on falsehoods, what then will be the result? Will they not say that since these things are myth and our Church has permitted them to be perpetuated…might not the other fundamentals to the actual story of the Church, the things in which it had its origin, might they not all be lies and nothing but lies? … [Some say that] because one repudiates the false he stands in danger of weakening, perhaps losing the truth. I have no fear of such results. I find my own heart strengthened in the truth by getting rid of the untruth, the spectacular, the bizarre, as soon as I learn that it is based upon worthless testimony. (Defender of the Faith: The B. H. Roberts Story, p. 363.)

As Elder Roberts explained, avoiding this outcome requires a willingness to search out and let go of false traditions while holding fast to what withstands investigation.

The words of God through Isaiah describe what happens when traditions overcome revealed religion:

> But my Lord says, Because these people approach me with the mouth and pay me homage with their lips, while their heart remains far from me—their piety toward me consisting of commandments of men learned by rote—therefore it is that I shall again astound these people with wonder upon wonder, rendering void the knowledge of their sages and the intelligence of their wise men insignificant….What a contradiction you are! (Isaiah 29:13-14, 16, Gileadi Translation.)

My hope is that, in some small way, this book can be one of the wonders of the Lord that renders void the supposed knowledge of the self-proclaimed sage and wise among us. They truly are a contradiction who, as the Pharisees of old, pay great homage to God with their lips, while their hearts are far from him. Though they are blinded to this fact by their acts of devotion to God, as they suppose, they are equally blind to the fact that their lives and works are an abomination before God.

Searching for Further Knowledge

The scriptures are replete with commandments to search out new truth. There is a finite amount of knowledge that is required before an individual can conquer the sins of this world. Joseph said, "Knowledge saves a man; and in the world of spirits no man can be exalted but by knowledge." (Joseph Smith, TPJS, p. 357.) If we have not yet come back into God's presence, it is because we have not yet attained this saving portion of knowledge.

Evaluation of candidate truth is neither easy nor fast. Mormon said, "Search diligently in the light of Christ that ye may know good from evil" (Moroni 7:19). It is not a passive activity.

Obtain Evidence for What You Believe

Peter taught that we should "be ready always to give an answer to every man that asketh you a reason of the hope that is in you with meekness and fear." (1 Peter 3:15) "A reason" implies that there are true facts behind a given belief. Embracing a belief simply because someone else (a friend, family member, or church leader) maintains that belief is often not compelling enough to convert others or to maintain your own adherence during trials.[1] We should not believe something just because we were told it by our parents. Nor should we assume that something is true if it is repeated enough.[2] Those

---

[1] It is unwise to believe something just because someone else believes it. "It seems frequently to be the case that the cohesiveness that promotes survival is fostered just as effectively by shared belief systems...whether those beliefs be true or not....You can fool yourself if you want, and you can fool as many as will follow for as long as you can get away with it. But you can't fool reality. If your design is wrong, your plane won't fly." (James Hogan, "Kicking the Sacred Cow", p9) You can say that a church is led by God, but that won't make him speak to it. You can say that a church is true, but that won't correct falsehoods proclaimed by it. You can say your active status in a church means your calling and election is made sure, but that won't open God's presence to you. The fruits prove the claims. Without fruits, the claims are necessarily false.

[2] "Future shock occurs when you are confronted by the fact that the world you were educated to believe in doesn't exist. Your images of reality are apparitions that disappear on contact. There are several ways of responding to such a condition, one of which is to withdraw and allow oneself to be overcome by a sense of impotence.

who are off the strait and narrow path far outnumber those who are on it. Truth always stands in the minority, and therefore will always be the exception to what is heard most often.

Instead, we should seek to follow the advice of men of God in the scriptures, who have invited us to "try the spirits." "Trying the spirits" is an antiquated way to refer to an active search for truth. Salvation is not a passive activity. One must be anxiously engaged in discerning between truth and error if there is to be any hope for salvation.[3]

We have no right to feel strongly about something for which we can not provide either charismatic or rational evidence. Feelings are insufficient. Emotion is not revelation. Instead, emotions tend to mirror prior held beliefs. When prior held beliefs are reinforced, the believer feels good. When prior held beliefs are contradicted, the believer feels bad (this is called cognitive dissonance). When truth evaluation is reduced to feelings, it becomes impossible to persuade, no matter how certain and clear the facts. Instead of debating the correctness or incorrectness of doctrine, which can be established through scriptural, rational, and historical investigation, one must defend against the feelings comments caused to those with status quo beliefs, whether or not those beliefs are true. The doctrine itself ceases to be the focus. Instead, the feelings of the believer become the focus. (See "Revelation.") The natural man is an enemy to God; finding truth requires us to yield our emotive response—which is carnal—to the voice of the Holy Ghost.

More commonly, one continues to act as if his apparitions were substantial, relentlessly pursuing a course of action that he knows will fail him. You may have noticed that there are scores of political, social and religious leaders who are clearly suffering from advanced cases of future shock. They repeat over and over again the words that are supposed to represent the world about them. But nothing seems to work out. And then they repeat the words again and again." (Postman and Weingartner, "Teaching as a Subversive Activity", p. 26) Elder Andersen and Elder Packer have both taught that repetition is a valid method of learning truth. For example, "This is Joseph's own testimony of what actually occurred. Read it often. Consider recording the testimony of Joseph Smith in your own voice, listening to it regularly, and sharing it with friends. Listening to the Prophet's testimony in your own voice will help bring the witness you seek." (Elder Neil Andersen, "Joseph Smith," Oct 2014 General Conference)

[3] In recent years, information available online has caused challenges to the official narrative. In response, leaders of the church have encouraged church members to "doubt their doubts," or refrain from a diligent analysis of the traditions they hold in light of this new and sometimes contradictory information (see Dieter F. Uchtdorf, "Come, Join with Us," October 2013 General Conference.) This attitude assures that the individual will never draw closer to Christ, which requires the acquisition of further light and truth.

We search in order to find two kinds of evidence: charismatic evidence and rational evidence. Charismatic evidence consists of experiences we have had that support a principle. In this category, we could place Paul's witness of Christ: He saw; therefore, he knew. We could place Joseph of Egypt's dream of the 14 years of plenty and famine in this category. In fact, the scriptures are full of visitations, visions, dreams, and voices that all serve as charismatic evidence for a particular idea. We should exercise extreme caution in considering emotional experiences as charismatic evidence.[4]

Rational evidence is a historical, scriptural, or logical argument that supports or contradicts a given principle. Rational evidence can be evaluated absent of experience. Rational evidence is a powerful tool for disproving principles, since only one counterexample is needed to disprove something. But it has another more important use. Charismatic experience is how we gain unshakeable testimonies of truth. However, charismatic experiences come largely as the result of experimenting on God's word. When one has no logical, scriptural, or historical reason to believe on a proffered principle, they will not have enough faith to experiment on it. Rational evidence provides a bridge between where we stand and where we need to stand in order to receive a charismatic witness.

We are testing the word when we refrain from considering a teaching true until the Lord proves it to us through a charismatic experience. Asking questions and doubting are essential to provide the real intent necessary to learn new truth through study and revelation. Since one cannot have faith in a false principle, the evaluation of potential truth is a task of utmost importance to those of faith, for the attempted exercise of faith in false principles will perpetuate ignorance, stall progression, and further delay a first-hand experience with God.

Seeking Truth Requires Considering Other Views

If one assumes that they lack knowledge, the next step is to seek it. If we want to learn more than we know, we will have to investigate points of view that don't belong to us already. We ought not fear reading or hearing information that doesn't agree with what we believe.

Fear of searching was not present historically. Consider the following:

> If we have the truth, it cannot be harmed by investigation. If we have not the truth, it ought to be harmed. (President J. Reuben Clark)

> Convince us of our errors of Doctrine, if we have any, by reason, by logical arguments, or by the Word of God and we will ever be

---

[4] Emotions are taught in modern Mormonism to be a vehicle for the Holy Ghost, when the scriptures negate instead of support the claim. See "Revelation."

grateful for the information and you will ever have the pleasing reflections that you have been instruments in the hands of God of redeeming your fellow beings. (Orson Pratt, "The Seer," p. 15.)

[t]he man who cannot listen to an argument which opposes his views either has a weak position or is a weak defender of it. No opinion that cannot stand discussion or criticism is worth holding. And it has been wisely said that the man who knows only half of any question is worse off than the man who knows nothing of it. He is not only one-sided but his partisanship soon turns him into an intolerant and a fanatic. In general it is true that nothing which cannot stand up under discussion or criticism is worth defending. (James E. Talmage Improvement Era, Jan 1920, p. 204)

If a faith will not bear to be investigated; if its preachers and professors are afraid to have it examined, their foundation must be very weak. (President George A. Smith)

I think a full, free talk is frequently of great use; we want nothing secret nor underhanded, and I for one want no association with things that cannot be talked about and will not bear investigation. (Journal of Discourses, 20:264)

I admire men and women who have developed the questioning spirit, who are unafraid of new ideas and stepping stones to progress. We should, of course, respect the opinions of others, but we should also be unafraid to dissent - if we are informed. Thoughts and expressions compete in the marketplace of thought, and in that competition truth emerges triumphant. Only error fears freedom of expression. This free exchange of ideas is not to be deplored as long as men and women remain humble and teachable. Neither fear of consequence nor any kind of coercion should ever be used to secure uniformity of thought in the church. People should express their problems and opinions and be unafraid to think without fear of ill consequences. We must preserve freedom of the mind in the church and resist all efforts to suppress it. (Hugh B. Brown, counselor in First Presidency, Speech at BYU, March 29, 1958.)

As you accept the responsibility to seek after truth with an open mind and a humble heart, you will become more tolerant of others, more open to listen, more prepared to understand, (Dieter F. Uchtdorf, https://www.lds.org/broadcasts/article/ces-devotionals/2013/01/what-is-truth)

Many have noted the strong tendency of Latter-day Saints to avoid making waves. They seem strangely touchy on controversial issues.

This begets an extreme lack of candor among the Saints, which in turn is supported by a new doctrine, according to which we have a Prophet at our head who relieves us of all responsibility for seeking knowledge beyond a certain point, making decisions, or taking action on our own. (Hugh Nibley, Temples of the Ancient World, p. 610)

...while I believe all that God has revealed, I am not quite sure that I understand what he has revealed, and the fact that he has promised further revelation is to me a challenge to keep an open mind and be prepared to follow wherever my search for truth may lead....We have been blessed with much knowledge by revelation from God which, in some part, the world lacks. But there is an incomprehensibly greater part of truth which we must yet discover. Our revealed truth should leave us stricken with the knowledge of how little we really know. It should never lead to an emotional arrogance based upon a false assumption that we somehow have all the answers--that we in fact have a corner on truth....Preserve...the freedom of your mind in education and in religion, and be unafraid to express your thoughts and to insist upon your right to examine every proposition. We are not so much concerned with whether your thoughts are orthodox or heterodox as we are that you shall have thoughts. (Hugh B. Brown, BYU May 13, 1969 address, "An Eternal Quest: Freedom of the Mind.")

Despite the historical record of church leaders advocating exactly that, we find ourselves in a paradigm that challenges us to not only avoid consideration of opposing positions, but to avoid even the idea of rational evaluation of our own position.[5]

Searching for truth requires a willingness to investigate both sides of a position as objectively as possible. If you are merely arguing for your position, you cannot honestly say you are searching for truth. You do not know all things, and therefore you cannot ever be totally sure that you are right. If you aren't willing to be wrong about something, you can only go so far in your search for truth.

There ought not be any fear of losing what you already have—a rational mind will only replace a previous position with a more solid position. An open mind and a desire to know truth will only ever lead a person closer to God.

Knowledge of opposing views is absolutely necessary both in order to convince one supporting that view of your own contrary view, and also in

---

[5] Such a comment is deserving of proof; Yet, the case is significant enough that it cannot be treated here. Evidence supporting this position is provided in later chapters in context of specific topics.

order for you to hold a rational position. Knowing the alternative point of view is necessary to be able to persuade others and to reaffirm one's position. Without knowing the contrary view, how can you have any confidence that your position is right? Why would anyone ever consider your position persuasive without your being able to frame it as rational in context of what they know? It would be like arguing that one variety of apple is the tastiest while admitting you've never tried another variety. Anyone who has tried more than one variety would consider it folly to listen to anything you had to say on the matter. Merely knowing that your counterpart holds an opposing view is not sufficient to be able to persuade them. Rather, you must know *why* they hold that opposing view. Once you know why, you can construct a persuasive argument that shows your position to be more rational by removing the perceived benefit in their position and convincing them of the benefit of yours.

Remember, though, that rational evaluation is a two-edged sword. Just as you could possess evidences of your position that your counterpart had never considered, so could they. You could very well end up supporting their position should their evidence prove stronger than yours. Yet, such a situation is to be desired, not feared, for those in possession of greater truth have drawn closer to God.

Fear of finding new truth is simply not well founded. As a camera focuses, the image becomes more clear. Although the view certainly changes, the progress is always a refinement. A focused camera picture represents only information gain, not loss. Perhaps this is why Nephi said,

> I know that the words of truth are hard against all uncleanness; but the righteous fear them not, for they love the truth and are not shaken. (2 Nephi 9:40.)

Nephi himself was no stranger to uncomfortable new truth. His life was a constant barrage of paradigm shifts. These showed him that he could always confide in God, even if it meant abandoning things he previously thought were true, or blazing paths unfamiliar to his culture and heritage.

You Don't Know Everything

In context of what is at stake, it becomes evident just how important it is to always welcome new truth. Nephi warned that in our day many would not be interested in more truth.

> Yea, wo be unto him that saith: We have received, and we need no more! And in fine, wo unto all those who tremble, and are angry because of the truth of God! For behold, he that is built upon the rock receiveth it with gladness; and he that is built upon a sandy foundation trembleth lest he shall fall. Wo be unto him that shall say: We have received the word of God, and we need no more of the

11

word of God, for we have enough! For behold, thus saith the Lord God: I will give unto the children of men line upon line, precept upon precept, here a little and there a little; and blessed are those who hearken unto my precepts, and lend an ear unto my counsel, for they shall learn wisdom; for unto him that receiveth I will give more; and from them that shall say, We have enough, from them shall be taken away even that which they have. (2 Nephi 28:27-30.)

We are told that those who adopt this position will not be given any additional truth, and thus will never reach the point where they can come back into God's presence. The attitude of satisfaction is damning. One way of wording this is that those who consider themselves wise will never accept new truth. Nephi's declaration of the same is frequently used as a caution to those who study the gospel more than the usual cursory amount:

And whoso knocketh, to him will he open; and the wise, and the learned, and they that are rich, who are puffed up because of their learning, and their wisdom, and their riches—yea, they are they whom he despiseth; and save they shall cast these things away, and consider themselves fools before God, and come down in the depths of humility, he will not open unto them. (2 Nephi 9:42.)

However, a careful reading will show that Nephi is not blasting the same acquisition of real knowledge he advocates for throughout his writings. Instead, he is condemning the feeling of supposing you know all there is to know. In fact, in order to consider yourself a fool before God, and yet relentlessly seek and obtain further light and truth from him, you must adopt the difficult position of at once being perceptive and faithful enough to act on everything you have been taught thus far while also being ready at a moments notice to cast it aside in favor of greater light and truth.

Joseph stated that when individuals assume that their preconceived notions about the gospel encompass all there is to know, they will be sorely disappointed:

It is the constitutional disposition of mankind to set up stakes and set bounds to the works and ways of the Almighty. But I will give you a more painful thought. Suppose you have an idea of a resurrection, etc., and yet know nothing at all of the Gospel, nor comprehend one principle of the order of heaven, but find yourselves disappointed—yes, at last find yourselves disappointed in every hope or anticipation, when the decision goes forth from the lips of the Almighty. Would not this be a greater disappointment—a more painful thought than annihilation....Why be so certain that you comprehend the things of God, when all things with you are so uncertain. (TPJS, p. 229-230.)

While spiritual stagnation is comfortable, it is also damning. It is easy and comfortable to live your religion when you assume that it will always be the same: your spiritual practices will never change, nor will the requirements of salvation. However, every saved person in the scriptures—every person with whom God made covenant—was constantly subjected to principles that were beyond their previous comprehension despite their righteous lives. Abraham was asked to sacrifice Isaac, Moses was astounded by things he had never before supposed, etc. This is because we are not like God. The glory we possess is associated with the law pertaining to that glory. In order to ascend to a higher degree of glory, we will always need to embrace a set of laws that we are ignorant of. If you live the law you know perfectly, and have not been brought back into God's presence, the law you currently know does not possess the power to bring you back into God's presence as did the law that Moses, Abraham, Isaac, Jacob, Adam, Joseph Smith, and all other saved men.[6]   Therefore, coming up to a celestial glory will require letting go of things you currently hold as true. You cannot close yourself to ideas you perceive as contradictory to what you currently believe and simultaneously let in further light and truth. God can only teach us a

> portion of his word…according to the heed and diligence which they give unto him. And therefore, he that will harden his heart, the same receiveth the lesser portion of the word; and he that will not harden his heart, to him is given the greater portion of the word, until it is given unto him to know the mysteries of God until he know them in full. And they that will harden their hearts, to them is given the lesser portion of the word until they know nothing concerning his mysteries; and then they are taken captive by the devil, and led by his will down to destruction. Now this is what is meant by the chains of hell. (Alma 12:9-11.)

Not even Jesus himself possessed all there was to know in the beginning.

> And he received not of the fulness at first, but continued from grace to grace, until he received a fulness; And thus he was called the Son of God, because he received not of the fulness at the first. (D&C 93:13-14).

Those that believe that they already know all the doctrines necessary to be saved presume they know more that Jesus did, as he had to progress from one teaching to the next. They presume that, while Enoch and his city

---

[6] Gospel knowledge is not just additive; it also is progressive (meaning you will replace things you currently think you know with things that are more true). Consider the Sermon on the Mount.

required hundreds of years to become Zion, they can do it with what little we have handed to us through Joseph Smith. Enoch was in heaven with God for generations, yet still learned new fundamental truths about God's character.[7] Frankly, no one knows everything there is to know. As the Lord said,

> For my thoughts are not your thoughts, neither are your ways my ways, saith the Lord. For as the heavens are higher than the earth, so are my ways higher than your ways, and my thoughts than your thoughts. (Isaiah 55:8-9.)

If Jesus, Enoch, and others still had a lot to learn, we should be very cautious in our assertions of what we "know" to be true. Otherwise, we fall into the category of those who think they are wise, which incidentally means precisely that we do not hearken to God:

> O that cunning plan of the evil one! O the vainness, and the frailties, and the foolishness of men! When they are learned they think they are wise, and they hearken not unto the counsel of God, for they set it aside, supposing that they know of themselves, wherefore, their wisdom is foolishness and it profiteth them not. And they shall perish. (2 Nephi 9:28.)

It may seem difficult to imagine that thinking you know something and failing to hearken to God are the same. Yet, Jacob equates it to being deaf (2 Nephi 9:31) and blind (2 Nephi 9:32), probably because God continues to reveal new things to everyone as long as they continue to listen to him. Therefore, if you become set in your idea of the truth, you could only have done so by ignoring what God is continuing to say to you. Living revelation means constant revelation. We should expect to frequently displace our current understanding with something better. You should not assume something is false simply because you have never heard it before. Anyone who does not believe they know everything ought to expect to hear something that they've never heard before, or something that contradicts what they have been told previously.

Situations that fail to find a solution in orthodoxy are fertile ground for receiving revelation. Postman and Weingartner wrote,

---

[7] "And after that Zion was taken up into heaven, Enoch beheld, and lo, all the nations of the earth were before him....And there came generation upon generation; and Enoch was high and lifted up, even in the bosom of the Father, and of the Son of Man....And it came to pass that the God of heaven looked upon the residue of the people, and he wept; and Enoch bore record of it, saying: How is it that the heavens weep, and shed forth their tears as the rain upon the mountains? And Enoch said unto the Lord: How is it that thou canst weep, seeing thou art holy, and from all eternity to all eternity?" (Moses 7:23-24, 28)

We are unlikely to alter our perceptions until and unless we are frustrated in our attempts to do something based on them. If our actions seem to permit us to fulfil our purposes, we will not change our perceptions no matter how often we are told that they are 'wrong'. (Postman and Weingartner, "Teaching as a Subversive Activity", p. 93.)

As long as we are satisfied by our current understanding of what is true, we never really have a reason to marshal real intent, a necessary prerequisite to receiving revelation. President Uchtdorf said, "How often has the Holy Spirit tried to tell us something we needed to know but couldn't get past the massive iron gate of what we thought we already knew?"[8]

Jesus taught we should be like children.[9] Children are inquisitive. They never stop wondering and testing. They are never satisfied.

Abraham found himself unsatisfied in the orthodoxy of his time. He somehow noticed that there were greater blessings available to him than the theology of his father offered him.

> In the land of the Chaldeans, at the residence of my fathers, I, Abraham, saw that it was needful for me to obtain another place of residence; And, finding there was greater happiness and peace and rest for me, I sought for the blessings of the fathers, and the right whereunto I should be ordained to administer the same; having been myself a follower of righteousness, desiring also to be one who possessed great knowledge, and to be a greater follower of righteousness, and to possess a greater knowledge, and to be a father of many nations, a prince of peace, and desiring to receive instructions, and to keep the commandments of God, I became a rightful heir, a High Priest, holding the right belonging to the fathers. (Abraham 1:1-2.)

Abraham clearly had heard stories that described religious experiences far exceeding those he observed in the religion of his father. Thus, he believed that there had to be a better system available than what he had experienced.[10]

---

[8] Dieter F. Uchtdorf, "Acting on the Truths of the Gospel of Jesus Christ," Worldwide Leadership Training, 2/11/12

[9] "And again I say unto you, ye must repent, and become as a little child, and be baptized in my name, or ye can in nowise receive these things. And again I say unto you, ye must repent, and be baptized in my name, and become as a little child, or ye can in nowise inherit the kingdom of God." (3 Nephi 11:37-38)

[10] For a similar experiment, read JST Genesis 14. Does this describe the priesthood you possess? If not, what does that imply?

A Willingness to be Wrong

Nephi's example underscores the importance of accepting the possibility that your understanding of what God wants is wrong. Nephi demonstrated this humility when he was willing to accept God's command to slay Laban despite it contradicting his understanding of God's commandments. He taught that we should not "set aside" God's counsel on account of our "supposing [we] know of [ourselves]." (2 Nephi 9:28.) In other words, we ought to be willing to be wrong, and willing to have God correct us.

The Lord does not despise those who acquire knowledge. He despises those who assume they know something despite their ignorance. He despises those who think they know more than God, and ignore what he tries to teach them, assuming they already know what he wants. Nephi states that the antidote to the poison of pride is to "hearken unto the counsels of God." (2 Nephi 9:29.)

In order to be recipients of new truth, we must be willing to be wrong. A proper response to an invitation from another to consider a different point of view should always be met with patient, unbiased consideration. Joseph displayed this attitude throughout his life, despite continuously accruing evidence that he knew more about God than anyone alive at the time.

Should you find yourself getting angry at such an invitation, it should serve as a signal that you have cut yourself off from the learning process, and have become one who thinks they are wise.

> And it came to pass as he began to expound these things unto them they were angry with him, and began to mock him; and they would not hear the words which he spake....And it came to pass that they saw that the people would harden their hearts, therefore they departed and came over into the land of Middoni. And they did preach the word unto many, and few believed on the words which they taught. (Alma 21:10,12.)

Anger is never a result of rational consideration of evidence. It causes God to withdraw the opportunity to learn more.

We are taught plainly that we are not even excused to become angry when the novel position we are invited to consider is that we are sinning:

> Behold ye say that I have agreed with a man that he should murder Seezoram, our chief judge. But behold, I say unto you, that this is because I have testified unto you that ye might know concerning this thing; yea, even for a witness unto you, that I did know of the wickedness and abominations which are among you. And because I have done this, ye say that I have agreed with a man that he should

do this thing; yea, because I showed unto you this sign ye are angry with me, and seek to destroy my life. (Helaman 9:23-24.)

This makes sense when you consider that the mission of prophets is to call men to repentance. Therefore, we ought not to take offense at supposed messengers when they come calling us to repentance. We ought to expect it. We ought to thank them for it, because their works are works of good. It is the response of the offended, and not the message of the preacher, that is wicked.

> For behold, at that day shall he rage in the hearts of the children of men, and stir them up to anger against that which is good. (2 Ne 28:20.)

Brigham Young was a particularly good example of the righteous reaction to a new candidate truth. He said he welcomed anyone who thought they could prove his beliefs incorrect:

> I will tell you who the real fanatics are: they are they who adopt false principles and ideas as facts, and try to establish a superstructure upon a false foundation...If our religion is of this character we want to know it; we would like to find a philosopher who can prove it to us. (Brigham Young, JD 13:270.)

He was not alone. It seemed early Mormons had studied both their own positions and the alternatives enough to be confident in their choice to the point of not fearing opposing argument:

> ...convince us of our errors of doctrine, if we have any, by reason, by logical arguments, or by the Word of God, and we will be ever grateful for the information, and you will ever have the pleasing reflection that you have been instruments in the hands of God of redeeming your fellow beings from the darkness which you may see enveloping their minds. (Apostle Orson Pratt, The Seer, pp. 15-16.)

This is perhaps not surprising, as all of the early brethren were converts to the restoration, and had to have at one point been willing to listen to opposing views in order to have accepted the gospel. In today's church, where almost half of members inherit the faith of their parents, this is not the case.

Avoiding Bias in Evaluation

For most, unbiased evaluation of opposing views is particularly difficult. No one wants to turn away from their life's work, or the legacy of their ancestors. What would that mean for the things you sacrificed to get there? It has to be true, or all that was for nothing. The loss isn't all philosophical, either. For example, suppose you were a General Authority.[11] Discovering truth that compromised your temple recommend status would mean not only great social stigma and familial troubles, but also a great financial loss.

In order to maintain objectivity, one must adopt an anthropological attitude.

> The [anthropological] perspective allows one to be part of his own culture and, at the same time, be out of it. One views the activities of his own group as would an anthropologist, observing its tribal rituals, its fears, its conceits, its ethnocentrism. In this way, one is able to recognize when reality begins to drift too far away from the grasp of the tribe. (Postman and Weingartner, "Teaching as a Subversive Activity", p. 17.)

The anthropological attitude helps one pause their cultural and experiential bias in evaluating new perspectives. The ability to unplug from the network of one's observations and conclusions is absolutely vital in order to logically consider alternative possibilities.

Once candidate truth has passed anthropological assessment, previously accumulated observations and conclusions must be folded back in to evaluate whether they still hold.

Falsifiability

Advancement in knowledge requires that one's position be falsifiable. Falsifiability is defined as "the logical possibility that an assertion could be shown false by a particular observation or physical experiment." (Karl Popper.) In other words, falsifiability means that your belief can be proven wrong. If no counter evidence could ever be sufficient to convince you that your position is wrong, your position is not falsifiable. A belief that is not falsifiable can never be abandoned, and thus an unfalsifiable position is always the last position you will ever hold on any given topic. This is, essentially, damnation, because you limit yourself to the glory associated with the current law you live.[12] You have drawn a line in the sand beyond which you are not willing to move, whether or not greater truth exists.

---

[11] General authorities are usually asked to give up lucrative employment to become full-time servants of the church. In return, at age 70 they are retired from church service and provided an income and health benefits for life—provided they maintain good standing in the church.

[12] Glory comes proportional to the degree of the law lived. Those who limit themselves to the law they currently understand cannot advance to higher states of glory. "And they who are not sanctified through the law which I have given unto you, even the law of Christ, must inherit another kingdom, even that of a terrestrial kingdom, or that of a telestial kingdom. For he who is not able to abide the law of a

Falsifiability highlights the danger in dogmatic assertions unattached from specific evidences. Suppose one says "the church is true." This is not a falsifiable statement. In order to make it falsifiable, one must define *what* "true" means and/or say *why* the church is true. Without a specification of what "the church is true" means, it is not falsifiable. Any attempt to assume a meaning (such as everything in the church is sanctioned by God) in order to provide a counterexample would result in the person saying, "but no one is saying that is what it means." Thus, a rational argument cannot take place. If someone says "the church is God's because he said so," that becomes a falsifiable statement. If someone wants to show this is false, they must simply present revelation where God said it was not his church at a later date than the statement cited by the believer. Another example lies in whether you believe the current church president is a prophet of God. Without define what a prophet is, whether he is or is not a prophet is impossible to prove.

A religion that cannot be proven false cannot be true. If you can think of no change in doctrine or policy that would cause you to conclude your religion is false, your religion cannot be true.

Truth Can Come from Anywhere

In the process of evaluating truth, candidate truth should never be dismissed out of hand. We dismiss candidate truth out of hand when we assume the church is the source of all truth, manifested by refusing to consider as true material not officially sanctioned by the church. Sometimes, we dismiss candidate truth out of hand through association with terms that generate an immediate emotive response. For example, when we associate material with "apostasy," do we immediately feel badly or set it aside? Supreme Court Justice Oliver Wendell Holmes said there were "phrases that serve as an excuse for not thinking." We must exercise caution and control our emotive responses. Vocabulary concepts can be a powerful means of thought control.[13]

---

celestial kingdom cannot abide a celestial glory. And he who cannot abide the law of a terrestrial kingdom cannot abide a terrestrial glory. And he who cannot abide the law of a telestial kingdom cannot abide a telestial glory; therefore he is not meet for a kingdom of glory. Therefore he must abide a kingdom which is not a kingdom of glory." (D&C 88:21-24.)

[13] The fictional book 1984 very accurately portrayed the power of vocabulary associations, a tactic used without exception in modern cults: "The purpose of Newspeak was not only to provide a medium of expression for the world-view and mental habits proper to the devotees of [the party], but to make all other modes of thought impossible." (George Orwell, 1984) In modern Mormonism, if a person has been labeled as an apostate, members struggle to believe that anything they say can be true, or that anything they do can be of God.

Dismissing a matter out of hand was specifically forbidden under the law of Moses. "Doth our law judge any man, before it hear him, and know what he doeth?" (John 7:51) How can one honestly evaluate whether a position is true without first hearing why someone holds it? "He that answereth a matter before he heareth it, it is folly and shame unto him." (Proverbs 18:13.)

The idea that truth can come from anywhere is not only true, but was once a founding principle of Mormonism. Joseph Smith wrote:

> Mormonism is truth; and every man who embraces it feels himself at liberty to embrace every truth: consequently the shackles of superstition, bigotry, ignorance, and priestcraft, fall at once from his neck; and his eyes are opened to see the truth, and truth greatly prevails over priestcraft....Mormonism is truth, in other words the doctrine of the Latter-day Saints, is truth....The first and fundamental principle of our holy religion is, that we believe that we have a right to embrace all, and every item of truth, without limitation or without being circumscribed or prohibited by the creeds or superstitious notions of men, or by the dominations of one another, when that truth is clearly demonstrated to our minds, and we have the highest degree of evidence of the same. (Letter from Joseph Smith to Isaac Galland, Mar. 22, 1839, Liberty Jail, Liberty, Missouri, published in Times and Seasons, Feb. 1840, pp. 53–54; spelling and grammar modernized.)

This principle endured at least into Brigham Young's administration. It was a frequent theme in his sermons:

> I want to say to my friends that we believe in all good. If you can find a truth in heaven, earth or hell, it belongs to our doctrine. We believe it; it is ours; we claim it. (Brigham Young, DBY, p. 2).

In Joseph's day, and for decades thereafter, it was well established that Mormonism was not the source of all truth, but a collection of men and women who sought all truth no matter where it came from. As time has passed, Mormons have shifted to assuming that the church is the source of all truth. One noted exception was Dr. Henry Eyring, the prominent scientist and father of President Henry B. Eyring. He took a position very consistent with Joseph Smith. He recognized that he was "obliged, as a Latter-day Saint, to believe whatever is true, regardless of the source." (Henry Eyring, "The Faith of a Scientist," Bookcraft 1969, p. 31) He took the position that the leaders of the church do not define what the church is. Rather, truth defines what the church is: "The Gospel is not the people in the Church. The Gospel is not even the people who direct it. The Gospel is the truth." (Henry Eyring, "The Faith of a Scientist," Bookcraft 1969, p. 23.)

The idea that all truth belongs *in* the church is much different from the idea that all truth comes *from* the church. In the former, members are expected to evaluate candidate truth from any source, including the need to evaluate what is said by their leaders. In the latter, members are expected to reject anything as false unless they hear it from their leaders while also assuming everything spoken by their leaders is true.

The former was taught by Joseph Smith and, after him, Brigham Young.

> Be willing to receive the truth, let it come from whom it may; no difference, not a particle. Just as soon receive the Gospel from Joseph Smith as from Peter, who lived in the days of Jesus. Receive it from one man as soon as another. If God has called an individual and sent him to preach the Gospel that is enough for me to know; it is no matter who it is, all I want is to know the truth (DBY, p. 11).

The latter is taught by modern Mormonism: [14]

> ...the Lord speaks to the church through the Prophet....no one can be appointed to an office without a vote of the church....no one is to receive revelation for the church except the prophet....no one is to preach or build up the church except he be regularly ordained by the head of the church.[15]

The belief that if it isn't preached in the church or it is contrary to something preached in the church, it is not true is false.[16] The idea of the church as the source of all truth seems to have been created by President Harold B. Lee as the foundational idea behind his correlation program—placing the entire church in a hierarchical form under the president of the

---

[14] As recently as 1978 there were General Authorities who did would not agree with the new doctrine: "...it is so important for us to learn all the truth we can from all the sources we can." (Elder N. Eldon Tanner, April 1978 General Conference.)

[15] Richard Turley, assistant church historian, in a joint sermon delivered with Elder Dallin H. Oaks June 17, 2105 in Boise, Idaho. Though Elder Oaks appealed to D&C 42 as support for this position, it is hard to believe any would be able to read D&C 42:11-13 in a way that would a) deny that those appointed by God directly would somehow not have God's authority to preach the gospel, or b) invalidate the authority of even one true prophet in scripture, let alone most, as nearly none of the true messengers in scripture were called by their church or recognized by them as legally appointed.

[16] We will avoid the obvious problem here of what exactly "the church" is. Who defines what the church's position is? The LDS Newsroom? A single member of the 15? The church president? As will be examined later in this book, the church states emphatically that none of these people have the authority to proclaim doctrine for the church. In essence, "the church" means the scriptures and signed proclamations from the combined 15 apostles. It is very rarely used in this sense, however.

church. In the church, the correlation committee have the exclusive right to define what is true and what isn't, and members need not seek anywhere but in correlation-approved materials for what is useful in one's return to Christ. This invisible group of academically-trained theologians decide what is taught in CES classes, what appears in the church manuals, and what is allowed to be said at conference. The proclaimed purpose of this committee is to ensure that doctrinal errors do not appear in church settings, yet their material is fraught with errors and egregious omissions. They are the source of what "the church" teaches. They define orthodoxy.

The Lord taught in D&C 121 that an appeal to authority to convince of truth is unrighteous dominion. A principle should not be considered true simply because it is endorsed by the church[17] or any individual or group within the church. Absent convincing arguments that withstand critical investigation, no principle ought to be accepted. Or, as the apostle John put it, "Dear friends, don't believe everyone who claims to have the Spirit of God. Test them all to find out if they really do come from God." (1 John 4:1-2, CEV.)

Orthodoxy is at odds with an open cannon. It cannot co-exist with the expectation that God will yet reveal great things to the church and that he will reveal things never before revealed to individuals. Progress towards God is marked by invitations to do things you had either never before considered (as Moses was) or things you thought were previously wrong (as Nephi was when he was told to kill Laban). God will consistently challenge your paradigms. Ironically, orthodoxy is used as the measuring stick for apostasy, when the idea of a closed cannon is itself apostate.

Orthodoxy is the antithesis of seeking truth from God[18]. The latter requires a constant search for new facts, new observations, and new theories. The former " tenaciously defend[s] beliefs in the face of what would appear to be verified fact and plain logic… doggedly closing eyes and minds to ideas whose time has surely come." (James Hogan, "Kicking the Sacred Cow", p8)

Joseph Smith not only preached to consider candidate truth from all sources—he also practiced it. One morning a man came into his house and introduced himself as Joshua. Joseph asked Joshua questions about his interesting ideas on religion. Despite obvious differences, he invited him to give them a lecture on his beliefs to assist him in his evaluation of what he was preaching. It was not until two days of his association that his doctrine was not correct. He did not dismiss Joshua out of hand. He listened and patiently evaluated his message.

---

[17] Which, incidentally, would at a minimum require a signed statement from the combined 15 apostles, and may even have to include a unanimous vote of acceptance from the body of the church, something not done for a long time.

[18] In Joseph's day, it was truth that determined orthodoxy. In correlated modern Mormonism, it is orthodoxy that determines what is true.

Unbelief

Refusing to believe something is true is a sin called unbelief. Prophets of the Book of Mormon taught that unbelief came because people dismissed out of hand candidate truth that contradicted the false traditions of their fathers:

> For behold, had the mighty works been shown unto them which have been shown unto you, yea, unto them who have dwindled in unbelief because of the traditions of their fathers, ye can see of yourselves that they never would again have dwindled in unbelief. (Helaman 15:15.)

In order to repent of unbelief, then, we have to be willing to consider that the traditions of our fathers, which we believe are correct, may be false.[19] We must be willing to objectively evaluate what we are told by others, even if it contradicts what we already believe. The only way God can help us overcome our false traditions is by sending true messengers that contradict them. When true messengers preach to us, it as first seems painfully contradictory to our false traditions.[20] But, if we heed Jesus' commandment to be like a child by considering the new doctrine, we will find that it makes more sense the longer we consider it.[21] The longer a true doctrine is studied, the more it makes sense. The more a false doctrine is studied, the more it crumbles.[22]

True Doctrine Bears Fruit

The Savior taught that true doctrine can be proven by the fruits it

---

[19] "The honest investigator must be prepared to follow wherever the search of truth may lead. Truth is often found in the most unexpected places. He must, with fearless and open mind 'insist that facts are far more important than any cherished, mistaken beliefs." (President Hugh B. Brown, Hugh B. Brown, General Conference October 1962.)

[20] Jesus' good works were offensive to his church leaders: "And, behold, they brought to him a man sick of the palsy, lying on a bed: and Jesus seeing their faith said unto the sick of the palsy; Son, be of good cheer; thy sins be forgiven thee. And, behold, certain of the scribes said within themselves, This man blasphemeth." (Matthew 9:2-3)

[21] "Now, we will compare the word unto a seed. Now, if ye give place, that a seed may be planted in your heart, behold, if it be a true seed, or a good seed, if ye do not cast it out by your unbelief, that ye will resist the Spirit of the Lord, behold, it will begin to swell within your breasts; and when you feel these swelling motions, ye will begin to say within yourselves—It must needs be that this is a good seed, or that the word is good, for it beginneth to enlarge my soul; yea, it beginneth to enlighten my understanding, yea, it beginneth to be delicious to me." (Alma 32:28.)

[22] False doctrines do not stand up to scripture, logic, or history. For example, Sherem taught both that man "cannot tell of things to come" and also that he knew that Christ would never come (Jacob 7:7,9).

produces.[23] He taught that it was both necessary and possible to prove candidate truth.

> If any man will do his will, he shall know of the doctrine, whether it be of God, or whether I speak of myself. (John 7:17.)

He taught that true doctrine taught by true messengers is always accompanied by signs.[24]

> And these signs shall follow them that believe—In my name they shall do many wonderful works; In my name they shall cast out devils; In my name they shall heal the sick; In my name they shall open the eyes of the blind, and unstop the ears of the deaf; And the tongue of the dumb shall speak; And if any man shall administer poison unto them it shall not hurt them; And the poison of a serpent shall not have power to harm them. (D&C 84:65-72.)

Despite this truth being presented in the D&C, the New Testament (Mark 16:17-18), the Book of Mormon (Mormon 9:24), and the temple endowment, modern leaders have taught that signs are not necessary to evidence true messengers:

> Show me Latter-day Saints who have to feed upon miracles, signs and visions in order to keep them steadfast in the Church, and I will show you members of the Church who are not in good standing before God, and who are walking in slippery paths. It is not by marvelous manifestations unto us that we shall be established in the truth, but it is by humility and faithful obedience to the commandments and laws of God. (Joseph F. Smith, Gospel Doctrine.)

By showing fruit that could only come through God's approbation, Jesus showed he was a true messenger:

> And Jesus knowing their thoughts said, Wherefore think ye evil in your hearts? For whether is easier, to say, Thy sins be forgiven thee; or to say, Arise, and walk? But that ye may know that the Son of man hath power on earth to forgive sins, (then saith he to the sick of the palsy,) Arise, take up thy bed, and go unto thine house. And he arose, and departed to his house. (Matthew 9:4-7.)

In attributing the fruits of examined doctrine, we need to be cognizant of common causes. Any member can cite a list of positive outcomes associated with a doctrinal point according to their understanding.

---

[23] "But wisdom is justified of all her children." (Luke 7:35.)
[24] This is also taught in the endowment, where true messengers present signs to prove that their message comes from God.

The idea is that someone can't challenge one of your beliefs if you have experienced blessings that you attribute to that belief. The weakness of this position is that it is possible that the blessings came from something else.

Blessings come due to the law they are predicated upon. However, isn't it possible that the blessings were predicated one some sub-piece of the commandment we believe in? For example, if I believed in paying 11% tithing, would I not receive the same blessings as you do for paying 10% tithing? Yet, my believe in 11% tithing being a commandment is wrong.

Another fallacy is non sequitor, or misattributing a conclusion to a given premise. For example, although God said the constitution was inspired, it does not follow that he endorses everything the country does, whether it is in accordance with the constitution or not. However, modern Mormons invite investigators to pray about the Book of Mormon, saying that if God says it is true, everything the church does is endorsed by him.

> Here, then, is a procedure to handle most objections through the use of the Book of Mormon….if the Book of Mormon is true, then Jesus is the Christ, Joseph Smith was his prophet, The Church of Jesus Christ of Latter-day Saints is true, and it is being led today by a prophet receiving revelation. (President Ezra Taft Benson, April 1975 General Conference, also quoted in "Preach My Gospel.")

This logical fallacy can also extend to conflating the source of blessings. What if in addition to paying tithing, I also did home teaching? Would I be correct in assuming that the windows of heaven were being opened because I was home teaching? Yet, the incorrectness of a theory doesn't mean that nothing good can come of it. Home teaching may be a good thing even if it does not result in the same set of blessings predicated upon tithing.

One security in the otherwise uncomfortable position of considering that one's evidences of treasured beliefs are in fact ascribable to another belief, leaving the sacred cows exposed to slaughter is that any experiences of value or true observations must still be accounted for in any replacement belief. "Disproving an opponent's premises does nothing to refute his conclusions." ("Popper", Bryan Magee, 1973, p42) In other words, in searching for truth, there is no risk of losing anything of value—it all has to be accounted for in any change that occurs. I've heard people say, "I just can't refute x, y, and z" without realizing that x, y, and z could in fact still be true if the points being argued are not true. We all have positive experiences in the church. Yet, having a positive experience with a Muslim would not lead you to conclude the Muslim is part of the Lord's church, that there is only one such incorporated body, and that everything a Muslim does which did not play a role in your positive experience is sanctioned by the Lord. Any observations or experiences of value within a later-proved theory must be reconciled in a replacement theory.

The Source of a Message Does Not Impact its Truthfulness

Jesus' authority did not come from the church authorities of his day. Nor did it come from the fact that he was the Son of God.[25] Jesus' authority came through the provenance of his message. He spoke the words of the Father. Those who judged the truthfulness of his message based on earthly authority incorrectly rejected him.

> And when [Jesus] was come into his own country, he taught them in their synagogues, insomuch that they were astonished, and said, Whence hath this Jesus this wisdom and these mighty works? Is not this the carpenter's son? Is not his mother called Mary? And his brethren, James, and Joses, and Simon, and Judas? And his sisters, are they not all with us? Whence then hath this man all these things? And they were offended at him. (Matthew 14:55-57, Inspired Version.)

We ought to assume that those who use the same false standards will also reject God's true messengers today. If we reject true messengers, we too will be rejected.

> My people are destroyed for lack of knowledge: because thou hast rejected knowledge, I will also reject thee, that thou shalt be no priest to me: seeing thou hast forgotten the law of thy God, I will also forget thy children. (Hosea 4:6.)

Modern Mormonism teaches that that no true messenger will come without church recognition and church authority.[15] Applying this standard would reject not only most of the true messengers in the scriptures, but Christ himself.

Open Problems are Fertile Ground for Discovery.

Situations that fail to find a solution in orthodoxy are fertile ground for receiving revelation. Postman and Weingartner wrote,

> We are unlikely to alter our perceptions until and unless we are frustrated in our attempts to do something based on them. If our actions seem to permit us to fulfil our purposes, we will not change our perceptions no matter how often we are told that they are 'wrong'. (Postman and Weingartner, "Teaching as a Subversive Activity", p. 93.)

As long as we are satisfied by our current understanding of what is true, we never really have a reason to marshal real intent, a necessary prerequisite to receiving revelation. President Uchtdorf said, "How often has

---

[25] Satan is also a son of God.

the Holy Spirit tried to tell us something we needed to know but couldn't get past the massive iron gate of what we thought we already knew?"[26]

Jesus taught we should be like children.[27] Children are inquisitive. They never stop wondering and testing. They are never satisfied.

Abraham found himself unsatisfied in the orthodoxy of his time. He somehow noticed that there were greater blessings available to him than the theology of his father offered him.

> In the land of the Chaldeans, at the residence of my fathers, I, Abraham, saw that it was needful for me to obtain another place of residence; And, finding there was greater happiness and peace and rest for me, I sought for the blessings of the fathers, and the right whereunto I should be ordained to administer the same; having been myself a follower of righteousness, desiring also to be one who possessed great knowledge, and to be a greater follower of righteousness, and to possess a greater knowledge, and to be a father of many nations, a prince of peace, and desiring to receive instructions, and to keep the commandments of God, I became a rightful heir, a High Priest, holding the right belonging to the fathers. (Abraham 1:1-2.)

Abraham clearly had heard stories that described religious experiences far exceeding those he observed in the religion of his father. Thus, he believed that there had to be a better system available than what he had experienced.[28]

Seek to Criticize What You Believe to Be True

To find truth, you must be your belief's hardest critic. You must be informed. How can you satisfactorily persuade someone who does not believe you without being prepared to answer any criticism of your belief? If what we believe is true, seeking to contradict it can only improve our ability to persuade others. Of course, it will also lead to situations where we discover that what we previously believed was false. While self-investigation will sometimes lead to disproving previously held notions, letting go of false beliefs draws one closer to God. Therefore, whether resulting in affirmation or disproof, honest questioning can only lead closer to God.

Sir Carl Popper wrote,

---

[26] Dieter F. Uchtdorf, "Acting on the Truths of the Gospel of Jesus Christ," Worldwide Leadership Training, 2/11/12

[27] "And again I say unto you, ye must repent, and become as a little child, and be baptized in my name, or ye can in nowise receive these things. And again I say unto you, ye must repent, and be baptized in my name, and become as a little child, or ye can in nowise inherit the kingdom of God." (3 Nephi 11:37-38)

[28] For a similar experiment, read JST Genesis 14. Does this describe the priesthood you possess? If not, what does that imply?

For all of us, in all our activities, the notions that we can do better only by finding out what can be improved and then improving it; and therefore that shortcomings are to be actively sought out, not concealed or passed over; and that critical comment from others, far from being resented, is an invaluable aid to be insisted on and welcomed, are liberating to a remarkable degree. It may be difficult to get people—conditioned to resent criticism and expect it to be resented, and therefore to keep silent about both their own mistakes and others'—to provide the criticisms on which improvement depends; but no one can possibly give us more service than by showing us what is wrong with what we think or do; and the bigger the fault, the bigger the improvement made possible by its revelation. The man who welcomes and acts on criticism will prize it almost above friendship: the man who fights it out of concern to maintain his position is clinging to non-growth. (Sir Carl Popper quoted in "Popper", Bryan Magee, 1973, p. 39.)

Seek for Contradictions

Every belief structure can be thought of as a map. Our observational experience is akin to the actual terrain. For whatever reason, most people of faith are not very apt at comparing their map to the surrounding terrain. Any difference in the two is contradiction.

Modern Mormons suppress contradictions to their model, but they aren't alone in the practice. This behavior is the result of confirmation bias or cognitive dissonance. Confirmation bias occurs when we see all evidence as support for what we already believe when some of it is actually evidence that opposes what we believe. Cognitive dissonance is a negative emotive response that occurs when our experiences contradict our belief system, causing us to flee from or ignore situations that do not support our belief system. We see examples of these phenomena not only in the way we selectively remember things, but also in the way we interpret evidence. This is why one scripture can be read that directly contradicts a tenet of someone's faith, yet that person can contort it to fit.

It only takes a single contradiction or counterexample to prove an idea false. For instance, if I said all pigs fly, I would only need to find one pig that did not, in fact, fly, to show that all pigs do not fly. For a scriptural example, look at Corihor. He said that no man can know of things future, but also said that there should be no Christ, which he couldn't possibly know unless men *could* know of things future. (see Alma 30). Contradictions can be a powerful tool for discerning between truth and error.

Search for Questions Without Answers

Jesus repeatedly said, "ask and ye shall receive." The restoration of the gospel occurred because a boy didn't accept the answers he was given by religious leaders, but asked God directly. The Book of Mormon is punctuated by a promise that God will answer any sincere question. Beware of any who tell you not to ask questions or that certain questions are off limits.

In forming questions, we should be specific. Ill-formed questions yield less effective. They reveal the bias and/or ill preparation of the asker. For example, asking "is the church true" reveals that the asker errantly believes that either everything the church does is sanctioned by God, or nothing the church does is sanctioned by God. A better question would be to ask what is really wanted. As Heisenberg said, "We have to remember that what we observe is not nature itself, but nature exposed to our methods of questioning." For example, "should I be baptized into the LDS church, given that at least some doctrines it teaches are true" is a much more effective question than "is the church true." The Spirit has to answer your question: even if your question is ill-posed, he will tell you the answer that will bring you closer to God.[29] The way we ask questions will inform what we believe more than anything else.

Search to Understand the Meaning of Words

Every faith group has developed a vocabulary of words whose meaning goes beyond the ordinary meaning for outsiders. In the LDS church, words like authority, prophet, sustain, atonement, and apostasy have very different meanings than they do to non-LDS. While it is easy to adopt the vocabulary of the status quo, we should strive to use more precise words. There are experiences and situations that simply cannot be described with the status-quo vocabulary:

> The level of abstraction at which one uses language in any context is an index of the extent to which one is in touch with reality. The higher the level, the less is the contact with reality. (Postman and Weingartner, "Teaching as a Subversive Activity", p. 120.)

Using an imprecise religious vocabulary limits the degree of thought and introspection that one can have. As an example, there are those in the church who think that the definition of "prophet" is "someone whose words you obey without question," while some in the church define "prophet" as "someone who repeats words God spoke to him." Say what you actually mean, and you will have a new source of questions to ask. Vague questions

---

[29] Aaron's discourse with the Lamanite king is a great example. God isn't really the great spirit, and there isn't really just one God. However, given the needs of the Lamanite king, that was the appropriate answer. Truth is circumstantial.

can only lead to vague answers. An articulate, precise question will lead to an articulate, precise answer.

Although unintentional, the verbal biases of LDS vocabulary have the unfortunate effect of preventing members from obtaining anything but a superficial and vague understanding of the doctrines and an inability to distinguish them from tradition. Loaded, biased vocabularies have the side effect not only of evoking negative emotions in response to critical thinking, but also of preventing such thinking in the first place through inability of expression.[30] Parsing semantics will sidestep the emotive responses engrained in the broader unspoken definitions of common terms and open the door to a deeper understanding of doctrine and traditions. We see what we say, but we must learn to say what we see.[31] Specificity in terms unfortunately brings negative responses from those who are not interested in more accurate expression, who will see your efforts of verbal precision as subversion.[32]

Don't Assume an Answer is the Final Answer

Alma taught:

> It is given unto many to know the mysteries of God; nevertheless they are laid under a strict command that they shall not impart only according to the portion of his word which he doth grant unto the children of men, according to the heed and diligence which they give unto him. And therefore, he that will harden his heart, the same receiveth the lesser portion of the word; and he that will not harden his heart, to him is given the greater portion of the word, until it is given unto him to know the mysteries of God until he know them in full. (Alma 12:9-10.)

God can only reveal as much truth to a person as they are prepared to receive. What happens, then, if one asks a question whose answer they are

---

[30] "The purpose of Newspeak was not only to provide a medium of expression for the world-view and mental habits proper to the devotees of Ingsoc, but to make all other modes of thought impossible." (George Orwell, 1984)

[31] "There is a basic scheme of classification built into our common speech and language. This built-in classification system directs us so that we observe the things we can readily classify with the names we know, while we tend strongly to overlook or disregard everything else. We see with our categories." (W. Johnson, "Verbal Man")

[32] "Those who are sensitive to the verbally built-in biases of their 'natural' environment seem 'subversive' to those who are not. There is probably nothing more dangerous to the prejudices of the latter than a man in the process of discovering that the language of his group is limited, misleading, or one-sided. Such a man is dangerous because he is not easily enlisted on the side of one ideology or another, because he sees beyond the words to the processes which give an ideology its reality." (Postman and Weingartner, "Teaching as a Subversive Activity", p. 18)

not ready to receive? God's answer to such a person will be partial—it will consist of what they are ready to receive.[33] To the person who is fully ready, the full answer will be given. This is one reason why two people can pray over the same question and receive two seemingly different answers.

God said, "All truth is independent in that sphere in which God has placed it."[34] The Spirit can reveal something that is true in your "sphere" of understanding, but to someone who has attained to a different "sphere," or a higher degree of knowledge, would be false. This concept is hard for some to accept,[35] but consider a decimal point number as an analogy. Additional digits of precision are true, as are less digits of precision. However, to the engineer possessing the decimal of ten digits' precision, the decimal of two digits' precision is less true. Just as one could add digits of precision infinitely, God's truth never ceases (even though there is a finite limit to telestial knowledge). Then there are those who round off and receive even less precision.

Nephi experienced the progressive nature of God's law when God amended "thou shalt not kill" with some particulars that indicated, in the case of Laban, it was indeed correct to kill. There was a higher law, an additional digit of precision. As an example, consider the group of disciples in the New Testament that had received the authoritative baptism of John, but had not yet received the baptism of the apostles.[36] They recognized a higher law, and submitted to rebaptism to gain the gift of the Holy Ghost.

Because the degree of glory we enjoy in life is dictated by the degree of God's law that we live,[37] we should always be willing and eager to receive

---

[33] One way God answers us when we ask for knowledge or experiences we are not prepared for is by sending us experiences that will prepare us if we are faithful through them.

[34] D&C 93:30.

[35] Joseph Smith: "Many men will say, 'I will never forsake you, but will stand by you at all times.' But the moment you teach them some of the mysteries of the kingdom of God that are retained in the heavens and are to be revealed to the children of men when they are prepared for them they will be the first to stone you and put you to death. It was this same principle that crucified the Lord Jesus Christ, and will cause the people to kill the prophets in this generation." (Joseph Smith, TPJS; p. 309.)

[36] "...Paul having passed through the upper coasts came to Ephesus: and finding certain disciples, He said unto them, Have ye received the Holy Ghost since ye believed? And they said unto him, We have not so much as heard whether there be any Holy Ghost. And he said unto them, Unto what then were ye baptized? And they said, Unto John's baptism. Then said Paul, John verily baptized with the baptism of repentance, saying unto the people, that they should believe on him which should come after him, that is, on Christ Jesus. When they heard this, they were baptized in the name of the Lord Jesus. And when Paul had laid his hands upon them, the Holy Ghost came on them; and they spake with tongues, and prophesied. (Acts 19:1-6.)

[37] "And again, verily I say unto you, that which is governed by law is also preserved by law and perfected and sanctified by the same." (D&C 88:34.)

further light and truth to expand and clarify the law we currently have. This will likely cause us to change what we are doing. And to facilitate this process, we should always be willing to ask questions to further our understanding of answers we have already received—like a child. We should never judge someone who fully believes that their actions are in accordance with God's word when we have received a different answer to the same question, knowing that it is very possible that they have progressed passed us in knowledge. Instead, we should do as Nephi did when presented with his father's strange claims of having a vision that contradicted Nephi's understanding: we should pray and ask God. Even if we are not prepared for the answer, God will mobilize the necessary experiences in our life to bring us to the point where we can receive the same knowledge.

Conclusion

A true search for truth must be a consistent rational evaluation of new evidences, both those that support and those that refute currently held positions. In order to search for truth, then, one must be able to enumerate the reasons for their currently held beliefs. Anyone who preaches the gospel must already be able to give reasons for what they believe, yet a surprising number of people both attempt to preach the gospel and defend their own beliefs without any substance at all. Instead, their entire argument consists of a few tired logical fallacies. These ineffective attempts fail to convert. Moreover, failure to substantiate one's beliefs guarantees that they cannot improve in their beliefs, because you cannot argue against evidences that do not explicitly exist.[38]

Asking questions is among the most important skills we must develop in our quest to know God. Good askers have confidence in God's willingness to respond. They are suspicious of what others say. They realize that the vast majority of people have no idea what they are talking about most of the time. They are also suspicious of what they already believe they know. They are willing to be wrong. They are able to suspend judgment on an issue until more facts are gathered. Because their belief is constructed based on their observations over time, they expect that their belief will change as they make more observations.

Each principle stands or falls on its own. It is a false tradition to assume that because one principle is true, all principles bundled together by some person or group are also true.[39] The truthfulness of the Book of

---

[38] Incidentally, failure to substantiate one's beliefs is in itself a logical fallacy named "appeal to ignorance." This fallacy shifts the burden of proving what is proposed from the teacher who is preaching it to the recipient.

[39] "Well, it's either true or false. If it's false, we're engaged in a great fraud. If it's true, it's the most important thing in the world. Now, that's the whole picture. It is either right or wrong, true or false, fraudulent or true. And that's exactly where we stand,

Mormon does not imply that everything the church ever did or will do is inspired by God any more than the Constitution being inspired implies that everything the U.S. government did or will do is inspired. We must learn how to ask specific questions, which might have limited application.

We make a grave mistake when we assume that questioning leads to doubts. In reality, questioning not only leads to faith, but it is the only path that leads to faith, since faith cannot be had in false principles, and the only way to establish which principles are true is to ask God.

We ought to believe what we have found to be true, not evaluate what is true based on what we already believe.[40] Moses' journey closer to God was punctuated with moments where he learned things he had never before supposed. We are no different. We progress towards God not only by learning new things but also by rejecting old things we previously believed in that are false. If we limit our investigation to what we already believe to be true, we will never approach closer to God than we currently are.

---

with a conviction in our hearts that it is true: that Joseph went into the [Sacred] Grove; that he saw the Father and the Son; that he talked with them; that Moroni came; that the Book of Mormon was translated from the plates; that the priesthood was restored by those who held it anciently. That's our claim. That's where we stand, and that's where we fall, if we fall. But we don't. We just stand secure in that faith." (Hinckley, PBS)

[40] David Ausubel defined learning as "the process of adjusting our mental models to accommodate new experiences." (Scientific Teaching, p7) Under that definition, using our mental models to shut out new experiences would be the opposite of learning. In spiritual terms, this is known as damnation, or the cessation of learning.

Persuasion and Argument

Both in the scriptures and in our personal lives, it is clear that when God teaches, he employs persuasion. He follows the same law that he gives to all teachers:

> No power or influence can or ought to be maintained by virtue of the priesthood, only by persuasion, by long-suffering, by gentleness and meekness, and by love unfeigned; By kindness, and pure knowledge, which shall greatly enlarge the soul without hypocrisy, and without guile. (D&C 121:41-42.)

God himself teaches this way, and he instructs all teachers to apply the same methods. Guileless persuasion, long-suffering, gentleness, meekness, love, kindness, and pure knowledge is the *only* way the gospel can be preached. The only other option is "to exercise control or dominion or compulsion upon the souls of the children of men." This is strictly forbidden. When that is done, "the heavens withdraw themselves; the Spirit of the Lord is grieved; and when it is withdrawn, Amen to the priesthood or the authority of that man." (D&C 121:37.)

We are warned in this same section that

> ...it is the nature and disposition of almost all men, as soon as they get a little authority, as they suppose, they will immediately begin to exercise unrighteous dominion. (D&C 121:38-39.)

We should carefully discern when teachers are using persuasion and when they are using unrighteous dominion. What are the hallmarks of unrighteous dominion? We are told in this revelation that exercising control or dominion or compulsion is unrighteous dominion. A true messenger will not preach the gospel by appealing to his authority (for example, a calling in the church) or by declaring a policy or program by edict. To do so would not only prove to everyone that they were not true messengers, but would automatically annul (if a man) his priesthood commission from God. Joseph Smith proclaimed that he never appealed to his authority in teaching the gospel, but that the goodness of the truth he taught was persuasive in and of itself:

> President Joseph Smith again arose & said in relation to the power over the minds of mankind which I hold, I would say it is in

34

consequence of the power of truth in the doctrins which I have been an instrument in the hands of God of presenting unto them & not because of any Compulsion on my part. I will ask if I ever got any of it unfair. If I have not reproved you in the gate, I ask did I ever exerise any compulsion over any man. did I not give him the liberty of disbelieveing any doctrin I have preached if he saw fit, why do not my enemies strike a blow at the doctrin, they cannot do it, it is truth, And I am as the voice of one Crying in the wilderness repent of your sins & prepare the way for the Coming of the Son of Man, for the Kingdom of God has Come unto you and hence forth the ax is laid unto the root of the tree and evry tree that bringeth not forth good fruit, God Almighty (and not Jo Smith) shall hew down & cast it into the fire. (Wilford Woodruff Journal, March 24, 1844) (Original spelling)

What are the hallmarks of godly teaching? Persuasion, longsuffering, gentleness, meekness, love, kindness, and pure knowledge, all without guile. Here we critically note that these characteristics inescapably connote an exchange of unaligned positions—an argument. Of what use is persuasion when two parties already agree? Of what use is longsuffering when the receiver of knowledge already understands? Why are gentleness, love and kindness required if the lesson only consists of a reminder of what is already known? Of what use is pure knowledge if the student knows what the teacher knows? In what situation is guile employed, if not to convince? Teaching the gospel does not mean the rote recitation of what the student has already heard. This would require no persuasion. Teaching the gospel does not mean a one-way presentation of something new. This would be unrighteous dominion because a fiat demand to change does not include persuasion, longsuffering gentleness, meekness, or pure knowledge. *These attributes require a two-way exchange.*

Contrary to our modern aversion to the idea, argument, when done with persuasion, longsuffering gentleness, meekness, love, kindness, and pure knowledge, is actually *the* method for teaching the gospel.

While we ought to most readily associate persuasive argument with gospel teaching, the words argument and debate have a strong negative connotation in modern Mormonism. Modern Mormons identify rote recitation of what is already known or dogmatic assertion by those with a little authority, as they suppose, as gospel teaching. In reality, this is opposite of what it should be.

Imagine two Sunday school environments. In the first class, everyone sits quietly and listens to the teacher read the same lines from the manual that have been read in years past, or reads a conference talk that may not only be a repeat in terms of phrases and topics, but may in fact have been given in its entirety at least once before. In the second class, a class member disagrees with something that it said in the course of the lesson, citing historical evidence for her position. In which of the two classes would most modern Mormons rather be? The prevailing feeling in the first would be comfort, and in the second anxiety or perhaps annoyance and anger. The soundness of the position of the dissenter is not a factor in the reaction to her words.

As another example, imagine two different outcomes of a sustaining during sacrament. In the first, the presiding official reads the calling to be made, and there is unanimous support out of deference to the authority of the presiding official. In the second, a member voices concern over the appropriateness of the individual. Discussion ensues. In the end, all concerns are vetted and the member is sustained. What modern Mormon would be comfortable with the second scenario? Yet, this is a scenario that repeated itself frequently in Joseph Smith's day.[41]

Having discussed how the gospel is taught through argument, we now move to a discussion of why it must be this way. If truth were self-evident, there would be no need for argument. All gospel teaching could be repetition of what we already know. However, many different groups believe many different (and opposing) things to be true, and the natural man—our own best effort to know what is right—is an enemy to God.

> For the natural man is an enemy to God, and has been from the fall of Adam, and will be, forever and ever, unless he yields to the enticings of the Holy Spirit, and putteth off the natural man and becometh a saint through the atonement of Christ the Lord, and becometh as a child, submissive, meek, humble, patient, full of love, willing to submit to all things which the Lord seeth fit to inflict upon him, even as a child doth submit to his father. (Mosiah 3:19.)

We are told what the antidote to man's fallacious reasoning is: the Holy Ghost. Only by yielding to God can a man overcome his innate inability to judge righteously. Men are incapable, of their own accord, to know what is right and what is wrong. We need the intervention of God, and that frequently comes through the ministry of true human messengers.

The assumption of man that he possesses sufficient wisdom to discern whether some new thing is true or not is foolhardy. It is also anti-scriptural. We are given countless examples of men like Moses who, having received more revelation in a life of faithfulness than most of us can even dream of, are left in subsequent visits to admit that they had never before supposed what God had just revealed.[42]

---

[41] For example, Joseph himself led the contrary vote on one occasion when Sidney Rigdon was being sustained as his counselor. The people continued to vote in support of Sidney despite Joseph's contrary position.

[42] Moses 1:10. See also Lehi's reaction to his vision in Jerusalem (1 Nephi 1:6).

Having found that, even among men and women spiritually stout enough to sacrifice and endure much more than we would today, members were generally unable to assess candidate truth properly, Joseph wrote a long editorial to the membership in "Times and Seasons," the church periodical. In it, he explained that throughout time it has been impossible to judge the veracity of acts or principles based solely on subjective personal opinion:

> The Egyptians were not able to discover the difference between the miracles of Moses and those of the magicians until they came to be tested together; and if Moses had not appeared in their midst, they would unquestionably have thought that the miracles of the magicians were performed through the mighty power of God, for they were great miracles that were performed by them—a supernatural agency was developed, and great power manifested....The witch of Endor is a no less singular personage; clothed with a powerful agency she raised the Prophet Samuel from his grave, and he appeared before the astonished king, and revealed unto him his future destiny. Who is to tell whether this woman is of God, and a righteous woman—or whether the power she possessed was of the devil, and she a witch as represented by the Bible? It is easy for us to say now, but if we had lived in her day, which of us could have unraveled the mystery? It would have been equally as difficult for us to tell by what spirit the Apostles prophesied, or by what power the Apostles spoke and worked miracles. Who could have told whether the power of Simon, the sorcerer, was of God or of the devil? (HC 4:571.)

Joseph goes on to say that evaluating new possible truth by comparing it to some doctrinal creed, or the status quo of what the individual currently believes, is "preposterous folly," "sheer ignorance," and "madness":

> "Try the spirits," but what by? Are we to try them by the creeds of men? What preposterous folly—what sheer ignorance—what madness! Try the motions and actions of an eternal being (for I contend that all spirits are such) by a thing that was conceived in ignorance, and brought forth in folly—a cobweb of yesterday! Angels would hide their faces, and devils would be ashamed and insulted... (HC 4:572.)

Note that it is quite common in modern Mormonism to measure new truth against some creed such as a quote from an authority, a citation from the current handbook, a reference to a cultural norm, or an appeal to the "Articles of Faith." None of these items, according to Joseph, ought to be used as a measuring stick. In fact, he says, even the scriptures are questionable because all the different sects cite the same volume of scripture to support their opposing view. "The Articles of Faith" is quite an interesting item to use as a creed, since its author was so vehemently opposed to creeds. Said Joseph,

> I cannot believe in any of the creeds of the different denominations, because they all have some things in them I cannot subscribe to, though all of them have some truth. I want to come up into the presence of God, and learn all things; but the creeds set up stakes, and say, 'Hitherto shalt thou come, and no further'; which I cannot subscribe to. (TPJS, p. 235)[43]

Joseph said the devil has an "angelic form, [a] sanctified look and gesture," and that he even feigns "zeal…for the glory of God, together with the prophetic spirit, the gracious influence, the godly appearance, and the holy garb," and that these would cause most who are judging of themselves to assume he is a heavenly messenger.

> A man must have the discerning of spirits before he can drag into daylight this hellish influence and unfold it unto the world in all its soul-destroying, diabolical, and horrid colors; (HC 4:573.)

Most people would assume that any angelic messenger appearing with grace, godly appearance, and holy garb, would be a veritable heavenly angel. But they would be wrong. A man's eyes, experience, and preconceived notions can certainly lead him just as astray in ascertaining truth in any other case as it could in determining whether the devil is a heavenly messenger. **New truth cannot be evaluated through the lens of the current beliefs of an individual**. Jesus taught, "Judge not according to your traditions, but judge righteous judgment." (John 7:24, JST.) It is not the false traditions of our fallen flesh that will teach us the truth of all things, but the Holy Ghost (see Moroni 10:5). **Candidate truth can only be evaluated through individual revelation from God.**

Now, if the only way to identify truth is to ask God, why does God view rational argument as so important in teaching that he revealed a commandment to describe it? In other words, if all that can be done to

---

[43] In context of the Articles of Faith, this position might seem hypocritical. However, it should be realized that the Articles of Faith, a portion of a larger letter detailing the origin of the church founded by Joseph, was a snapshot in time portraying the current beliefs espoused by members. Note that the Articles themselves reveal the anticipation of beliefs changing ("…and everything he will yet reveal…"). Joseph said that he wrote them in hopes of not having to repeat the history of the church or answer "what do you believe" so often. Joseph's frequent railing against creeds is plain evidence that he never intended them to become canon in the church. They were not canonized until 1880 (see L. Tom Perry "The Articles of Faith" April 1998 General Conference).

identify truth is to ask God, why bother doing anything but dictating a principle and ending with an invitation to pray? First, as any missionary who has tried the tactic knows, most people will not actually pray. Why would they, when they don't believe what you are saying could ever be true? Second, even if they pray, their preconception of the falsehood of what you are saying will make it impossible to exercise real intent. Real intent is the belief that what is being prayed about is possible and the individual is willing to act on it if told it is true. Moroni explains that God will not answer prayers that are not offered with real intent: "And likewise also is it counted evil unto a man, if he shall pray and not with real intent of heart; yea, and it profiteth him nothing, for God receiveth none such." (Moroni 7:9.) Lastly, even if an individual is able to marshal real intent, the more an individual clings to his preconceived notions, the more likely he is to conflate his own ideas with revelation from the Spirit. After all, discerning the Spirit is difficult. As Joseph stated, great care must be taken to ensure that the response an individual believes comes from God is actually from God,

> ...for nothing is a greater injury to the children of men than to be under the influence of a false spirit when they think they have the Spirit of God. Thousands have felt the influence of its terrible power and baneful effects. Long pilgrimages have been undertaken, penances endured, and pain, misery and ruin have followed in their train; nations have been convulsed, kingdoms overthrown, provinces laid waste, and blood, carnage and desolation are habiliments in which it has been clothed....without a divine communication they must remain in ignorance. (Joseph Smith, HC 4:571-581.)

Without gospel teaching in the form described by God in D&C 121, a person will not be equipped to evaluate candidate truth with unbiased real intent, and therefore will not be able to obtain revelation from God on whether or not it is true.

From this brief overview, we can distill a few takeaways:
1) Truth cannot be ascertained except through the Holy Ghost.
2) To evaluate truth, a man must pray with real intent.
3) Real intent cannot be achieved without the individual considering that the candidate truth to be evaluated could possibly be true, and having faith that if it is true, they will reconcile their lives to it.
4) For these reasons, God commands gospel teaching to take the form of providing a rational argument with the qualities given in D&C 121.
5) Even when truth is prayed about with real intent, it requires mature discernment to distinguish between the Spirit of God and other conflicting sources, such as one's emotions.

In context of the foregoing, it should be clear that teaching truth requires a rationally supported argument.

The Lord has said, on more than one occasion, "let us reason together, that ye may understand;" (D&C 50:10, see also Isaiah 1:18.) To reason is to consider logical arguments with the intent of coming to a conclusion. In order to be rational, the conclusion must reconcile all addressed evidences. Reasoning is a two-way process. The teacher can expect protests from the student, and must be prepared to respond to every rational reason the student might have to disbelieve the teacher's message.

What does this look like in practice? We have a wonderful example of the Lord's persuasion of Nephi, who was commanded to slay Laban:

> And it came to pass that I was constrained by the Spirit that I should kill Laban; but I said in my heart: Never at any time have I shed the blood of man. And I shrunk and would that I might not slay him. And the Spirit said unto me again: Behold the Lord hath delivered him into thy hands. Yea, and I also knew that he had sought to take away mine own life; yea, and he would not hearken unto the commandments of the Lord; and he also had taken away our property. And it came to pass that the Spirit said unto me again: Slay him, for the Lord hath delivered him into thy hands; Behold the Lord slayeth the wicked to bring forth his righteous purposes. It is better that one man should perish than that a nation should dwindle and perish in unbelief. And now, when I, Nephi, had heard these words, I remembered the words of the Lord which he spake unto me in the wilderness, saying that: Inasmuch as thy seed shall keep my commandments, they shall prosper in the land of promise. Yea, and I also thought that they could not keep the commandments of the Lord according to the law of Moses, save they should have the law. And I also knew that the law was engraven upon the plates of brass. And again, I knew that the Lord had delivered Laban into my hands for this cause—that I might obtain the records according to his commandments. Therefore I did obey the voice of the Spirit, and took Laban by the hair of the head, and I smote off his head with his own sword. (1 Nephi 4:10-18.)

The exchange between God and Nephi is notable. It is a two-way conversation. God welcomes challenges to what he commands. He invites them. He is prepared to make counterarguments or, in some cases, to cede his ground.[44] As God is, we must also "...be ready always to give an answer to

---

[44] For instance, when God commanded Ezekiel to bake his bread with fire fueled by human waste as a sign to Israel, Ezekiel protested "Ah Lord God! behold, my soul hath not been polluted: for from my youth up even till now have I not eaten of that which dieth of itself, or is torn in pieces; neither came there abominable flesh into my mouth. Then he said unto me, Lo, I have given thee cow's dung for man's dung, and thou shalt prepare thy bread therewith." (Ezekiel 4:14-15.)

every man that asketh you a reason of the hope that is in you with meekness and fear:" (1 Peter 3:15.)

It is not enough to be in the right. A true messenger must be able to deliver his message skillfully enough that it stands as a witness, beyond reproach. A true messenger must ensure that, should the message be rejected, it is not due to the fault of the messenger. Providing a reason for what you posit is not an abstract activity. A skillful teacher must ground each teaching attempt in the context of the hearer. Jesus showed ample examples of this skill during his mortal ministry. Perhaps it is best summed up by Paul's description:

> And unto the Jews I became as a Jew, that I might gain the Jews; to them that are under the law, as under the law, that I might gain them that are under the law; To them that are without law, as without law, (being not without law to God, but under the law to Christ,) that I might gain them that are without law. To the weak became I as weak, that I might gain the weak: I am made all things to all men, that I might by all means save some. And this I do for the gospel's sake. (1 Corinthians 9:20-23.)

By grounding his argument in the context of the beliefs of his audience, Paul was able to anticipate and address the concerns his audience would express that prevented them from believing his message could be true. This required Paul to know his audience. Ideally, this always consists of a two-way exchange. In practice this is not always possible, and gospel teachers have to anticipate—hopefully with the guidance of discernment through the Holy Ghost—what concerns their audience have.

While new truth will sometimes be compatible with that which is already understood, it frequently opposes the extant beliefs of the hearer. In this case, before new truth is expounded, contrary false tradition must be addressed. Without incompatible ideas in the mind of the receiver, teaching the gospel would be easy and comfortable. However, because they almost always exist, preaching the gospel almost always consists primarily in disabusing the recipient of false tradition. This is both difficult and unpleasant. The prominent reticence towards direct confrontation with ideas comes at a great loss. Without uprooting false tradition, the individual's ability to have faith on the Lord unto repentance is greatly limited.

> And behold, ye do know of yourselves, for ye have witnessed it, that as many of them as are brought to the knowledge of the truth, and to know of the wicked and abominable traditions of their fathers, and are led to believe the holy scriptures, yea, the prophecies of the holy prophets, which are written, which leadeth them to faith on the Lord, and unto repentance, which faith and repentance bringeth a change of heart unto them— (Helaman 15:7.)

This scripture does not overstate the importance of helping people (including yourself) realize that many of their preconceived notions are wicked and abominable. As the scripture states, they prevent belief in the scriptures, belief in the prophecies of the prophets, faith in God, and repentance. It is not enough to skip over the false traditions people hold. False traditions will damn anyone who holds them. There are not other, more readily acceptable gospel truths that can be taught in hopes that the false traditions will work themselves out.

How can one directly address false tradition in the beliefs of others? Contention is not the only way. God has commanded us not to contend with each other:

> For verily, verily I say unto you, he that hath the spirit of contention is not of me, but is of the devil, who is the father of contention, and he stirreth up the hearts of men to contend with anger, one with another. (3 Nephi 11:29.)

Yet, not all argument is contention. Nephi described contention as "teach[ing] with their learning, and deny the Holy Ghost, which giveth utterance." (2 Nephi 28:4.) Incidentally, he correctly warned that this would be prominent in our day. In other words, Nephi says that gospel persuasion is not about convincing the hearer that you are right. It is about convincing the hearer to pray to God believing that it *could* be right.

The word "argue" sometimes connotes anger and disrespect, and not just in modern context. Lehi explained to Laman and Lemuel that they were incorrect in assuming that Nephi's arguments towards them were motivated by anger:

> And I exceedingly fear and tremble because of you, lest he shall suffer again; for behold, ye have accused him that he sought power and authority over you; but I know that he hath not sought for power nor authority over you, but he hath sought the glory of God, and your own eternal welfare. And ye have murmured because he hath been plain unto you. Ye say that he hath used sharpness; ye say that he hath been angry with you; but behold, his sharpness was the sharpness of the power of the word of God, which was in him; and that which ye call anger was the truth, according to that which is in God, which he could not restrain, manifesting boldly concerning your iniquities. And it must needs be that the power of God must be with him, even unto his commanding you that ye must obey. But behold, it was not he, but it was the Spirit of the Lord which was in him, which opened his mouth to utterance that he could not shut it. (2 Nephi 1:25-27.)

Arguments, then, are not contentious by definition, but only when they are motivated by anger. Even here, we have to separate the subtle difference between anger and "sharpness." Arguing truth for the purpose of persuasion can include sharpness (D&C 121:43). In fact, Jesus frequently employed sharpness. In one typical example, he said:

> And the Lord said unto him, Now do ye Pharisees make clean the outside of the cup and the platter; but your inward part is full of ravening and wickedness. Ye fools, did not he that made that which is without make that which is within also? But rather give alms of such things as ye have; and, behold, all things are clean unto you. But woe unto you, Pharisees! for ye tithe mint and rue and all manner of herbs, and pass over judgment and the love of God: these ought ye to have done, and not to leave the other undone. Woe unto you, Pharisees! for ye love the uppermost seats in the synagogues, and greetings in the markets. Woe unto you, scribes and Pharisees, hypocrites! for ye are as graves which appear not, and the men that walk over them are not aware of them. Then answered one of the lawyers, and said unto him, Master, thus saying thou reproachest us also. And he said, Woe unto you also, ye lawyers! for ye lade men with burdens grievous to be borne, and ye yourselves touch not the burdens with one of your fingers. Woe unto you! for ye build the sepulchres of the prophets, and your fathers killed them. Truly ye bear witness that ye allow the deeds of your fathers: for they indeed killed them, and ye build their sepulchres. (Luke 11:39-48.)

How would you react if someone called you a fool, full of wickedness, a hypocrite, and a murderer? Would you consider that contention? Yet, Jesus' example shows it is not.[45] While it is true that Jesus was gentle with the meek, he was also very sharp with the prideful. He is the perfect example to follow. You can't emulate Jesus without arguing and, at times, with sharpness. Sharpness is often the only way to crack through false tradition, an ideological film that is almost always based on an inherited position (by definition, one not based on reasoning or evidences, but an emotive connection to parents). It is very difficult to reason with someone who is arguing from an emotive position.

The definition of argue is to give reasons or cite evidence in support of an idea, action, or theory, typically with the aim of persuading others to share one's view. When argument is used in the literal sense of the word, the intrinsic motivation will always be persuasion. Argue is the best word to

---

[45] Joseph Smith said, "I have not the least idea, if Christ should come to the earth and preach such rough things as He preached to the Jews, but that this generation would reject Him for being so rough." (Joseph Smith, History of the Church, 5:423–25.)

describe *how* one persuades: producing evidence; reasoning. In contrast, to contend means to strive in order to prove one's position is correct; to defend one's position in order to preserve it, or to oppose. All of these senses have at their heart the intent to remain in one's former position---not, as in the case of argument or debate, to seek out truth, even if it means letting go of one's former position. Contention, then, is *not* the presence of argument, but the lack thereof, where an individual refuses to give or receive reasons supporting a position.

Contention is about *who* is right, whereas debate is about *what* is right. Two persons who are unwilling to change their current position are unable to argue—unable to present evidence to determine *what* is right, they must take turns asserting *who* is right. They can only contend with one another.

Contention is enmity: the state or feeling of being actively opposed or hostile to someone or something. It is a feeling, not a position informed by reasoning or evidences. It is a non-neutral, non-objective, emotional, irrational practice. It is a reaction against a position rather than a defense against the evidences or reasons behind that position.

Persuasive argument, as instructed in D&C 121, should consist in pure knowledge, that is, true facts. A person should be able to expound a position using scripture and, as Jesus did, common sense.[46] Persuasive argument ought not to employ guile. Guile is sly craftiness. It is dishonest—not a lie, but an attempt to distract rational reasoning by distraction and device that draws attention away from a simple analysis of the issue at hand. There is a long list of these devices (called logical fallacies) that everyone interested in truth should be aware of. Among them are appeal to authority, appeal to common practice, appeal to tradition. None of these devices ought to be considered when evaluating truth. However, let's address one example of guile in detail due to the frequency of its use: *ad hominem*.

An ad hominem is when someone dismisses a group of evidences or reasons because of their impression of the person who is giving the evidences or reasons. By labeling the person as incapable of possessing truth, they can be ignored without objective consideration of their evidences or reasons. Ad hominem is libel by label—an avoidance of the issue via an up front (upfront) dismissal of the person connected to the issue. In the church, this is done by labeling the person an apostate. For example, Michael Quinn was perhaps the greatest LDS historian of all time at the time of his excommunication. A

---

[46] Many of the devil's designs do not hold up to reasoning. For instance, Sherem stated that no man could know that Jesus was to come, but failed to realize that this also implied that he could not know that Jesus *wasn't* to come (see Jacob 7:7). Jesus artfully pointed out nonsensical positions using stories of everyday life. For example, he chided the Pharisees' application of the Law of Moses' Sabbath day prohibition of work to his healing an invalid by asking them if they fed and watered their cattle on the Sabbath (see Luke 13:15).

professor of history at Brigham Young University, he had a lifetime of church service under his belt, was an associate and advocate of the brethren and close friend of Spencer W. Kimball, who, in a blessing, promised him he would one day be an apostle. Yet, his two volume history on the church is openly dismissed as inadmissible, despite the fact that that the books are so well documented that around half of the text consists of footnotes to minutes of the meetings of the Quorum of the Twelve, First Presidency minutes, journals, and other official sources. Ironically, due to Quinn's access to and diligence in studying those publicly unavailable sources, his volumes continue to be the best resource of their contents, which the church has opted to keep closed to the public. By ignoring Quinn due to his excommunication, an individual can completely avoid having to present evidence suggesting a position alternative to what Quinn's historical analyses suggest without the burden of providing a rational argument for doing so.

For some reason, it is particularly easy to derail a modern Mormon from honest inquiry by employing ad hominem. It ought to be more difficult. After all, no one suggests that Ghandi's movement was not as beautiful as it was effective, despite the fact that he was racist against blacks. Dr. Martin Luther King, Jr.—whose entire program of peaceful resistance was borrowed from Ghandi—could evaluate the efficacy of Ghandi's precepts on peaceful protests independently from Ghandi's racism. Many, in turn, see the value of Dr. King's teachings on civil rights despite his serial adultery. God holds us accountable to our acceptance of truth regardless of whether or not it is provided by an imperfect messenger.

Some may seek to avoid opportunities to argue truth with others. It is definitely difficult and unpleasant. Joseph described it as trying to split hemlock knots with a wedge made of corn bread and a pumpkin for a sledge hammer.[47] However, it is not optional for a disciple of Christ who has covenanted "to stand as witnesses of God at all times and in all things, and in all places" (Mosiah 18:9). Beyond an obligatory condition of the covenant, refraining from sharing truth brings penalties upon one's head:

---

[47] "But there has been a great difficulty in getting anything into the heads of this generation. It has been like splitting hemlock knots with a corn dodger for a wedge, and a pumpkin for a beetle. Even the Saints are slow to understand. I have tried for a number of years to get the minds of the Saints prepared to receive the things of God; but we frequently see some of them, after suffering all they have for the work of God, will fly to pieces like glass as soon as anything comes that is contrary to their traditions: they cannot stand the fire at all. How many will be able to abide a celestial law, and go through and receive their exaltation, I am unable to say, as many are called, but few are chosen." (DHC 6:183 185, Jan. 20, 1844.) Hemlock is among the hardest wood to split. Knots are harder to split than straight wood, pumpkins explode when struck, and corn bread crumbles when picked up.

When I say unto the wicked, Thou shalt surely die; and thou givest him not warning, nor speakest to warn the wicked from his wicked way, to save his life; the same wicked man shall die in his iniquity; but his blood will I require at thine hand. Yet if thou warn the wicked, and he turn not from his wickedness, nor from his wicked way, he shall die in his iniquity; but thou hast delivered thy soul....Nevertheless if thou warn the righteous man, that the righteous sin not, and he doth not sin, he shall surely live, because he is warned; also thou hast delivered thy soul. (Ezekiel 3:18-19,21.)

Though fear can be a motivator, the better reason for willingly attempting to help another overcome false tradition is love. Jesus taught that the greatest demonstration of love is to give one's life for another, suggesting that love can be measured by what one is willing to sacrifice for the benefit of another.

Revelation

There is a discrete portion of knowledge that every person must receive before they can be saved. Joseph said,

> A man is saved no faster than he gets knowledge, for if he does not get knowledge, he will be brought into captivity by some evil power in the other world, as evil spirits will have more knowledge, and consequently more power than many men who are on the earth. Hence it needs revelation to assist us, and give us knowledge of the things of God. (Joseph Smith, TPJS, p. 154.)

It is not enough to simply follow the general commandments. What is publicly available is not sufficient to become like Jesus is. The purpose of what is publicly available is not to make someone like Jesus, but to bring them to the gate of personal revelation available through the Holy Ghost.

> ...For the gate by which ye should enter is repentance and baptism by water; and then cometh a remission of your sins by fire and by the Holy Ghost. And then are ye in this strait and narrow path which leads to eternal life; yea, ye have entered in by the gate; ye have done according to the commandments of the Father and the Son; and ye have received the Holy Ghost, which witnesses of the Father and the Son, unto the fulfilling of the promise which he hath made, that if ye entered in by the way ye should receive. And now, my beloved brethren, after ye have gotten into this strait and narrow path, I would ask if all is done? Behold, I say unto you, Nay; for ye have not come thus far save it were by the word of Christ with unshaken faith in him, relying wholly upon the merits of him who is mighty to save. Wherefore, ye must press forward with a steadfastness in Christ, having a perfect brightness of hope, and a love of God and of all men. Wherefore, if ye shall press forward, feasting upon the word of Christ, and endure to the end, behold, thus saith the Father: Ye shall have eternal life. (2 Nephi 31:17-20.)

It is the "unspeakable" teachings[48] revealed through the Holy Ghost that bring an individual to be like Jesus.

Assuming that the general commandments are sufficient to save is a common error. The Pharisees argued against Jesus' teachings because they "ha[d] the law for [their] salvation." He told his disciples to:

> Say unto them, Ask of God; ask, and it shall be given you; seek, and ye shall find; knock, and it shall be opened unto you. For everyone that asketh, receiveth; and he that seeketh, findeth; and unto him that knocketh, it shall be opened. And then said his disciples unto him, They will say unto us, We ourselves are righteous, and need not that any man should teach us. God, we know, heard Moses and some of the prophets; but us he will not hear. And they will say, We have the law for our salvation, and that is sufficient for us. Then Jesus answered, and said unto his disciples, Thus shall ye say unto them, What man among you, having a son, and he shall be standing out, and shall say, Father, open thy house that I may come in and sup with thee, will not say, Come in, my son; for mine is thine, and thine is mine? (JST Matthew 7:12-17.)

Jesus taught quite plainly, particularly in the book of John, that a direct, real relationship with him was required for eternal life. The pinnacle of eternal knowledge comes as a face to face relationship with God himself. As John put it, this knowledge is one and the same as eternal life. "And this is life eternal, that they might know thee the only true God, and Jesus Christ, whom thou hast sent." (John 17:3) As Nephi, Joseph, and other prophets have taught, the way we come up to this experience is by following the words of God given to the individual by the Holy Ghost.

Revelation through the Holy Ghost is the way appointed to take a man from his fallen state to the point where he receives the promise of eternal life. Nephi taught that this path is to "feast upon the words of Christ; for behold, the words of Christ will tell you all things what ye should do." (2 Nephi 32:3.) He said these words—those that tell us what to do to come back to his presence in this life—come through the Holy Ghost: "if ye will enter in by the way, and receive the Holy Ghost, it will show unto you all things what ye should do." (2 Nephi 32:5.) This path will lead a man to a face-to-face encounter with Christ, redeeming him from the fall.[49]

---

[48] "God shall give unto you knowledge by his Holy Spirit, yea, by the unspeakable gift of the Holy Ghost, that has not been revealed since the world was until now;" (D&C 121:26.)

[49] "And when he had said these words, behold, the Lord showed himself unto him, and said: Because thou knowest these things ye are redeemed from the fall; therefore ye are brought back into my presence; therefore I show myself unto you." (Ether 3:13)

> Behold, this is the doctrine of Christ, and there will be no more doctrine given until after he shall manifest himself unto you in the flesh. And when he shall manifest himself unto you in the flesh, the things which he shall say unto you shall ye observe to do. (2 Nephi 32:6.)

This experience of meeting Christ "in the flesh" is called the Second Comforter. What greater thing could Heavenly Father reveal to an individual than his son Jesus Christ? Some believe in the existence of this ordinance, but consider it to be either reserved for those of particular church office or otherwise unnecessary. This experience is not a voyeuristic endeavor, but a requirement to attain exaltation.[50]

The possession of knowledge provided through revelation is not optional. It is the means by which a fallen man obtains eternal life. Although others who have attained more can show us the path they travelled to get to where they are, one man's salvation is insufficient to save another man.[51] Just as the Holy Ghost can only lead us to the point where Christ himself must teach us, the teachings and witnesses of men can only lead us to the point where the Holy Ghost can teach us. Remaining forever in dependence to another man for spiritual knowledge can never yield eternal life. Joseph taught that it is not sufficient for us to merely believe the expression of others' knowledge. He said,

> Search the scriptures...and ask your Heavenly Father, in the name of His Son Jesus Christ, to manifest the truth unto you, and if you do it with an eye single to his glory nothing doubting, He will answer you

---

[50] See "The Gospel of Jesus Christ."

[51] God taught Ezekiel the principle that there are some judgments that cannot be avoided, even if the most righteous men who ever lived interceded on your behalf. "The word of the Lord came again to me, saying, Son of man, when the land sinneth against me by trespassing grievously, then will I stretch out mine hand upon it, and will break the staff of the bread thereof, and will send famine upon it, and will cut off man and beast from it: Though these three men, Noah, Daniel, and Job, were in it, they should deliver but their own souls by their righteousness, saith the Lord God. If I cause noisome beasts to pass through the land, and they spoil it, so that it be desolate, that no man may pass through because of the beasts: Though these three men were in it, as I live, saith the Lord God, they shall deliver neither sons nor daughters; they only shall be delivered, but the land shall be desolate. Or if I bring a sword upon that land, and say, Sword, go through the land; so that I cut off man and beast from it: Though these three men were in it, as I live, saith the Lord God, they shall deliver neither sons nor daughters, but they only shall be delivered themselves. Or if I send a pestilence into that land, and pour out my fury upon it in blood, to cut off from it man and beast: Though Noah, Daniel, and Job, were in it, as I live, saith the Lord God, they shall deliver neither son nor daughter; they shall but deliver their own souls by their righteousness." (Ezekiel 14:12-20)

by the power of His Holy Spirit. You will then know for yourselves and not for another. You will not then be dependent on man for the knowledge of God; nor will there be any room for speculation. No; for when men receive their instruction from Him that made them, they know how He will save... (Joseph Smith, TPJS, p. 5.)

Because all gospel progress relies upon one's ability to receive individual revelation, a correct understanding of revelation through the Holy Ghost is the single most important bit of knowledge to obtain in the gospel. As the conduit through which all knowledge is received, a misunderstanding of what revelation is, how it is received, by whom it is received, or upon what topics it can be received can damn a person more immediately than anything else.

Topics on Which Revelation is Given

Joseph taught that there is a discrete portion of knowledge required to be saved. What happens when an individual believes that God would never grant revelation on some bit of that required portion of knowledge? That person will be damned, because he can never acquire the knowledge necessary for salvation.

It is of utmost importance to understand a very simple fact: God will grant revelation on any truth. Put differently, "by the power of the Holy Ghost ye may know the truth of *all* things." (Moroni 10:5.) God will reveal *all* things. All means everything! Nothing is withheld. There were no caveats given here, and you won't find any throughout scripture. In every case, the topics are boundless. There is no exception made for "things outside of your stewardship," no exceptions made for doctrinal topics, and no exclusion of issues being considered by church leaders. You can know the truth of *all* things, including whether church policies are God's will, whether or not the home teaching lesson is true doctrine, whether or not your neighbor ought to take the job she's been mulling over,[52] and whether Joseph Smith practiced polygamy.

We are not only *allowed* to ask for revelation on any subject, we are *commanded* to. Besides all the explicit commands to ask, seek, and knock,[53] we are also commanded to be like children. The boundless questioning best

---

[52] Such a thought is anathema in the context of the false tradition that you can only receive revelation for "your stewardship." The scriptures demonstrate a virtually unlimited list of examples of people receiving revelation for others. Still, many find a way to explain it away, for example by saying "but we aren't prophets." The question is whether being a prophet entitles you to get revelation for others, or whether getting revelation for others makes you a prophet. Again, the examples abound where God asks unsuspecting normal people out of the blue to go deliver his word to others.
[53] See Matthew 7:7, Luke 11:9, 3 Nephi 14:7, and D&C 88:63.

characterized by children is the type of attitude that brought about Joseph's first encounter with God. He read James 1:5 and *really believed* that God would not upbraid—or scold—him for his questions, no matter how taboo, unpopular, or indiscrete his questions might be. Do you suppose that Joseph would have ever had the faith to ask such bold questions (notably pertaining to the religion of his parents) if he had been taught that only his church leaders could pray about church doctrines being true or not? Perhaps this is one element of God's command that we should be like children. "And said, Verily I say unto you, Except ye be converted, and become as little children, ye shall not enter into the kingdom of heaven." (Matthew 18:3.)

"All things" must necessarily include those things not currently known or understood. Many today are taught that it is only acceptable to question God when the answer is already known. For example, Elder Oaks equates "seeking answers to mysteries" with "a strong desire to understand everything about every principle of the gospel," which he calls an invitation for Satan to lead the seeker into apostasy. [54] Everything and all are synonymous, meaning that having "a strong desire to understand everything about every principle of the gospel" is *exactly* what God commands us to do! This position stands in direct defiance of God's word.

Meanwhile, the term "mysteries" merely means anything in the gospel that is not common knowledge. This can include both things that have never been revealed as well as things that have previously been revealed but which are presently misunderstood. Therefore, the advice of those who council you to avoid seeking the mysteries of the gospel is akin to someone telling you that you are not permitted to ask questions except when the answer to those questions is already known. Besides being illogical, this position stands in opposition to God's word on the topic, as he not only promises that mysteries will be revealed to those who are faithful,[55] but also commands us (twice) to seek for the mysteries of God:

> Seek not for riches but for wisdom; and, behold, the mysteries of God shall be unfolded unto you, and then shall you be made rich. Behold, he that hath eternal life is rich. (D&C 11:7 and D&C 6:7.)

Further support for an expectation that God will reveal that which has not yet been revealed is codified in the "Articles of Faith":

---

[54] Dallin Oaks, "Our Strengths Can Become Our Downfall," BYU Speeches June 7, 1992

[55] "Yea, he that repenteth and exerciseth faith, and bringeth forth good works, and prayeth continually without ceasing—unto such it is given to know the mysteries of God; yea, unto such it shall be given to reveal things which never have been revealed; yea, and it shall be given unto such to bring thousands of souls to repentance, even as it has been given unto us to bring these our brethren to repentance." (Alma 26:22)

> We believe all that God has revealed, all that He does now reveal, and we believe that He will yet reveal many great and important things pertaining to the Kingdom of God. (Article of Faith 9.)

In yet another example, Nephi is told that all who search the mysteries of God diligently will be answered, and also that this is the duty of the Holy Ghost:

> For he that diligently seeketh shall find; and the mysteries of God shall be unfolded unto them, by the power of the Holy Ghost, as well in these times as in times of old, and as well in times of old as in times to come; wherefore, the course of the Lord is one eternal round. (1 Nephi 10:19.)

Some claim that God limits his definition of "all things" to the church callings a person might have. These statements almost always inject legalistic phrases, such as "for the entire church", that are not present in God's description of "all things." For example,

> When one person purports to receive revelation for another person outside his or her own area of responsibility—such as a Church member who claims to have revelation to guide the entire Church or a person who claims to have a revelation to guide another person over whom he or she has no presiding authority according to the order of the Church—you can be sure that such revelations are not from the Lord. (Elder Dallin H. Oaks, "Eight Ways God Can Speak to You," Ensign Sept 2004.)

Another example:

> First, we should understand what can be called the principle of 'stewardship in revelation.' ....Only the president of the Church receives revelation to guide the entire Church. Only the stake president receives revelation for the special guidance of the stake. The person who receives revelation for the ward is the bishop. For a family, it is the priesthood leadership of the family. Leaders receive revelation for their own stewardships. Individuals can receive revelation to guide their own lives. But when one person purports to receive revelation for another person outside his or her own stewardship---such as a Church member who claims to have revelation to guide the entire Church or a person who claims to have a revelation to guide another person over whom he or she has no presiding authority according to the order of the Church---you can be sure that such revelations are not from the Lord. (Elder Dahlin H. Oaks, "Revelation", Sep 29, 1981 BYU devotional.)

Recall that God makes no mention of "the order of the church" or "authority" when he defines *all* things. When an individual believes God will not tell him something, he will not be able to ask in faith. Nor will he believe if the revelation comes without asking. Suppose you were minding your own business one evening, praying for the welfare of a neighbor you knew was going through hard times. Suppose further that God unexpectedly answered your prayer for the welfare of that person by giving you a message on their behalf with the command to deliver it. Would you do so? Would you believe God, or would you assume it was all a figment of your imagination?

In reality, God would rather us not set limits on what he can reveal. We are promised that he "upbraideth not," or in other words, does not balk at the topics of the questions we might ask him. What would have happened if young Joseph Smith presupposed that, because he was not a leader of a church, he could not ask which of all churches was true?

Instead, we are told that what a person learns from God is limited not by calling or stewardship, but by the heed and diligence an individual exerts to obtain all truth:

> And now Alma began to expound these things unto him, saying: It is given unto many to know the mysteries of God; nevertheless they are laid under a strict command that they shall not impart only according to the portion of his word which he doth grant unto the children of men, according to the heed and diligence which they give unto him. (Alma 12:9.)

How well you obey what you have been told and how hard you search for more are the only limiting factors in what God reveals to you. Joseph reiterated this principle when he taught that "if a person gains more knowledge and intelligence in this life through his diligence and obedience than another, he will have so much the advantage in the world to come." (D&C 130:19.) This is not limited in any way by what your leaders do or don't know. It is totally possible for you or anyone else to know more than your leaders know. Some balk at this possibility, but the situation is guaranteed if you exercise greater heed and diligence in searching than they do.[56] Joseph challenged others to learn more than he knew, if they could: "God hath not revealed anything to Joseph, but what he will make known unto the Twelve, and even the least Saint may know all things as fast as he is able to bear

---

[56] Some of the recent brethren (President Hinckley, President Packer, and Elder Haight, for example) have stated that General Authorities simply do not have much time to study the scriptures. If you study more than they do, it is likely you know more than they do. Also, recall that a willingness to be wrong and let go of previous beliefs is a big factor in how quickly you can learn. Mormon called this being "quick to observe," a trait observed in himself by Amaron, which resulted in his assignment to take the sacred records while only a young man.

them..."[57] If the most ignorant Saint exerts greater diligence and obedience than another, no matter whether the other be a Pope or a President, that ignorant Saint will soon be in possession of greater knowledge than the other in short order. God does not tether what an individual can know to what level of knowledge his church leaders have attained—such defies the law of heaven.

Brigham Young echoed the same sentiment. He said,

> My knowledge is, if you will follow the teachings of Jesus Christ and his Apostles, as recorded in the New Testament, every man and woman will be put in possession of the Holy Ghost; every person will become a Prophet, Seer, and Revelator, and an expounder of truth. They will know things that are, that will be, and that have been. They will understand things in heaven, things on the earth, and things under the earth, things of time, and things of eternity, according to their several callings[58] and capacities. (Brigham Young, JD 1:243.)

If Joseph was right in teaching that there is a discrete portion of knowledge required to be saved, and an individual came to believe that God would never grant revelation on some bit of that required portion, that person could never be saved. This is why it is critically important to understand that God has not, does not, and will not ever limit the topics on which revelation can be received. Any man who teaches that he does is not only anti-scriptural, he is anti-Christ, and the degree to which you listen to him will be the degree to which you are damned.

Revelation can Contradict Traditions

The Catholics have long believed that revelation that counters the tradition of their elders cannot be from God:

> A true mystic or visionary will always obey the legitimate religious superiors and authorities in the Church. We can be sure that if a mystic or seer is in any way disobedient to the local Bishop or their religious Superiors, then the alleged revelations and messages cannot be authentic. God's graces flow through His Church in union with

---

[57] "Discourses of the Prophet Joseph Smith," p. 150-151.

[58] The word calling here does not have the modern LDS meaning (church assignment). The 1828 Webster definition gives the following options: 1) A naming, or inviting; a reading over or reciting in order, or a call of names with a view to obtain an answer, as in legislative bodies. 2) Vocation; profession; trade; usual occupation, or employment. 3) Class of persons engaged in any profession or employment. 4) Divine summons, vocation, or invitation."

the legitimate authority (ie—Pope, Bishops, Religious Superiors) that He Himself has established.[59]

To claim that revelation cannot contradict tradition is to claim that leaders are infallible, a position that is overwhelmingly refuted by historical examples of repeated deviation of religious tradition from God's revealed law. For example, Jesus showed through precept and example that the leaders of his time lived a tradition that contradicted God's. When asked why his disciples "transgress[ed] the tradition of the elders," "he answered and said unto them, "Why do ye also transgress the commandment of God by your tradition?" (Matthew 15:2-3.) In this case Jesus was referring to God's word as recorded in the scriptures.

Unfortunately, the LDS church has adopted[60] the same position as the Catholics:

> In 1912 the first presidency warned, ""When visions, dreams, tongues, prophecy, impressions or an extraordinary gift or inspiration, convey something out of harmony with the accepted revelations of the Church or contrary to the decisions that its constituted authorities, latter-day saints may know that it is not of God no matter how plausible it may appear. (1912 First Presidency Letter, recently quoted by Elder Oaks.)

Besides contradicting God's word and logic, it seems it seems rather ironic that any in the church would adopt a position that would discredit the experience of its founder by arguing the impossibility of anyone having a similar experience. Joseph's "visions, dreams, and prophecies" strongly opposed the position of the constituted authorities of his time. God uses revelation to point out the false traditions that have been embraced contrary to the scriptures. Without allowing such corrections, an institution cuts itself off from God's attempts to point out errors that have crept in.[61]

---

[59]   http://www.mysticsofthechurch.com/2009/11/obedience-to-catholic-church-judging.html, retrieved 24 Sept 2015.

[60] Although Elder Oaks' position has been the status quo for many decades, there was a time when Joseph's position of trusting the Spirit above all was still accepted by some leaders in the church. "You must work through the Spirit. If that leads you into conflict with the program of the Church, you follow the voice of the Spirit." (S. Dilworth Young (First Council of Seventy), quoted in Benson Y. Parkinson, "S. Dilworth Young: General Authority, Scouter, Poet" (American Fork, UT: Covenant Communications, 1994), 297; Deseret News 1995-1996 Church Almanac, 68, for Young.)

[61] Apostasy does not require the wholesale abandonment of truth. Instead, it merely requires slow, small corruptions to the truths delivered through a dispensation head. "Apostasy never came by renouncing the gospel, but always by corrupting it." (Hugh Nibley, Temples and Cosmos, pg. 395.)

The Book of Mormon clearly teaches that the Spirit supersedes man's traditions. Nephi was taught why his understanding was incorrect in assuming that God prohibited all killing. He was commanded to kill Laban by the Spirit despite the tradition that killing was always a sin. King Benjamin openly credited his people's access to the scriptures as having prevented their adoption of traditions that would have contradicted God's word:

> I say unto you, my sons, were it not for these things, which have been kept and preserved by the hand of God, that we might read and understand of his mysteries, and have his commandments always before our eyes, that even our fathers would have dwindled in unbelief, and we should have been like unto our brethren, the Lamanites, who know nothing concerning these things, or even do not believe them when they are taught them, because of the traditions of their fathers, which are not correct. (Mosiah 1:5.)

Merely having the scriptures was insufficient. They had to have them "always before [their] eyes." Not only that, but they obviously had to believe that the scriptures held precedent to any innovations by their leaders. They had to take God's word as a higher authority than man's word, or words from men claimed to be God's. To King Benjamin's people, the Spirit was the supreme authority of truth.

Although the scriptures can and should be used to separate God's word from man's tradition, they are not the supreme source of distinction. It is the Spirit—and only the Spirit—that can divide truth from error and reveal the truth of all things.[62]

If we accept that men, even leaders, can be incorrect, and we know that the Spirit can and does reveal the truth of all things, we must accept that the Spirit can and will reveal to us discrepancies between the positions espoused by church leaders and God's will.

The "great apostasy" occurred because church leaders made changes based on committee decisions instead of revelation.[63] Unwilling to follow the

---

[62] "And by the power of the Holy Ghost ye may know the truth of all things." (Moroni 10:5) "For behold, again I say unto you that if ye will enter in by the way, and receive the Holy Ghost, it will show unto you all things what ye should do." (2 Nephi 32:5) "For they that are wise and have received the truth, and have taken the Holy Spirit for their guide, and have not been deceived—verily I say unto you, they shall not be hewn down and cast into the fire, but shall abide the day." (D&C 45:57)

[63] See "The Great Apostasy" by Elder Talmage. Talmage's book used to be part of the missionary library. However, Talmage's book and Talmage's correct conclusion has been replaced with the false idea that Christ's original church apostatized because apostles died without passing on their authority. History shows that the apostles did continue to call leaders of the church before their death, including Linus, the priesthood leader from whom the Catholics trace their authority. The modern LDS

doctrines as given by their dispensation head, they were unable to receive new revelation, and therefore substituted their own ideas for God's word.[64] As innovations and the commandments of men replace the commandments of God, the need for an individual to sift through the philosophies of men to reveal and reclaim the revelations given to the dispensation head increases. In short, the importance of personal revelation increases as the receipt of institutional revelation decreases.

Frequency of Revelation

The Book of Mormon describes how often Nephi and Lehi from the book of Helaman received revelation:

> And in the seventy and ninth year there began to be much strife. But it came to pass that Nephi and Lehi, and many of their brethren who knew concerning the true points of doctrine, having many revelations daily, therefore they did preach unto the people, insomuch that they did put an end to their strife in that same year. (Helaman 11:23.)

The Book of Mormon not only tells us that these two received many revelations daily, but that their knowledge depended upon those revelations. They are not alone in experiencing a high frequency of revelation. Jesus himself, our supreme example, said that God commanded him in all things.[65] Such consummate guidance would surely require many revelations daily.

---

church says Linus didn't hold enough of the priesthood, despite the fact that this situation is almost exactly identical to the succession from Joseph Smith to Brigham Young; Joseph did not appoint Brigham as his successor, but in a junior office of the priesthood. With Joseph's death, the quorum held the highest remaining priesthood, and decided that was equivalent to what Joseph held and have been continuing the precession as if that were the case ever since. The LDS church does not have a superior claim to priesthood keys than the Catholic church. Any superior authority is a result of more correct doctrine; any claim to being "the Lord's" (see 2 Nephi 28:3) stands or falls proportional to how much of Joseph's revelations we ignore or replace.
[64] "All historical Christian churches agree that revelation for the direction of the church ceased with the last of the apostles," one author has written. History shows, in fact, that after the first century, church leaders, in order to decide important issues, could not (and did not) appeal to heaven for authoritative direction because they did not possess the keys of the kingdom. There were still honorable people on the earth who received personal inspiration for their individual lives. But the church was run largely by men who gathered in councils and held debates, letting their decisions rest on the collected wisdom of mortal beings." ("Apostasy, Restoration, and Lessons in Faith," Ensign, December 1995)
[65] "The Son can do nothing of himself, but what he seeth the Father do: for what things soever he doeth, these also doeth the Son likewise. For the Father loveth the Son, and sheweth him all things that himself doeth." (John 5:19-20)

Are individuals who receive frequent revelations rare? The Book of Mormon is a wonderful experiment for this question. How often do we see God communicating with individuals in the Book of Mormon? If you were to highlight every passage that describes God communicating with individuals, you will find that almost every verse of almost every page is highlighted. The Book of Mormon is an overwhelming evidence that God is exceedingly willing—even anxious—to communicate to individuals through revelation. So why don't we receive more revelations?

The frequency of revelation is diminished under certain circumstances. Nephi received the Liahona, which would give them instruction from time to time
"according to the faith and diligence and heed which we did give unto [it]." (1 Nephi 16:28.) Alma later taught that revelation works the same way:

> And now Alma began to expound these things unto him, saying: It is given unto many to know the mysteries of God; nevertheless they are laid under a strict command that they shall not impart only according to the portion of his word which he doth grant unto the children of men, according to the heed and diligence which they give unto him. (Alma 12:9.)

To heed is to take notice of. Diligence means persistent effort. Those who believe God speaks only infrequently, and that revelations are something exceptional and out of the norm will never exercise sufficient heed and diligence. Consequently, they will receive revelation far less often than they otherwise could. If you want more revelation, believe and obey the revelation you already have.[66]

Unbelief in God's expressed desire to give us many revelations dramatically hinders its receipt. Modern Mormons teach that revelation is infrequent and unnecessary:

> Revelation is not constant. The Lord's way puts limits on how often He will speak to us by His Spirit. Not understanding this, some have been misled by expecting revelations too frequently. (Elder Dahlin H. Oaks, "In his own time, in his own way," Ensign August 2013.)

> I have learned that strong, impressive spiritual experiences do not come to us very frequently. (President Boyd K. Packer, "The Candle of the Lord," January 1983.)

> Let me say first that we have a great body of revelation, the vast majority of which came from the prophet Joseph Smith. We don't

---

[66] There are many revelations which, if received by a modern Mormon, would be rejected as "from the devil." One example was given previously: God giving you an instruction "outside of your stewardship."

need much revelation. We need to pay more attention to the revelation we've already received. (SF Gate, "SUNDAY INTERVIEW—Musings of the Main Mormon / Gordon B. Hinckley" April 13, 1997.)

If you believe that God will not give many revelations, you will not seek to have many revelations, and you will not believe them if you do receive them.

Nephi warned of those in our day who would state that we have enough revelation. "Wo be unto him that shall say: We have received the word of God, and we need no more of the word of God, for we have enough!" (2 Nephi 28:29.) Such satiety is a contrasting emotion to that expressed by the Book of Mormon prophets, whose desire for the word of God was never quenched. When left to choose between the modern examples quoted, and Lehi and Nephi, we must ask ourselves which example will draw us closer to the example given by the Lord? It is wrong to be satisfied in the consequences of living below our privileges.

If an individual believes that God does not want to be bothered with our questions, will he bother asking? Will God answer a question that remains unanswered? Jesus commands his followers to seek, ask, and knock an absurd number of times (see, for example, Matthew 7:7, D&C 11:5, D&C 4:7, Luke 11:9, D&C 6:5, 3 Nephi 27:29, etc.). Those who teach that God has limited how often he will give revelation, and encourage individuals not to ask, seek, and knock stand in opposition to Christ.

Revelation is Information, Not Emotion

As described at the outset, there is a discrete quantity of knowledge that has to be gained via personal revelation in order for a man to be saved. You cannot get there through accumulating emotion, but rather knowledge. The exclusive mechanism designed to convey that knowledge is individual revelation through the Holy Ghost. Therefore, it is supremely important to understand what is and what is not revelation.

The 2014 priesthood and relief society manual quotes President Benson as teaching "We hear the words of the Lord most often by a feeling. If we are humble and sensitive, the Lord will prompt us through our feelings."[67] This is false doctrine.

Revelation is informational, not emotional. It consists of the conveyance of knowledge, intelligence, light, and truth. As Joseph taught, "This first comforter or Holy Ghost has no other effect than pure intelligence."

Joseph taught that it wasn't easy to recognize the Holy Ghost's effect. He said that the key to learning to recognize the Holy Ghost is to notice when pure intelligence flows into you:

---

[67] Teachings of Presidents of the Church: Ezra Taft Benson, (2014), 156–66

A person may profit by noticing the first intimation of the spirit of revelation; for instance, when you feel pure intelligence flowing into you, it may give you sudden strokes of ideas, so that by noticing it, you may find it fulfilled the same day or soon; (i.e.,) those things that were presented unto your minds by the Spirit of God, will come to pass; and thus by learning the Spirit of God and understanding it, you may grow into the principle of revelation, until you become perfect in Christ Jesus. (Joseph Smith, TPJS, p. 151.)

Joseph indicated that at least some of the intelligence conveyed through revelation consists of predictions about the future. These predictions serve as signposts to validate the other instructions received in the same "sudden strokes of ideas." Notice that Joseph omits the description of feelings as an indicator of the Holy Ghost or revelation. To Joseph, revelation was informational, not emotional. It is this information that is required to bring a fallen man up to the character of Christ, which is required to merit salvation. For, as quoted before,

A man is saved no faster than he gets knowledge, for if he does not get knowledge, he will be brought into captivity by some evil power in the other world, as evil spirits will have more knowledge, and consequently more power than many men who are on the earth. Hence it needs revelation to assist us, and give us knowledge of the things of God. (Joseph Smith, TPJS, p. 154.)

The essentiality of personal revelation for salvation is the driving force behind the need for baptism. Baptism gives access to the channel through which God will teach us what we need to know to come up from our lost and fallen state to where we need to be to merit salvation. Nephi describes baptism as the entrance to the way or path to eternal life. The receipt of constant additional knowledge through the Holy Ghost advances us along this path, which culminates in a personal encounter with Christ:

For behold, again I say unto you that if ye will enter in by the way, and receive the Holy Ghost, it will show unto you all things what ye should do. Behold, this is the doctrine of Christ, and there will be no more doctrine given until after he shall manifest himself unto you in the flesh. And when he shall manifest himself unto you in the flesh, the things which he shall say unto you shall ye observe to do. (2 Nephi 32:5-6.)

This same journey is depicted in the endowment ceremony, where Adam and Eve progress along the path by heeding the light and truth they have already received, and receiving more. Never in the endowment does God send Adam and Eve feelings to advance them along this path. Instead, God sends messages consisting of new information that helps them become more like Christ.

One stumbling block that prevents recognition that revelation is not emotion is the concept that the fruits of the Spirit are "love, joy, peace, longsuffering, gentleness, goodness, faith, meekness, and temperance." (Galatians 5.) Therefore, one may conclude, if I feel love, joy, or peace (all feelings), I am receiving revelation and/or am under the persuasion of the Holy Ghost. Unfortunately, this common understanding is taken out of context and, as will be explained momentarily, has damning consequences. Because emotions are a product of the carnal natural man, they lead one in a course away from God by both encouraging ungodly behavior that feels good and by discouraging godly behavior that is difficult or painful. Receiving emotions as revelation blinds the individual to their true state before God: they cannot see that they do not receive any or much real revelation, yet are shielded from the productive conclusion that repentance of false tradition or willful sin is required in order to receive real revelation.

When Paul uses the words love, joy, and peace, he is not describing what it feels like to have the Spirit with you. He is describing the works of one who is guided by the Spirit, and contrasting that to the works of one who is guided by the flesh:

> Now the works of the flesh are manifest, which are these; Adultery, fornication, uncleanness, lasciviousness, Idolatry, witchcraft, hatred, variance, emulations, wrath, strife, seditions, heresies, Envyings, murders, drunkenness, revellings, and such like: of the which I tell you before, as I have also told you in time past, that they which do such things shall not inherit the kingdom of God. But the fruit of the Spirit is love, joy, peace, longsuffering, gentleness, goodness, faith, Meekness, temperance: against such there is no law. (Galatians 5:19-23.)

Just as the fruit of the tree of life is not the iron rod, but the result of walking the iron rod, peace, love, and joy are the fruits received by those who respond obediently to the information conveyed by the Holy Ghost. Incidentally, Paul also describes the "fruit" of the Spirit in another letter, here again speaking of them as what a person guided by the Spirit will produce in their lives, not what it feels like to have the Spirit communicate something to you:

> Let no man deceive you with vain words: for because of these things cometh the wrath of God upon the children of disobedience. Be not ye therefore partakers with them. For ye were sometimes darkness, but now are ye light in the Lord: walk as children of light: (For the fruit of the Spirit is in all goodness and righteousness and truth;) Proving what is acceptable unto the Lord. (Ephesians 5:6-10.)

Emotion, peace, or love are not the voice of the Spirit. Rather, a person might respond with these emotions upon hearing the information communicated by the voice of the Spirit. Emotions are not the content of revelation, although they can be a reaction to it.

A telltale sign that a message is from God is that a person is edified afterward. What is edification? God told Oliver and Joseph:

> Verily, verily, I say unto thee, blessed art thou for what thou hast done; for thou hast inquired of me, and behold, as often as thou hast inquired thou hast received instruction of my Spirit. If it had not been so, thou wouldst not have come to the place where thou art at this time. Behold, thou knowest that thou hast inquired of me and I did enlighten thy mind; and now I tell thee these things that thou mayest know that thou hast been enlightened by the Spirit of truth; (D&C 6:14-15.)

In other words, you can know you were enlightened by the Spirit of truth, because your mind received instruction that you did not have before. Edification, then, is knowing more than you did previously.

The most pure and noble emotions can be summoned on demand, and then can evaporate just as quickly as they came, all without causing any lasting change in the person, all without effecting a change in that person's character. A mundane movie can elicit high emotion, but the effects are fleeting. Truth, on the other hand, changes people. It edifies them, because as a result of embracing it they become more like Jesus in thought, word, and deed. If it comes by any other way, it is not of God.

Real Revelation Frequently Causes Negative Feelings

A misunderstanding that peace and love are the message from God leads men to reject the sizeable quantity of revelations from God that evoke negative emotions. Deep sorrow, fear, or distress are not signals that the message received is not from God. They are valid responses to real revelation. For example, the response of Lehi's family upon reading the words on the Liahona:

> And it came to pass that when my father beheld the things which were written upon the ball, he did fear and tremble exceedingly, and also my brethren and the sons of Ishmael and our wives. (1 Nephi 16:27.)

Considering peace, love, and joy to always accompany God's messages[68] is damning. Consider the prophets of the scriptures. How many

---

[68] "When you do good, you feel good, and that is the Holy Ghost speaking to you." (Teachings of Presidents of the Church: Ezra Taft Benson, (2014), 156–66)

messages did they receive from God that gave them peace, love, and joy? Isaiah described his horror when God revealed to him his nothingness. Moses collapsed in weakness after being in the presence of God. Isaiah certainly did not click his heels in joy when God instructed him to travel naked for three years as a sign to Israel. Hosea was instructed to marry a whore. Peter was shown how he would die ignominiously. Young Hezekiah, who had served God at great travail in a time of abhorrent wickedness, was told he would shortly die. All of these messages were from God, and none conveyed anything close to peace, love, and joy. If these men of God used modern Mormonism's criteria for revelation, they would have dismissed God's instructions to them as false revelation. They would have cut themselves off from God through disobedience to his word, being in open rebellion against God.

Negative feelings from revelation can come because God is revealing a difficult assignment to us, like asking Isaiah to go without clothing for three years as a sign to Israel. But it can also come because you are being presented with something that is so radically different to what you currently believe. Interpreting negative emotions as a negative signal from God assures that the most important revelations—those that call us to abandon our false idols and false traditions—will be rejected due to misinterpreting negative feelings as a negative sign from God. These negative feelings can be cognitive dissonance, a well-known and well-studied phenomenon that occurs when one's actions, beliefs, and understanding of truth jolt out of alignment, usually as the result of learning something new. If we believe that the purpose of individual revelation is to teach us the things we currently do not know, or point out the things about which we are mistaken, we ought to expect cognitive dissonance as a regular occurrence and a hallmark of spiritual growth.[69] An absence of this feeling would indicate a lack of spiritual growth. The solution for it is to bring your actions and beliefs into accord with your newly expanded understanding of truth.

It is not negative feelings, but positive ones, that are a rare commodity among men of God in the scriptures. The Spirit led those men from one tragedy to another, not from one exuberant ecstasy to another. The treasure of these men was in heaven—found in a face-to-face encounter with angels and God himself—not on earth in the form of temporal happiness or worldly peace. Jesus said plainly that the peace he gives is NOT as the world gives. It is to be found in the personal promise of eternal life from him to you, a peace that can remain present even in a deluge of earthly discord

---

[69] A few brief examples of cognitive dissonance in the scriptures: Jonah when God chastened him for desiring the destruction of Babylon, Nephi when God told him to slay Laban, Laman and Lemuel when told Jersulalem was wicked, Noah and his priests when Abinadi delivered God's rebuke of their religion, the Pharisees when Jesus rebuked their religion, etc.

consisting of immense personal suffering, insecurity, loneliness, and loss. This is the fruit of the Spirit: the peace that Abinadi felt as he delivered his last sermon, knowing he would be burned at the stake for doing so; the peace Peter felt even after Jesus told him he would be crucified for his ministry; the peace Alma and Amulek felt as they watched their converts burn at the stake and lay on the ground naked, bound for a seemingly interminable time; the peace felt by Paul as he endured several shipwrecks, privations, and trials before potentates, finally facing his death.

Treating negative feelings as a sign of displeasure from God, or assuming it signals the withdrawal of the Spirit, is tantamount to self-inflicted damnation. This is like a plant hiding from the sun—the result will always be a withering away from required nutrients for growth. God warned us against this gross misjudgment:

> Woe to those who suppose what is evil to be good and what is good, evil! They put darkness for light and light for darkness; they make bitterness sweet and the sweet bitter. Woe to those who are wise in their own eyes and clever in their own view! (Isaiah 5:20-21, Gileadi Translation.)

Although our reaction to God's revelations frequently includes negative feelings, the fruits of these messages are something very different. They are what occurs when one heeds the message—not the fruit of hearing the message but of doing what the message says. The fruits of heeding even God's hardest messages caused peace, love, and joy because they were all drawn closer to God, whose companionship with the righteous always produces those fruits.

An over focus on emotion as a substitute for real spiritual experiences is nothing new in modern Mormonism. In 1981 the Academic Vice-President of BYU said,

> ...too much of the literature used, seen, and quoted in the Church today is just sentimental trash which is designed to pull our heart strings or to moisten our eyes—but it is not born of true spiritual experience. The tendency of our youth to use sentimental stories in Church talks creates a culture of spiritual misunderstanding in which thinking and learning are discouraged. Because our youth often respond positively to sentimentalism, there is a danger that we might cater to that in the Church instruction more generally...It [emotional sentimentalism] should never be leaned upon as a substitute for spirituality. Reliance on sentimentality will stunt our own spiritual growth by misleading us and filling our understanding with false experiences. ("Reason and Revelation," Noel B. Reynolds, BYU, Summer 1981.)

Relying on emotions as revelation is an invitation to be led astray. After all, emotion is a carnal sense, and while the carnal sense, which also include sight and smell, are indispensible tools in our lives, they are channels loaded with deceptive noise from Satan and his followers. Korihor admitted that the devil deceived him by teaching him false doctrines that were pleasing to his carnal senses, and he taught them successfully for the same reason:

> But behold, the devil hath deceived me; for he appeared unto me in the form of an angel, and said unto me: Go and reclaim this people, for they have all gone astray after an unknown God. And he said unto me: There is no God; yea, and he taught me that which I should say. And I have taught his words; and I taught them because they were pleasing unto the carnal mind; and I taught them, even until I had much success, insomuch that I verily believed that they were true; and for this cause I withstood the truth, even until I have brought this great curse upon me. (Alma 30:53.)

Thus we see that those who teach doctrine through "pleasing the carnal mind" are operating from the devil's playbook. Unfortunately, for over a century modern Mormonism has plied this tack in venues ranging from the sacred with temple movies to the public with television commercials and public films shown by missionaries and visitors centers. The construction of the Legacy theater in the now Joseph Smith Memorial Building was a pioneering effort in this agenda. President Hinckley instructed the director: "I want them to leave the theater crying."[70] In fact, Bonneville Communications, one of the church's many businesses, has trademarked the concept of coercing people into action based on emotional manipulation. They call it "HeartSell."[71] Recipients of pleas to the carnal mind should ask themselves, is it the Spirit or is it "strategic emotional advertising"?

---

[70] See http://onthisdayinmormonhistory.blogspot.com/2008/10/june-27th.html

[71] "For more than 30 years, our creative professionals have designed public service and direct response messages for national nonprofit organizations such as the Huntsman Cancer Institute, Boy Scouts of America, National Hospice Foundation, The Church of Jesus Christ of Latter-day Saints and The Salvation Army.
Our unique strength is the ability to touch the hearts and minds of our audiences, evoking first feeling, then thought and, finally, action. We call this uniquely powerful brand of creative 'HeartSell'® - strategic emotional advertising that stimulates response." (http://www.bonneville.com/?nid=32) There are those in the church who continue to encourage members to substitute real revelation with powerful emotional ritual. For example, Elder Andersen suggested repeating the testimony of Joseph Smith until you get a "witness" that it is true: "Gain a personal witness of the Prophet Joseph....read the testimony of the Prophet Joseph....Read it often. Consider recording the testimony of Joseph Smith in your own voice, listening to it regularly, and sharing it with friends. Listening to the Prophet's testimony in your own voice

Remember that revelation is the link that attaches us to God and instructs us on how to return to him. It is the most important concept of the gospel to get right, because it is the only thing that prevents us from getting everything else wrong. That is why Joseph said,

> ...nothing is a greater injury to the children of men than to be under the influence of a false spirit when they think they have the Spirit of God. Thousands have felt the influence of its terrible power and baneful effects. Long pilgrimages have been undertaken, penances endured, and pain, misery and ruin have followed in their train; nations have been convulsed, kingdoms overthrown, provinces laid waste, and blood, carnage and desolation are habiliments in which it has been clothed. (Joseph Smith, TPJS, p. 205.)

Perhaps foreseeing that this ancient tactic emotional misdirection would continue to be used in our day, Paul guided us to hearken to our spiritual—not our fleshy—guidance systems:

> That the righteousness of the law might be fulfilled in us, who walk not after the flesh, but after the Spirit. For they that are after the flesh do mind the things of the flesh; but they that are after the Spirit the things of the Spirit. For to be carnally minded is death; but to be spiritually minded is life and peace. Because the carnal mind is enmity against God: for it is not subject to the law of God, neither indeed can be. So then they that are in the flesh cannot please God. (Romans 8:4-8.)

Note that he says that the carnal mind is enmity against God, or stands in opposition to him. He says the carnal senses cannot be subject to the law of God. This idea is paralleled by Alma who taught that you don't acquire revelatory knowledge through your feelings, but through the Spirit: "And I would not that ye think that I know of myself—not of the temporal but of the spiritual, not of the carnal mind but of God." (Alma 36:4.)

Revelation is Composed of Words

Personal revelation prevents deception because the Holy Ghost "speaketh of things as they really are, and of things as they really will be" (Jacob 4:13).

> For they that are wise and have received the truth, and have taken the Holy Spirit for their guide, and have not been deceived—verily I say

---

will help bring the witness you seek." (Oct 2014 GC.) Elder Andersen did not mention prayer or the Holy Ghost as part of receiving a witness of Joseph Smith.

unto you, they shall not be hewn down and cast into the fire, but shall abide the day. (D&C 45:57.)

Again, the Holy Ghost *speaks*. It projects informational ideas, not feelings.

In the scriptures, we are given countless examples of revelation received. None of them indicate the reception of an emotion or feeling. God describes the mechanisms of revelation in plainness:

> Verily I say unto you, he that is ordained of me and sent forth to preach the word of truth by the Comforter, in the Spirit of truth, doth he preach it by the Spirit of truth or some other way? And if it be by some other way it is not of God. And again, he that receiveth the word of truth, doth he receive it by the Spirit of truth or some other way? If it be some other way it is not of God. Therefore, why is it that ye cannot understand and know, that he that receiveth the word by the Spirit of truth receiveth it as it is preached by the Spirit of truth? Wherefore, he that preacheth and he that receiveth, understand one another, and both are edified and rejoice together. And that which doth not edify is not of God, and is darkness. That which is of God is light; and he that receiveth light, and continueth in God, receiveth more light; and that light groweth brighter and brighter until the perfect day. And again, verily I say unto you, and I say it that you may know the truth, that you may chase darkness from among you; (D&C 50:17-25.)

The Spirit of truth teaches not by issuing a feeling, but by giving the *word* of truth. "Therefore, whoso readeth it, let him understand, for the Spirit manifesteth truth;" (D&C 91:4.) It is truth and it is conveyed through words. Though revelatory ideas can come, as Joseph described, in a sudden rush, they are writable. You can translate those ideas into words.

The Lord does not say we should live by every feeling that proceeds from the mouth of God. He says:

> For you shall live by every word that proceedeth forth from the mouth of God. For the word of the Lord is truth, and whatsoever is truth is light, and whatsoever is light is Spirit, even the Spirit of Jesus Christ. (D&C 84:44-45.)

Words come out of one's mouth, not feelings. *Voices* are heard, not felt.

> Behold, that which you hear is as the voice of one crying in the wilderness—in the wilderness, because you cannot see him—my voice, because my voice is Spirit; my Spirit is truth; truth abideth and hath no end; and if it be in you it shall abound. (D&C 88:66.)

Some may quip that God's voice and the Holy Ghost are two separate things. However, the Book of Mormon prophets would disagree. Mormon wrote:

> For immediately after I had learned these things of you I inquired of the Lord concerning the matter. And the word of the Lord came to me by the power of the Holy Ghost, saying: Listen [not feel] to the words of Christ, your Redeemer, your Lord and your God. Behold, I came into the world not to call the righteous but sinners to repentance; the whole need no physician, but they that are sick; wherefore, little children are whole, for they are not capable of committing sin; wherefore the curse of Adam is taken from them in me, that it hath no power over them; and the law of circumcision is done away in me. And after this manner did the Holy Ghost manifest the word of God unto me; wherefore, my beloved son, I know that it is solemn mockery before God, that ye should baptize little children. (Moroni 8:7-9.)

After what manner did the Holy Ghost manifest the word of God to Mormon? Through an audible voice.

Another popular misconception is to equate "still small voice" with a feeling, despite the fact that the phrase is not "still small feeling." The phrase itself comes from the story of Elijah seeking God in a cave after much persecution. In response to his prayer, there was an earthquake,

> And after the earthquake a fire; but the Lord was not in the fire: and after the fire a still small voice. And it was so, when Elijah heard it, that he wrapped his face in his mantle, and went out, and stood in the entering in of the cave. And, behold, there came a voice unto him, and said, What doest thou here, Elijah? (1 Kings 19:12-13.)

Even the example from which the phrase is lifted plainly describes the hearing of an actual voice. It communicated information, in this case causing him to leave the cave. In modern times, Joseph described the still small voiced in our canonized scriptures this way:

> Yea, thus saith the still small voice, which whispereth through and pierceth all things, and often times it maketh my bones to quake while it maketh manifest, saying: And it shall come to pass that I, the Lord God, will send one mighty and strong, holding the scepter of power in his hand, clothed with light for a covering, whose mouth shall utter words, eternal words; while his bowels shall be a fountain of truth, to set in order the house of God, and to arrange by lot the inheritances of the saints whose names are found, and the names of their fathers, and of their children, enrolled in the book of the law of God; While that man, who was called of God and appointed, that

putteth forth his hand to steady the ark of God, shall fall by the shaft of death, like as a tree that is smitten by the vivid shaft of lightning. And all they who are not found written in the book of remembrance shall find none inheritance in that day, but they shall be cut asunder, and their portion shall be appointed them among unbelievers, where are wailing and gnashing of teeth. These things I say not of myself; therefore, as the Lord speaketh, he will also fulfil. (D&C 85:6-10.)

Note that here Joseph attributes a paragraph of God's writeable word to the still small voice. To Joseph, the still small voice of the Holy Ghost was an actual voice that conveyed information. The detail here exceeds what an emotion or feeling could convey.

Conclusion

If you believed that God did not give much revelation, would you ask for it? If you believed that God limited what kind of revelation you could receive, would you believe revelations not fitting that description? Would you pray about doctrine if you didn't think God allowed you to do so? Would you expect God to give you revelations about your day-to-day life if you did not believe such was necessary?

Would you trust in what God says to you in revelation, even if it disagrees with something you've heard before? Would you believe God's word to you, even if it is hard to hear and causes negative feelings?

I hope it is abundantly clear that the false traditions regarding revelation embraced in modern Mormonism will prevent an individual from hearing God's voice and returning to his presence. Well did Jesus say about those who taught such damning doctrine in his day:

Woe unto you, lawyers! for ye have taken away the key of knowledge: ye entered not in yourselves, and them that were entering in ye hindered. (Luke 11:52.)

No Poor Among Them

One of the qualifying properties of Zion is that there be no poor there.[72] Because our ability to achieve Zion is inescapably tied to our ability to care for the poor, our effort to achieve Zion can be measured by how much effort we expend in care for the poor.

Care for the poor may seem to some to be an auxiliary commandment. After all, Jesus said that loving our neighbor was the second commandment, second to the commandment to love God.[73] And yet, King Benjamin taught that "when ye are in the service of your fellow beings ye are only in the service of your God,"[74] suggesting that the way that we serve God is through serving our neighbor. Therefore, in a sense, there is only one real great commandment, and it has to do with caring for the poor.[75] This suggests that a significant indication of how well we are living the first great commandment is through analyzing how well we are living the second great commandment. Proverbs 14:31 suggests that the relationship holds in reverse as well: "He that oppresseth the poor reproacheth his Maker: but he that honoureth him hath mercy on the poor." We can measure our love of God by the love we have for our neighbor, and we can measure our disobedience towards God by the degree of poor treatment that we dispense on our neighbor.

Jesus taught it this way:

When the Son of man shall come in his glory, and all the holy angels with him, then shall he sit upon the throne of his glory: And before

---

[72] "And the Lord called his people Zion, because they were of one heart and one mind, and dwelt in righteousness; and there was no poor among them." (Moses 7:18.)

[73] "Master, which is the great commandment in the law? Jesus said unto him, Thou shalt love the Lord thy God with all thy heart, and with all thy soul, and with all thy mind. This is the first and great commandment. And the second is like unto it, Thou shalt love thy neighbour as thyself. On these two commandments hang all the law and the prophets." (Matthew 22:36-40.)

[74] Mosiah 2:17.

[75] As an aside, modern Mormons often criticize those who say that their religion is to try to be a good person. Modern Mormons point out the necessity of ordinances despite the fact that Jesus did not include ordinances among the great commandments. Perhaps this is because, while provision exists for ordinances, there is no route that I am aware of to become charitable by proxy. One lost heathen who is kind means more to heaven than ninety-nine close-fisted Pharisees.

him shall be gathered all nations: and he shall separate them one from another, as a shepherd divideth his sheep from the goats: And he shall set the sheep on his right hand, but the goats on the left. Then shall the King say unto them on his right hand, Come, ye blessed of my Father, inherit the kingdom prepared for you from the foundation of the world: For I was an hungred, and ye gave me meat: I was thirsty, and ye gave me drink: I was a stranger, and ye took me in: Naked, and ye clothed me: I was sick, and ye visited me: I was in prison, and ye came unto me. Then shall the righteous answer him, saying, Lord, when saw we thee an hungred, and fed thee? or thirsty, and gave thee drink? When saw we thee a stranger, and took thee in? or naked, and clothed thee? Or when saw we thee sick, or in prison, and came unto thee? And the King shall answer and say unto them, Verily I say unto you, Inasmuch as ye have done it unto one of the least of these my brethren, ye have done it unto me. Then shall he say also unto them on the left hand, Depart from me, ye cursed, into everlasting fire, prepared for the devil and his angels: For I was an hungred, and ye gave me no meat: I was thirsty, and ye gave me no drink: I was a stranger, and ye took me not in: naked, and ye clothed me not: sick, and in prison, and ye visited me not. Then shall they also answer him, saying, Lord, when saw we thee an hungred, or athirst, or a stranger, or naked, or sick, or in prison, and did not minister unto thee? Then shall he answer them, saying, Verily I say unto you, Inasmuch as ye did it not to one of the least of these, ye did it not to me. (Matthew 25:31-45.)

These instructions appeared in the New Testament. Do they apply to our dispensation? It turns out that we have been directly commanded in this dispensation to care for the poor. The Lord said,

Remember in all things the poor and the needy (D&C 52:40.)

Therefore, if any man shall take of the abundance which I have made, and impart not his portion, according to the law of my gospel, unto the poor and the needy, he shall, with the wicked, lift up his eyes in hell, being in torment. (D&C 104:18.)

And they shall look to the poor and the needy, and administer to their relief that they shall not suffer... (D&C 38:35.)

And the storehouse shall be kept by the consecrations of the church; and the widows and orphans shall be provided for, as also the poor. (D&C 83:6.)

Verily, thus saith the Lord, in addition to the laws of the church concerning women and children, those who belong to the church, who have lost their husbands or fathers: Women have claim on their husbands for their maintenance, until their husbands are taken; and if they are not found transgressors they shall have fellowship in the church. And if they are not faithful they shall not have fellowship in the church; yet they may remain upon their inheritances according to the laws of the land. All children have claim upon their parents for their maintenance until they are of age. And after that, they have claim upon the church, or in other words upon the Lord's storehouse, if their parents have not wherewith to give them inheritances. And the storehouse shall be kept by the consecrations of the church; and widows and orphans shall be provided for, as also the poor. Amen. (D&C 83:1-6.)

The Lord has been clear and repetitive in his admonition to care for the poor. It is one fulfillment of both the first and second great commandments. It is how he has told us he will interpret our fidelity to him. Modern Mormonism answers this charge through tithing and fast offerings.

The Doctrine of Tithing

D&C 119 provides a revelation on tithing. It reads:

Verily, thus saith the Lord, I require all their surplus property to be put into the hands of the bishop of my church in Zion, For the building of mine house, and for the laying of the foundation of Zion and for the priesthood, and for the debts of the Presidency of my Church. And this shall be the beginning of the tithing of my people. And after that, those who have thus been tithed shall pay one-tenth of all their interest annually; and this shall be a standing law unto them forever, for my holy priesthood, saith the Lord. Verily I say unto you, it shall come to pass that all those who gather unto the land of Zion shall be tithed of their surplus properties, and shall observe this law, or they shall not be found worthy to abide among you. And I say unto you, if my people observe not this law, to keep it holy, and by this law sanctify the land of Zion unto me, that my statutes and my judgments may be kept thereon, that it may be most holy, behold, verily I say unto you, it shall not be a land of Zion unto you. And this shall be an ensample unto all the stakes of Zion. Even so. Amen. (D&C 119:1-7.)

God states that tithing consists of two phases. Those new to the law are to donate all surplus property to the church. Thereafter, they are to pay a tenth of their interest annually. It is important to note that those who have not donated all their surplus property to the church at some point in their lives do not live the law of tithing as given by the Lord.

The Lord said that "this shall be a standing law" forever, or that it would not change. It turns out that this commandment is not new. It was restored anew, but it existed in the same exact form at least since the time of Abraham. As Joseph restored to Genesis 14 in the JST, when Abraham paid tithes to Melchizedek, "Abram paid unto him tithes of all that he had, of all the riches which he possessed, which God had given him more than that which he had need." (JST Gen 14:39.) Clearly, one tenth of one's interest is defined as one tenth of what God gives you over what you need. In other word's, God has said that tithing is one tenth of your net income, not one tenth of your gross income.

The expenses authorized by this section 119 are not very clear. This passage enumerates what the Lord has authorized tithing to be spent on:

1) "The building of mine house." The revelation does not specify what "mine house" means. Does it mean the group of people that follow God? Does it mean the Far West temple, the one temple that was the focus of the church in 1838 when this revelation was received? Does it extend to the many subsequent temples built after Joseph's death? Does it include the thousands of chapels the church has built? Does it include any building the church builds?

2) "The laying of the foundation of Zion." What does this mean?

3) "The priesthood." What aspect of the priesthood requires property?

4) "The debts of the Presidency of my Church." Does this extend to future expenses?

From JST Gen 14, we learn that tithing in Abraham's day was "for the poor" (JST Gen 12:38). Members donate tithing, estimated at over $7 billion per year[76] with an understanding that their donation is the fulfillment of a commandment. How well does their understanding match reality?

The Practice of Tithing

The church has not published an accounting of the receipt or expenditure of tithing funds since the 60s when President Henry D. Moyle of the 1st presidency successfully lobbied President David O. McKay to cease the practice of providing an accounting of funds to the membership at each annual conference.[77] However, private estimates of the amount donated are about $7 billion per year.[78] Where does this money go?

---

[76] "Insight: Mormon church made wealthy by donations", Reuters.com Aug 12, 2012.

[77] At that time, the church finances were overseen by a member of the First Presidency (in this case, Henry D. Moyle). Moyle's motivation was to hide the fact that he had spent the church into tremendous debt by building chapels in areas where there was insufficient membership to occupy them in hopes of bringing in enough members to fill them. Eventually, N. Eldon Tanner was called to the 12 because of his business acumen. President Tanner seems to have initiated the practice of

Although a complete accounting is impossible to reconstruct, there are sufficient morsels of information that have been released that allow inference.

The largest recipient of tithing, according to Gordon B. Hinckley, is the operation of church universities: "[BYU] is the single most expensive entity funded by the tithes of the Church."[79] The church universities (BYU Provo, BYU Hawaii, BYU Idaho, LDS Business School, and BYU Salt Lake Campus) are a very expensive enterprise. Using actual BYU tuition rates and comparative private tuition figures published by BYU ($24,000 more in tuition per year), as well as current enrollment numbers, we can estimate the tithing cost of the church universities at $1.1 billion. In addition to the church universities, the Church Educational System retains over 1,000 institute directors (see full list at institute.lds.org). Each director receives a significant salary in addition to perks such as a company car, a cost of living allowance, and a lifetime retirement at 30 years of service. The annual cost of the institute directors easily exceeds $10 million before counting the cost of those on retirement. Additionally, the church employs up to 24,000 lesser-paid full-time seminary teachers, which would cost a bare minimum of $600 million per year (assuming $24,000 per year salaries and conservative employer tax contributions). Thus, the CES annual budget is at least $1.5 billion per year, or 21% of tithing, and could be higher than $2 billion per year, or 29% of tithing.

After the CES system, the next highest tithing expense is most likely the salaries, benefits, and office space costs of full-time employees of the church (excluding CES). The church has not publicly released the number of workers it employs globally. However, a consideration of the number of entities and the work they do can assist in getting an idea of the order of magnitude of church employment. We typically think of the ecclesiastical employees who receive a salary for their work, such as the First Presidency, the Quorum of the 12, and the General Authorities. Each of these men also have secretaries. Also, there are over 400 mission presidents who are salaried and 25 area office staffs that consist of a collection of full-time employees to handle welfare, finance, facilities, etc. There are also facilities management personnel for the church buildings worldwide. Temple recorders are paid positions. There are also those who make garments, print scriptures and manuals, etc. There are a large number of professionals that provide support functions for church administration: lawyers, accountants, editors,

---

investing tithing into the stock market, which at the time became a wildly successful enterprise.

[78] "Insight: Mormon church made wealthy by donations", Reuters.com Aug 12, 2012.
[79] Gordon B. Hinckley, "Out of Your Experience Here," October 16, 1990 BYU Speeches.

programmers, electricians, janitors, and the like. Finally, there are the emeritus 70s, who receive pay and benefits for life.

Beyond the ecclesiastical employees of the church, the church wholly owns and operates an array of for-profit businesses. The employees of these operations are church employees. These companies include Deseret Management Corporation, Beneficial Financial Group, Bonneville International, Bonneville Communications, Bonneville Interactive Services, Bonneville Satellite, 35 different radio stations, KSL Television Station, Deseret Book, Excel Entertainment, Deseret Morning News, Hawaii Reserves, Polynesian Cultural Center, La'ie Shopping Center, La'ie Water Company, La'ie Treatment Works, Temple Square Hospitality and Temple Square restaurants, Zions Securities Corporation, Ensign Peak Advisors, Farm Management Corporation, Deseret Land and Livestock, Sun Ranch, Deseret Ranches of Florida, Deseret Farms of California, West Hills Orchards, Cactus Lane Ranch, Deseret Trust Company, LDS Family Services, Property Reserves Inc., and Deseret Mutual Benefit Administrators (DMBA).

Again, quantifying the amount of money spent on these employees is not possible. However, to get an idea, we can consider the legally mandated financial information published by the LDS church in the UK. In 2012, the church in the UK had 188,029 members and spent 12,350,000 pounds on staff. This number did not include "missionary work," the category which would tally the cost of mission president salaries and expense accounts, as well as associated employees at the area office, totaling about 7 million pounds. However, just using the exclusionary 12.3 million pounds number, that equates to sixty five pounds per member, or about $103 per member. This figure is the cost for local administration and does not include the army of lawyers, accountants, IT professionals, and General Authorities who are on the headquarters payroll. It likewise does not include any of the for-profit businesses, many of which are operated in the USA. However, it provides a very conservative lower bound. Extrapolating to the 15 million members reported by the church worldwide, we can estimate that LDS non-business salaries and benefits worldwide cost at least $1.5 billion per year, or approximately 21% of tithing.

Temples and chapels are another large item of expenditure for the church. The church publicizes the sparing of no expense in the construction of its temples. In the October 2012 General Conference, Elder Scott D. Whiting recounted how, during the renovation of the Laie Hawaii Temple, he watched a delegation of Church leaders indicate that certain parts of the construction would have to be redone. These included a large custom made stained glass window where a two-inch square was one eighth of an inch crooked and how several walls felt gritty to the touch. Elder Whiting later realized that the walls had always been intended to be wallpapered, and the small, crooked glass square was planned to sit behind a large potted plant.

This level of exactness costs a lot of money to achieve. This is besides the materials themselves, which are lauded as being top of the line. On an open house tour of the Draper Utah temple, the tour guide showed me the astounding number of costly materials used to construct the 57,000 sqft building. The abundant granite facing, counters and floor molding come from China. The wooden panels, doors, and molding come from Africa. The limestone floors are from France. There are over 35,000 hand-cut pieces of glass in the building. The church has not disclosed the cost of the Draper temple, though unofficial estimates are all over $100 million. The only temple whose cost has been partially disclosed is the Washington, D.C. temple, which leaders said would cost an estimated $15 million in the late 1960s, or about $88 million today. The D.C. temple is much larger than the Draper temple, but the materials used inside and out are significantly less costly than those in recent temples. The Preston England temple complex cost around $165 million in 1998, according to a Stake President there. The smaller temples are estimated to cost much less, around $16-20 million. Each temple has maintenance costs for the grounds, utilities, etc. that are considerable. Since 1998, the church has built or is building a total of 66 temples. Assuming the non-local contribution of each temple is $16 million (a conservative estimate), that equates to over a billion dollars, or around $62 million per year, excluding the cost of renovations or maintenance of existing temples. In total, the church could easily spend a billion dollars per year in temple operations and construction. This is at least 14% of annual tithing.

The church also builds about one chapel per day. According to the Zwick Construction (a firm that has built many temples and chapels for the church) website, a standard, US chapel costs 2-3 million dollars (excluding land cost and landscaping).[80] A standard stake center costs around $4 million. Like temples, chapels built in the first world are built of considerably more expensive materials than in the developing world. If we assume that international chapels cost half what US chapels do (a very conservative factor), and that 1 in 10 new chapels are stake centers (also a conservative estimate), the church spends at least $400 million on new chapels per year. But what about the land cost? Although in some areas, like the UK, land costs exceed construction costs, we can conservatively estimate the cost of the land occupied by new chapels at 50% of the construction cost, or $200 million per year.[81] It is harder to estimate utilities and renovation costs. However, the church is required by law to release financials for operations in the UK. From this information, we can gather that chapel renovations usually cost half what

---

[80] From Zwick Construction's website: The Mona Chapel cost $2,202,790, the Payson Chapel $2,735,813, and the Stansbury Park Benson Mill Chapel $2,313,518.
[81] I realize that many chapels are rented. The costs of rents are assumed to be reflected in the conservative inference figures.

a new chapel would cost.[82] We assume $200 million annually for these renovations, and for the sake of being conservative, ignore the costs of utilities and maintenance. This brings the total chapel cost estimation at $800 million per year. This is about 11% of tithing.

It is commonly understood in the church that one of the uses for tithing is to care for the poor. However, that is a false understanding. The LDS.org topics essay of "Tithing" does not list care for the poor as one of its uses: "Tithing funds are always used for the Lord's purposes—to build and maintain temples and meetinghouses, to sustain missionary work, to educate Church members, and to carry on the work of the Lord throughout the world." President Monson recently explained that money spent on the poor in the church comes completely from fast offerings.[83] The portion of tithing spent on the poor comes in the form of the humanitarian aid fund. In 2011, the church disclosed exactly how much money was spent in the preceding 26 years on humanitarian aid: $1.4 billion.[84] This amounts to $53.8 million per year, or 0.76% of tithing per year.

In conclusion, approximately 29% of tithing goes to CES, 21% in ecclesiastic and administrative salaries, 14% to temple construction and operation, 11% to chapel construction and maintenance, 0.76% to humanitarian aid.[85]

The Practice of Fast Offerings

Fast offerings in the church are prescribed to be donated the first Sunday of each month. They are meant to be at least the amount of two consecutive meals, but generosity is encouraged.

The concept is that, by fasting, the funds saved on food can be reallocated to the poor in the church. Using publicly disclosed data from the church in the UK, fast offerings are around 10% of tithing donations, or

---

[82] According to the 2013 UK financial report, there were 5 chapel renovations costing about 1 million pounds each, while each of the two new meetinghouses cost 2,346,455 and 2,600,000 pounds each, excluding land costs (see http://apps.charitycommission.gov.uk/Accounts/Ends51/0000242451_AC_201312 31_E_C.pdf).

[83] "Our sacred fast offerings finance the operation of storehouses, supply cash needs of the poor, and provide medical care for the sick who are without funds." (Thomas S. Monson, "Basic Principles of Welfare and Self-Reliance," (2009), 11–13)

[84] See "Welfare Services Fact Sheet—2011." It is unclear whether this amount is limited to goods provided (e.g., money spent by the church) or whether it also includes a market valuation for the 872,721 hours donated by church members enumerated on the sheet, which would not have caused money to be spent by the church.

[85] It is unclear what the other 24% of tithing is appropriated to. Our estimates are conservative, which would absorb some portion of the unaccounted amount. There is also an undisclosed amount that goes to the rainy day fund (explained below).

approximately $700 million per year. Local units dispense fast offerings to the poor, and local leaders are encouraged to find people on whom to spend the donations. Funds that remain unspent at the local unit level are forwarded to the stake, where they can be reapportioned to other units in the stake. Like the bishops, stake presidents are counseled to find a use for the funds they have. If the stake has excess funds, they go to church headquarters. Although there is a mechanism for needy wards to obtain extra fast offering funds, it requires the approval of the stake president, the area president, and even the presiding bishop, meaning it is a very rare occurrence.

The Doctrine of Fast Offerings

The Lord has never given a revelation on fast offerings. The doctrines pertaining to the concept of caring for the poor in relation to fasting are individual instructions, not connected to an institution. Both the commandment and the promised blessings are individual.

> Is not this the fast that I have chosen? to loose the bandsof wickedness, to undo the heavy burdens, and to let the oppressed go free, and that ye break every yoke? Is it not to deal thy bread to the hungry, and that thou bring the poor that are cast out to thy house? when thou seest the naked, that thou cover him; and that thou hide not thyself from thine own flesh? Then shall thy light break forth as the morning, and thine health shall spring forth speedily: and thy righteousness shall go before thee; the glory of the Lordshall be thy rearward. Then shalt thou call, and the Lord shall answer; thou shalt cry, and he shall say, Here I am. If thou take away from the midst of thee the yoke, the putting forth of the finger, and speaking vanity; And if thou draw out thy soul to the hungry, and satisfy the afflicted soul; then shall thy light rise in obscurity, and thy darkness be as the noonday: And the Lord shall guide thee continually, and satisfy thy soul in drought, and make fat thy bones: and thou shalt be like a watered garden, and like a spring of water, whose waters fail not. (Isaiah 58:6-11.)

In principle, the church's fast offering program could be used to facilitate mobilization of resources from affluent members to areas of the world that are more destitute. In practice, since the church's fast offerings are encouraged to be consumed locally, and since it takes approval from the stake, area, and presiding bishop levels before funds can be obtained from headquarters, the fast offering program does not have many advantages compared to the scriptural practice of individuals directly donating their money to needy parties. In fact, given the abundance of all-volunteer organizations who care for the poor internationally, it could be argued that direct contributions through international charities have greater impact on the plight of the poor than traditional church fast offerings, which are almost guaranteed to be consumed locally in comparatively affluent areas.

The Plight of Poor LDS

Only 51% of the LDS membership lives in the first world.[86] For the rest, poverty is a surprisingly ubiquitous condition. In 2013, I attended a meeting with LDS leaders and members from several stakes and districts in Guatemala, Peru, and Ecuador described the norm among members: one meal per day, consisting of perhaps some rice one day, a tomato another day, and a tortilla the third day. In Zimbabwe, interviews I conducted in early 2014 with the stake/district and ward/branch leadership yielded a consistent picture: the 90% unemployment in the country applied equally to the membership. Measured malnutrition rates in LDS children in these and other countries like the Philippines and Cambodia are staggering. In the developing world, making up 49% of church membership, many LDS children are starving. Several hundred die every year,[87] while those who survive will suffer the ill effects of their childhood hunger during a lifetime of physical and cognitive problems that reduce or prevent workforce participation, increasing the probability that future generations will find themselves in the same condition. There **are** poor among us—millions of them.

According to the church, fast offerings are a local program.[88] Unlike tithing, fast offerings are not sent to headquarters to be redistributed according to need. Instead, Bishops are instructed to seek out the most needy members in the congregation and offer them assistance.[89] When Bishops cannot find members in need, they send the excess offerings to the stake. Stake presidents are in turn instructed to send those offerings to other Bishops in the stake whose needs exceed their donations. Funds are sent to headquarters only when there is surplus as the stake level. These funds do not necessarily get used on the poor at all, as "all donations become the Church's property and will be used at the Church's sole discretion."[90]

---

[86] http://www.deseretnews.com/article/865613347/LDS-spokesman-breaks-down-membership-demographics.html

[87] Bradley Walker, "Spreading Zion Southward," Dialogue. https://www.dialoguejournal.com/wp-content/uploads/sbi/articles/Dialogue_V35N04_105.pdf

[88] "In addition to tithing, most faithful members donate fast offerings, which consist of at least the money saved by fasting for two meals each month. These proceeds go directly to supporting each **local** congregation's poor and needy." (http://www.mormonnewsroom.org/article/tithing, retrieved 9 Jun 2015)

[89] "The bishop directs welfare work in the ward. He has a divine mandate to seek out and care for the poor" (Handbook 2:6.2.1)

[90] From the tithing slip as of 2015.

But what about tithing? As discussed, tithing represents some $7 billion per year in member donations. How much of that is spent on caring for the poor membership of the church? The basic answer is simple: none of it. President Monson said that the church's welfare program is funded not by tithing, but by fast offerings.[91] Some tithing is spent on the world's poor through the humanitarian aid program. This aid comes in the form of disaster relief supplies, not in the normal course of life. The church revealed that $1.4 billion was spent in humanitarian aid over 26 years ending in 2011.[92] This amounts to $53.8 million per year, or 0.76% of tithing per year. Why?

Church Reasoning for Neglecting the Poor

Recently, a couple traveled to the Philippines recently in order to volunteer to help rebuild from the natural disaster they had suffered. This couple was not only shocked by the first-hand witness of the poverty of active LDS members, but noted the extra helping of irony provided by a story told in General Conference six months prior. Elder Teh told the story of a widow having paid her tithing despite having lost her family and home in the earthquake. She was forced to live in a tent and go back to work in order to afford food. This couple happened to meet the widow from Elder Teh's story and help rebuild her house. Six months after being mentioned in conference, the widow was still homeless, and only regained housing through the actions of people outside the church.

How is it possible that modern Mormonism can speak so often about helping the poor, and yet leave so much undone? How is it that members can skip two meals a month in the name of helping the poor, raising much more money than needed to provide the necessities of life for all members who struggle, yet those members still go without? How is it that members are so incredulous when presented with this information?

If tithing and offerings are not spent on the poor, what are they spent on? The gross majority is spent annually on buildings and salaries for church officers and employees. In order to spend money on the poor, one or more of those expenses would have to be reduced or eliminated. The church therefore judges subsidized education for first world members, salaries for full time ecclesiastical officers and professionals, and the building and

---

[91] "Our sacred fast offerings finance the operation of storehouses, supply cash needs of the poor, and provide medical care for the sick who are without funds." (Thomas S. Monson, "Basic Principles of Welfare and Self-Reliance," (2009), 11–13)

[92] See "Welfare Services Fact Sheet—2011." It is unclear whether this amount is limited to goods provided (e.g., money spent by the church) or whether it also includes a market valuation for the 872,721 hours donated by church members enumerated on the sheet, which would not have caused money to be spent by the church.

maintenance of chapels and temples to be more important than the lives of the poor members of the church.[93]

> The preeminence of the spiritual over the temporal, which Jesus taught, has many applications in our own day. For example, it explains why our church spends great sums preaching the restored gospel and building temples to perform the ordinances of eternity rather than (as some advocate) devoting these same resources to temporal concerns already being pursued by others, such as preserving the environment, researching cures for diseases, or administering to other physical needs that can be accomplished without priesthood power or direction. ("The Lord's Way," Dallin H. Oaks, p.111.)

The prevailing belief in the hierarchy seems to be that the only responsibility they have toward the poor LDS is to act when doing so would also improve their spirituality. As Elder Oaks expounded upon the use of the pricey ointment on Jesus,

> Thus, while the care of the poor was important, its importance should be seen in a spiritual context. In this instance, there was something more important to do with this ointment than to give its value to the poor. The things of eternity, including what Jesus could teach his followers concern the salvation of their souls and what he could do for them by his death and resurrection, were more important than the temporal care of the poor. ("The Lord's Way" Dallin H. Oaks, p. 110.)

At least some of the brethren believe that what the church spends its money on is more important than caring for the poor because, well, other Christians without "priesthood power" can attend to that. There are two significant problems with this attitude. First, God has not described the building of temples, or the building of chapels, or the operation of heavily subsidized church universities, or full time stipends for ecclesiastical ministers, or a litany of church employees as the key to bringing Zion. Instead, Zion will come when people keep God's commandments. Caring for the poor is one of those commandments.

> But whoso hath this world's good, and seeth his brother have need, and shutteth up his bowels of compassion from him, how dwelleth the love of God in him? (I John 3:17.)

---

[93] "The Lord will enter into judgment with the ancients of his people, and the princes thereof: for ye have eaten up the vineyard; the spoil of the poor is in your houses." (Isaiah 3:14.)

Building modern temples, building chapels, providing nearly free education for North American LDS, and paying thousands and thousands of employees were never given as commandments.[94] Chapels cannot be argued to be necessary for the advancement of the gospel. Joseph did everything he did without the aid of a single chapel. Temples seem justified. But it would be a mistake to assume that their presence is always an indication of God's approbation. Jeremiah says otherwise:

> But don't be fooled by those who promise you safety simply because the LORD's Temple is here. They chant, "The LORD's Temple is here! The LORD's Temple is here!" (New Living Translation, Jeremiah 7:4)

Second, if the issue is focusing on the segment of what we could do as a church that no one else could do, then why spend approximately $1 billion per year on subsidizing U.S. members' education, when the U.S. government already provides programs that put an education within reach for all North Americans? Why spend billions per year on salaries for church officers and church professional employees? Are there really no members who would teach seminary as a calling for free or volunteer legal services for free? Is there a reason these people can't support themselves while simultaneously offering their time to the church, as did King Benjamin? It seems that the rule of prioritizing the things that only LDS can do does not explain what the church *does* spend its money on as much as it justifies what it *does not* spend its money on.

When God's basic commandments are ignored in order to build temples, will he honor them? As Paul said, "if any provide not for his own, and specially for those of his own house, he hath denied the faith, and is worse than an infidel." (1 Tim 5:8) We focus so much on the idea that we cannot be spiritually saved without the salvation of our dead. However, we seem to ignore that we cannot be spiritually saved without the temporal salvation of our fellow LDS. "The rich cannot be saved without Charity, giving to feed the poor when and how God requires as well as building." (Joseph Smith, 1 May 1842, Manuscript History of the Church.) Is it the existence of the building that sanctifies it, or is it God who sanctifies it? Will

---

[94] The last temple a church president claimed was specified by revelation was the Nauvoo temple. The only church employees specified in our scriptures are Bishops, who ironically are no longer paid. Just one for-profit entity of the church, DMC, has "2,000 to 3,000 employees" according to CEO and former Presiding Bishop Keith McMullin (http://www.bloomberg.com/bw/articles/2012-07-10/how-the-mormons-make-money). This number does not include any of the dozens of other for-profit companies the church owns or the ecclesiastical employees and their support (General Authorities, their secretaries, CES employees, lawyers, accountants, IT specialists, maintenance, security, food service, etc.).

he sanctify a building that is built through opposition to his commandments? As God said through Jeremiah, a temple can't be efficacious if those who attend it oppress the poor:

> Trust ye not in lying words, saying, The temple of the Lord, The temple of the Lord, The temple of the Lord, are these. For if ye throughly amend your ways and your doings; if ye throughly execute judgment between a man and his neighbour; If ye oppress not the stranger, the fatherless, and the widow, and shed not innocent blood in this place, neither walk after other gods to your hurt: Then will I cause you to dwell in this place, in the land that I gave to your fathers, for ever and ever. Behold, ye trust in lying words, that cannot profit. Will ye steal, murder, and commit adultery, and swear falsely, and burn incense unto Baal, and walk after other gods whom ye know not; And come and stand before me in this house, which is called by my name, and say, We are delivered to do all these abominations? Is this house, which is called by my name, become a den of robbers in your eyes? Behold, even I have seen it, saith the Lord. But go ye now unto my place which was in Shiloh, where I set my name at the first, and see what I did to it for the wickedness of my people Israel. And now, because ye have done all these works, saith the Lord, and I spake unto you, rising up early and speaking, but ye heard not; and I called you, but ye answered not; Therefore will I do unto this house, which is called by my name, wherein ye trust, and unto the place which I gave to you and to your fathers, as I have done to Shiloh. And I will cast you out of my sight, as I have cast out all your brethren, even the whole seed of Ephraim. Therefore pray not thou for this people, neither lift up cry nor prayer for them, neither make intercession to me: for I will not hear thee. (Jeremiah 7:4-16.)

It displays great hubris and hypocrisy beyond measure for modern Mormons to pray in the most holy posture to ask the Lord to hear their pleas while necessarily ignoring the pleas of the poor in order to build the temples they pray in. The Lord say through Isaiah, referring to this very act:

> When you spread forth your hands, I will conceal my eyes from you; though you pray at length, I will not hear—your hands are filled with blood. (Isaiah 1:15.)

We also are warned about this in the Book of Mormon:

> Behold, O God, they cry unto thee, and yet their hearts are swallowed up in their pride. Behold, O God, they cry unto thee with their mouths, while they are puffed up, even to greatness, with the vain things of the world. Behold, O my God, their costly apparel, and

their ringlets, and their bracelets, and their ornaments of gold, and all their precious things which they are ornamented with; and behold, their hearts are set upon them, and yet they cry unto thee and say— We thank thee, O God, for we are a chosen people unto thee, while others shall perish. (Alma 31:27-28.)

When there are yet poor among us, and we build temples instead of caring for them, we cause LDS members to die by building temples. This is perhaps of what Nephi was prophesying of when he said:

Because of pride, and because of false teachers, and false doctrine, their churches have become corrupted, and their churches are lifted up; because of pride they are puffed up. They rob the poor because of their fine sanctuaries; they rob the poor because of their fine clothing; and they persecute the meek and poor in heart, because in their pride they are puffed up. They wear stiff necks and high heads; yea, and because of pride, and wickedness, and abominations, and whoredoms, they have all gone astray save it be a few, who are the humble followers of Christ; nevertheless, they are led, that in many instances they do err because they are taught by the precepts of men. (2 Ne. 28: 12-14.)

It is **because** of our building fine sanctuaries that we rob the poor. In other words, we rob the poor when we build fine sanctuaries, or we rob the poor in order to build fine sanctuaries. Therefore, when we go to temples and "spread forth" our hands, they are filled with the blood of those we have killed and continue to kill in order to sustain our vain worship. God does not hear such prayers, and the offerers of such prayers bring down cursing instead of blessing on their own heads through their idolatrous hypocrisy.

Ironically, the claim is sometimes made that the purpose of dotting the land with temples is to make temples accessible to the poor, who cannot afford to travel to the temples already in existence. The preference of building temples that cost many times what it would cost to alleviate poverty among members is an example of the embodiment of the church policy to focus only on the spiritual welfare of members. But again, this is not an either or scenario. The church can provide both spiritual *and* temporal salvation to its poor members. Proposals have been made (and rejected) to convert a cruise ship or a large airplane into a temple. Such an approach would result in a tremendous cost savings that could be allocated to the poor while also providing them with the temple ordinances.

It seems appropriate to recall that the covetousness of the Saints in being unwilling to give their time, talents, etc. to the poor was what invoked the ire of the Lord in Kirtland.

I, the Lord, am not well pleased with many who are in the church at Kirtland; For they do not forsake their sins, and their wicked ways, the pride of their hearts, and their covetousness, and all their detestable things, and observe all things whatsoever I have said unto them. (D&C 98:19-21, see also D&C 104:4, 52.)

The same argument could be made about the failure to achieve Zion in Missouri and Illinois. Joseph Smith implied this was a regular problem: "God had often sealed up the heavens because of covetousness in the Church." (Joseph Smith, TPJS, p. 9.) This begs the question of how the Lord feels with us as an institution when we have many times more wealth than these brethren in Ohio, Missouri, and Illinois ever dreamed of, yet our members are so poor they are actually dying (a calamity unknown to the early Saints).

In a time of great comparative poverty the Lord said,

> There is even now already in store sufficient, yea, even an abundance, to redeem Zion, and establish her waste places, no more to be thrown down, were the churches, who call themselves after my name, willing to hearken to my voice. (D&C 101:75.)

What would he say now, when the church has tens of billions of dollars in equity, yet has failed to build Zion? Could it be because they continue to attempt to build Zion without eradicating the plight of the poor among us?

> ...were it not for the transgressions of my people, speaking concerning the church and not individuals....they have not learned to be obedient to the things which I required at their hands, but are full of all manner of evil, and do not impart of their substance, as becometh saints, to the poor and afflicted among them; ...Zion cannot be built up unless it is by the principles of the law of the celestial kingdom; otherwise I cannot receive her unto myself. (D&C 105:1-5.)

Purpose: Self Sufficiency for Some But not Others?

The various handbooks instructing Bishops and Stake Presidents on administering church welfare are clear in explaining that the purpose of the church welfare program isn't about alleviating suffering: "The bishop provides welfare assistance to members to help them develop spirituality, become self-reliant, and learn to provide for others." Self-reliance, or the ability of a member to provide for the needs of himself and his family without outside intervention, is the keystone of modern church welfare.[95] However, the necessary precondition for self-reliance is the economic possibility of

---

[95] God has never made the recipient's ability to come out of poverty a pre-requisite for giving; "… the righteous giveth and spareth not." (Proverbs 21:25-26)

supporting yourself and your family. Unknown to most U.S. members, including far too many in church leadership, is the fact that in many developing nations, sufficient employment does not exist—no matter your training—to meet the needs of your family. For example, in most of Guatemala, even the most industrious may only be able to find work 3 days of the week, while one day's wages are insufficient to purchase one day's food.[96] The same is the case in many parts of Mexico.[97] In Zimbabwe, there are no real employment opportunities.[98] These situations stress the limitations of the church welfare program under the current guidelines that instruct church leaders to avoid the situation where the church is being relied upon to provide the staples of life.

Of course, the doctrines provided by God to alleviate the poor are not limited by local economic circumstances. God instructed the Saints to physically gather into one place specified by revelation. They were instructed to buy up land and donate it to the church. The church then allowed the poor to work the donated land to feed themselves. The only resource that had to be provided by the church was limited training on how to farm and welfare for those very few who were physically or mentally disabled and did not have family that could provide for them. The system as prescribed cannot be fully implemented in modern Mormonism, since the gathering was ended by fiat in stages in the early 1900s. However, buying farms in the developing world and allowing the poor to work them in exchange for the food that is produced on them would be a much closer approximation to the Lord's instructions that the modern welfare system. It would certainly alleviate the concerns of the Brethren who have reservations about creating a system where members are not self-reliant.

Beyond the mechanical limitations of the program in the realities of economies outside of the first world, a deeper philosophical problem exists: Why is it acceptable for church leaders to receive a comfortable and guaranteed living while it is not acceptable for the poor to do the same?

The First Presidency, Quorum of the Twelve, all other General Authorities,[99] and mission presidents receive money as a result of their calling from the church. General Authority Seventies who have reached the age of 70 continue to receive benefits until death, despite a release from their duties. It is important to note that the church insists that "There is no paid or

---

[96] From interviews between the author and local Guatemalan church leaders.

[97] From interviews between the author and day laborers in various locations.

[98] The author's interviews with LDS and non-LDS Zimbabweans throughout the country suggested unemployment at 90%, with no employment opportunities for either skilled or unskilled individuals.

[99] Unlike their General Authority counterparts, Area Seventies are called only for a brief period, and are expected to support themselves in addition to their calling.

professional ministry."[100] Until 1995, General Authorities' salaries came not from their ecclesiastical work, but from their membership on the boards of church-owned businesses.[101] After 1995, when General Authorities ceased to sit on such boards, there are only two possible ways of describing the money given to them.[102] Either they are being paid for the ministry, which is priestcraft, or they are being paid for doing nothing, which would present an awfully hypocritical situation given the persistence of avoiding giving handouts to the poor. Why is it acceptable to stress that the poor not be given assistance without working for it, when we freely give many times the welfare budget of entire Stakes in the each paycheck to a 70 or apostle without any work requirement?[103]

The scriptures, particularly the Book of Mormon, teach plainly that ecclesiastical officers should support themselves. Alma "…commanded them that the priests whom he had ordained should labor with their own hands for their support." (Mosiah 18:24.). We are also told that the priests received

---

[100] President Gordon B. Hinckley, "What of the Mormons?," p. 4.

[101] Until 1995, General Authorities were paid to sit on the boards of church-owned businesses in addition to their ecclesiastical duties. "I should like to add, parenthetically for your information, that the living allowances given the General Authorities, which are very modest in comparison with executive compensation in industry and the professions, come from this business income and not from the tithing of the people." (President Gordon B. Hinckley, "Questions and Answers," Ensign (November 1985), 49.) Thus, they were technically not being paid for preaching the gospel. After 1995, the General Authorities no longer sat on these boards and therefore were paid in exchange for work they did for the church (see http://en.fairmormon.org/Mormonism_and_church_finances/No_paid_ministry/G eneral_Authorities_living_stipend). Of course whether the money comes from church-owned businesses or tithing has no impact on whether or not it could or should be used on the poor, but is only brought up to illustrate the hypocrisy of anyone paid by the church to claim that the poor should not be given assistance because it would violate their self-reliance.

[102] The church has not released how much General Authorities are paid. In 1996, it was revealed that at least some of the General Authorities received "in the neighborhood of $50,000.00 a year" (see http://en.fairmormon.org/Mormonism_and_church_finances/No_paid_ministry/G eneral_Authorities_living_stipend). In terms of today's dollars, that would be around $100,000 per year. They also receive non-pay benefits such as free cars.

[103] The church has not published the salaries of the General Authorities. However, a search of publicly available records shows that President Monson owns over $1 million in personal real estate. Recall that President Monson was called into the Twelve in his 30s after just 2 years as an advertising executive, thus it is logical to conclude that his wealth comes solely from his time as a member of the Twelve. President Packer, a man who has spent his entire life as either a CES employee or a General Authority, owns over $2 million in privately owned real estate.

power and authority in their teaching as a result of their not being paid to do it:

> And the priests were not to depend upon the people for their support; but for their labor they were to receive the grace of God, that they might wax strong in the Spirit, having the knowledge of God, that they might teach with power and authority from God. (Mosiah 18:26.)

King Mosiah also adopted this law: "Yea, and all their priests and teachers should labor with their own hands for their support, in all cases save it were in sickness, or in much want..." (Mosiah 27:5.) Leaders in the Book of Mormon did not use their many ecclesiastical responsibilities as an excuse not to support themselves. Alma explained how he supported himself despite his litany of responsibilities as the presiding officer of both the church and the government,

> ...I have labored even from the commencement of the reign of the judges until now, with mine own hands for my support, notwithstanding my many travels round about the land to declare the word of God unto my people. (Alma 30:32.)

Neither workload nor physical age was used as an excuse worthy of earning the people's support by King Benjamin, who not only had to lead the church, but rule the secular kingdom:

> And even I, myself, have labored with mine own hands that I might serve you, and that ye should not be laden with taxes, and that there should nothing come upon you which was grievous to be borne... (Mosiah 2:14.)

Arguments supporting the church's paying clergy are found in the Book of Mormon, but unfortunately they are offered up by apostates and anti-Christs. Nehor, for example,

> had gone about among the people, preaching to them that which he termed to be the word of God...declaring unto the people that every priest and teacher ought to become popular; and they ought not to labor with their hands, but that they ought to be supported by the people. (Alma 1:3.)

These behaviors are described by Samuel the Lamanite as becoming only a false proophet:

> Yea, ye will lift him up, and ye will give unto him of your substance; ye will give unto him of your gold, and of your silver, and ye will clothe him with costly apparel; and because he speaketh flattering words unto you, and he saith that all is well, then ye will not find fault

with him. O ye wicked and ye perverse generation; ye hardened and ye stiffnecked people, how long will ye suppose that the Lord will suffer you? Yea, how long will ye suffer yourselves to be led by foolish and blind guides? Yea, how long will ye choose darkness rather than light? (Helaman 13:28-29.)

Even if church leaders will not support themselves with their own hands, couldn't they at least reduce their standard of living? Does the average member of the church get a new luxury car every year, have multiple homes, have personal assistants, have a cook, a gardener, or expensive suits? The royalties they receive for their books should be sufficient alone to maintain an affluent standard of living. Why do they need lavish salaries to have sufficient for their needs?

The discrepancy between the living situation of many members and the poverty of other members is reminiscent of the description Amos gave of leaders at his time living in opulence while others lived in squalor:

> Woe to them that are at ease in Zion, and trust in the mountain of Samaria, which are named chief of the nations, to whom the house of Israel came! Pass ye unto Calneh, and see; and from thence go ye to Hamath the great: then go down to Gath of the Philistines: be they better than these kingdoms? or their border greater than your border? Ye that put far away the evil day, and cause the seat of violence to come near; That lie upon beds of ivory, and stretch themselves upon their couches, and eat the lambs out of the flock, and the calves out of the midst of the stall; That chant to the sound of the viol, and invent to themselves instruments of musick, like David; That drink wine in bowls, and anoint themselves with the chief ointments: but they are not grieved for the affliction of Joseph. (Amos 6:1-6.)

How can we live so opulently when billions of the inhabitants of the earth live in dire poverty? How can modern Mormons not be repulsed by the contrast between the fineries of church leaders and the poor half of the church?

The Rainy Day Fund

An undisclosed amount of church offerings are invested. For example, all donations to the perpetual aid fund are invested. Awards are made in the form of interest-bearing loans out of the interest on the principle endowment. Similarly, church leaders have built what they call a "rainy day" fund in the anticipation of a drop in tithes significant enough to disrupt the regular financial obligations of the church (salaries and rents). Michael Purdy, church spokesman, said,

The church teaches its members to live within their means and put a little money aside for life's unexpected events. As a church, we live by the same principle. ("Insight: Mormon church made wealthy by donations," Reuters.com, Aug 12, 2012.)

In defense of this position, President Hinckley taught:

For years, the Church has taught its membership the principle of setting aside a reserve of food, as well as money, to take care of emergency needs that might arise. We are only trying to follow the same principle for the Church as a whole. (April 1991 General Conference.)

In this same talk he explained that,

In the financial operations of the Church, we have observed two basic and fixed principles: One, the Church will live within its means. It will not spend more than it receives. Two, a fixed percentage of the income will be set aside to build reserves against what might be called a possible 'rainy day.'

We do not know what this fixed percentage is. However, we know at least some of the things that have been purchased as part of the rainy day fund.

Stocks. Ensign Peak Advisors is an investment company owned by the church. It's sole mission is to invest church money. Ensign Peak Advisors employee Laurence R. Stay told the Deseret News in 2006 that "billions of dollars change hands every day."

Real estate. In recent history, the church has accelerated its acquisition of real estate holdings. The City Creek Center, whose costs exceeded a billion dollars, joins with the construction of a large luxury apartment complex in Philadelphia and increases in ranch holdings in Florida. To date, the church owns more ranch land in the United States than any other private entity. It owns a chunk of Florida the size of Rhode Island in addition to large ranches in California, Utah, Nebraska, and Hawaii.

The rainy day fund seems like a good idea on the surface. Just as Joseph stored excess grain in times of surplus, the church can save up money and land in order to use it for good in a time of scarcity. Yet, the money is not surplus. We are surrounded both in and out of the church with those who do not have sufficient food to eat. This is not surplus money—this is money that is optionally assigned to investment rather than fulfilling the needs of the poor, including active LDS poor. We are taking food out of the mouths of members in order to invest it for future use. The question is, future use for whom? If the money comes from ignoring the plight of the poor in the developing world, is it any doubt that the proceeds will not be spent on the developing world?

The rainy day fund is respect of persons. It is saving for the benefit of members in the United States at the expense of international members. As with chapels, temples, and universities, it is another example of how the church treats developing world members differently than those in the United States.

The rainy day fund is a curious program when compared with the scriptures. It is based on many assumptions that are anti-scriptural. When needed, leaders assume that:

- Money will still exist. God says it will not. "Your silver and gold will be thrown into the streets like garbage, because those are the two things that led you into sin, and now they cannot save you from my anger. They are not even worth enough to buy food." (Ezekiel 7:19, CEV.)

- The stock market will persist. Just in lieu of the recent regular crashes of the stock market in response to comparatively minor events, this is ludicrous.

- Transportation mechanisms will still exist. God says they will not. "The highways are desolate, travel is at an end." (Isaiah 33:8)

- Civil law and order will be sufficient to protect and distribute the goods. Isaiah says it will not.

Even if God approved of the idea of a rainy day fund, the likelihood that it will be of use when the events God has promised come to pass is essentially zero. All the stockpiled wealth will disappear in an instant, and the stored material goods will be mobbed by local vandals.

The Lord taught amply that his disciples were to give what they had to the poor, not store it up for themselves in a latter time of need:

> Lay not up for yourselves treasures upon earth, where moth and rust doth corrupt, and where thieves break through and steal: But lay up for yourselves treasures in heaven, where neither moth nor rust doth corrupt, and where thieves do not break through nor steal: For where your treasure is, there will your heart be also. (Matthew 6:19-21.)

In Luke 12:33-34, Jesus gives us an idea of treasure in heaven when he says:

> Sell that ye have, and give alms; provide yourselves bags which wax not old, a treasure in the heavens that faileth not, where no thief approacheth, neither moth corrupteth. For where your treasure is, there will your heart be also.

Where is modern Mormonism's treasure? Is there any doubt that the heart of modern Mormonism is to be found in Babylon, where it's treasure lies? It is certainly not in alms to the poor.

The business model of investing to then later spend a share of whatever profits may come is antithetical to the model the Savior employed while on the earth. He took a boy's few loaves and fishes and distributed them among the hungry. After receiving all the crowd had to give, he made it enough to meet their needs. Their needs were met through faith in God and not security in the bank.

> Cast thy bread upon the waters: for thou shalt find it after many days. (Ecclesiastes 1:11.)

The Lord spoke derisively of those who would build bigger barns to store their amassed wealth instead of caring for the poor:

> And he said unto them, Take heed, and beware of covetousness: for a man's life consisteth not in the abundance of the things which he possesseth. And he spake a parable unto them, saying, The ground of a certain rich man brought forth plentifully: And he thought within himself, saying, What shall I do, because I have no room where to bestow my fruits? And he said, This will I do: I will pull down my barns, and build greater; and there will I bestow all my fruits and my goods. And I will say to my soul, Soul, thou hast much goods laid up for many years; take thine ease, eat, drink, and be merry. But God said unto him, Thou fool, this night thy soul shall be required of thee: then whose shall those things be, which thou hast provided? So is he that layeth up treasure for himself, and is not rich toward God. (Luke 12:15-21.)

Let us remember that God has promised widespread destruction at our doors. Any one of these prophesied calamities will render our bigger barns worthless. Isaiah predicted that, in our day, the presiding officers of Ephraim would be drunk on delusion and craft a plan to avoid the suffering to precede the second coming not by righteousness, but by creating secret refuges:

> Woe to the garlands of glory of the drunkards of Ephraim! Their crowning splendor has become as fading wreaths on the heads of a the opulent a overcome with wine....These too have indulged in wine and are giddy with strong drink: priests and prophets have gone astray through liquor. They are intoxicated with wine and stagger because of strong drink; they err as seers, they blunder in their decisions....Therefore hear the word of Jehovah, you scoffers who preside over these people in Jerusalem. You have supposed, by taking refuge in deception and hiding behind falsehoods, to have covenanted with Death, or reached an understanding with Sheol, that, should a flooding scourge sweep through the earth, it shall not reach you. I will make justice the measure, righteousness the weight; a

> hail shall sweep away your false refuge and waters flood the hiding place. Your covenant with Death shall prove void, your understanding with Sheol have no effect: when the flooding scourge sweeps through, you shall be overrun by it. As often as it sweeps through, you shall be seized by it: by day and by night it shall seize you; it shall cause terror merely to hear word of it. Then shall come to pass the proverb: The couch is too short to stretch out on, the covering too narrow to wrap oneself in. (Isaiah 28: 1,7-20.)

The Lord told Isaiah that the leaders' attempts at avoiding the punishment coming would fail. This isn't surprising to anyone who has read the scriptures. Is a cattle ranch any good when darkness covers the earth for a long time? Will food deposits do anyone any good when God has taken our modern transportation away, or when men are encompassed by plague? Does it not go without saying that real estate holdings and stock market equities will be worthless when Babylon is fallen? The church may claim to preach the gospel, but it certainly does make decisions predicated upon its truthfulness. The only way these programs make any rational sense is if you completely ignore the fact that there are people who are dying now because of lack of very cheap intervention and you believe that the Lord delays his coming (see Matthew 24:48). Not only are we neglecting our brothers and sisters in Christ in order to build bigger barns, but we are building the barns knowing full well they will not be accessible when the prophesied destruction is poured out.

At the time of destruction, it will be righteousness (giving to the poor) and not storage (rainy day fund) that will save.

> Treasures of wickedness profit nothing: but righteousness delivereth from death. The Lord will not suffer the soul of the righteous to famish: but he casteth away the substance of the wicked. (Proverbs 10:2-3.)

> Riches profit not in the day of wrath: but righteousness delivereth from death....The righteousness of the upright shall deliver them: but transgressors shall be taken in their own naughtiness. (Proverbs 11:4,6.)

> He that trusteth in his riches shall fall: but the righteous shall flourish as a branch. (Proverbs 11:28.)

This covenant with death will surely fail, and when it does, the repercussion will be that God will not hear the cries of those who oppressed the poor in order to set up security for their own time of need. "Whoso stoppeth his ears at the cry of the poor, he also shall cry himself, but shall not be heard." (Proverbs 21:13.)

There was a certain rich man, which was clothed in purple and fine linen, and fared sumptuously every day: And there was a certain beggar named Lazarus, which was laid at his gate, full of sores, And desiring to be fed with the crumbs which fell from the rich man's table: moreover the dogs came and licked his sores. And it came to pass, that the beggar died, and was carried by the angels into Abraham's bosom: the rich man also died, and was buried; And in hell he lift up his eyes, being in torments, and seeth Abraham afar off, and Lazarus in his bosom. And he cried and said, Father Abraham, have mercy on me, and send Lazarus, that he may dip the tip of his finger in water, and cool my tongue; for I am tormented in this flame. But Abraham said, Son, remember that thou in thy lifetime receivedst thy good things, and likewise Lazarus evil things: but now he is comforted, and thou art tormented. (Luke 16:19-25.)

And again,

Therefore thus saith the Lord; Ye have not hearkened unto me, in proclaiming liberty, every one to his brother, and every man to his neighbour: behold, I proclaim a liberty for you, saith the Lord, to the sword, to the pestilence, and to the famine; and I will make you to be removed into all the kingdoms of the earth. (Jeremiah 24:17.)

And again,

Rob not the poor, because he is poor: neither oppress the afflicted in the gate: For the Lord will plead their cause, and spoil the soul of those that spoiled them. (Proverbs 22:22-23.)

And again,

I will punish you for your sins and treat you the same way you have treated others. (Ezekiel 7:27, CEV.)

The Lord's "rainy day" plan is to give to the poor—now—in whatever way we can.

Withhold not good from them to whom it is due, when it is in the power of thine hand to do it. Say not unto thy neighbour, Go, and come again, and to morrow I will give; when thou hast it by thee. (Proverbs 3:27-28.)

Then, and only then, we will have a right to call on him for protection when the destruction comes, not as slothful servants who ignored his commission and counted on his prolonged absence, but as faithful stewards who anticipated his return.

Modern Mormons would do well to heed Mormon's warning to them, having seen our day:

And I know that ye do walk in the pride of your hearts; and there are none save a few only who do not lift themselves up in the pride of their hearts, unto the wearing of very fine apparel, unto envying, and strifes, and malice, and persecutions, and all manner of iniquities; and your churches, yea, even every one, have become polluted because of the pride of your hearts. For behold, ye do love money, and your substance, and your fine apparel, and the adorning of your churches, more than ye love the poor and the needy, the sick and the afflicted. O ye pollutions, ye hypocrites, ye teachers, who sell yourselves for that which will canker, why have ye polluted the holy church of God? Why are ye ashamed to take upon you the name of Christ? Why do ye not think that greater is the value of an endless happiness than that misery which never dies—because of the praise of the world? Why do ye adorn yourselves with that which hath no life, and yet suffer the hungry, and the needy, and the naked, and the sick and the afflicted to pass by you, and notice them not? Yea, why do ye build up your secret abominations to get gain, and cause that widows should mourn before the Lord, and also orphans to mourn before the Lord, and also the blood of their fathers and their husbands to cry unto the Lord from the ground, for vengeance upon your heads? Behold, the sword of vengeance hangeth over you; and the time soon cometh that he avengeth the blood of the saints upon you, for he will not suffer their cries any longer. (Mormon 8:36-41.)

Tithing the Poor

While it is quite repugnant that the church withholds assistance to the poor who have no opportunity to work while giving salaries to General Authorities and Mission Presidents, it would be well if that were the only problem in the matter. What is more egregious still is that the doctrine of tithing has been modified to enable the extraction of money from the poor.

As detailed earlier, God states in D&C 119 and JST Gen 14 that tithing consists of 1) a one-time donation of all surplus property to God's representative, and 2) an annual payment of one tenth of net income.

In today's church, there is no mechanism for or instruction to give a one-time donation of all surplus property. There is instruction, however, to pay one tenth of one's gross annual income, instead of one tenth of one's net income.

As God said in D&C 119, and as is confirmed by the consistency of the law given to Abraham and that given through Joseph Smith, tithing as revealed in D&C 119 is to be a standing law forever. God himself said that it would not change. So how did modern Mormons come to practice a different law?

It is apparent that during Joseph's life, the law was lived as written. The church newspaper featured an article that said:

> The celestial law requires one-tenth part of all a man's substance which he possesses at the time he comes into the church (See D&C 119:1), and one-tenth part of his annual increase ever after (See D&C 119:4). If it requires all man can earn to support himself and his family, he is not tithed at all. The celestial law does not take the mother's and children's bread, neither ought else which they really need for their comfort. The poor that have not of this world's good to spare, but serve and honor God according to the best of their abilities in every other way, shall have a celestial crown in the Eternal Kingdom of our Father. (The Millenial Star, 1847.)

Another contemporary source reads:

> If a man gives for the benefit of the Church, it is considered a voluntary offering. Yet the law requires or enjoins a consecration of the overplus, after reserving for himself and family to carry on his business. (John Corrill, A Brief History of the Church of Latter Day Saints, p. 45.)

Less than two months after Joseph's death, the brethren issued a proclamation demanding a one time payment of 1/10th of their property to the church, without exemptions for those who had already done so per D&C 119. That started an incessant shift to tithing as it is practiced today. In 1873, Orson Hyde preached that tithing was 1/10 of your income, instead of 1/10 of your surplus. In 1874, Orson Pratt preached that tithing was separate from the initial consecration commanded in D&C 119. In 1892, Joseph F. Smith publicly taught that tithing ought to be paid before the necessities of life. In 1899, Lorenzo Snow ended the practice of an initial consecration. In 1910, tithing on one's income became a requirement to enter the temple.

As the Lord said through Ezekiel:

> There is a conspiracy of her prophets in the midst thereof, like a roaring lion ravening the prey; they have devoured souls; they have taken the treasure and precious things; they have made her many widows in the midst thereof. Her priests have violated my law, and have profaned mine holy things...Her princes in the midst thereof are like wolves ravening the prey, to shed blood, and to destroy souls, to get dishonest gain. And her prophets have daubed them with untempered mortar, seeing vanity, and divining lies unto them, saying, Thus saith the Lord God, when the Lord hath not spoken. The people of the land have used oppression, and exercised robbery, and have vexed the poor and needy: yea, they have oppressed the stranger wrongfully. (Ezekiel 22:25-29.)

Today, the church constantly preaches that individuals must pay 10% of their gross income in order to consider themselves full tithe payers, and that this payment should come even if it means one cannot pay their bills.[104] This policy is obviously much more difficult for the poor than for the rich. The rich are no longer required to make a one-time consecration of their surplus. The church commands the poor to give what little they have to finance expenditures not authorized by God and for which the poor receive nothing on the one hand, and then refuses to support the poor on the other. All the while, the Brethren themselves do not work. Is it any question what Jesus would say about this, when he said the following about the rulers in his day?

> …The scribes and the Pharisees sit in Moses' seat…they bind heavy burdens and grievous to be borne, and lay them on men's shoulders; but they themselves will not move them with one of their fingers….Woe unto you, scribes and Pharisees, hypocrites! for ye devour widows' houses, and for a pretense make long prayer: therefore ye shall receive the greater damnation. (Matthew 23:2,4,14.)

Is it any wonder whether the church today is a fulfillment of Isaiah's prophecy?

> …O my people, your leaders mislead you, abolishing your traditional ways. Jehovah will…bring to trial the elders of his people and their rulers, and say to them, It is you who have devoured the vineyard; you fill your houses by depriving the needy. What do you mean by oppressing my people, humbling the faces of the poor? says Jehovah of Hosts. (Isaiah 3:12-15, Gileadi Translation.)

The leaders of ancient Israel treated the poor the same as the church does today.[105] God called their actions "manifold transgressions" and "mighty

---

[104] For example, "Pay [tithing] first, even when you think you do not have enough money to meet your other needs. Doing so will help you develop greater faith, overcome selfishness, and be more receptive to the Spirit." ("For the Strength of Youth (2011), p. 38.) "Pay your tithing first, and you will be blessed in helping your family." ("Tithing," Family Home Evening Manual, 1997, p. 227.) "We should always first set aside our tithing from our earnings, and then we will find that our Father in Heaven will bless us to be able to manage what is left so we will have enough for our needs." (Gospel Fundamentals Manual, Chapter 28.)

[105] The Lord insulted the leaders who oppressed the poor fat cows, who had become fat from eating the goods of the poor. " 1 Hear this word, ye kine of Bashan, that are in the mountain of Samaria, which oppress the poor, which crush the needy, which say to their masters, Bring, and let us drink." (Amos 4:1) God spoke harsh things of the leaders who took food out of the mouths of the poor: " 11 Forasmuch therefore as your treading is upon the poor, and ye take from him burdens of wheat: ye have built houses of hewn stone, but ye shall not dwell in them; ye have planted pleasant

sins." He promised their destruction as a result. In Micah, God promises that leaders who neglect the poor will not have visions, prophecies, or answers to prayers, causing one to wonder whether the church's neglect of the poor today might have something to do with the complete lack of prophecy, visions, and revelations from those who are sustained as prophets, seers, and revelators.

> And I said, Hear, I pray you, O heads of Jacob, and ye princes of the house of Israel; Is it not for you to know judgment? Who hate the good, and love the evil; who pluck off their skin from off them, and their flesh from off their bones; Who also eat the flesh of my people, and flay their skin from off them; and they break their bones, and chop them in pieces, as for the pot, and as flesh within the caldron. Then shall they cry unto the Lord, but he will not hear them: he will even hide his face from them at that time, as they have behaved themselves ill in their doings. Thus saith the Lord concerning the prophets that make my people err, that bite with their teeth, and cry, Peace; and he that putteth not into their mouths, they even prepare war against him. Therefore night shall be unto you, that ye shall not have a vision; and it shall be dark unto you, that ye shall not divine; and the sun shall go down over the prophets, and the day shall be dark over them. Then shall the seers be ashamed, and the diviners confounded: yea, they shall all cover their lips; for there is no answer of God. But truly I am full of power by the spirit of the Lord, and of judgment, and of might, to declare unto Jacob his transgression, and to Israel his sin. Hear this, I pray you, ye heads of the house of Jacob, and princes of the house of Israel, that abhor judgment, and pervert all equity. They build up Zion with blood, and Jerusalem with iniquity. The heads thereof judge for reward, and the priests thereof teach for hire, and the prophets thereof divine for money: yet will they lean upon the Lord, and say, Is not the Lord among us? none evil can come upon us. Therefore shall Zion for your sake be plowed as a field, and Jerusalem shall become heaps, and the mountain of the house as the high places of the forest. (Micah 3:1-12.)

As God said through Micah, it is as if leaders think that they can build Zion with the blood of the poor extracted through a wresting of the law of tithing, all while teaching the gospel for money. And yet, the leaders do claim that the Lord is among them, and that no evil can come upon them.[106]

---

vineyards, but ye shall not drink wine of them. 12 For I know your manifold transgressions and your mighty sins: they afflict the just, they take a bribe, and they turn aside the poor in the gate from their right." (Amos 5:11-12)

[106] Elder Jeffery R. Holland said the following on Facebook on May 27th, 2015: "The gospel of Jesus Christ is the most certain, the most secure, the most reliable, and the

The following two passages of scriptures are necessary reading on the topic, though they will be presented without commentary.

And the word of the Lord came unto me, saying, Son of man, prophesy against the shepherds of Israel, prophesy, and say unto them, Thus saith the Lord God unto the shepherds; Woe be to the shepherds of Israel that do feed themselves! should not the shepherds feed the flocks? Ye eat the fat, and ye clothe you with the wool, ye kill them that are fed: but ye feed not the flock. The diseased have ye not strengthened, neither have ye healed that which was sick, neither have ye bound up that which was broken, neither have ye brought again that which was driven away, neither have ye sought that which was lost; but with force and with cruelty have ye ruled them. And they were scattered, because there is no shepherd: and they became meat to all the beasts of the field, when they were scattered. My sheep wandered through all the mountains, and upon every high hill: yea, my flock was scattered upon all the face of the earth, and none did search or seek after them. Therefore, ye shepherds, hear the word of the Lord; As I live, saith the Lord God, surely because my flock became a prey, and my flock became meat to every beast of the field, because there was no shepherd, neither did my shepherds search for my flock, but the shepherds fed themselves, and fed not my flock; Therefore, O ye shepherds, hear the word of the Lord; Thus saith the Lord God; Behold, I am against the shepherds; and I will require my flock at their hand, and cause them to cease from feeding the flock; neither shall the shepherds feed themselves any more; for I will deliver my flock from their mouth, that they may not be meat for them. For thus saith the Lord God; Behold, I, even I, will both search my sheep, and seek them out. As a shepherd seeketh out his flock in the day that he is among his sheep that are scattered; so will I seek out my sheep, and will deliver them out of all places where they have been scattered in the cloudy and dark day. And I will bring them out from the people, and gather

---

most rewarding truth on earth and in heaven, in time and in eternity. Nothing—not anything, not anyone, not any influence—will keep this Church from fulfilling its mission and realizing its destiny declared from before the foundation of the world. Ours is that fail-safe, inexorable, indestructible dispensation of the fulness of the gospel. There is no need to be afraid or tentative about the future.Unlike every other era before us, this dispensation will not experience an institutional apostasy; it will not see a loss of priesthood keys; it will not suffer a cessation of revelation from the voice of Almighty God. Individuals will apostatize or turn a deaf ear to heaven, but never again will the dispensation collectively do so. What a secure thought! What a day in which to live!"

them from the countries, and will bring them to their own land, and feed them upon the mountains of Israel by the rivers, and in all the inhabited places of the country. I will feed them in a good pasture, and upon the high mountains of Israel shall their fold be: there shall they lie in a good fold, and in a fat pasture shall they feed upon the mountains of Israel. I will feed my flock, and I will cause them to lie down, saith the Lord God. I will seek that which was lost, and bring again that which was driven away, and will bind up that which was broken, and will strengthen that which was sick: but I will destroy the fat and the strong; I will feed them with judgment. And as for you, O my flock, thus saith the Lord God; Behold, I judge between cattle and cattle, between the rams and the he goats. Seemeth it a small thing unto you to have eaten up the good pasture, but ye must tread down with your feet the residue of your pastures? and to have drunk of the deep waters, but ye must foul the residue with your feet? And as for my flock, they eat that which ye have trodden with your feet; and they drink that which ye have fouled with your feet. Therefore thus saith the Lord God unto them; Behold, I, even I, will judge between the fat cattle and between the lean cattle. Because ye have thrust with side and with shoulder, and pushed all the diseased with your horns, till ye have scattered them abroad; Therefore will I save my flock, and they shall no more be a prey; and I will judge between cattle and cattle. And I will set up one shepherd over them, and he shall feed them, even my servant David; he shall feed them, and he shall be their shepherd. And I the Lord will be their God, and my servant David a prince among them; I the Lord have spoken it. And I will make with them a covenant of peace, and will cause the evil beasts to cease out of the land: and they shall dwell safely in the wilderness, and sleep in the woods. And I will make them and the places round about my hill a blessing; and I will cause the shower to come down in his season; there shall be showers of blessing. And the tree of the field shall yield her fruit, and the earth shall yield her increase, and they shall be safe in their land, and shall know that I am the Lord, when I have broken the bands of their yoke, and delivered them out of the hand of those that served themselves of them. And they shall no more be a prey to the heathen, neither shall the beast of the land devour them; but they shall dwell safely, and none shall make them afraid. And I will raise up for them a plant of renown, and they shall be no more consumed with hunger in the land, neither bear the shame of the heathen any more. Thus shall they know that I the Lord their God am with them, and that they, even the house of Israel, are my people, saith the Lord God. And ye my flock, the flock of my pasture, are men, and I am your God, saith the Lord God. (Ezekiel 34:1-31)

There is a voice of the howling of the shepherds; for their glory is spoiled: a voice of the roaring of young lions; for the pride of Jordan is spoiled. Thus saith the Lord my God; Feed the flock of the slaughter; Whose possessors slay them, and hold themselves not guilty: and they that sell them say, Blessed be the Lord; for I am rich: and their own shepherds pity them not. For I will no more pity the inhabitants of the land, saith the Lord: but, lo, I will deliver the men every one into his neighbour's hand, and into the hand of his king: and they shall smite the land, and out of their hand I will not deliver them. And I will feed the flock of slaughter, even you, O poor of the flock. (Zechariah 11:3-7.)

Respect of Persons

The Lord has commanded us to be one.[107] Until we are one, we cannot be Zion. One way we can be one is by treating all our brothers and sisters in the developing world the same way we treat those in the first world. Throughout the scriptures, the Lord commands us to do exactly that. He indicates that it would not be right to treat one group of members better than another group:

And again I say unto you, let every man esteem his brother as himself. For what man among you having twelve sons, and is no respecter of them, and they serve him obediently, and he saith unto the one: Be thou clothed in robes and sit thou here; and to the other: Be thou clothed in rags and sit thou there—and looketh upon his sons and saith I am just? Behold, this I have given unto you as a parable, and it is even as I am. I say unto you, be one; and if ye are not one ye are not mine. (D&C 38:25-27.)

Elder Glenn L. Pace once said, "There is a state of human misery below which no Latter-day Saint should descend as long as others are living in abundance." This is a laudatory thought. We ought to be just as concerned about those Saints in the developing world as we are the Saints in our own ward.

Jacob strongly chastened his brethren because they thought they were better than the poor among them due to their riches:

And the hand of providence hath smiled upon you most pleasingly, that you have obtained many riches; and because some of you have

---

[107] "For if ye are not equal in earthly things ye cannot be equal in obtaining heavenly things;" (D&C 78:6)

101

obtained more abundantly than that of your brethren ye are lifted up in the pride of your hearts, and wear stiff necks and high heads because of the costliness of your apparel, and persecute your brethren because ye suppose that ye are better than they. And now, my brethren, do ye suppose that God justifieth you in this thing? Behold, I say unto you, Nay. But he condemneth you, and if ye persist in these things his judgments must speedily come unto you....Think of your brethren like unto yourselves, and be familiar with all and free with your substance, that they may be rich like unto you. (Jacob 2:13-14,17.)

Although it is doubtful that anyone will ever self-identify as thinking they are better than others, or as treating one group differently than another, Jacob gives us a clue of how to tell: Are you familiar with *all* and free with your substance? Or, do you partition more of your substance to some than others? Are their qualifiers placed on your giving?

Alma taught that we suppose we "are better one than another" when we turn our "backs upon the poor, and the needy" and withhold our substance from them. He said those who do so have set their hearts upon riches.[108]

The Lord has indicated that if we are not equal, and we do not treat others equally, that he will withhold his Spirit. "Nevertheless, in your temporal things you shall be equal, and this not grudgingly, otherwise the abundance of the manifestations of the Spirit shall be withheld." (D&C 70:14.) We ought to pay strict heed, therefore, to whether or not we treat the poor among us as well as we do the rich.

One way modern Mormons treat the poor differently that the rich is in how we spend fast offerings. Estimated at $400 million per annum, only 2% of that goes to the developing world, where almost half of members live. About 25% of members in the developing world live on less than $1.25 per day in areas where the cost of food is not very different from the United States.[109] The issue with the manner of distributing fast offerings is that the poorest nations house both the members with the greatest financial need and the members with the least ability to donate fast offerings. Without a globally

---

[108] "...will ye still persist in the wearing of costly apparel and setting your hearts upon the vain things of the world, upon your riches? Yea, will ye persist in supposing that ye are better one than another; yea, will ye persist in the persecution of your brethren, who humble themselves and do walk after the holy order of God, wherewith they have been brought into this church, having been sanctified by the Holy Spirit, and they do bring forth works which are meet for repentance---Yea, and will you persist in turning your backs upon the poor, and the needy, and in withholding your substance from them?" (Alma 5:53-55.)

[109] Bradley Walker MD "Spreading Zion Southward", Dialogue.

equal standard of need, Bishops instead define need based on local norms.[110] Thus, families in Zimbabwe are turned away from the few dollars in fast offerings the Bishops there have to spend per month because hunger is not a sufficiently emergent need in Zimbabwe, while a member in the United States can easily receive $1500 per month in aid to pay his mortgage when he is laid off of work. In places like Zimbabwe, the needs far exceed the welfare budget. Because of the nearly ubiquitous unemployment, nearly the entire ward is in need. In my interviews with leaders there, Bishops told me that they rotate their assistance allotment among perhaps 3 families each month.[111] A month's assistance consists of perhaps a 2 lb. bag of corn flour and a bar of soap. There are no bishop's storehouses in the developing world. There is no budget available for medical needs, as even the most minor medical need, such as a course of inexpensive antibiotic treatment chronic diarrhea, exceeds the ward and stake welfare budgets. Although there is a codified mechanism to gain access to welfare funds beyond the ward/stake fast offerings collected, the need must be clearly recognizable as beyond the norm for the local area in order to gain the required approval of Stake President, Area President, and Presiding Bishop.[112] Thus, there is no direct mechanism to distribute fast offerings from affluent areas such as the United States to areas of great poverty. In short, fast offerings are not designed to alleviate poverty in the church, but rather to provide short term assistance in local congregations.

Would it really be so difficult to make the welfare budget like the ward budget, where all funds go to headquarters to be redistributed globally by ward size, instead of anchoring the offerings to the unit that donated them? This would not be as advantageous as allocating welfare budgets according to global weighted need, but it would be a change that could occur overnight and would be many times more efficacious (and equitable) than the current system.

Another way modern Mormons treat the poor differently is in the excuses they use not to donate to them. The biggest excuse is self-reliance. The counsel to be self-reliant is present in every manual discussing caring for the poor. In fact, it is listed first in order of duty before actually caring for the poor in every case. Self-reliance is a mantra of church welfare. For instance:

---

[110] The church is well aware of this disparity, as leaders are instructed in handbook 1 that "the temporal circumstances and needs of members vary from country to country. A family that might be considered needy in one location might not be considered so if they lived elsewhere." (2010 handbook 1 5.2.3)

[111] In March 2014 I toured each of the stakes and districts in Zimbabwe save one for Liahona Children's Foundation, a charity that provides free nutrition supplements for malnourished LDS children. I gathered these facts personally from stake/district presidents and bishops/branch presidents.

[112] For example, see Handbook 1:5.1.2.

the Lord only helps those who are willing to help themselves. He expects His children to be self-reliant to the degree they can be. (L. Tom Perry, "Becoming Self-Reliant", Oct 1991.)

Many programs have been set up by well-meaning individuals to aid those who are in need. However, many of these programs are designed with the shortsighted objective of "helping people," as opposed to "helping people help themselves." Our efforts must always be directed toward making able-bodied people self-reliant. (Marion G. Romney October 1982 General Conference.)

the Church is not satisfied with any system which leaves able people permanently dependent, and insists, on the contrary, that the true function and office of giving, is to help people [get] into a position where they can help themselves and thus be free. (The Church Welfare Plan, Gospel Doctrine manual, 1946, p. 77.)

While there is nothing wrong with helping people avoid laziness, the mantra of self-reliance is based on the assumption that it is, in fact, possible to obtain self-sufficiency in all countries. The fact is—it isn't. The United States has been an economically productive land since it's inception. The modern reasons for this surround the value of our currency. It is not possible for all other nations, or even a majority of nations, to enjoy the economic prosperity we do. This is why their comments about the poor sound regrettably similar to Korihor, who was an antichrist. He preached that:

...every man fared in this life according to the management of the creature; therefore every man prospered according to his genius, and that every man conquered according to his strength... (Alma 30:17.)

Unfortunately, most church members (including the leaders) are from the United States, and have never experienced real poverty. Because the only poverty they have experienced has been from those who could work but choose not to, you hear church members saying the following about the poor:
- "They are poor because they don't pay tithing."
- "They are poor because they keep electing corrupt governments."
- "They are poor because they are lazy and won't work."

No one who has met these members, visited their homes, or even heard their story could say such foolishly arrogant things. The mantra of self-reliance is one possible fulfillment of Isaiah's prophecy:

For the godless utter blasphemy; their heart ponders impiety: how to practice hypocrisy and preach perverse things concerning Jehovah, leaving the hungry soul empty, depriving the thirsty soul of drink. And rogues scheme by malevolent means and insidious devices to ruin the poor, and with false slogans and accusations to denounce the needy. But the noble are of noble intent, and stand up for what is virtuous. (Isaiah 32:6-8, Gileadi Translation.)

Here, the false accusations are those above enumerated. The false slogan is "self-reliance." Hypocrisy includes the fact that the Brethren receive salaries without working from the church, but they say it wouldn't be righteous to give money to the poor without their working for it. Their programs leave the hungry soul empty. The idea of requiring 10% of a poor persons income, in contradiction to God's word on the subject, and withhold temple worship from those who cannot comply, can only be described as malevolent and insidious.

God did not ask us only to care for certain of the poor. He did not make it conditional. In fact, if he specified any group on whom we should have mercy, he said it was those who cannot repay us, those who will never be self-reliant.

> But when thou makest a feast, call the poor, the maimed, the lame, the blind: And thou shalt be blessed; for they cannot recompense thee: for thou shalt be recompensed at the resurrection of the just. (Luke 14:13-14.)

There are those who say, "well, given to the wretchedly poor is not a permanent solution. You are just fighting the symptoms." Yet, no parent ever looks at a baby who has just soiled their diaper and said, "I will not change them because they will just dirty the new diaper as well." God knows that the most poor people will never cease to be poor. Yet, he commands us to be liberal even with these:

> For the poor shall never cease out of the land: therefore I command thee, saying, Thou shalt open thine hand wide unto thy brother, to thy poor, and to thy needy, in thy land. (Deuteronomy 15:11.)

God teaches that we should not give to others based on their capacity to give back. Rather, our generosity to those who cannot repay characterizes our generosity with God. "He that hath pity upon the poor lendeth unto the Lord; and that which he hath given will he pay him again." (Proverbs 19:17.)

Another way we show preference to the rich in the church today is through how we spend on education. The church's universities and the perpetual education fund provide a staggering juxtaposition. President Hinckley said that "[BYU] is the single most expensive entity funded by the tithes of the Church." ("Out of Your Experience Here," October 16, 1990 BYU Speeches.) While we do not know how much tithing is spent on church universities, we can infer an estimate using BYU's comparison of tuition at comparable private universities at $24,000 per year per student more than BYU tuition, or over $1 billion per year for the more than 49,000 full-time students in church universities. That comes out to $96,000 in tithing per student assuming the student graduates in 4 years, a feat only accomplished by 31% of students at BYU according to US News.

The PEF costs roughly $1,000 per completed participant.[113] Since inception in 2001, the program has only consumed around $60 million dollars. The PEF is not a grant program. Participants are loaned the money. They are required to pay it back at a healthy interest rate.[114] Since every penny of that money came from interest on the donations from members earmarked for the PEF, no tithing has been spent on the PEF. During that same time, roughly $13 billion dollars in tithing have been spent on church schools.

While PEF entrants are required to complete a class on finance and choose a training program for which employment is available,[115] there are no such requirements at church universities. In fact in 2014, 46% of graduates from BYU received degrees in fields for which there is little to no demand for jobs.[116] PEF tuition is an interest-bearing loan, not a gift, and the terms of repayment are contracted prior to receipt of the money. Meanwhile, church university students are trusted to repay the church's substantially greater investment (around 100 times greater) in them without any interest and no principle. PEF students are held to strict timelines. BYU students are not rushed in any way.[117]

Education is quite affordable in the United States, Canada, and Europe, where government subsidies and job opportunities in sensible fields mean that tuition can be repaid within a year of graduating, even if the entire degree was financed. In most countries where the PEF is a church member's only hope at church education assistance, there are limited or no subsidies, and financing is not available. So with the church spending 100 times more per student with no strings attached, why would any member of the church choose to go through the PEF instead of BYU? Because they can't afford to. Acceptance rates aside, BYU costs prohibitively more for international students than for first world students. International students must not only

---

[113] "the average cost for each student is $1,112, while the average length of time spent in the program is 2.3 years" (Deseret News, "Perpetual Education Fund a Sucess but with Challenges," April 13, 2009)

[114] The propriety of charging the poor interest is questionable. See for instance Ezekiel 18 and Ezekiel 22:1-2, 12.

[115] PEF loans are only given for jobs that "are in demand in the local economy." (see pef.lds.org/pef/faqhome).

[116] In 2014, about 21% of graduates recieved degrees in Family, Home and Social Sciences, 13% in Fine Arts, and 12% in Humanities, totaling about 46% of graduates getting degrees in fields for which there is slight or no employment demand (see registrar.byu.edu/registrar/graduation/statistics.php).

[117] The Department of Education reports that traditional students (those not attending part-time) take five years and 10 months to finish a bachelor's degree. (http://nces.ed.gov/pubs2013/2013150.pdf) While specific figures are not provided by BYU, US News reported that only 31% of BYU students graduate in 4 years.

pay tuition, room, and board at rates that are many times higher than their native countries, but they also must come up with a $4,000 to deposit into a BYU-controlled escrow account in order to be admitted, which cannot be spent for tuition, room, or board.[118] Finally, passing the English fluency requirement is usually only possible after years of expensive English classes, something only the relatively wealthy can afford. As President Hinckley once said, the exclusion of members who wish to go to BYU but cannot is an "injustice."[119] Yet, neither he nor his successor have done anything to make it more fair. Simply subjecting BYU students to the same terms as the PEF would be a marked improvement.

Joseph said, "God had often sealed up the heavens because of covetousness in the Church." (TPJS, p. 9) Is there any wonder whether the church today is covetous? Do modern Mormons treat the poor members of the church the same as they treat the rich? No wonder Jesus said, "For it is easier for a camel to go through a needle's eye, than for a rich man to enter into the kingdom of God." (Luke 18:25) If such is true for a man, what of an institution?

To Get Gain

In modern Mormonism, salvation comes in and through the temple ordinances (see "Temples"). Because of this, all aspects of the church point to the temple. Financial aspects of the church are no different. Because temples are taught as necessary to salvation, and because temples cost so much to build, it is understandable that the church puts so much emphasis on the acquisition of money.

---

[118] See https://admissions.byu.edu/deposit-policy

[119] "I remember many years ago, when Ernest L. Wilkinson was president, we had an important discussion in our board meeting. For some years prior to that, the university had vigorously recruited students, with General Authorities at stake conferences being a part of that effort. Then, suddenly, there were more applicants than could be accommodated, and there was much discussion concerning enrollment ceilings. There was talk about who should be eligible to come and what should be the qualifying factors. That meeting was conducted by President Harold B. Lee, who was then serving as a counselor in the First Presidency. As the discussion went on, I remember saying, "The basic question we face now and will continue to face is simply this, 'Who will the Church educate, and who will it turn away?'...If the major portion of the costs of operating BYU come from the tithing funds of the Church, then why are not the children of longtime faithful tithe payers eligible to attend as long as they meet reasonable qualifications? In his letter, the stake president continued, "Is it our objective to turn out of this school an elitist group, snobbish about their intellectual superiority? These are difficult questions to answer. There is an injustice. This is the single most expensive entity funded by the tithes of the Church. Should not all who are honest and generous in their tithing be eligible for its benefits?" (Gordon B. Hinckley, "Out of Your Experience Here," October 16, 1990 BYU Speeches)

Of course, the temple model for salvation does not require the army of professionals employed by the church, nor the smaller contingent of paid ministers employed by the church (CES, General Authorities, and mission presidents). Oddly, the annual combined cost of all church employees easily exceeds the cost to build and maintain temples. To labor for money in the name of building Zion is explicitly identified by Nephi as priestcraft: "the laborer in Zion shall labor for Zion; for if they labor for money they shall perish" (2 Ne. 26:31).

Nephi prophesied that "the Gentiles" would do exactly these things. Though modern Mormons comfortably shrug off this prophecy to the Catholics, it is unquestionable that the church's actions fit the bill.

> And the Gentiles are lifted up in the pride of their eyes, and have stumbled, because of the greatness of their stumbling block, that they have built up many churches; nevertheless, they put down the power and miracles of God, and preach up unto themselves their own wisdom and their own learning, that they may get gain and grind upon the face of the poor. (2 Nephi 26:20.)

Has the church build many churches? The church breaks ground on one chapel per day. Have the leaders put down the power and miracles of God? They have preached consistently that revelation is just your feelings,[120] that only the unrighteous seek spiritual manifestations,[121] that spiritual gifts are

---

[120] Under a bold heading reading "If we are humble and sensitive, the Lord will prompt us through our feelings," the 2015 Priesthood and Relief Society manual quotes President Ezra Taft Benson saying "When you do good, you feel good, and that is the Holy Ghost speaking to you....We hear the words of the Lord most often by a feeling. If we are humble and sensitive, the Lord will prompt us through our feelings." (Teachings of Presidents of the Church: Ezra Taft Benson, (2014), 156–66)

[121] Moroni clearly taught that the absence of spiritual manifestations indicated a lack of faith and was a condition that called for repentance. "And now I speak unto all the ends of the earth—that if the day cometh that the power and gifts of God shall be done away among you, it shall be because of unbelief. And wo be unto the children of men if this be the case; for there shall be none that doeth good among you, no not one. For if there be one among you that doeth good, he shall work by the power and gifts of God. (Moroni 10:24-25) Behold I say unto you, Nay; for it is by faith that miracles are wrought; and it is by faith that angels appear and minister unto men; wherefore, if these things have ceased wo be unto the children of men, for it is because of unbelief, and all is vain. (Moroni 7:37) Yet, Elder Bednar recently taught that it was normal to "not receive frequent, miraculous, or strong impressions." He said "as we consider the experiences of Joseph in the Sacred Grove, of Saul on the road to Damascus, and of Alma the Younger, we come to believe something is wrong with or lacking in us if we fall short in our lives of these well-known and spiritually striking examples. If you have had similar thoughts or doubts, please know that you are quite normal." (April 2011 General Conference) Elder Bednar quoted Joseph F.

often from the devil,[122] and that, contrary to God's word on the subject, one should not actually seek the face of Jesus in this life.[123]

Have the leaders "preached up unto themselves their own wisdom and their own learning?" They have truly set themselves up as the light of the world, proclaiming that revelation can't be from God if it disagrees with them,[124] that we should trust in them for salvation,[125] that their opinions should be accepted as God's word,[126] and that a man's allegiance to Christ is measured by his allegiance to them.[127]

Smith who taught much earlier "Show me Latter-day Saints who have to feed upon miracles, signs and visions in order to keep them steadfast in the Church, and I will show you members…who are not in good standing before God, and who are walking in slippery paths. It is not by marvelous manifestations unto us that we shall be established in the truth, but it is by humility and faithful obedience to the commandments and laws of God" (in Conference Report, Apr. 1900, 40).

[122] "I believe that if one wants revelations enough to crave them beyond the rightness of it, that eventually he will get his revelations but they may not come from God. I am sure that there may be many spectacular things performed because the devil is very responsive." President Spencer W. Kimball, quoted by Richard Turley, Church Historian, in June 2015 Boise Meeting with Elder Oaks.

[123] "Of course, all of the righteous desire to see the face of our Savior, but the suggestions that this must happen in mortality is a familiar tactic of the adversary. To identify a worthy goal, such as to achieve exaltation, and then to use the desirability of that goal and people's enthusiasm for it to obscure the new means the adversary suggests to achieve it." (Elder Dallin H. Oaks, June 2015 Boise Meeting.)

[124] "When visions, dreams, tongues, prophecy, impressions or an extraordinary gift or inspiration convey something out of harmony with the accepted revelations of the Church or contrary to the decisions of its constituted authorities, Latter-day Saints may know that it is not of God, no matter how plausible it may appear. Also, they should understand that directions for the guidance of the Church will come, by revelation, through the head. All faithful members are entitled to the inspiration of the Holy Spirit for themselves, their families, and for those over whom they are appointed and ordained to preside. But anything at discord with that which comes from God through the head of the Church is not to be received as authoritative or reliable." (First Presidency Letter, August 1913, repeated often since and as recently as June 2015 by Richard Turley, Church Historian with Elder Oaks in a Boise regional meeting)

[125] "The calling of 15 men to the holy apostleship provides great protection for us as members of the Church. Why? Because decisions of these leaders must be unanimous.13 Can you imagine how the Spirit needs to move upon 15 men to bring about unanimity?… Trust me! These 15 men—prophets, seers, and revelators—know what the will of the Lord is when unanimity is reached!" (Elder Russell M. Nelson, "Sustaining the Prophets," April 2014 General Conference.)

[126] See "Prophet: Title or Description?"

[127] "…the key question on who's on the Lord's side is how they feel about the church's current prophetic leadership. If those feelings are sufficiently negative, they take members into what we call apostasy." (Dallin Oaks, Boise, Idaho, June 17, 2105.)

But have these teachings been demonstrably for the purpose of getting gain at the expense of the poor? If a poor man can obtain salvation directly from Christ, he does not need to worry about selling his house or working away from his family for years in order to obtain salvific ordinances from the church while the rich can obtain it without any such sacrifice.[128] If a poor man can obtain salvation directly from Christ, he would not have to go without food, medicine, or shelter to pay 10% of his already insufficient income to the church in order to finance luxury living standards for church employees and obscenely ornate temples.[129] Turning the people away from Christ and towards themselves in order to maintain their dependence upon them is a literal fulfillment of this prophecy, and it is particularly harmful to the poor, whose sacrifices to maintain membership in the system must far exceed that of the rich.

Therefore, there is no doubt that the following lament is directly squarely upon the leaders of modern Mormonism as much as any other group:

> O ye wicked and perverse and stiffnecked people, why have ye built up churches unto yourselves to get gain? Why have ye transfigured the holy word of God, that ye might bring damnation upon your souls? Behold, look ye unto the revelations of God; for behold, the

---

[128] "May I share with you the account of Tihi and Tararaina Mou Tham and their 10 children. The entire family except for one daughter joined the Church in the early 1960s....Soon they began to desire the blessings of an eternal family sealing in the temple. At that time the nearest temple to the Mou Tham family was the Hamilton New Zealand Temple, more than 2,500 miles (4,000 km) to the southwest, accessible only by expensive airplane travel. The large Mou Tham family, which eked out a meager living on a small plantation, had no money for airplane fare, nor was there any opportunity for employment on their Pacific island. So Brother Mou Tham and his son Gérard made the difficult decision to travel 3,000 miles (4,800 km) to work in New Caledonia, where another son was already employed. The three Mou Tham men labored for four years. Brother Mou Tham alone returned home only once during that time, for the marriage of a daughter. After four years, Brother Mou Tham and his sons had saved enough money to take the family to the New Zealand Temple. All who were members went except for one daughter, who was expecting a baby. They were sealed for time and eternity, an indescribable and joyful experience. Brother Mou Tham returned from the temple directly to New Caledonia, where he worked for two more years to pay for the passage of the one daughter who had not been at the temple with them—a married daughter and her child and husband." (President Thomas S. Monson, "The Holy Temple—a Beacon to the World," April 2011 General Conference.)

[129] The church maintains that the gilded nature of temple construction is necessary for God to accept them. The scriptures and history prove otherwise, as discussed in "Temples."

time cometh at that day when all these things must be fulfilled. (Mormon 8:33.)

The change of tithing from a one-time consecration with 10% of annual surplus thereafter to 10% of annual income with no consecration of surplus was a change made by fiat with the intent to bring in more money.[130] Because God gave no revelation to change his standing law forever (D&C 119); this was and is a transfiguration of the holy word of God.

Changes to align church policy more closely to God's revealed word would not need to be drastic (though many church employees would lose high paying jobs). For example, the church is already buying massive tracts of farmland. Would it be that much of a change to buy it in the developing world instead of the United States, and give poor members the opportunity to farm their own food? Simply by moving these land holdings to the developing world, the church could save millions of church members from poverty.

Other, more drastic changes, would be needed to bring about complete compliance with God's word. He doesn't provide a mechanism for priestcraft or for a for-profit church. He doesn't provide for a way to have both rich and poor members.

> And it is my purpose to provide for my saints, for all things are mine. But it must needs be done in mine own way; and behold this is the way that I, the Lord, have decreed to provide for my saints, that the poor shall be exalted, in that the rich are made low. For the earth is full, and there is enough and to spare; yea, I prepared all things, and have given unto the children of men to be agents unto themselves. Therefore, if any man shall take of the abundance which I have made, and impart not his portion, according to the law of my gospel, unto the poor and the needy, he shall, with the wicked, lift up his eyes in hell, being in torment. (D&C 104:15-18.)

He did not say, "my way is that the rich remain rich and the poor remain poor." The way he has appointed is that the money flow from the rich to the poor. If this is true of individuals, should it not be true of the church itself? Does God approve of a rich church whose members are still poor?

In the end, it is abundantly clear that the model of the church is that salvation comes in and through temples and the paid personnel of the church, and therefore the objective of the church is to gain as much money as

---

[130] President Lorenzo Snow made this calculated change to reverse the difficulty of paying the innovative repetitive 10% consecrations exacted by his predecessors. Many, knowing that they could not comply with this excessive request, had simply stopped paying anything. Restoring tithing to 10% of annual surplus made paying tithing possible again. The dropping of the revealed initial consecration made it a lot easier still.

possible in order to finance the temple-church employee complex because, under this model, the more money gained, the more souls can be saved. As a result, the poor are disproportionately deprived of welfare that would otherwise be their due under the gospel, and also disproportionately deprived of the little they have as a result of priestcraft. While the church decides against proselyting activities that will only add poor members to the church, such as baptizing thousands of Africans who have petitioned for missionaries,[131] the church infrastructure is filled with entities whose sole purpose is to get gain.

> First among its for-profit enterprises is DMC, which reaps estimated annual revenue of $1.2 billion from six subsidiaries, according to the business information and analysis firm Hoover's Company Records (DNB). Those subsidiaries run a newspaper, 11 radio stations, a TV station, a publishing and distribution company, a digital media company, a hospitality business, and an insurance business with assets worth $3.3 billion. AgReserves, another for-profit Mormon umbrella company, together with other church-run agricultural affiliates, reportedly owns about 1 million acres in the continental U.S., on which the church has farms, hunting preserves, orchards, and ranches. These include the $1 billion, 290,000-acre Deseret Ranches in Florida, which, in addition to keeping 44,000 cows and 1,300 bulls, also has citrus, sod, and timber operations. Outside the U.S., AgReserves operates in Britain, Canada, Australia, Mexico, Argentina, and Brazil. Its Australian property, valued at $61 million in 1997, has estimated annual sales of $276 million, according to Dun & Bradstreet. The church also runs several for-profit real estate arms that own, develop, and manage malls, parking lots, office parks, residential buildings, and more. Hawaii Reserves, for example, owns or manages more than 7,000 acres on Oahu, where it maintains commercial and residential buildings, parks, water and sewage infrastructure, and two cemeteries. Utah Property Management Associates, a real estate arm of the church, manages portions of City Creek Center. According to Spencer P. Eccles from the Utah Governor's Office of Economic Development, the mall cost the church an estimated $2 billion. It is only one part of a $5 billion church-funded revamping of downtown Salt Lake City, according to the Mormon-owned news site KSL. (http://www.bloomberg.com/bw/articles/2012-07-10/how-the-mormons-make-money.)

---

[131] This is referred to as the "centers of strength" policy. See http://www.cumorah.com/index.php?target=view_other_articles&story_id=569&cat_id=30

The article goes on to list Ensign Peak Advisors, a multi-billion dollar hedge fund whose sole purpose is to invest money for the church. Since this article was published, the church has accelerated the acquisition of real estate holdings, including the construction of a luxury apartment complex on the site of the new Philadelphia temple.

In the end, the following criticism from Moroni seems to fit well:

> For behold, ye do love money, and your substance, and your fine apparel, and the adorning of your churches, more than ye love the poor and the needy, the sick and the afflicted....Yea, why do ye build up your secret abominations to get gain, and cause that widows should mourn before the Lord, and also orphans to mourn before the Lord, and also the blood of their fathers and their husbands to cry unto the Lord from the ground, for vengeance upon your heads? Behold, the sword of vengeance hangeth over you; and the time soon cometh that he avengeth the blood of the saints upon you, for he will not suffer their cries any longer. (Mormon 8:36-41.)

Conclusion

The Lord explained that the reason the Saints in Joseph's day failed to attain Zion was because of their institutional neglect of the poor.

> Behold, I say unto you, were it not for the transgressions of my people, speaking concerning the church and not individuals, they might have been redeemed even now. But behold, they have not learned to be obedient to the things which I required at their hands, but are full of all manner of evil, and do not impart of their substance, as becometh saints, to the poor and afflicted among them. (D&C 105:2-3.)

Notice how the Lord was explicitly in saying this was not a problem with individuals, but with the church organization itself.

When the institution is failing to care for the poor, who is at fault? Certainly not individual members, who are donating substantial sums to the organization every year. The Lord said:

> If thou lovest me thou shalt serve me and keep all my commandments. And behold, thou wilt remember the poor, and consecrate of thy properties for their support that which thou hast to impart unto them, with a covenant and a deed which cannot be broken. And inasmuch as ye impart of your substance unto the poor, ye will do it unto me; and they shall be laid before the bishop of my church and his counselors, two of the elders, or high priests, such as he shall appoint or has appointed and set apart for that purpose. (D&C 42:29-31.)

It is the leaders' responsibility to distribute the offerings given from the people to the poor. Ironically, the oft-quoted passage from Malachi used to chide poor members into paying 10% of their gross income to the church is actually directed towards the priests who quote it. It is they who are robbing God by refusing to spend tithing and offerings on the poor.

> Will a man rob God? Yet ye have robbed me. But ye say, Wherein have we robbed thee? In tithes and offerings. Ye are cursed with a curse: for ye have robbed me, even this whole nation. Bring ye all the tithes into the storehouse, that there may be meat in mine house, and prove me now herewith, saith the Lord of hosts, if I will not open you the windows of heaven, and pour you out a blessing, that there shall not be room enough to receive it. (Malachi 3:8-10.)

The church leaders are commanded today to

> ...remember in all things the poor and the needy, the sick and the afflicted, for he that doeth not these things, the same is not my disciple. (D&C 52:40.)

Are they? How can we be the Lord's church if he wouldn't even call us his disciples? Jesus said that "a rich man shall hardly enter into the kingdom of heaven...It is easier for a camel to go through the eye of a needle, than for a rich man to enter into the kingdom of God." (Matthew 19:23-24.) If a rich man can't get into the Celestial Kingdom, can a rich church ever become Celestial? Can a rich church ever bring forth Zion?

We are told in the Book of Mormon that if we do not care for the poor, God will not hear our prayers:

> And now behold, my beloved brethren, I say unto you, do not suppose that this is all; for after ye have done all these things, if ye turn away the needy, and the naked, and visit not the sick and afflicted, and impart of your substance, if ye have, to those who stand in need—I say unto you, if ye do not any of these things, behold, your prayer is vain, and availeth you nothing, and ye are as hypocrites who do deny the faith. Therefore, if ye do not remember to be charitable, ye are as dross, which the refiners do cast out, (it being of no worth) and is trodden under foot of men. (Alma 34:28-29.)

Perhaps this is one reason there is a drought of the word of God among the leadership of the church. Isaiah instructs us how we can again begin to receive institutional revelation. He notes how we pray to the Lord consistently and observe the rituals of our religion, as if we were doing the things we are meant to do. Yet, the Lord does not speak to us:

> Proclaim it aloud without restraint; raise your voice like a trumpet! Declare to my people their transgressions, to the house of Jacob its

sins. 2 Yet they importune me daily, eager to learn my ways, like a nation practicing righteousness and not forsaking the precepts of its God. They inquire of me concerning correct ordinances, desiring to draw nearer to God: Why, when we fast, do you not notice? We afflict our bodies and you remain indifferent! It is because on your fast day you pursue your own ends and constrain all who toil for you. You fast amid strife and contention, striking out savagely with the fist. Your present fasts are not such as to make your voice heard on high. (Isaiah 58:1-4, Gileadi Translation.)

And he won't, until we repent and care for the poor:

Is not this the fast I require: To release from wrongful bondage, to untie the harness of the yoke, to set the oppressed at liberty and abolish all forms of subjection? Is it not to share your food with the hungry, to bring home the wretchedly poor, and when you see men underclad to clothe them, and not to neglect your own kin? Then shall your light break through like the dawn and your healing speedily appear; your righteousness will go before you, and the glory of Jehovah will be your rearguard. Then, should you call, Jehovah will respond; should you cry, he will say, I am here. Indeed, if you will banish servitude from among you, and the pointing finger and offensive speech, if you will give of your own to the hungry and satisfy the needs of the oppressed, then shall your light dawn amid darkness and your twilight become as the noonday. Jehovah will direct you continually; he will satisfy your needs in the dearth and bring vigor to your limbs. (Isaiah 58:6-11, Gileadi Translation.)

The Lord expects the church to take care of the poor, but he does not find that happening. As Isaiah prophesied,

The vineyard of Jehovah of Hosts is the house of Israel and the people of Judah his cherished grove. He expected justice, but there was injustice; he expected righteousness, but there was an outcry. (Isaiah 5:7, Gileadi Translation.)

Today, as an institution, we commit the same sins for which Sodom was destroyed.

Behold, this was the iniquity of thy sister Sodom, pride, fulness of bread, and abundance of idleness was in her and in her daughters, neither did she strengthen the hand of the poor and needy. And they were haughty, and committed abomination before me: therefore I took them away as I saw good. (Ezekiel 16:49-50.)

Do you expect the Lord to deal with us any differently than he did Sodom?

In General Conference of April 2011, the Presiding Bishop said,

> The commitment of church leaders to relieve human suffering was as certain as it was irrevocable. President Grant wanted 'a system that would... reach out and take care of the people no matter what the cost.' He said he would even go so far as to 'close seminaries, shut down missionary work for a period of time, or even close temples, but they would not let the people go hungry.

If true, how far the church has fallen in only 100 years.

Of course, we can still repent. How would the Lord have us to repent? He has already told us: "Jesus said unto him, If thou wilt be perfect, go and sell that thou hast, and give to the poor, and thou shalt have treasure in heaven: and come and follow me." Will the church do this, or will it go "away sorrowful: for [it] had great possessions"? (Matthew 19:21.)

When Zion does come, it will come to the same type of people it always has: those with all things in common.

> And it came to pass in the thirty and sixth year, the people were all converted unto the Lord, upon all the face of the land, both Nephites and Lamanites, and there were no contentions and disputations among them, and every man did deal justly one with another. And they had all things common among them; therefore there were not rich and poor, bond and free, but they were all made free, and partakers of the heavenly gift. (4 Nephi 1:2-3.)

That people will not oppress the poor by manipulating tithing to take the little they have. That people will not treat members from the developing world differently than first world members by providing them second rate education programs and withholding the welfare program from them. That people will not pay their leaders to preach the word. That people will not engage in extensive for profit business to get gain. That people will not be lying as they sing, "We've shared our bread with those in need, Relieved the suffring poor. The stranger we have welcomed in—Wilt thou impart thy store?" ("Bless Our Fast, We Pray," Hymn 138.)

That people will be Zion.

The Preeminence of Joseph Smith's Teachings

In the conference center at BYU there is a hallway adorned with portraits of the presidents of the church. Each portrait includes key developments from that president's tenure. President Lee's portrait includes a big book that says, "PRIESTHOOD CORRELATION." President G. Smith's portrait has a Boy Scout medal. Gordon B. Hinckley's portrait has the Huntsman jet on it and a satellite dish. President Monson's has a printing press and some pigeons. The first painting, that of the prophet Joseph Smith, features only a portrayal of the gold plates from which the Book of Mormon was translated.

Perhaps the artist did not think the Doctrine and Covenants was not significant. Or the many visitations of heavenly beings to Joseph. Or the revelation that informed us that God once was a man. Or the revelation of the three kingdoms. I can completely understand that, for someone like David O. McKay, the lack of significant doctrinal developments during his tenure would necessitate a space occupier like a picture of his childhood home. I would expect the opposite problem with Joseph, that of not having enough space and needing to be selective. But one thing? God said that Joseph Smith was his spokesman to our generation. He was and is a really big deal.

Joseph was appointed to hold the keys of this dispensation. The Lord told him:

> Therefore, thou art blessed from henceforth that bear the keys of the kingdom given unto you; which kingdom is coming forth for the last time. Verily I say unto you, the keys of this kingdom shall never be taken from you, while thou art in the world, neither in the world to come; (D&C 90:2-3.)

God told Joseph that his keys would not be taken from him until the Second Coming.

> rebel not against my servant Joseph; for verily I say unto you, I am with him, and my hand shall be over him; and the keys which I have given unto him...shall not be taken from him till I come. (D&C 112:15.)

God said that our dispensation would receive his word through Joseph: "But this generation shall have my word through you;" (D&C 5:11.) God gave the church a very singular commandment regarding Joseph, telling them to treat his words as God's own.

> Wherefore, meaning the church, thou shalt give heed unto all his words and commandments which he shall give unto you as he receiveth them, walking in all holiness before me; For his word ye shall receive, as if from mine own mouth, in all patience and faith. (D&C 21:4-5.)

This was an exceedingly rare thing for God to say. There are no scriptures that indicate he's ever said it to anyone else. God also said that Joseph was the only one appointed to receive commandments and revelations for the church:

> But, behold, verily, verily, I say unto thee, no one shall be appointed to receive commandments and revelations in this church excepting my servant Joseph Smith, Jun., for he receiveth them even as Moses. (D&C 28:2)

God told the church officers that it was Joseph's words that they should preach: "my servants, whom I shall call and ordain...shall go forth with my words that are given through you." (D&C 5:11.)

Every promise listed here was made to Joseph. It was not made to the office of the president of the church, and it was not promised to the successors of Joseph. Perhaps knowing this would be the case, God instructed that "there is none other appointed unto you to receive commandments and revelations" except Joseph Smith and those appointed "through him," and that "ye receive not the teachings of any that shall come before you as revelations or commandments." (D&C 43:1-7.) In spite of the clarity of these verses, modern Mormonism allocates what God said to Joseph to all other presidents of the church.[132] It is important to note that God never did so.

---

[132] This pattern developed soon after Joseph's death. "When I say that Priesthood, I mean the individual who holds the keys thereof. He is the standard—the living oracle to the Church....the revelations of God command us plainly that we shall hearken to the living oracles. Hence, if we undertake to follow the written word, and at the same time do not give heed to the living oracles of God, the written word will condemn us...'Wherefore, meaning the church, thou shalt give heed unto his words and commandments which he shall give unto you as he receiveth them, walking in all holiness before me; For his word shall ye receive, as if from mine own mouth, in all patience and faith.' Here, then, we perceive what is binding upon the Church of the living God, what was binding upon them thirty years ago, and what has been binding upon them ever since, from the day that it was given, until the day the Prophet was

In a revelation recorded in D&C 124, the Lord said:

I give unto you my servant Joseph to be a presiding elder over all my church, to be a translator, a revelator, a seer, and prophet. I give unto him for counselors my servant Sidney Rigdon and my servant William Law, that these may constitute a quorum and First Presidency, to receive the oracles for the whole church. I give unto you my servant Brigham Young to be a president over the Twelve traveling council; Which Twelve hold the keys to open up the authority of my kingdom upon the four corners of the earth, and after that to send my word to every creature.

The prerogative of Joseph (by name) and his counselors (appointed by name) was to receive oracles [133] —answers from God to questions pertaining to the whole church. The prerogative of the twelve, designed as an independent and equal quorum and not a subordinate feeder pool for the First Presidency, was not to receive answers to questions, but to preach the gospel outside of the stakes of Zion.[134] To Joseph, *oracles* were revelations, not

---

martyred, down until the year 1860, and until the present moment of time." (Orson Pratt, JD 7:373)

[133] In all known uses by Joseph Smith, the definition of "oracle" was that of the answers provided by God in response to a question. For example, "Some start on the revelations to come…This is the place that is appointed for the oracles of god to be revealed." (WOJS 13 April 1843) Joseph used the word interchangeably with "scripture." For example, "…men, in previous generations, have with polluted hands and corrupt hearts, taken from the sacred oracles many precious items which were plain of comprehension…" (JS History 1834-1836, p84) "…to further the great work of the Lord, and to establish the children of the kingdom, according to the oracles of God, as they are had among us." (MHC 1838-1856, B-1, p207)

[134] Although, since Brigham Young, the LDS have followed a pattern of refilling First Presidency vacancies from the pool of apostles, the Lord established the First Presidency as a quorum independent from the Quorum of the Twelve, "Of necessity there are presidents, or presiding officers growing out of, or appointed of or from among those who are ordained to the several offices in these two priesthoods: Of the Melchizedek Priesthood, three Presiding High Priests, chosen by the body, appointed and ordained to that office, and upheld by the confidence, faith, and prayer of the church, form a quorum of the Presidency of the Church. The twelve traveling councilors are called to be the Twelve Apostles, or special witnesses of the name of Christ in all the world—thus differing from other officers in the church in the duties of their calling. And they form a quorum, equal in authority and power to the three presidents previously mentioned. (D&C 107:21-24) During Joseph's life, despite almost constant vacancies in the First Presidency, God never called a member of the Twelve to the First Presidency.

revelators.[135] Joseph was told that through him the oracles would be given to the church:

> Therefore, thou art blessed from henceforth that bear the keys of the kingdom given unto you; which kingdom is coming forth for the last time. Verily I say unto you, the keys of this kingdom shall never be taken from you, while thou art in the world, neither in the world to come; Nevertheless, through you shall the oracles be given to another, yea, even unto the church. And all they who receive the oracles of God, let them beware how they hold them lest they are accounted as a light thing, and are brought under condemnation thereby, and stumble and fall when the storms descend, and the winds blow, and the rains descend, and beat upon their house. (D&C 90:2-5.)

Importantly, Joseph was told that the answers God had provided through him to questions regarding doctrine and church administration would be passed on, *not* the ability to receive oracles. This distinction is critical to understanding the importance of what God provided through Joseph.

Joseph's dispensation was a body of oracles, not a perpetual process to receive oracles. An understanding of that fact places an inexpressible importance on the revelations Joseph received. Inasmuch as we ignore, misinterpret, or replace the oracles given by Joseph, we cut ourselves off from the kingdom of God and the blessings offered by the restoration.

> What Constitutes the Kingdom of God Whare there is a Prophet a priest or a righteous man unto whom God gives his oracles there is the Kingdom of God, & whare the oracles of God are not there the Kingdom of God is not...The plea of many in this day is that we have no right to receive revelations, But if we do not get revelations

---

[135] The usage of "oracles" to mean "a person" was employed by others after Joseph's death. For example, John Taylor said, "We have got to follow the oracles of heaven in all things; there is no other way but to follow him God has appointed to lead us and guide us into eternal salvation." (JD 1:375, John Taylor, April 19, 1854) The shift not only changed the word to mean the person who reveals, but the person who is expected to reveal. This shift was significant, causing the focus to be on a man rather than the word of God—which need not be present. For example, from the above cited discourse: "But there is one thing you may set down for a certainty − if a man has not confidence in one revelation of God, he has not in another; and if a man feels right in one, he will in all the revelations from that source...He is either delegated from heaven to do this, or he is not; if he is, we will follow his counsel; if he is not, then we may kick up our heels, and every man help himself the best way he can." In actuality, a man can be inspired some or none of the time, and this has no bearing over whether he will continue to be inspired or not.

we do not have the oracles of God & if they have not the oracles of God they are not the people of God But say you what will become of the world or the various professors of religion who do not believe in revelation & the oracles of God as Continued to the Church in all ages of the world when he has a people on earth I Tell you in the name of Jesus Christ they will be damned & when you get into the eternal world you will find it to be so they cannot escape the damnation of hell (Words of Joseph Smith, 22 Jan 1843.)

The issue of succession is too complex to address here. Suffice it to say that Brigham Young's succession victory over Sidney Rigdon at the hand of a majority public vote, should not be viewed in the same light as the appointments that were made to the First Presidency during Joseph's life. Every single one of the ten appointments to the First Presidency in Joseph's life were made through written explicit commandment from God. The same applies for appointments to the Twelve. In none of the many appointments to the First Presidency during Joseph's life did God select a member of the Quorum of the Twelve. The Quorum of the Twelve was not designed as a feeder pool for the First Presidency. Apostles had special jurisdiction limited to areas where stakes had not been organized. Their authority was equal (but separate) to that of a Stake President's (see D&C 107.)

It is rather odd that a God who thought it necessary to vocally enumerate each member of these quorums from heaven would suddenly make two radical changes: First, to the order of their appointment, as the Quorum of the Twelve was selected to lead the church by self-suggestion and a majority vote of the church; Second, to fill the office of the presidency of the high priesthood with members of a lower priesthood office—that of apostle—without an ordination to the higher office (Brigham Young was never ordained to be president of the church).[136]

---

[136] Brigham Young said, "when a man is ordained to the office of an Apostle, he is ordained to the fullest extent a man can be on earth." (JD 9:281.) Yet, only one of the ten men serving as Joseph's counselors (Oliver Cowdery) were ordained as apostles. Still, somehow, they held sufficient authority to serve as presidents of the high priesthood, holding the authority to do all things in the priesthood, while members of the quorum of the Twelve had no authority outside the organized stakes of Zion. The post-martyrdom brethren taught that "apostle" was the highest office in the priesthood: "I bear this testimony this day, that Joseph Smith was and is a Prophet, Seer, and Revelator—an Apostle holding the keys of this last dispensation and of the kingdom of God, under Peter, James, and John." (Elder Parley P. Pratt, JD 5:195.) Yet, Joseph taught that he had advanced past the office of apostle, and had been ordained by both God and men to be a prophet, priest, and king. During the years after the martyrdom, ordination was not considered necessary since the apostles governed by the keys of the apostleship. Apostle Erastus Snow, quoting Brigham Young, said: "Joseph is still my leader; he is still my President; he still bears the keys

Brigham Young did not preside as the president of the church, but as the president of the quorum of the Twelve, which continues to preside over the church today, a role it has never been given in revelation. Prior to and up to Joseph's death, the Twelve had no priesthood authority within any organized stake of the church.[137] They could not organize a new stake, nor ordain anyone within an organized stake. They did not have the authority to call any stake presidents, any stake patriarch, the presiding patriarch, or even replacements in their quorum. Yet, somehow, they considered themselves to possess the authority to do all this and more at the moment of Joseph's death.

Knowing all this, does an Apostle (even one sitting as church president) have the authority to receive revelation that supersedes that received by a President of the High Priesthood ordained by God's commandment? Joseph Smith said,

---

before me. I am still following after him to carry out his counsel, to accomplish the work of which he laid the foundation, under God. I am still as he appointed, an Apostle to bear off this kingdom, to bear witness of the work which God by him did accomplish, and to carry it forward by the power of God and the help of my brethren and fellow laborers, and I am still an Apostle and President of the Twelve Apostles." (JD 19:102) One of Brigham Young's counselors explained, "In relation to ordination, a great many people have imagined that it was necessary to ordain a man to succeed another, that it would impart a particular efficacy or endow him with some additional power. Ordination is always good and acceptable; blessings and setting apart are always desirable to those who have to go forth to prepare them for God's service; but it is not necessary that an Apostle should be ordained to stand at the head of the people. When the exigency arises, he has already got the fulness of authority, and the power of it.... As I have stated, it is not necessary for a man who has received this power and these keys to be ordained and set apart to act; he can act in any position. President Young, when he chose brother George A. Smith to be his First Counselor, in the place of Heber C. Kimball, did not lay his hands upon his head to confer upon him any additional power or authority for the position, because brother George A. held the Apostleship in its fulness, and by virtue of that Priesthood he could act in that or in any other position in the Church. He chose other assistant Counselors; he did not set them apart, there was no necessity for it, as they already held the Apostleship. And if he had, he could only have blessed them; he could not bestow upon them any more than they already had, because they had all that he himself had, that is when he chose them from the same Quorum." (George Q. Cannon (Counselor to Brigham Young), JD 19:235)

[137] "During Joseph Smith's lifetime, the Quorum of the Twelve Apostles never had authority to ordain even a stake patriarch, and certainly not the Presiding Patriarch, as Pratt alleged concerning Hyrum Smith. As of 1840, the apostles ordained patriarchs in England, one of the 'large branches of the Church.' The vast missionfield outside LDS stakes was the only place where the Quorum of the Twelve had authority to officiate according to Smith's revelations and instructions of 1835." (Quinn, "Mormon Heirarchy: Origins of Power," pp. 46-47.)

> I will inform you that it is contrary to the economy of God for any member of the church, or any one, to receive instruction for those in authority, higher than themselves, therefore you will see the impropriety of giving heed to them: but if any have a vision or a visitation from a heavenly messenger, it must be for their own benefit and instruction, for the fundamental principles, government, and doctrine of the church is vested in the keys of the kingdom. (Joseph Smith, HC, 1:338.)

Joseph Fielding Smith wrote that no man, no matter his office, has the authority to teach doctrines that conflict with Joseph's revelations:

> When prophets write and speak on the principles of the gospel, they should have the guidance of the Spirit. If they do, then all that they say will be in harmony with the revealed word. If they are in harmony then we know that they have not spoken presumptuously. Should a man speak or write, and what he says is in conflict with the standards which are accepted, with the revelations the Lord has given, then we may reject what he has said, no matter who he is. (Joseph Fielding Smith, Doctrines of Salvation, 1:187.)

If we are to believe and listen to God's instructions, Joseph's teachings ought to hold preeminence in Mormonism. They ought to be considered of chief importance. God's words through Joseph are to us. They ought to be studied. They ought to be heeded.

A Covenant was Revealed Through Joseph

Through Moses, a covenant was given to Israel. [138] It consisted of commandments and promises contingent on their keeping them. While the full weight of God's blessings cannot be obtained without a covenant from him, neither can the full weight of his wrath. Christians mistakenly think that the God of the Old Testament was more severe than the God of the New Testament. In reality, the curses that fell upon those who disobeyed God in the Old Testament were a consequence of breaking the covenant given from God through Moses. The New Testament does not contain the consequences of the people rejecting the new covenant offered through Christ, with the exception of the couple that disobeyed the law of consecration after having received it. [139] The consequence for the general rejection of the covenant came after the conclusion of the accounts, and was every bit as horrific as anything

---

[138] "These are the words of the covenant, which the Lord commanded Moses to make with the children of Israel in the land of Moab, beside the covenant which he made with them in Horeb." (Deuteronomy 9:21.)
[139] See Acts chapter 5.

in the Old Testament.[140] The God of the Old Testament is the same as the God of the New, and he will consistently treat all who disobey a received covenant with the degree of penalty observed in the past.

There is a consequence of breaking a covenant.

> For of him unto whom much is given much is required; and he who sins against the greater light shall receive the greater condemnation. (D&C 82:3.)

This was well-understood in ancient times, as evidenced by the fact that the Nephites would allow their mortal enemies to escape unharmed if they swore a covenant that they would not return to fight again.[141] Every time God extends a covenant, he also extends a cursing if the conditions are not met. For example, when God dispensed the gospel to Israel through Moses with a covenant, he said:

> Behold, I set before you this day a blessing and a curse; A blessing, if ye obey the commandments of the Lord your God, which I command you this day: And a curse, if ye will not obey the commandments of the Lord your God, but turn aside out of the way which I command you this day... (Deuteronomy 11:26-28.)

We see the results of the cursing played out in the death penalty and similarly steep consequences prescribed in the law of Moses. For example, in Ezekiel we read that the Pharaoh will be taken captive, beg his life, and yet all his company will be destroyed, all as a consequence of breaking a covenant:

> Neither shall Pharaoh with his mighty army and great company make for him in the war, by casting up mounts, and building forts, to cut off many persons: Seeing he despised the oath by breaking the covenant, when, lo, he had given his hand, and hath done all these things, he shall not escape. Therefore thus saith the Lord God; As I live, surely mine oath that he hath despised, and my covenant that he hath broken, even it will I recompense upon his own head. And I will spread my net upon him, and he shall be taken in my snare, and I will bring him to Babylon, and will plead with him there for his trespass that he hath trespassed against me. And all his fugitives with all his bands shall fall by the sword, and they that remain shall be scattered toward all winds: and ye shall know that I the Lord have spoken it. (Ezekiel 17:17-21)

Jeremiah provided an example of the issuance of a covenant from God to the people and the consequence of their breaking it:

---

[140] Josephus tells of maddening hunger with mothers eating children ("Wars of the Jews," Book VI:4).
[141] See Alma 44:15, for example.

The word that came to Jeremiah from the Lord, saying, Hear ye the words of this covenant, and speak unto the men of Judah, and to the inhabitants of Jerusalem; And say thou unto them, Thus saith the Lord God of Israel; Cursed be the man that obeyeth not the words of this covenant, Which I commanded your fathers in the day that I brought them forth out of the land of Egypt, from the iron furnace, saying, Obey my voice, and do them, according to all which I command you: so shall ye be my people, and I will be your God: Yet they obeyed not, nor inclined their ear, but walked every one in the imagination of their evil heart: therefore I will bring upon them all the words of this covenant, which I commanded them to do; but they did them not...Therefore thus saith the Lord, Behold, I will bring evil upon them, which they shall not be able to escape; and though they shall cry unto me, I will not hearken unto them. (Jeremiah 11:1-4,8,11.)

The principle of penalties for breaking a covenant are in just as much force today as they ever were in the past. This used to be taught in the temple with prescribed penalties for breaking the covenant of the dispensation of the gospel given to Joseph Smith.[142]

One way we can break covenants is through changing ordinances. God has clearly expressed that no man—not even a church leader—has the right to change ordinances. In Malachi 1, the Lord blasts the priests for having changed the ordinances he had revealed to them:

A son honoureth his father, and a servant his master: if then I be a father, where is mine honour? and if I be a master, where is my fear? saith the Lord of hosts unto you, O priests, that despise my name. And ye say, Wherein have we despised thy name? Ye offer polluted bread upon mine altar; and ye say, Wherein have we polluted thee? In that ye say, The table of the Lord is contemptible. And if ye offer the blind for sacrifice, is it not evil? and if ye offer the lame and sick, is it not evil? offer it now unto thy governor; will he be pleased with thee, or accept thy person? saith the Lord of hosts. And now, I pray you, beseech God that he will be gracious unto us: this hath been by your means: will he regard your persons? saith the Lord of hosts. Who is there even among you that would shut the doors for nought? neither do ye kindle fire on mine altar for nought. I have no pleasure in you, saith the Lord of hosts, neither will I accept an offering at your hand. For from the rising of the sun even unto the going down of the same my name shall be great among the Gentiles; and in every place

---

[142] These were removed in 1990 because surveys showed that the majority of LDS found the penalties offensive.

incense shall be offered unto my name, and a pure offering: for my name shall be great among the heathen, saith the Lord of hosts. (Malachi 1:6-11.)

The Lord states that, because they modified his ordinances, he will not bless them (v9), he will not accept their offerings (v10), and he will take the covenant from them and give it to another people (v11). The Lord always punishes those who have broken a covenant through changing the ordinances.

The sons of Eli changed the ordinances, and took greater than their portion from that which was dedicated to the Lord. In addition, through their syphoning off of the offering, they made the people loathe giving their offerings:

And the priests' custom with the people was, that, when any man offered sacrifice, the priest's servant came, while the flesh was in seething, with a fleshhook of three teeth in his hand; And he struck it into the pan, or kettle, or caldron, or pot; all that the fleshhook brought up the priest took for himself. So they did in Shiloh unto all the Israelites that came thither. Also before they burnt the fat, the priest's servant came, and said to the man that sacrificed, Give flesh to roast for the priest; for he will not have sodden flesh of thee, but raw. And if any man said unto him, Let them not fail to burn the fat presently, and then take as much as thy soul desireth; then he would answer him, Nay; but thou shalt give it me now: and if not, I will take it by force. Wherefore the sin of the young men was very great before the Lord: for men abhorred the offering of the Lord. (1 Samuel 2:13-17.)

As we learn from the account of the sons of Eli, one consequence of changing the ordinances is that it trains men to "abhor the offering of the Lord" because they fail to receive God's blessings despite their religious practice, as God does not bless men for conducting adulterated ordinances.

Isaiah described that the latter day people would change the ordinances and reject the covenant:

The earth lies polluted under its inhabitants: they have transgressed the laws, changed the ordinances, set at nought the ancient covenant. (Isaiah 24:5, Gileadi Translation.)

In the past, God unleashed terrible punishments upon those who rejected a covenant once offered.[143] Will an unchanging God treat this generation any

---

[143] For example, God said the following to a group who changed the ordinances he had provided: "Because my people hath forgotten me, they have burned incense to vanity, and they have caused them to stumble in their ways from the ancient paths, to

differently? "For thus saith the Lord God; I will even deal with thee as thou hast done, which hast despised the oath in breaking the covenant." (Ezekiel 16:59.)

We Lose light and Truth if we Don't Heed what Joseph Received

King Benjamin taught that his people were preserved from "dwindl[ing] in unbelief" because they had read and understood the scriptures. (Mosiah 1:5.) He defined unbelief as 1) not knowing what the scriptures say, 2) not believing what the scriptures say when you are taught them, and 3) allowing incorrect traditions[144] to overrule what the scriptures say. Those who do not obtain, read, and understand the words God revealed to Joseph are dwindling in unbelief. They are in a state where they 1) do not know what God revealed through Joseph, 2) do not believe what God revealed through Joseph when someone teaches them, and 3) have replaced what God revealed through Joseph with false traditions.[145]

In the church today, do we know what God revealed through Joseph? How many members have read "Teachings of the Prophet Joseph Smith?" How many have read "Words of Joseph Smith"? How many study "The Joseph Smith Papers"? Do we fare any better as an institution? How do leaders regard Joseph's teachings? Do they revere them as primal, or do they

---

walk in paths, in a way not cast up; To make their land desolate, and a perpetual hissing; every one that passeth thereby shall be astonished, and wag his head. I will scatter them as with an east wind before the enemy; I will shew them the back, and not the face, in the day of their calamity." (Jeremiah 18:15-17)

[144] Lance B. Wickman of the Seventy, in a face-to-face conversation a few years ago, answered my question of why the church's policy on war is different than the Lord's revelation on the subject in D&C 98 by saying that that revelation does not apply today. When I asked if God had given a revelation to supersede what appeared to be an eternal law given to Abraham, Nephi, and Joseph Smith, he said "you will find the current doctrine of the church in my talks."

[145] History shows that the great apostasy did not happen because those with keys died without passing them, or even because those who remained failed to obtain revelation. The great apostasy happened because men substituted their own words for God's word when their attempts to get revelation that contradicted former revelation failed. "He that turneth away his ear from hearing the law, even his prayer shall be abomination." (Proverbs 28:9.) The councils of early Christianity attempted to formulate innovated doctrines that included those advocated by society. When revelation is sought to gain God's permission to substitute his word with societal sensibilities, revelation will not be received. "Thus saith the Lord, Stand ye in the ways, and see, and ask for the old paths, where is the good way, and walk therein, and ye shall find rest for your souls. But they said, We will not walk therein. Also I set watchmen over you, saying, Hearken to the sound of the trumpet. But they said, We will not hearken." (Jeremiah 6:16-17)

relegate them to history? How many times are his words taught in manuals[146] or General Conference? Instead, we are warned not to pay attention to the differences between what he taught and what we are taught today.[147] We are taught that only what is taught by today's leaders is important.

Joseph Smith taught that it is not a light thing for God to reveal his word to men:

> If we have direct revelations given us from heaven, surely those revelations were never given to be trifled with, without the trifler's incurring displeasure and vengeance upon his own head, if there is any justice in heaven; (Joseph Smith, TPJS, p. 54.)

We have been taught what happens when we neglect to heed the light and truth that God dispenses:

> And now Alma began to expound these things unto him, saying: It is given unto many to know the mysteries of God; nevertheless they are laid under a strict command that they shall not impart only according to the portion of his word which he doth grant unto the children of men, according to the heed and diligence which they give unto him. And therefore, he that will harden his heart, the same receiveth the lesser portion of the word; and he that will not harden his heart, to him is given the greater portion of the word, until it is given unto him to know the mysteries of God until he know them in full. (Alma 12:9-10.)

To the degree we ignore or disobey God's word as revealed through Joseph, we will degrade in our understanding of the truth and be cut off from the blessings associated with a higher law.

> Through the kind providence of our Father a portion of His word which he delivered to His ancient saints, has fallen into our hands, is presented to us with a promise of a reward if obeyed, and with a penalty if disobeyed. (Joseph Smith, TPJS, p. 61.)

---

[146] Even when Joseph's teachings are cited, they are mangled. The "Teachings of the Presidents of the Church" series does not produce manuals that embody the teachings of the featured church president. Instead, quotes are selected and edited to fit within a pre-made outline reflecting current church doctrine, making it possible to have a manual bearing the name and likeness of a church president that is completely devoid of the hallmark teachings of his tenure. The Joseph Smith manual was originally two volumes, but was reduced by half when quotes offensive to modern Mormonism were removed. Furthermore, many current-church-policy-sustaining quotes are falsely attributed to Joseph Smith from dubious sources (see "Church History").

[147] Members are routinely instructed to avoid church history, except what they find in correlated materials.

God commanded the Latter-day Saints to give head to Joseph's words and warned them not to replace God-given revelations to Joseph with pretended revelations:

> And they shall give heed to that which is written, and pretend to no other revelation; and they shall pray always that I may unfold the same to their understanding. And they shall give heed unto these words and trifle not, and I will bless them. Amen. (D&C 32:4-5.)

In the church today, we do just that (see "Prophet: Title or Description?").

The Saints in Joseph's day had already begun to take lightly the revelations God had given them. God said of them:

> And your minds in times past have been darkened because of unbelief, and because you have treated lightly the things you have received—Which vanity and unbelief have brought the whole church under condemnation. And this condemnation resteth upon the children of Zion, even all. And they shall remain under this condemnation until they repent and remember the new covenant, even the Book of Mormon and the former commandments which I have given them, not only to say, but to do according to that which I have written—That they may bring forth fruit meet for their Father's kingdom; otherwise there remaineth a scourge and judgment to be poured out upon the children of Zion. (D&C 84:54-58.)

If this was said then, what must God think of today, when we have unprecedented access to God's word through Joseph Smith, yet probably know it less than any of those who came before us?

Living President vs. Dead Prophet

Joseph's special commission as the head of this dispensation was not without substance. As is the case with all dispensation heads, Joseph was given special experiences with heaven that provided him with uncommon knowledge about the gospel. His experiences were described well in an editorial he wrote for the "Evening and Morning Star":

> Wherefore, we again say, search the revelations of God; study the prophecies, and rejoice that God grants unto the world Seers and Prophets. They are they who saw the mysteries of godliness; they saw the flood before it came; they saw angels ascending and descending upon a ladder that reached from earth to heaven; they saw the stone cut out of the mountain, which filled the whole earth; they saw the Son of God come from the regions of bliss and dwell with men on earth; they saw the deliverer come out of Zion, and turn away ungodliness from Jacob; they saw the glory of the Lord when he showed the transfiguration of the earth on the mount; they saw every

mountain laid low and every valley exalted when the Lord was taking vengeance upon the wicked; they saw truth spring out of the earth, and righteousness look down from heaven in the last days, before the Lord came the second time to gather his elect; they saw the end of wickedness on earth, and the Sabbath of creation crowned with peace; they saw the end of the glorious thousand years, when Satan was loosed for a little season; they saw the day of judgment when all men received according to their works, and they saw the heaven and the earth flee away to make room for the city of God, when the righteous receive an inheritance in eternity. And, fellow sojourners upon earth, it is your privilege to purify yourselves and come up to the same glory, and see for yourselves, and know for yourselves. Ask, and it shall be given you; seek and ye shall find; knock, and it shall be opened unto you. (E&MS August, 1832. DHC 1:282-284.)

Joseph's life and teachings are perhaps the most proximate resource we have in getting to know Jesus. In order to draw closer to Jesus, you have to know him. And yet, Jesus is not wholly accessible. What the world knows about him is limited to the little contained in the Bible. He comes to those who seek him without limitation, but seeking him requires us to already know him, to an extent, creating a paradox. The role of true witnesses is that they serve as signposts along the way. Joseph Smith interfaced more with Jesus than any man we know of after his mortal ministry. While Peter, James, and John may have spent more time with him, their contributions to our understanding of him are limited in volume and subject to a host of factors that dilute their effect. These include cultural and historical context that is unfamiliar to us, as well as limitations in translation and preservation. In Joseph Smith we find a more proximate example of a saved man than, say, Abraham, Isaac, and Jacob. While we have very scant information on the life of the patriarchs, we have an almost constant record of Joseph's later life: not just of the spiritual high points, but of the seemingly mundane events. With these accounts we have many firsthand accounts of those who observed him in his day-to-day life, providing exterior frames of reference. We also have, of course, a very large body of recorded revelation that reveals much more doctrinally about God when placed in the context of the events surrounding them.

How much time do people in the church, from the president of the high priesthood down to the newest member, spend searching out the words of Joseph Smith—the words God gave him to deliver? What proportion of their time is spent on that source compared to others? It is odd that we would sing "Praise to the Man" while simultaneously completely ignoring what that man actually taught, not to mention that which God has commanded us to study.[148]

It is beyond dispute that Joseph possessed the ability to ask and receive the oracles of God. In D&C 77 we have an example of how Joseph could ask God questions and receive categorical answers. For example, he asks (about John's vision in the Book of revelation) "What are we to understand by the eyes and wings, which the beasts had?" In response, the Lord says, "Their eyes are a representation of light and knowledge, that is, they are full of knowledge; and their wings are a representation of power, to move, to act, etc." (D&C 77:4.) What was a routine process for Joseph in obtaining revelation on seemingly any question is markedly absent from the experience of modern Mormons. Who among us today can ask questions like these questions and receive answers to them?

Modern Mormon leaders do not share the same experiences Joseph had. They do not have the visions Joseph had. They do not have the revelations Joseph had. They have not displayed the ability to ask questions and receive answers from God. Joseph was a dispensation head. Through him God revealed the gospel of Jesus Christ. Because of this, we can use the scriptures and the words of Joseph to vet modern teachings.[149] Joseph wrote:

> If any man writes to you, or preaches to you, doctrines contrary to the Bible, the Book of Mormon, or the Book of Doctrine and Covenants, set him down as an imposter. (Joseph Smith, Times & Seasons, April 1, 1844.)

President Joseph Fielding Smith taught:

> When prophets write and speak on the principles of the gospel, they should have the guidance of the Spirit. If they do, then all that they say will be in harmony with the revealed word. If they are in harmony then we know that they have not spoken presumptuously. Should a man speak or write and what he says is in conflict with the standards which are accepted, with the revelations the Lord has given, then we may reject what he has said, no matter who he is. (Joseph Fielding Smith, Doctrines of Salvation, Vol. 1 p. 187.)

---

[148] This is reminiscent of the chiding the Lord gave to the Pharisees who built monuments to the prophets that their fathers had killed (See Matt 23:29).

[149] Joseph Smith said that this rule was so firm that we could use it to distinguish between angels from God and angels from the devil: "How, it may be asked, was this known to be a bad angel?...by his contradicting a former revelation." (Joseph Smith, TPJS, pp. 214-215.)

When a man teaches that they have the authority to overrule revelation given through Joseph Smith,[150] you can "set him down as an imposter." When a man teaches that he is a higher authority than scripture,[151] you can "reject what he has said, no matter who he is." God's word does not have an expiration date. What he said at any time in the past is just as valid today as it was then.

> What I the Lord have spoken, I have spoken, and I excuse not myself; and though the heavens and the earth pass away, my word shall not pass away, but shall all be fulfilled, whether by mine own voice or by the voice of my servants, it is the same. (D&C 1:38.)

When there is a difference[152] between what Joseph taught and what is taught today, you will have to decide who you will believe:[153] the man who communed with Jehovah, through whom God said he would speak, who—though he be taken—would leave to us God's oracles, or the man who says

---

[150] For instance, "When there is to be anything different from that which the Lord has told us already, he will give it to his prophet..." (Harold B. Lee, "The Place of the Living Prophet, Seer, and Revelator," address to CES religious educators, July 8, 1964).

[151] For instance, "The living prophet is more vital to us than the standard works. The living prophet is more important to us than a dead prophet." (Ezra Taft Benson, "Fourteen Fundamentals of Following the Prophet")

[152] Elder Oaks, among others, has taught that any differences in teachings between modern Mormon leaders and Joseph Smith is due to circumstance. He taught, "the most important difference between dead prophets and living ones is that those who are dead are not here to receive and declare the Lord's latest words to his people. If they were, there would be no differences among the messages of the prophets." (Dallin Oaks, "Our Strengths Can Become Our Downfall," General Conference October 1994.) This creates an apparent contradiction. If God does not change, why would his commandments change? Why would he revoke his words concerning Joseph Smith, whom he said would be the only one among us to reveal his commandments? The contradiction disappears when it is realized that the changes do not come from God, but from men who believe their feelings are the same as God's word, and who are willing to bow to societal pressures. See "Revelation" and "Prophets, Seers, Revelators?"

[153] "A desire to follow a prophet is surely a great and appropriate strength, but even this has its potentially dangerous manifestations. I have heard of more than one group who are so intent on following the words of a dead prophet that they have rejected the teachings and counsel of the living ones." (Spencer W Kimball, The Teachings of Spencer W. Kimball (Salt Lake City: Bookcraft, 1982), p. 462) The issue is not whether we are listening to men who call themselves prophets, but whether we are listening to God.

he stands above Joseph,[154] yet who cannot speak of any of the same experiences, of whom God has not testified, who contradicts God's words by saying that they are no longer valid,[155] but without offering any revelations to back up the claim. When men pray for a revelation that contradicts what God already said through Joseph, you can be sure they will not receive it.[156] When doctrines taught by Joseph Smith are removed from the doctrines of the church, you will have to decide who knows better: Joseph Smith, who received it from God, or a group of men who find that Joseph's doctrine contradicts their tradition.[157]

---

[154] "Beware of those who would set up the dead prophets against the living prophets, for the living prophets always take precedence." (Ezra Taft Benson, "Fourteen Fundamentals of Following the Prophet")

[155] "Soon after President David O. McKay announced to the Church that members of the First Council of the Seventy were being ordained high priests...a seventy I met...was very much disturbed. He said to me, 'Didn't the Prophet Joseph Smith say that this was contrary to the order of heaven to name high priests as presidents of the First Council of the Seventy?' And I said, 'Well, I have understood that he did, but have you ever thought that what was contrary to the order of heaven in 1840 might not be contrary to the order of heaven in 1960?' He had not thought of that. He again was following a dead prophet, and he was forgetting that there is a living prophet today. Hence the importance of our stressing that word living....We have some today willing to believe someone who is dead and gone and to accept his words as having more authority than the words of a living authority today." (Stand Ye in Holy Places [1974], 152–53.)

[156] "And again we never inquire at the hand of God for special revelation only in case of their being no previous revelation to suit the case;" (Joseph Smith, TPJS, p 22.)

[157] "The Lectures on Faith defined the Holy Ghost as the mind of the Father and the Son, a member of the Godhead, but not a personage, who binds the Father and Son together. This view of the Holy Ghost reinforced Trinitarian doctrine by explaining how personal beings like the Father and Son become one God through the noncorporeal presence of a shared mind." In the fall of 1898, the First Presidency asked him to rewrite the lectures and present them for approval as an exposition of Church doctrines. In the process, Talmage reconsidered and reconstructed the doctrine of the Holy Ghost....By January 1915, Apostle Charles W Penrose had completed a revision of Parley E Pratt's Key to the Science of Theology. Penrose deleted or altered passages that discussed the Holy Ghost as non-personal and that posited a sort of 'spiritual fluid' pervading the universe....The clarification of the doctrine of the Holy Ghost and the relationship between the three members of the Godhead also made necessary the revision of the Lectures on Faith....the First Presidency appointed a committee consisting of Apostles George F. Richards, Anthony W. Ivins, James E. Talmage, and Melvin J. Ballard to review and revise the entire Doctrine and Covenants.....The committee proposed to delete the Lectures on Faith on the grounds that they were 'lessons prepared for use in the School of the Elders, conducted in Kirtland, Ohio, during the winter of 1834-35; but they were never presented to nor accepted by the Church as being otherwise than theological lectures or lessons.' How the committee came to this conclusion is uncertain. The

All men are liars who say they are of the true Church without the revelations of Jesus Christ and the Priesthood of Melchizedek, which is after the order of the Son of God. It is in the order of heavenly things that God should always send a new dispensation into the world when men have apostatized from the truth and lost the priesthood, but when men come out and build upon other men's foundations, they do it on their own responsibility, without authority from God; and when the floods come and the winds blow, their foundations will be found to be sand, and their whole fabric will crumble to dust. Did I build on any other man's foundation? I have got all the truth which the Christian world possessed, and an independent revelation in the bargain... (Joseph Smith, TPJS, pp. 375-376.)

Some men teach that the words of a living prophet are more important than those of a dead one. God commissioned Jeremiah to provide an interesting test to a group of people called the Rechabites. God said:

Go unto the house of the Rechabites, and speak unto them, and bring them into the house of the Lord, into one of the chambers, and give them wine to drink. And I set before the sons of the house of the Rechabites pots full of wine, and cups, and I said unto them, Drink ye wine. But they said, We will drink no wine: for Jonadab the son of Rechab our father commanded us, saying, Ye shall drink no wine, neither ye, nor your sons for ever.....we have...obeyed, and done according to all that Jonadab our father commanded us.....Then came the word of the Lord unto Jeremiah, saying, Thus saith the Lord of hosts, the God of Israel; Go and tell the men of Judah and the inhabitants of Jerusalem, Will ye not receive instruction to hearken to my words? saith the Lord. The words of Jonadab the son of Rechab, that he commanded his sons not to drink wine, are performed; for unto this day they drink none, but obey their father's commandment: notwithstanding I have spoken unto you, rising early and speaking; but ye hearkened not unto me. I have sent also unto you all my servants the prophets, rising up early and sending them, saying, Return ye now every man from his evil way, and amend your doings, and go not after other gods to serve them, and ye shall dwell in the land which I have given to you and to your

---

general conference of the Church in April 1835 had accepted the entire volume, including the Lectures, not simply the portion entitled 'Covenants and Commandments,' as authoritative and binding upon Church members." (Thomas G. Alexander, "The Reconstruction of Mormon Doctrine," Sunstone, August, 1980.)
This is just one example of rejecting God's word to keep their own tradition. (Mark 7:8–9)

fathers: but ye have not inclined your ear, nor hearkened unto me. Because the sons of Jonadab the son of Rechab have performed the commandment of their father, which he commanded them; but this people hath not hearkened unto me: Therefore thus saith the Lord God of hosts, the God of Israel; Behold, I will bring upon Judah and upon all the inhabitants of Jerusalem all the evil that I have pronounced against them: because I have spoken unto them, but they have not heard; and I have called unto them, but they have not answered. And Jeremiah said unto the house of the Rechabites, Thus saith the Lord of hosts, the God of Israel; Because ye have obeyed the commandment of Jonadab your father, and kept all his precepts, and done according unto all that he hath commanded you: Therefore thus saith the Lord of hosts, the God of Israel; Jonadab the son of Rechab shall not want a man to stand before me for ever. (Jeremiah 35:2,5-6,10,12-19.)

God seemed very pleased that the Rechabites had preserved the commandment they had received for generations, and he blessed them for it. He also cursed those who had ignored the commandments received from prophets from generations past. That Zechariah preached the principle of the persistence of God's word suggests this is a standing doctrine:

Should ye not hear the words which the LORD hath cried by the former prophets, when Jerusalem was inhabited and in prosperity, and the cities thereof round about her, when men inhabited the south and the plain?...But they refused to hearken, and pulled away the shoulder, and stopped their ears, that they should not hear. Yea, they made their hearts as an adamant stone, lest they should hear the law, and the words which the LORD of hosts hath sent in his spirit by the former prophets: therefore came a great wrath from the LORD of hosts. (Zechariah 7:7,11-12.)

The former prophets hold just as much authority today as they did in their day. God's word does not have an expiration date. If there is a contradiction between former prophets and current prophets, we must analyze the source of each message. In 1 Kings 13 we read of a prophet who was commanded of God to fast for a prescribed time. As the LDS chapter heading states, he was "led astray by a prophet" who convinced him to disobey the original commandment, claiming God had told given him a new commandment that overruled the previous one. God destroyed the deceived prophet, who refused to analyze the source of the new, contradictory commandment or ask God about it before accepting it. When men claiming to be prophets encourage us to act contrary to God's commandments given by the former prophets, we are obligated to ask God to ensure we are not being led astray, as the deceived prophet in 1 Kings 13 was. Only then will we be taking measures to avoid substituting the philosophies of men mingled with scripture for the word of God received by the former prophets.[158] Nephi warned that

> Cursed is he that putteth his trust in man, or maketh flesh his arm, or shall hearken unto the precepts of men, save their precepts shall be given by the power of the Holy Ghost. (2 Nephi 28:31.)

Joseph Smith possesses a unique claim as *the* head of the dispensation, *the* source of God's word to this generation. As long as this dispensation stands, any "living prophet" ought to preach in favor of—not contradict—God's dispensation of the gospel through Joseph Smith. True messengers contradict—not invent—false traditions, restoring teachings to their original, undefiled state. Their teachings should not contradict scripture, but support it.

Conclusion

Through Ezekiel, God summarized his relationship with the Israelites to that point. He said:

> In the day that I lifted up mine hand unto them, to bring them forth of the land of Egypt into a land that I had espied for them, flowing with milk and honey, which is the glory of all lands: Then said I unto them, Cast ye away every man the abominations of his eyes, and defile not yourselves with the idols of Egypt: I am the Lord your God. But they rebelled against me, and would not hearken unto me: they did not every man cast away the abominations of their eyes, neither did they forsake the idols of Egypt: then I said, I will pour out my fury upon them, to accomplish my anger against them in the midst of the land of Egypt. But I wrought for my name's sake, that it should not be polluted before the heathen, among whom they were, in whose sight I made myself known unto them, in bringing them forth out of the land of Egypt. Wherefore I caused them to go forth out of the land of Egypt, and brought them into the wilderness. And I gave them my statutes, and shewed them my judgments, which if a man do, he shall even live in them. Moreover also I gave them my

---

[158] "For although a man may have many revelations, and have power to do many mighty works, yet if he boasts in his own strength, and sets at naught the counsels of God, and follows after the dictates of his own will and carnal desires, he must fall and incur the vengeance of a just God upon him. Behold, you have been entrusted with these things, but how strict were your commandments; and remember also the promises which were made to you, if you did not transgress them. And behold, how oft you have transgressed the commandments and the laws of God, and have gone on in the persuasions of men." (D&C 3:4-6)"

sabbaths, to be a sign between me and them, that they might know that I am the Lord that sanctify them. But the house of Israel rebelled against me in the wilderness: they walked not in my statutes, and they despised my judgments, which if a man do, he shall even live in them; and my sabbaths they greatly polluted: then I said, I would pour out my fury upon them in the wilderness, to consume them. But I wrought for my name's sake, that it should not be polluted before the heathen, in whose sight I brought them out. Yet also I lifted up my hand unto them in the wilderness, that I would not bring them into the land which I had given them, flowing with milk and honey, which is the glory of all lands; Because they despised my judgments, and walked not in my statutes, but polluted my sabbaths: for their heart went after their idols. Nevertheless mine eye spared them from destroying them, neither did I make an end of them in the wilderness. But I said unto their children in the wilderness, Walk ye not in the statutes of your fathers, neither observe their judgments, nor defile yourselves with their idols: I am the Lord your God; walk in my statutes, and keep my judgments, and do them; And hallow my sabbaths; and they shall be a sign between me and you, that ye may know that I am the Lord your God. Notwithstanding the children rebelled against me: they walked not in my statutes, neither kept my judgments to do them, which if a man do, he shall even live in them; they polluted my sabbaths: then I said, I would pour out my fury upon them, to accomplish my anger against them in the wilderness. Nevertheless I withdrew mine hand, and wrought for my name's sake, that it should not be polluted in the sight of the heathen, in whose sight I brought them forth. I lifted up mine hand unto them also in the wilderness, that I would scatter them among the heathen, and disperse them through the countries; Because they had not executed my judgments, but had despised my statutes, and had polluted my sabbaths, and their eyes were after their fathers' idols. Wherefore I gave them also statutes that were not good, and judgments whereby they should not live; And I polluted them in their own gifts, in that they caused to pass through the fire all that openeth the womb, that I might make them desolate, to the end that they might know that I am the Lord. Therefore, son of man, speak unto the house of Israel, and say unto them, Thus saith the Lord God; Yet in this your fathers have blasphemed me, in that they have committed a trespass against me. For when I had brought them into the land, for the which I lifted up mine hand to give it to them, then they saw every high hill, and all the thick trees, and they offered there their sacrifices, and there they presented the provocation of their offering: there also they made their sweet savour, and poured out there their drink offerings. Then I said unto them, What is the high place whereunto ye go? And the name thereof is called Bamah unto this day. Wherefore say unto the house of Israel, Thus saith the Lord God; Are ye polluted after the manner of your fathers? and commit ye whoredom after their abominations? For when ye offer your gifts, when ye make your sons to pass through the fire, ye pollute yourselves with all your idols, even unto this day: and shall I be inquired of by you, O house of Israel? As I live, saith the Lord God, I will not be inquired of by you. And that which cometh into your mind shall not be at all, that ye say, We will be as the heathen, as the families of the countries, to serve wood and stone. As I live, saith the Lord God, surely with a mighty hand, and with a stretched out arm, and with fury poured out, will I rule over you: And I will bring you out from the people, and will gather you out of the countries wherein ye are scattered, with a mighty hand, and with a stretched out arm, and with fury poured out. And I will bring you into the wilderness of the people, and there will I plead with you face to face. Like as I pleaded with your fathers in the wilderness of the land of Egypt, so will I plead with you, saith the Lord God. And I will cause you to pass under the rod, and I will bring you into the bond of the covenant: And I will purge out from among you the rebels, and them that transgress against me: I will bring them forth out of the country where they sojourn, and they shall not enter into the land of Israel: and ye shall know that I am the Lord. As for you, O house of Israel, thus saith the Lord God; Go ye, serve ye every one his idols, and hereafter also, if ye will not hearken unto me: but pollute ye my holy name no more with your gifts, and with your idols. For in mine holy mountain, in the mountain of the height of Israel, saith the Lord God, there shall all the house of Israel, all of them in the land, serve me: there will I accept them, and there will I require your offerings, and the firstfruits of your oblations, with all your holy things. I will accept you with your sweet savour, when I bring you out from the people, and gather you out of the countries wherein ye have been scattered; and I will be sanctified in you before the heathen. And ye shall know that I am the Lord, when I shall bring you into the land of Israel, into the country for the which I lifted up mine hand to give it to your fathers. And there shall ye remember your ways, and all your doings, wherein ye have been defiled; and ye shall lothe yourselves in your own sight for all your evils that ye have committed. And ye shall know that I am the Lord, when I have wrought with you for my name's sake, not according to your wicked ways, nor according to your corrupt doings, O ye house of Israel, saith the Lord God. (Ezekiel 20:6-44.)

This passage serves as a fitting analog to the behavior of modern Israel in how they have treated the revelations of Joseph, and God's response to them because of it.

The task of Joseph's successors was to teach what Joseph gave them. How well they have or continue to do so is an open question. Joseph said "...if any man preach any other gospel than that which I have preached, he shall be cursed..." (Joseph Smith, Historical Record 7:548.)

A brief survey of milestones in the administrations of Joseph Smith's successors punctuates some of the very many differences in the gospel of modern Mormonism and the gospel restored by Joseph Smith. Brigham Young made plural marriage a general practice, created first presidency succession from the 12, subjugated the authority of stake presidents, the 70, and patriarchs to the 12, banned blacks from having the priesthood, began the practice of ordaining children as teachers, deacons, and priests, created Adam-God doctrine and blood atonement. I am not aware of changes John Taylor made. Wilford Woodruff revoked the law of adoption, invented white temple clothing, and had the interesting experiences of receiving a revelation saying polygamy would never end, then a revelation that said it had ended, all without actually ending it. Lorenzo Snow changed the law of tithing, removing the initial consecration. In his defense, this was necessary to spur dwindling tithing receipts due to the continual abuse of asking for additional consecrations exercised by Brigham Young and others over the years when funds were low. Joseph F. Smith mandated the use of the word of wisdom as a commandment with some exceptions for the elderly and new converts, changed the sacrament ordinance from using wine to water, and ended plural marriage by fiat. Heber J. Grant modified the garment, significantly changed the endowment and changed the way men were ordained. George A. Smith issued a letter saying Brigham Young's priesthood ban was a direct commandment from God without any evidence that it was. David O. McKay revoked the commandment to gather and began the building of many temples, mostly to keep members in their home countries. Joseph Fielding Smith created many volumes of writings containing the philosophies of men mingled with scripture, many of which the church has subsequently disavowed. Harold B. Lee created correlation, a program whose consequences are beyond what can be discussed here.[159] Spencer W. Kimball modified the garment, reversed Brigham Young's priesthood ban, refuted Adam-God doctrine, taught missionaries sales tactics, ended practice of the true order of prayer outside of temples, and removed the office of presiding patriarch. Ezra Taft Benson and Howard W. Hunter were incapacitated for most of their

---

[159] The reader is referred to "David O. McKay and the Rise of Modern Mormonism," Chapter 7. Anyone member of the LDS church who has not read this book really should.

presidencies. Gordon B. Hinckley significantly modified the endowment ceremony as a result of surveys showing dissatisfaction with the contents and modified the structure and function of the 70s quorums. So far, Thomas S. Monson has modified the endowment ceremony and changed the classification of homosexual desires from a sin to acceptable.

The successors of Joseph Smith have ignored his oracles, and claimed his authority in spite of not receiving more revelation. Modern leaders not only fail to claim new revelation, but they claim that new revelation is not important.

> I have learned that strong, impressive spiritual experiences do not come to us very frequently. (President Boyd K. Packer, "The Candle of the Lord," January 1983.)

> Let me say first that we have a great body of revelation, the vast majority of which came from the prophet Joseph Smith. We don't need much revelation. We need to pay more attention to the revelation we've already received. (SF Gate, "SUNDAY INTERVIEW -- Musings of the Main Mormon / Gordon B. Hinckley" April 13, 1997.)

> Revelation is not constant. The Lord's way puts limits on how often He will speak to us by His Spirit. Not understanding this, some have been misled by expecting revelations too frequently. (Elder Dahlin H. Oaks, "In his own time, in his own way," Ensign August 2013.)

Joseph once directed the following to the Apostles and members:

> O ye Twelve! and all Saints! profit by this important Key—that in all your trials, troubles, temptations, afflictions, bonds, imprisonments and death, see to it, that you do not betray heaven; that you do not betray Jesus Christ; that you do not betray the brethren; that you do not betray the revelations of God, whether in Bible, Book of Mormon, or Doctrine and Covenants, or any other that ever was or ever will be given and revealed unto man in this world or that which is to come. Yea, in all your kicking and flounderings, see to it that you do not this thing, lest innocent blood be found upon your skirts, and you go down to hell. (Joseph Smith, TPJS, p. 156.)

Would Joseph consider that those claiming to be his successors have remained true and faithful to what God revealed through him? Would he judge them faithful to the revelations of God? To the Bible, Book of Mormon, and Doctrine and Covenants?[160] Or, would he find that they have

---

[160] A read of the Doctrine and Covenants will reveal that few, if any, instructions for church administration match what is practiced today.

betrayed him and God by replacing, adding to, and removing the revelations for the commandments of men, as Jeremiah prophesied:

> For my people have committed two evils; they have forsaken me the fountain of living waters, and hewed them out cisterns, broken cisterns, that can hold no water. (Jeremiah 2:13.)

The figurative cisterns that hold the commandments of men are broken because their contents are not sound: they always change.

God is testing us to see how completely we will live his commandments as given through Joseph Smith.[161] Individuals will only be taught the revelations in the sealed portion of the Book of Mormon as we hearken unto what we have already received, which is currently hid up because of our unbelief in what God has revealed to us already:

> For the Lord said unto me: They shall not go forth unto the Gentiles until the day that they shall repent of their iniquity, and become clean before the Lord. And in that day that they shall exercise faith in me, saith the Lord, even as the brother of Jared did, that they may become sanctified in me, then will I manifest unto them the things which the brother of Jared saw, even to the unfolding unto them all my revelations, saith Jesus Christ, the Son of God, the Father of the heavens and of the earth, and all things that in them are. And he that will contend against the word of the Lord, let him be accursed; and he that shall deny these things, let him be accursed; for unto them will I show no greater things, saith Jesus Christ; for I am he who speaketh. Come unto me, O ye Gentiles, and I will show unto you the greater things, the knowledge which is hid up because of unbelief. (Ether 4:6-8, 13.)

God punished the Israelites with the removal of the higher blessings of the covenant when they rejected the covenant offered through Moses:

> When God offers a blessing or knowledge to a man, and he refuses to receive it, he will be damned. The Israelites prayed that God would speak to Moses and not to them; in consequence of which he cursed them with a carnal law. (Teachings of the Presidents of the Church: Joseph Smith, Chapter 22.)

If, as a church, we have rejected the covenant offered by God through Joseph, what is our condition?

---

161 "And when they shall have received this, which is expedient that they should have first, to try their faith, and if it shall so be that they shall believe these things then shall the greater things be made manifest unto them. And if it so be that they will not believe these things, then shall the greater things be withheld from them, unto their condemnation." (3 Nephi 26:9-10)

The Gospel of Christ

Joseph said that "a man could get nearer to God by abiding by [the Book of Mormon's] precepts, than by any other book." (DHC 4:461.) The Book of Mormon and other restoration scriptures clearly lay out what the authors of the respective books label "the doctrine of Christ." For example, Nephi writes:

> Wherefore, the things which I have written sufficeth me, save it be a few words which I must speak concerning the doctrine of Christ; wherefore, I shall speak unto you plainly, according to the plainness of my prophesying. (2 Nephi 31:2.)

According to Nephi, the gospel of Christ begins with repentance, baptism by water, and baptism by fire:

> ...the gate by which ye should enter is repentance and baptism by water; and then cometh a remission of your sins by fire and by the Holy Ghost. (2 Nephi 31:17.)

Nephi teaches that, while baptism by water and fire are events, faith and repentance are processes—they must be practiced throughout life. Nephi teaches that we must continue to practice faith and repentance[162] until God says to us that we have obtained eternal life:

> And then are ye in this strait and narrow path which leads to eternal life; yea, ye have entered in by the gate; ye have done according to the commandments of the Father and the Son; and ye have received the Holy Ghost, which witnesses of the Father and the Son, unto the fulfilling of the promise which he hath made, that if ye entered in by the way ye should receive. And now, my beloved brethren, after ye have gotten into this strait and narrow path, I would ask if all is done? Behold, I say unto you, Nay; for ye have not come thus far save it were by the word of Christ with unshaken faith in him, relying wholly upon the merits of him who is mighty to save. Wherefore, ye must press forward with a steadfastness in Christ, having a perfect brightness of hope, and a love of God and of all men. Wherefore, if

---

[162] Notice that Nephi chooses to describe repentance as obtaining and implementing the word of God in your life. He omits any description of remorse or self-inflicted guilt.

ye shall press forward, feasting upon the word of Christ, and endure to the end, behold, thus saith the Father: Ye shall have eternal life. (2 Nephi 31:18-20.)

Nephi is clear that there is no other version of the doctrine of Christ, and no other pathway to salvation.

And now, behold, my beloved brethren, this is the way; and there is none other way nor name given under heaven whereby man can be saved in the kingdom of God. And now, behold, this is the doctrine of Christ, and the only and true doctrine of the Father, and of the Son, and of the Holy Ghost, which is one God, without end. Amen. (2 Nephi 31:21.)

Faith[163]

Although much could be said about faith, we focus on the overarching purpose of faith: obtaining eternal life. We learn from Joseph that "faith is the assurance which men have of the existence of things which they have not seen, and the principle of action in all intelligent beings." (Lectures on Faith 1:9.) From Paul we learn, that "faith cometh by hearing, and hearing by the word of God." (Romans 10:17.) If we put these two statements together, we see that faith is believing in God's word enough to act on it. It requires, first, the receipt of God's word, and second, action. As an example, a person exercises faith in baptism by hearing God's instruction about baptism, then repenting and being baptized, believing he will receive the gift of the Holy Ghost as promised.

Faith, then, is not mere belief, nor can it be exercised on commandments of men that are incorrectly assumed or purported to be God's word. When men understand faith as mere belief, or when they attempt to exercise it on commandments of men, they engage in vain religion; their efforts will never bring them closer to God. At best, they distract them from those actions that would bring about salvation. At worst, they move away from God through beliefs and actions that are antithetical to the gospel of Christ.

Repentance

Repentance means simply to move closer to God. It is to rid oneself of error in belief, or sin in action, through the acquisition of and reconciliation to knowledge from God.[164] Repentance is not a matter of beginning a checklist

---

[163] Faith is seen as a simple principle. In reality, books and books could be filled on the topic. Justice cannot be done in the space allotted here.

[164] "… A man is saved no faster than he gets knowledge, for if he does not get knowledge, he will be brought into captivity by some evil power in the other world, as evil spirits will have more knowledge, and consequently more power than many men

of actions while omitting another checklist of actions. One must align their whole soul to Christ, which requires not only a reconciliation to one's current understanding of God's will, but to anything he might reveal to the individual in the future:

> Not every one that saith unto me, Lord, Lord, shall enter into the kingdom of heaven; but he that doeth the will of my Father which is in heaven. Many will say to me in that day, Lord, Lord, have we not prophesied in thy name? and in thy name have cast out devils? and in thy name done many wonderful works? And then will I profess unto them, I never knew you: depart from me, ye that work iniquity. (Matthew 7:21-23.)

Note that here Jesus did not say "he that doeth what he believes to be the will of my Father." Instead, he said he who does the actual will of God. Getting to know God is very different than completing a checklist of actions. It requires persistent revelation to acquire knowledge of what God is like and what he actually wants. That's why Moses, despite being fully committed to God, came away from a conversation with him in such shock, having learned things he never would have supposed.[165] The frequency of our surprise at the difference between what we thought we knew of God and his commandments and what he is currently teaching us through personal revelation is a good indication of our degree of repentance.

Many mistakenly believe that repentance is about desire and willpower; that men sin because they don't want to abstain from sin, or they don't have enough will to abstain from sin. This is, in reality, a distraction from the real problem. There is a reason that one main purpose of our mortal probation is to learn to distinguish between truth and error; it is difficult! Are failure to choose what is true is almost always due to ignorance, not a lack of willpower. Human beings are rational beings. As we acquire knowledge, we act according to it. Our misconception that sin comes from a lack of willpower is tied to our misunderstanding of faith (see the definition above). When we acquire knowledge from God, and we have faith in him, we act according to that knowledge. If we act contrary to it, it is most often because we don't really believe it. Therefore, it has not become real knowledge, and is still merely belief. Acting against something you honestly know is so rare that it is called the unpardonable sin. Those in sin do not lack will power, they either lack knowledge, faith, or both. Those who spend their efforts to repent in willpower-gaining exercises will not make the same progress of those who recognize repentance as knowledge acquisition. Even those with incredible

---

who are on the earth." (Joseph Smith, HC 4:588.) "To become a joint heir of the heirship of the Son, one must put away all his false traditions." (Joseph Smith, HC 5:554.)

[165] Moses 1:10

will power have moments of weakness, because will power is not constant. Knowledge, however, does not wane except through disobedience. If will power could make a man perfect, knowledge would not be required for salvation. But knowledge is required for salvation, and it is the key to repentance.

In the days of Alma there were a significant number of members who were sinning exceedingly. They were so wicked that "there were many witnesses against them; yea, the people stood and testified of their iniquity in abundance." (Mosiah 26:9.) In response to Alma's query about what to do about these people, God said[166] that he retains the role of judge to decide who it is that is forgiven, since he is the one who paid the price:

> For it is I that taketh upon me the sins of the world; for it is I that hath created them; and it is I that granteth unto him that believeth unto the end a place at my right hand. (Mosiah 26:23.)

God then gives Alma the answer to his question of what to do with members in sin. It is as powerful as it is simple:

> Therefore I say unto you, Go; and whosoever transgresseth against me, him shall ye judge according to the sins which he has committed; and if he confess his sins before thee and me, and repenteth in the sincerity of his heart, him shall ye forgive, and I will forgive him also. Yea, and as often as my people repent will I forgive them their trespasses against me. And ye shall also forgive one another your trespasses; for verily I say unto you, he that forgiveth not his neighbor's trespasses when he says that he repents, the same hath brought himself under condemnation. Now I say unto you, Go; and whosoever will not repent of his sins the same shall not be numbered among my people; and this shall be observed from this time forward. (Mosiah 26:29-31.)

God teaches plainly that if a man confesses and says they repent, they are to be immediately forgiven. Perhaps anticipating the innovation of stigmatic statuses (disfellowshipped, etc.), he gives only a binary status: a member of his church, or not. Perhaps anticipating the innovation of a prescribed one year waiting period for those whose status has changed, he identifies the switching between the two as instantaneous. To put some weight behind it, he says that those who do not accept the person's statement of repentance "hath brought himself under condemnation." It is important to note that Alma immediately

---

[166] This was the second thing God said. The first was "For behold, this is my church; whosoever is baptized shall be baptized unto repentance. And whomsoever ye receive shall believe in my name; and him will I freely forgive." (Mosiah 26:23.) This is the simple and plain doctrine of Christ, and is taught plainly throughout the Book of Mormon.

implemented these instructions. When we see the application of statuses beyond "member" and "non-member" or waiting periods associated with repentance, we ought to realize that these are innovations never defined in God's word.[167]

This understanding has implications for baptism. God never ordained a baptismal interview, and never prescribed most if not all of the baptismal requirements printed in "Preach My Gospel". Jesus laid out the requirement for pre-baptismal repentance in crystal clarity, as well as providing a curse for any that modify that definition:

> And again I say unto you, ye must repent, and become as a little child, and be baptized in my name, or ye can in nowise receive these things. And again I say unto you, ye must repent, and be baptized in my name, and become as a little child, or ye can in nowise inherit the kingdom of God. Verily, verily, I say unto you, that this is my doctrine, and whoso buildeth upon this buildeth upon my rock, and the gates of hell shall not prevail against them. And whoso shall declare more or less than this, and establish it for my doctrine, the same cometh of evil, and is not built upon my rock; but he buildeth upon a sandy foundation, and the gates of hell stand open to receive such when the floods come and the winds beat upon them. (3 Nephi 11:37-40.)

The use of the word "atonement" has come into vogue in modern Mormonism. We "apply" the atonement, and even "apply it generously," as if it were soap.[168] We "embrace" the atonement" as if were a person.[168] We "use" the atonement, as if were a tool.[169] Yet, our subjects and verbs are erroneous. It is Jesus who forgives us, period. We do not apply his sacrifice, rather we apply *to* him, and he has power by virtue of his sacrifice to forgive us. We do not embrace the atonement. We embrace Jesus, through the veil, and receive greater light and knowledge that allows us to overcome sin and, in this life, re-enter his presence to embrace him face-to-face. We do not use his

---

[167] "The Miracle of Forgiveness," a very popular book by President Spencer W. Kimball, is as antithetical to the doctrine revealed through Alma as can be. Deseret Book recently stopped printing the book, but the continuation of statuses and waiting periods suggests this was more for the political incorrect ideas in the book rather than an admission of it containing false doctrine.

[168] Elder Jorg Klebingat, "Approaching the Throne of God with Confidence," October 2014 General Conference.

[169] Elder Shayne M. Bowen, "The Atonement Can Clean, Reclaim, and Sanctify Our Lives," October 2006 General Conference.

sacrifice. Rather, we emulate his example in sacrificing. Jesus saves us, not his atonement.[170]

Modern Mormonism not only personifies Jesus' action as its own entity, but it also transfigures it into mainstream Christianity's "saved by Grace" construct. In place of Christianity's simplistic "confessing Jesus," modern Mormons simply must accept the atonement.[171] Like a laundry machine, the church takes the sinner, puts him into the atonement, adds a sprinkling of "saving ordinances," rotates him through a few years in good standing in the church doing his best,[172] and out comes a Saint!

---

[170] "…the Savior's Atonement overcame original sin so that we can be born into this world yet not be punished for Adam's transgression" (Elder D. Todd Christofferson, "Free Forever, to Act for Themselves," October 2014 General Conference.)

[171] Mormon.org provides a limitless source of common understandings of doctrines among the membership. An entry under "grace" reads: "We are saved by grace, through the Atonement of Jesus Christ, after all that we can do. Because we are not perfect it is only through Jesus Christ that we can return through Heavenly Father. But he asks us to have faith, repent, be baptized, receive the gift of the Holy Ghost, and endure to the end. When we do this, which is all that we can do, then we are forgiven. Then we can return to our Heavenly Father." Joseph taught that "all we can do" exceeds performing ordnances and maintaining church membership. See "Lectures on Faith" 5:2, quoted in the text of this chapter.

[172] "We don't need to get a complex or get a feeling that you have to be perfect to be saved. You don't. There's only been one perfect person, and that's the Lord Jesus, but in order to be saved in the Kingdom of God and in order to pass the test of mortality, what you have to do is get on the straight and narrow path—thus charting a course leading to eternal life—and then, being on that path, pass out of this life in full fellowship. I'm not saying that you don't have to keep the commandments. I'm saying you don't have to be perfect to be saved. If you did, no one would be saved. The way it operates is this: You get on the path that's named the "straight and narrow." You do it by entering the gate of repentance and baptism. The straight and narrow path leads from the gate of repentance and baptism, a very great distance, to a reward that's called eternal life. If you're on that path and pressing forward, and you die, you'll never get off the path. There is no such thing as falling off the straight and narrow path in the life to come, and the reason is that this life is the time that is given to men to prepare for eternity. Now is the time and the day of your salvation, so if you're working zealously in this life—though you haven't fully overcome the world and you haven't done all you hoped you might do—you're still going to be saved. You don't have to do what Jacob said, "Go beyond the mark." You don't have to live a life that's truer than true. You don't have to have an excessive zeal that becomes fanatical and becomes unbalancing. What you have to do is stay in the mainstream of the Church and live as upright and decent people live in the Church—keeping the commandments, paying your tithing, serving in the organizations of the Church, loving the Lord, staying on the straight and narrow path. If you're on that path when death comes—because this is the time and the day appointed, this is the probationary estate—you'll never fall off from it, and, for all practical purposes, your calling and

The limiting factor in repentance is not obtaining forgiveness! God has already paid the price. Forgiveness is given instantly whenever it is asked for. The limiting factor is acquiring and applying new knowledge so that the sinner forsakes sin permanently. It is incorrect to teach or believe that God will admit into salvation any that have not yet become like him.[173] Obtaining forgiveness of one's sin is not sanctification—it is only justification. To obtain salvation, one must become like Christ in every way. When God commanded us to be perfect, he meant it. Doing your best is insufficient. The plan of salvation is not a classroom where select members of the class get an easier exam because they asked the teacher or participated in extra-curricular activities. The plan of salvation is like a classroom where no one is capable of passing the exam on the first round, but where students are permitted to retake the class as many times as it takes for them to be able to pass through an arrangement made between the teacher and the principle. [174] The atonement does not provide a bridge over the requirements of salvation. Rather, it provides infinite "resets" on the process, until we finally learn.

> For we labor diligently to write, to persuade our children, and also our brethren, to believe in Christ, and to be reconciled to God; for we know that it is by grace that we are saved, after all we can do. (2 Nephi 25:23.)

Doing our best does not reconcile us to God. There is yet more to be done "after all we can do." Jesus provides us greater space to repent and grow beyond what one mortal probation—an insufficient time for any of us—could provide.

Despite what is taught from the pulpit[175] and in best-selling books,[176] God cannot and will not save us *in* our sins.[177] You *must* deny yourself of all ungodliness and have a perfect love for God *before* his grace is sufficient.

---

election is made sure." (Bruce R. McConkie, "The Probationary Test of Mortality," University of Utah Jan 10, 1982)

[173] Elder Christofferson wrote, "Through the Atonement of Jesus Christ and His grace, our failures to live the celestial law perfectly and consistently in mortality can be erased and we are enabled to develop a Christlike character." ("Free Forever, to Act for Themselves," General Conference Oct 2014.) Actually, you cannot develop a Christlike character without Christlike obedience to God. Elder Christoferson attempts to lace together an array of scriptures that, when read in context, contradict church teachings on these topics. The dizzying gymnastics that result mischaracterize repentance, the atonement, justice, mercy, and grace.

[174] To carry the analogy a step further, in our case most students do not realize there even *is* an exam, and repeat the class without ever increasing, worlds without end.

[175] "Christ asks us to show faith in Him, repent, make and keep covenants, receive the Holy Ghost, and endure to the end. By complying, we are not paying the demands of justice—not even the smallest part. Instead, we are showing appreciation for what Jesus Christ did by using it to live a life like His. Justice requires immediate

> Yea, come unto Christ, and be perfected in him, and deny yourselves of all ungodliness; and if ye shall deny yourselves of all ungodliness, and love God with all your might, mind and strength, then is his grace sufficient for you, that by his grace ye may be perfect in Christ; and if by the grace of God ye are perfect in Christ, ye can in nowise deny the power of God. (Moroni 10:32.)

Mercy can *satisfy* justice in providing forgiveness to the sinner, but it cannot *rob* justice by providing the blessings of the obedient to the disobedient.[178] In other words, mercy can provide justification, but it cannot provide sanctification. Only justice can provide sanctification. Justice requires perfection. As Joseph wrote,

> [Jesus] descended in suffering below that which man can suffer, or in other words, suffered greater sufferings, and was exposed to more powerful contradictions than any man can be. But notwithstanding all this, he kept the law of God and remained without sin; showing thereby that it is in the power of man to keep the law and remain also

---

perfection or a punishment when we fall short. Because Jesus took that punishment, He can offer us the chance for ultimate perfection (see Matthew 5:48; 3 Nephi 12:48) and help us reach that goal. He can forgive what justice never could, and He can turn to us now with His own set of requirements (see 3 Nephi 28:35)." (Brad Wilcox, His Grace Is Sufficient, Ensign Sept 2013)

[176] "…the Savior says, in effect, All right, you're not perfect. But what can you do? Give me all you have, and I'll do the rest. He still requires our best effort. We must keep trying. But the good news is that having done all we can, it is enough. We may not be personally perfect yet, but because of our covenant with the Savior, we can rely on his perfection, and his perfection will get us through." (Stephen E. Robinson, Believing Christ, April 1992 General Conference.)

[177] Some do not believe this to be the case. From Mormon.org's entry on "grace," Kaylee Rose writes: "Because we are human and imperfect, no matter how hard we try our works alone are never sufficient to allow us to return to the presence of our Father in Heaven, because no unclean thing can dwell with him. It is only through the Atonement of our Savior Jesus Christ that our sins can be forgiven, our imperfections made perfect, and our weaknesses become strengths. If we exercise faith in the Lord Jesus Christ, repent and are baptized in his name and given the gift of the Holy Ghost through the laying on of hands, his grace is sufficient for us as long as we continue to exercise faith in him which is manifest as good works, obedience, and a repentant heart."

[178] It is not hard to find recent examples of this false doctrine: "Upon acknowledging our dedication and perseverance, the Lord will give us that which we are not able to attain due to our imperfections and human weaknesses." ("Be Meek and Lowly of Heart," Elder Ulisses Soares, Of the Presidency of the Seventy Oct 2013) "The miracle of the Atonement can make up for imperfections in our performance." ("Your Four Minutes", Bishop Gary E. Stevenson, Presiding Bishop, April 2014 General Conference.)

without sin. And also, that by him a righteous judgment might come upon all flesh, and that all who walk not in the law of God, may justly be condemned by the law, and have no excuse for their sins. (Lectures on Faith 5:2.)

There is no other way. One who does not keep the law God keeps cannot have the blessings God has.[179] He instead provides the environment for us to acquire the knowledge to stop sinning, if we will seek him and believe what he teaches us.

Baptism by Water

Baptism by water by one who has authority from the church is currently understood in the church to be the gateway to membership in the church. As alluded to, there are requirements from church authorities for baptismal candidates. These requirements have changed much over time, with the most recent change coming in November 2015, when the church announced that children of practicing homosexuals would be barred from baptism until they reached the age of 18.[180] However, before the church was legally founded in 1830, many were baptized unto repentance by the authority of the Aaronic Priesthood, which was restored in 1829. These candidates were baptized without a church and were not subject to any requirements except those given by Jesus in the Book of Mormon, namely to repent and believe in Christ.[181]

Since the Aaronic Priesthood existed outside of the church prior to 1830, it holds that the Aaronic Priesthood can be held outside of the church. Since legal baptisms were performed by Aaronic Priesthood holders prior to 1830, it holds that anyone with Aaronic Priesthood can legally baptize outside of the church. While those thus baptized would not be members of the Church of Jesus Christ of Latter-day Saints, they would still be legal recipients of the covenant of baptism.[182]

---

[179] "And unto every kingdom is given a law; and unto every law there are certain bounds also and conditions. All beings who abide not in those conditions are not justified." (D&C 88:38-39.) "...they who are not sanctified through the law which I have given unto you, even the law of Christ, must inherit another kingdom, even that of a terrestrial kingdom, or that of a telestial kingdom." (D&C 88:21.)

[180] https://www.washingtonpost.com/news/acts-of-faith/wp/2015/11/05/mormon-church-to-exclude-children-of-same-sex-couples-from-getting-blessed-and-baptized-until-they-are-18/

[181] "Verily I say unto you, that whoso repenteth of his sins through your words, and desireth to be baptized in my name, on this wise shall ye baptize them..." (3 Nephi 11:23.)

[182] The question raises of how someone not a member of the church could hold the Aaronic Priesthood. Since one can receive the covenant of baptism and the Aaronic Priesthood outside of the church, it holds that though one may receive both within the association of the church, the receipt and holding of those blessings stands

The wording of the ordinance is provided by Jesus in the Book of Mormon:

> And now behold, these are the words which ye shall say, calling them by name, saying: Having authority given me of Jesus Christ, I baptize you in the name of the Father, and of the Son, and of the Holy Ghost. Amen. And then shall ye immerse them in the water, and come forth again out of the water. And after this manner shall ye baptize in my name; for behold, verily I say unto you, that the Father, and the Son, and the Holy Ghost are one; and I am in the Father, and the Father in me, and the Father and I are one. (3 Nephi 11:24-27.)

This wording ("having authority") is the same used by Alma,[183] but is probably unfamiliar to modern Mormons, who use the words "having been commissioned by."

The history of the wording of the baptismal ordinance is interesting. The first mention of instruction comes from the "Articles of the Church," the original source for D&C 20, read and sustained by the church on 9 June 1830, and printed in the church's newspaper: "And the manner of baptism & the manner of administering the sacrament are to be done as is written in the Book of Morman [sic]"[184] The instructions in the Book of Mormon are to use

---

independent of one's relationship with the church, and is only a matter of one's relationship with God. If one then leaves the church, or is cast out of the church, as long as they continue to keep God's commandments, they retain both their baptismal covenant and the Aaronic Priesthood.

[183] "And when he had said these words, the Spirit of the Lord was upon him, and he said: Helam, I baptize thee, having authority from the Almighty God, as a testimony that ye have entered into a covenant to serve him until you are dead as to the mortal body; and may the Spirit of the Lord be poured out upon you; and may he grant unto you eternal life, through the redemption of Christ, whom he has prepared from the foundation of the world." (Mosiah 18:13.)

[184] The Joseph Smith Papers Project says about "The Articles of the Church," "The 'articles and covenants of the Church of Christ' set forth the offices, ordinances, and procedures that were to be part of the newly formed church. On 9 June 1830, at the first conference of the church following its organization, this document was presented to the membership for approval. The minutes of that meeting recorded, 'Articles and Covenants read by Joseph Smith jr. and recieved by unanimous voice of the whole congregation, which consisted of most of the male members of the Church.' The importance of Articles and Covenants to the church is suggested by the fact that it was the first revelatory document selected for printing in the church's earliest periodical, The Evening and the Morning Star, and the only one published there twice. In the 1835 edition of the Doctrine and Covenants, the compilers placed Articles and Covenants as the second section, preceded only by the revelatory

the phrase "having authority given me of Jesus Christ." Thus, all original members of the church were baptized with this ordinance. The next mention is in the church's newspaper in 1833, repeating the instruction in the Book of Mormon:

> And baptism is to be administered in the following manner unto all those who repent: Whosoever being called of God & having authority given them of Jesus Christ, shall go down into the water with them and shall say, calling them by name: Having authority given me of Jesus Christ, I baptize you in the name of the Father, and of the Son, and of the Holy Ghost. Amen. Then shall he immerse them in the water, and come forth again out of the water. (The Evening and Morning Star, 2:13, 1833.)

This account probably came from "Revelation Book 1," a handwritten journal of undated revelations received by Joseph Smith between 1828 and 1834. That source reads,

> And the way of Baptism is to be ministered in the following manner unto all those who Repent whosoever being called of God & having authority given them of Jesus Christ shall go down into the water with them & shall say calling them by name having authority given me of Jesus Christ I baptize thee in the name of Jesus Christ the Father & of the Son & of the Holy Ghost amen then Shall he immerse them in the water & come forth again out of the water

The next reference was the 1833 Book of Commandments, which reads:

> And baptism is to be administered in the following manner unto all those who repent: Whosoever being called of God and having authority given them of Jesus Christ, shall go down into the water with them, and shall say, calling them by name: Having authority given me of Jesus Christ, I baptize you in the name of the Father, and of the Son, and of the Holy Ghost. Amen. Then shall he immerse them in the water, and come forth again out of the water.

The first change to the instructions—which were consistent with the Book of Mormon until this point and twice canonized by vote of the church (once in 1830 and once in 1835)—came in June 1836 when the reprint of the earlier "Evening and Morning Star" article was printed with the phrase change.

> Baptism is to be administered in the following manner unto all those who repent: The person who is called of God and has authority from

---

'preface.'" (http://josephsmithpapers.org/paperSummary/articles-and-covenants-circa-april-1830-dc-20)

Jesus Christ to baptize, shall go down into the water with the person who has presented him or herself for baptism, and shall say, calling him or her by name: Having been commissioned of Jesus Christ, I baptize you in the name of the Father, and of the Son, and of the Holy Ghost, Amen. Then shall he immerse him or her in the water, and come forth again out of the water. ("Evening and Morning Star," 2:1, June 1836.)

About this reprint, the JSPP editors state,

The first issue of the reprinted newspaper, which appeared under the slightly modified title Evening and Morning Star, was published in January 1835. Though touted as a reprint that would correct typographical and other errors, "Evening and Morning Star" actually contained significant changes to the revelation texts. In the first issue, editor Oliver Cowdery explained the revisions he was making in the reprinted versions of the revelations: 'On the revelations we merely say, that we were not a little surprised to find the previous print so different from the original. We have given them a careful comparison, assisted by individuals whose known integrity and ability is uncensurable. Thus saying we cast no reflections upon those who were entrusted with the responsibility of publishing them in Missouri, as our own labors were included in that important service to the church, and it was our unceasing endeavor to have them correspond with the copy furnished us. We believe they are now correct. If not in every word, at least in principle.' Despite the implications of Cowdery's statement, very few of the changes in the reprint represent a restoration back to the earliest text, though Cowdery consulted early manuscript sources when reprinting some of the revelations. (http://josephsmithpapers.org/paperSummary/revelations-printed-in-evening-and-morning-star-january-1835-june-1836)

Whether intentional or not, Cowdery's scribal error was not approved by Joseph Smith. Unfortunately, it was perpetuated in the 1835 D&C, which was prepared by Cowdery with no evidence that Joseph proofread the typesetting and changes before publication.

Apart from Cowdery, Phelps, and Whitmer, these individuals were printing hands who likely had little to do with the composition, structure, or intellectual work of the Doctrine and Covenants. In addition to serving on the publication committee for the volume, JS solicited financial help for printing, helped secure the copyright, and signed the preface. He is listed on the title page, but his role in the day-to-day work of preparing the revelations for publication is not fully known. Some corrections in his hand that are reflected in the

Doctrine and Covenants are found on revelations in Revelation Books 1 and 2, and three notations in Revelation Book 2 indicate that he did at least some of the work of selecting items for publication. JS apparently relied on others to do the actual typesetting and printing and possibly the bulk of the editing, arranging, and other intellectual work needed to prepare the revelations for print. (http://josephsmithpapers.org/paperSummary/doctrine-and-covenants-1835)

Joseph's influence was limited to what he had written in Revelation Books 1 and 2 (which the 1835 D&C editors did not have, at least initially),[185] and what he had printed in the original run of "The Evening and Morning Star," which Oliver had modified in his reprinting of the series.

Though all of this has been available for discovery for over 150 years, and now explicitly written about in the Joseph Smith Papers Project, modern Mormons continue to perpetuate a modified version of the baptismal ordinance, an act that earlier church leaders argued made others' baptisms invalid.[186] Such would rightly argue that those baptized under an adulterated ordinance should be rebaptized with the ordinance in the form given by Christ.

Gift of Holy Ghost

Mormon.org provides a definition of receiving the gift of the Holy Ghost. It leaves out most of the gifts of the Spirit, stating that "the gift" is the constancy of the inspiration of the Holy Ghost, which is activated by the laying on of hands at confirmation, and wanes with disobedience to the commandments:

---

[185] The JSPP editors state "Those preparing the revelations for publication in the 1835 Doctrine and Covenants did not initially have access to Revelation Book 1 because it was in Missouri. After John Whitmer returned to Kirtland in the middle of May 1835, evidently bringing the manuscript book with him, it became a supplemental source for the publication effort." (http://josephsmithpapers.org/paperSummary/revelation-book-1)

[186] "[Apostate Churches] have changed many of the ordinances. For instance, they no longer baptize as Jesus was baptized when he went to John to be baptized of him." (Elder LeGrand Richards, "The Things of God and Man," Ensign, Nov. 1977, p. 21) "[Jesus Christ] instituted baptism to set forth this glorious thing unto men. But by degrees, yielding, as was supposed, to necessity, men depart from this manner of administering the ordinance of baptism for the remission of sins, until water sprinkled or poured upon the candidate was held to be sufficient for baptism. Whenever they did that, wherever they did it, they departed from the order established by the Son of God, they changed an ordinance of the Gospel." (Elder B. H. Roberts, Collected Discourses 5:385.)

The Holy Ghost can inspire you with thoughts and ideas, warn you, and comfort you in times of sorrow. Almost everyone has felt the Holy Ghost at some time. But there is a difference between experiencing the occasional influence of the Holy Ghost and receiving the gift of the Holy Ghost. Although the Holy Ghost may temporarily comfort someone or reveal truth to them, the gift of the Holy Ghost is reserved for those who have been baptized and confirmed into Christ's Church. This gift is the privilege of enjoying the constant companionship of the Holy Ghost conditional upon keeping the commandments. The gift of the Holy Ghost is given when a person is confirmed a member of the Church after baptism by someone having priesthood authority from God. It is given by the person having authority laying their hands upon the head of the person who was baptized and giving them a blessing to receive the Holy Ghost (Acts 8:14-18). Whether or not we then receive this great gift depends on our keeping the commandments of God. (https://www.mormon.org/faq/holy-ghost-blessings)

Another article is similar in content, adding that "receiving the gift of the Holy Ghost is often spoken of as a baptism by fire." (https://www.lds.org/scriptures/gs/gift-of-the-holy-ghost)

The gift of the Holy Ghost is not the constant companionship of the Holy Ghost. Anyone who keeps God's commandments will receive the Holy Ghost as often and to the degree that they keep the commandments. Instead, the gift is to receive the baptism by fire, which is an intense, overwhelming purging experience that changes a person by filling them with the love of God and their fellowman, purifying the recipient to an extent that they can more fully feel the influence of God in their lives.

And the Lord said unto me: Marvel not that all mankind, yea, men and women, all nations, kindreds, tongues and people, must be born again; yea, born of God, changed from their carnal and fallen state, to a state of righteousness, being redeemed of God, becoming his sons and daughters; (Mosiah 27:25.)

The gift of the Holy Ghost is always accompanied not only by internal feelings (which can be counterfeited), but also by outward signs.[187]

---

[187] At a minimum, every person who receives the Holy Ghost will receive the gift of revelation. Joseph Smith taught that "no man can receive the Holy Ghost without receiving revelations" (Joseph Smith, TPJS, p. 328.) Those who have not received spiritual gifts can know without a doubt that they have not yet received the gift of the Holy Ghost: "Whenever the Holy Ghost takes up its residence in a person, it not only cleanses, sanctifies, and purifies him, in proportion as he yields himself to its influence, but also imparts to him some gift, intended for the benefit of himself and

[The gift of the Holy Ghost's] internal fruits are faith, knowledge, wisdom, joy, peace, patience, temperance, long suffering, brotherly kindness and charity. Its external gifts are manifested in prophecies, visions, discernments, healings, miracles, power over evil spirits, speaking in various tongues, interpretation of tongues, etc. (First Presidency Counselor Charles W. Penrose, "Mormon Doctrine, Plain and Simple," p 17.)

No matter the definition in use for the phrase, the gift of the Holy Ghost does not come as a result of membership in the Church of Jesus Christ of Latter-day Saints. In the case of the companionship of the Holy Ghost, anyone who keeps God's commandments will enjoy the companionship of the Holy Ghost. Men were able to keep the commandments of God before 1830, and were blessed by the companionship of the Holy Ghost accordingly. Similarly, the Church of Jesus Christ of Latter-day Saints does not control who does or does not receive the baptism of fire. As demonstrated by Cornelius and the Lamanites, the baptism of fire comes by full purpose of heart in repentance.[190] It comes to all who fulfill this requirement, no matter their status in or out of the Church of Jesus Christ of Latter-day Saints.

Some in the church teach that baptism by fire is a process, not an event, and can be experienced without noticing it.[188] This is not true, and would only be taught by someone who had never experienced it. Perhaps one reason for the confusion is the misinterpretation of 3 Nephi 9:20: [189]

---

others. No one who has been born of the Spirit, and who remains sufficiently faithful, is left destitute of a Spiritual Gift. A person who is without a Spiritual Gift, has not the Spirit of God dwelling in him, in a sufficient degree, to save him; he cannot be called a Saint, or a child of God ; for all Saints who constitute the Church of Christ, are baptized into the same Spirit ; and .each one, without any exception, is made a partaker of some Spiritual Gift." (Orson Pratt, Masterful Discourses and Writings of Orson Pratt, comp. N. B. Lundwall [1946], pp. 539–41.)

[188] "Some people postpone acknowledging their testimony until they have experienced a miraculous event. They fail to realize that with most people—especially those raised in the Church—gaining a testimony is not an event but a process. Being born again is a gradual thing, except in a few isolated instances that are so miraculous that they get written up in the scriptures. As far as the generality of the members of the Church are concerned, conversion is a process; and it goes step by step, degree by degree, level by level, from a lower state to a higher, from grace to grace, until the time that the individual is wholly turned to the cause of righteousness." (Bruce R. McConkie, "Jesus Christ and Him Crucified," 1976 Devotional Speeches of the Year, 399.)

[189] For example, President Boyd K. Packer quoted this scripture and said, "It is not unusual for one to have received the gift [of the Holy Ghost] and not really know it." ("The Cloven Tongues of Fire," April 2000 General Conference.)

> And ye shall offer for a sacrifice unto me a broken heart and a contrite spirit. And whoso cometh unto me with a broken heart and a contrite spirit, him will I baptize with fire and with the Holy Ghost, even as the Lamanites, because of their faith in me at the time of their conversion, were baptized with fire and with the Holy Ghost, and they knew it not.

The story of the Lamanites spoken of is given in Helaman 5:

> And it came to pass that the Lamanites said unto him: What shall we do, that this cloud of darkness may be removed from overshadowing us? And Aminadab said unto them: You must repent, and cry unto the voice, even until ye shall have faith in Christ, who was taught unto you by Alma, and Amulek, and Zeezrom; and when ye shall do this, the cloud of darkness shall be removed from overshadowing you. And it came to pass that they all did begin to cry unto the voice of him who had shaken the earth; yea, they did cry even until the cloud of darkness was dispersed. And it came to pass that when they cast their eyes about, and saw that the cloud of darkness was dispersed from overshadowing them, behold, they saw that they were encircled about, yea every soul, by a pillar of fire. And Nephi and Lehi were in the midst of them; yea, they were encircled about; yea, they were as if in the midst of a flaming fire, yet it did harm them not, neither did it take hold upon the walls of the prison; and they were filled with that joy which is unspeakable and full of glory. And behold, the Holy Spirit of God did come down from heaven, and did enter into their hearts, and they were filled as if with fire, and they could speak forth marvelous words. And it came to pass that there came a voice unto them, yea, a pleasant voice, as if it were a whisper, saying: Peace, peace be unto you, because of your faith in my Well Beloved, who was from the foundation of the world. (Helaman 5:40-47.)

This Lamanites did indeed receive the baptism of fire. However, to imply that they did not know that something dramatic was happening to them is ridiculous. They were surrounded by fire, saw angels, and spoke forth marvelous words. Their testimony of that day was sufficient to cause them to immediately repent of their sins, go out preaching the gospel, and abandon the traditions of their fathers. They knew that something happened to them, and it was not a gradual process! They simply did not know *what* was happening at the time, which is completely understandable considering they had received the sum total of about five minutes of gospel instruction.

As quoted, the church teaches that the Holy Ghost is received at confirmation. However, President Snow taught that he did not receive the Holy Ghost until some time after his baptism:

> This manifestation did not immediately follow my baptism, as I expected....some two or three weeks after I was baptized...I began to feel very uneasy. I laid aside my books, left the house and wandered around through the fields under the oppressive influence of a gloomy, disconsolate spirit, while an indescribable cloud of darkness seemed to envelop me. I had been accustomed, at the close of the day, to retire for secret prayer to a grove...I had no sooner opened my lips in an effort to pray, than I heard a sound, just above my head, like the rustling of silken robes, and immediately the Spirit of God descended upon me, completely enveloping my whole person, filling me from the crown of my head to the soles of my feet, and O, the joy and happiness I felt! No language can describe the instantaneous transition from a dense cloud of mental and spiritual darkness into a refulgence of light and knowledge, as it was at that time imparted to my understanding. I then received a perfect knowledge that God lives, that Jesus Christ is the Son of God, and of the restoration of the Holy Priesthood, and the fulness of the gospel. It was a complete baptism—a tangible immersion in the heavenly principle or element, the Holy Ghost... ("Teachings of the Presidents: Lorenzo Snow")

As with the Apostles in Jesus' day, the baptism of fire rarely accompanies members at the time of their baptism, but comes some time later, when the member has truly submitted themselves to Christ.

For some few who are able to truly humble themselves before God at or prior to their baptism by water,[190] the baptism of fire comes immediately upon conversion:

> For as sure as thou livest, behold, I have seen my Redeemer; and he shall come forth, and be born of a woman, and he shall redeem all mankind who believe on his name. Now, when he had said these words, his heart was swollen within him, and he sunk again with joy;

---

[190] "Full purpose of heart" without hypocrisy is the requirement for the baptism by fire: "Wherefore, my beloved brethren, I know that if ye shall follow the Son, with full purpose of heart, acting no hypocrisy and no deception before God, but with real intent, repenting of your sins, witnessing unto the Father that ye are willing to take upon you the name of Christ, by baptism—yea, by following your Lord and your Savior down into the water, according to his word, behold, then shall ye receive the Holy Ghost; yea, then cometh the baptism of fire and of the Holy Ghost; and then can ye speak with the tongue of angels, and shout praises unto the Holy One of Israel." (2 Nephi 31:13) Those who have not yet been baptized by fire have not yet submitted to God with full purpose of heart without hypocrisy. Usually part of the problem is an unwillingness to accept all that God does and will reveal to the individual. Clinging to false traditions will always prevent the receipt of the baptism by fire.

and the queen also sunk down, being overpowered by the Spirit. (Alma 19:13.)

As in the case of the Lamanites in Helaman 5, Cornelius immediately received the gift of the Holy Ghost upon hearing the gospel, prior to baptism. As Joseph taught, Cornelius did not receive the constant companionship of the Holy Ghost before baptism, [191] but rather he received the converting, purifying event of justification of his sins and gifts of the Spirit.

Baptism by fire is not an optional event. Jesus taught:

> Verily, verily, I say unto thee, Except a man be born of water and of the Spirit, he cannot enter into the kingdom of God. That which is born of the flesh is flesh; and that which is born of the Spirit is spirit. Marvel not that I said unto thee, Ye must be born again. (John 3:5-7.)

Nephi explained that baptism by fire is merely the gate to the path which leads to eternal life. It is required but insufficient in order to obtain salvation:

> For the gate by which ye should enter is repentance and baptism by water; and then cometh a remission of your sins by fire and by the Holy Ghost. And then are ye in this strait and narrow path which leads to eternal life; yea, ye have entered in by the gate; ye have done according to the commandments of the Father and the Son; and ye have received the Holy Ghost, which witnesses of the Father and the Son, unto the fulfilling of the promise which he hath made, that if ye entered in by the way ye should receive. (2 Nephi 31:17-18.)

Baptism by fire is required for true justification, as well as to begin the process of sanctification which comes through the acquisition of knowledge through personal revelation only available for those who have been baptized by fire.

> And now, behold, my beloved brethren, I suppose that ye ponder somewhat in your hearts concerning that which ye should do after ye have entered in by the way....feast upon the words of Christ; for

---

[191] "Had he not taken [baptism] upon him, the Holy Ghost which convinced him of the truth of God, would have left him." (Joseph Smith, TPJS, p. 141.) Wilford Woodruff reports Joseph as having said: "Cornelius received the Holy Ghost before he was Baptized which was the convincing power of God unto him of the truth of the gospel but he could not receive the gift of the Holy Ghost untill after he was Baptized" (WOJS 20 March 1842, as written.) That this must have been a transcription error is shown by the plainness of the scripture, which states that "the gift of the Holy Ghost" was "poured out" on Cornelius and his house while Peter was yet preaching, before they had been baptized (Acts 10:44-48.) This is consistent with the experience of the Lamanites previously discussed that the Lord himself attested to.

behold, the words of Christ will tell you all things what ye should do. For behold, again I say unto you that if ye will enter in by the way, and receive the Holy Ghost, it will show unto you all things what ye should do. (2 Nephi 32:1,3,5.)

For this reason, Joseph taught that

You might as well baptize a bag of sand as a man, if not done in view of the remission of sins and getting of the Holy Ghost. Baptism by water is but half a baptism, and is good for nothing without the other half—that is, the baptism of the Holy Ghost. (History of the Church, 5:499.)

Nephi taught that there is no other way:

And now, my beloved brethren, after ye have gotten into this strait and narrow path, I would ask if all is done? Behold, I say unto you, Nay; for ye have not come thus far save it were by the word of Christ with unshaken faith in him, relying wholly upon the merits of him who is mighty to save. Wherefore, ye must press forward with a steadfastness in Christ, having a perfect brightness of hope, and a love of God and of all men. Wherefore, if ye shall press forward, feasting upon the word of Christ, and endure to the end, behold, thus saith the Father: Ye shall have eternal life. And now, behold, my beloved brethren, this is the way; and there is none other way nor name given under heaven whereby man can be saved in the kingdom of God}. And now, behold, this is the doctrine of Christ, and the only and true doctrine of the Father, and of the Son, and of the Holy Ghost, which is one God, without end. Amen. (2 Nephi 31:19-21.)

Audience with Christ: Second Comforter and Calling and Election Made Sure

After faith, repentance, and baptism comes endurance to the end. Most members believe that this means to simply continue as a faithful church member until death.

What you have to do is stay in the mainstream of the Church and live as upright and decent people live in the Church—keeping the commandments, paying your tithing, serving in the organizations of the Church, loving the Lord, staying on the straight and narrow path. If you're on that path when death comes—because this is the time and the day appointed, this is the probationary estate—you'll never fall off from it, and, for all practical purposes, your calling and election is made sure. (Bruce R. McConkie, "The Probationary Test of Mortality," University of Utah Jan 10, 1982.)

"The end" is not death, but the completion of the tests of mortality, a point that can (and ought) to occur prior to death, as in the case of Seth (D&C 107:43), Noah (Genesis 6:9), Job (Job 1:1), whom God called perfect men. The confusion of the meaning leads many to conclude their journey before they have even begun, assuming that they have somehow qualified for something after death that they have not qualified for before death, despite the plainly taught doctrine in the Book of Mormon that death does not change our character or the glory we have obtained.[192] Enduring to the end means proceeding in the tests of mortality until you have obtained the promise of eternal life from God.[193]

The doctrines of calling and election and the Second Comforter are, therefore, a crucial part of enduring to the end. Calling and election is the event where an individual receives the promise of eternal life from God.[194] The Second Comforter is the visitation of Jesus Christ to an individual.[195] These doctrines are taught plainly in scripture and in the teachings of Joseph Smith. Joseph explained the process of receiving these events:

> After a person has faith in Christ, repents of his sins, and is baptized for the remission of his sins and receives the Holy Ghost (by the

---

[192] "And assuredly, as the Lord liveth, for the Lord God hath spoken it, and it is his eternal word, which cannot pass away, that they who are righteous shall be righteous still, and they who are filthy shall be filthy still…" (2 Nephi 9:16.) "And, in fine, wo unto all those who die in their sins; for they shall return to God, and behold his face, and remain in their sins." (2 Nephi 9:38.) See also Alma 41.

[193] Wherefore, ye must press forward with a steadfastness in Christ, having a perfect brightness of hope, and a love of God and of all men. Wherefore, if ye shall press forward, feasting upon the word of Christ, and endure to the end, behold, thus saith the Father: Ye shall have eternal life." (2 Nephi 31:20.) "And I know that the Lord God will consecrate my prayers for the gain of my people. And the words which I have written in weakness will be made strong unto them; for it persuadeth them to do good; it maketh known unto them of their fathers; and it speaketh of Jesus, and persuadeth them to believe in him, and to endure to the end, which is life eternal." (2 Nephi 33:4.) "And, if you keep my commandments and endure to the end you shall have eternal life, which gift is the greatest of all the gifts of God." (D&C 14:7.)

[194] "The more sure word of prophecy means a man's knowing that he is sealed up unto eternal life, by revelation and the spirit of prophecy, through the power of the Holy Priesthood." (D&C 131:5.) For scriptural examples, see Alma 26:20, Enos 1:27, Mosiah 26:20, 3 Nephi 28:4–11, 3 Nephi 28: 1–3, Ether 12:37, D&C 124:19, HC 5:391, and D&C 132:49.

[195] "Wherefore, I now send upon you another Comforter, even upon you my friends, that it may abide in your hearts, even the Holy Spirit of promise; which other Comforter is the same that I promised unto my disciples, as is recorded in the testimony of John. This Comforter is the promise which I give unto you of eternal life, even the glory of the celestial kingdom;" (D&C 88:3-4.) This is an ordinance and there are details pertaining to it. These are intentionally glossed over here.

laying on of hands), which is the first Comforter, then let him continue to humble himself before God, hungering and thirsting after righteousness, and living by every word of God, and the Lord will soon say unto him, Son, thou shalt be exalted. When the Lord has thoroughly proved him, and finds that the man is determined to serve Him at all hazards, then the man will find his calling and election made sure, then it will be his privilege to receive the other Comforter, which the Lord hath promised the Saints. (DHC 3:380, TPJS, p. 150.)

And again,

Now what is this other Comforter? It is no more or less than the Lord Jesus Christ himself & this is the sum & substance of the whole matter, that when any man obtains this last Comforter he will have the personage of Jesus Christ to attend him or appear unto him from time to time. & even he will manifest the Father unto him & they will take up their abode with him, & the visions of the heavens will be opened unto him & the Lord will teach him face to face & he may have a perfect knowledge of the mysteries of the kingdom of God, & this is the state & place the Ancient Saints arrived at when they had such glorious vision Isaiah, Ezekiel, John upon the Isle of Patmos, St Paul in the third heavens, & all the Saints who held communion with the general Assembly & Church of the First Born &c (Words of Joseph Smith, 27 Jun 1839, original spelling.)

The D&C also explained the process:

Therefore, sanctify yourselves that your minds become single to God, and the days will come that you shall see him; for he will unveil his face unto you, and it shall be in his own time, and in his own way, and accord to his own will. (D&C 88:68.)

As does the Book of Mormon:

Therefore, I would that ye should be steadfast and immovable, always abounding in good works, that Christ, the Lord God Omnipotent, may seal you his, that you may be brought to heaven, that ye may have everlasting salvation and eternal life, through the wisdom, and power, and justice, and mercy of him who created all things, in heaven and in earth, who is God above all. Amen. (Mosiah 5:15.)

These are experiences that can be had by all under the prescribed conditions, no matter their gender, calling, or status:

Verily, thus saith the Lord: It shall come to pass that every soul who forsaketh his sins and cometh unto me, and calleth on my name, and obeyeth my voice, and keepeth my commandments, shall see my face and know that I am; (D&C 93:1.)

Joseph said that our power to "behold [God] face to face" depends "upon [our] diligence and faithfulness in seeking after him." (Lectures on Faith 2:55.) Since it is a promise, we can use it as a gauge of our spiritual progression. If we have not yet received a visit from the Lord, we can conclude that we are yet falling short on forsaking our sins, coming to Jesus, calling on his name, obeying his voice, and keeping his commandments.

Because these experiences are intended to be the pinnacle of what men can obtain in life and the signal that God approves of us, one would expect that modern leaders would focus on these key experiences just as Joseph Smith did.[196] As detailed in the chapter "Church History," modern LDS leaders do not teach members to seek an audience with Jesus Christ. Instead, they teach members *not* to seek such experiences, suggesting that the idea that this must happen in mortality is a tactic of the devil.

> Of course, all of the righteous desire to see the face of our Savior, but the suggestions that this must happen in mortality is a familiar tactic of the adversary. To identify a worthy goal, such as to achieve exaltation, and then to use the desirability of that goal and people's enthusiasm for it to obscure the new means the adversary suggests to achieve it. (Elder Dallin H. Oaks, Boise, Idaho, June 17, 2105.)

Yet, the necessity of these experiences is witnessed of not only by scriptures, but by the teachings of Joseph Smith. He explained that without these experiences, it is impossible to endure the trials required of every soul to receive eternal life:

> [The knowledge which persons must have that the course of life which they pursue is according to the will of God] supplies an important place in revealed religion; for it was by reason of it that the ancients were enabled to endure as seeing him who is invisible. An actual knowledge to any person that the course of life which he pursues is according to the will of God, is essentially necessary to enable him to have that confidence in God, without which no person can obtain eternal life...For a man to lay down his all, his character and reputation, his honor and applause, his good name among men, his houses, his lands, his brothers and sisters, his wife and children,

---

[196] Though Joseph Smith had obtained his calling and election and the Second Comforter, he did not consider them too sacred to teach about. Instead, his repeated teaching about them in public sermons (including to non-LDS people) indicate he thought it very important for all to know about.

and even his own life also, counting all things but filth and dross for the excellency of the knowledge of Jesus Christ, requires more than mere belief or supposition that he is doing the will of God, but actual knowledge; realizing that when these sufferings are ended he will enter into eternal rest, and be a partaker of the glory of God. For unless a person does know that he is walking according to the will of God, it would be offering an insult to the dignity of the Creator were he to say that he would be a partaker of his glory when he should be done with the things of this life. But when he has this knowledge, and most assuredly knows that he is doing the will of God, his confidence can be equally strong that he will be a partaker of the glory of God. Let us here observe, that a religion that does not require the sacrifice of all things, never has power sufficient to produce the faith necessary unto life and salvation...it is through the medium of the sacrifice of all earthly things, that men do actually know that they are doing the things that are well pleasing in the sight of God. When a man has offered in sacrifice all that he has for the truth's sake, not even withholding his life, and believing before God that he has been called to make this sacrifice, because he seeks to do his will, he does know most assuredly that God does and will accept his sacrifice and offering, and that he has not nor will not seek his face in vain. Under these circumstances then, he can obtain the faith necessary for him to lay hold on eternal life. It is in vain for persons to fancy to themselves that they are heirs with those, or can be heirs with them, who have offered their all in sacrifice, and by this means obtained faith in God and favor with him so as to obtain eternal life, unless they in like manner offer unto him the same sacrifice, and through that offering obtain the knowledge that they are accepted of him....Those then who make the sacrifice will have the testimony that their course is pleasing in the sight of God, and those who have this testimony will have faith to lay hold on eternal life, and will be enabled through faith to endure unto the end, and receive the crown that is laid up for them that love the appearing of our Lord Jesus Christ. But those who do not make the sacrifice cannot enjoy this faith, because men are dependent upon this sacrifice in order to obtain this faith; therefore, they cannot lay hold upon eternal life, because the revelations of God do not guarantee unto them the authority so to do; and without this guarantee faith could not exist. All the saints of whom we have account in all the revelations of God which are extant, obtained the knowledge which they had of their acceptance in his sight, through the sacrifice which they offered unto him. And through the knowledge thus obtained, their faith became sufficiently strong to lay hold upon the promise of eternal life, and to endure as seeing him who is invisible; and were enabled, through faith, to combat the powers of darkness, contend against the wiles of the adversary, overcome the world, and obtain the end of their faith, even the salvation of their souls. (Lectures on Faith 6:1-2,5-8,10-11.)

On another occasion he taught the same doctrine:

Though they might hear the voice of God and know that Jesus was the Son of God, this would be no evidence that their election and calling was made sure....They then would want that more sure word of prophecy, that they were sealed in the heavens and had the promise of eternal life in the kingdom of God. Then, having this promise sealed unto them, it was an anchor to the soul, sure and steadfast. Though the thunders might roll and lightnings flash, and earthquakes bellow, and war gather thick around, yet this hope and knowledge would support the soul in every hour of trial, trouble and tribulation. (Joseph Smith, TPJS, p. 298.)

The necessity of receiving one's calling and election and the Second Comforter in this life is not a teaching of the devil. It is a teaching laid out in scripture and by Joseph Smith. Jesus himself said: "And this is life eternal, that they might know thee the only true God, and Jesus Christ, whom thou hast sent." (John 17:3.) If you do not know[197] God, you do not have eternal life. If you do not know God here, why would you expect to be worthy to know him hereafter?

And assuredly, as the Lord liveth, for the Lord God hath spoken it, and it is his eternal word, which cannot pass away, that they who are righteous shall be righteous still, and they who are filthy shall be filthy still... (2 Nephi 9:16.)

Joseph taught that many who assume they are saved are in for a terrible surprise:

Suppose you have an idea of a resurrection, etc., and yet know nothing at all of the Gospel, nor comprehend one principle of the order of heaven, but find yourselves disappointed—yes, at last find yourselves disappointed in every hope or anticipation, when the decision goes forth from the lips of the Almighty. Would not this be a greater disappointment—a more painful thought than annihilation? (Joseph Smith, TPJS 229-230.)

---

[197] This is not a figurative phrase. "But if ye receive me in the world, then shall ye know me, and shall receive your exaltation; that where I am ye shall be also. This is eternal lives—to know the only wise and true God, and Jesus Christ, whom he hath sent. I am he. Receive ye, therefore, my law." (D&C 132:23-24.)

The Lord described those who have obtained Celestial, Terrestrial, and Telestial glory. By matching our current experience, we can determine what degree of glory we have obtained.[198] Receiving one's calling and election is required for those who will come forth in the first resurrection to inherit Celestial glory (D&C 76:53-62.) They have obtained the presence of the Father (D&C 76:71). If you have not received your calling and election, and have not been in the presence of the Father in this life, you are not Celestial. Were you to die today, you would inherit a lower degree of glory. Those who are Terrestrial "receive of the presence of the Son, but not of the fulness of the Father." (D&C 76:77.) If you have not obtained the presence of the Son, you are not Terrestrial.

Instead of teaching to literally seek the face of Jesus—a commandment given by the Lord himself[199]—the brethren teach that we do this figuratively by seeking after the brethren.

Everything in modern Mormonism focuses on following the brethren for one simple, but secret, reason: the second anointing. The second anointing is an ordinance that, in Brigham's day, was included in the endowment. As the authorization for endowments shifted from the church president to local authorities, the second half of the endowment was divided from the first, available only to those recommended by their Area Presidents on condition of a lifelong record of sacrifice for the church and dedication to the brethren. Apostles conduct the ordinance in local temples in the holy of holies or a sealing room set apart for the purpose. In this ordinance, a married pair is, among other things, sealed up to eternal life by the authority of the apostle. Thus, in the church today we see not only the figurative but literal fulfillment of Nephi's warning:

> And they deny the power of God, the Holy One of Israel; and they say unto the people: Hearken unto us, and hear ye our precept; for behold there is no God today, for the Lord and the Redeemer hath done his work, and he hath given his power unto men; Behold, hearken ye unto my precept; if they shall say there is a miracle wrought by the hand of the Lord, believe it not; for this day he is not a God of miracles; he hath done his work. (2 Nephi 28:5-6.)

---

[198] The Book of Mormon teaches that one is resurrected with the same degree of glory that one attained to in this life. The church teaches that progression from one degree of glory to another does not occur after death. Bruce R. McConkie listed the idea of "progression from one kingdom to another in the eternal worlds" or movement from "lower kingdoms...to...higher kingdoms" as a deadly heresy (see "Seven Deadly Heresies," BYU Speeches, June 1, 1980.) If both statements are true, one is resurrected to the same degree of glory they obtained in mortality.

[199] "And seek the face of the Lord always, that in patience ye may possess your souls, and ye shall have eternal life." (Doctrine and Covenants 101:38.)

These men act like "there is no God today" because they deny that God would personally promise an individual eternal life (a miracle, indeed), as they believe he will not do what he has given them the keys to do. They teach members to "hearken unto us" because that is the standard they use to judge whether they qualify for the second anointing. They disbelieve that Jesus would appear to lay members of the church, since he has not appeared to them (see "Witnesses").

The evidence that this ordinance is not effective comes from an analysis of the sealing power manifested by those who have the second anointing and those who give it. Those who receive this ordinance are given the sealing power by the apostle. Just like the apostles themselves, they fail to do *any* of the things done by those with the sealing power in scripture. From their own admissions, even their healing blessings are no more effectual than those without the sealing power, or those without any priesthood at all.[200]

Though it is true that Joseph used the sealing power to seal men to eternal life, he received it from God himself,[201] meaning that God knew that Joseph would not seal anyone up to eternal life against God's will. Modern leaders assume that they have the sealing power through Brigham Young.

---

[200] Elder Oaks' recent description of his experience in giving priesthood blessings could easily have been given by any priesthood holder without the sealing power, or any believer in Christ who heals the sick without any priesthood at all. It is a description of healing through faith, not priesthood. "Ideally, the elder who officiates will be so in tune with the Spirit of the Lord that he will know and declare the will of the Lord in the words of the blessing....When that happens, the spoken blessing is fulfilled literally and miraculously. On some choice occasions I have experienced that certainty of inspiration in a healing blessing and have known that what I was saying was the will of the Lord. However, like most who officiate in healing blessings, I have often struggled with uncertainty on the words I should say...Fortunately, the words spoken in a healing blessing are not essential to its healing effect. If faith is sufficient and if the Lord wills it, the afflicted person will be healed or blessed whether the officiator speaks those words or not. Conversely, if the officiator yields to personal desire or inexperience and gives commands or words of blessing in excess of what the Lord chooses to bestow according to the faith of the individual, those words will not be fulfilled. Consequently, brethren, no elder should ever hesitate to participate in a healing blessing because of fear that he will not know what to say. The words spoken in a healing blessing can edify and energize the faith of those who hear them, but the effect of the blessing is dependent upon faith and the Lord's will, not upon the words spoken by the elder who officiated." (Elder Dallin H. Oaks, "Healing the Sick", April 2010 General Conference.)

[201] "And verily, verily, I say unto you, that whatsoever you seal on earth shall be sealed in heaven; and whatsoever you bind on earth, in my name and by my word, saith the Lord, it shall be eternally bound in the heavens; and whosoever sins you remit on earth shall be remitted eternally in the heavens; and whosoever sins you retain on earth shall be retained in heaven." (D&C 132:46.)

Yet, Brigham Young did not receive it from Joseph,[202] as the sealing power never comes from a man, but always from God himself. Were it not so, Nephi would be liar when he said:

> ...Behold, the way for man is narrow, but it lieth in a straight course before him, and the keeper of the gate is the Holy One of Israel; and he employeth no servant there; and there is none other way save it be by the gate; for he cannot be deceived, for the Lord God is his name. (2 Nephi 9:41.)

Additionally, Joseph Smith would have been forgetting his own sealing power when he said:

> There is no safety, only in the arm of Jehovah. None else can deliver, and he will not deliver and he will not deliver unless we do prove ourselves faithful to him in the severest trouble. For he that will have his robes washed in the blood of the Lamb must come up through great tribulation, even the greatest of all affliction. (Teachings of the Presidents of the Church: Joseph Smith, p. 230.)

We all ought to repent and reconcile our course to obtaining our calling and election and seeing the Lord face-to-face:

> This has come in our day. Yet we find, even among those who have embraced the Gospel, hearts of unbelief. How many of you, my brethren and sisters, are seeking for these gifts that God has promised to bestow? ...How many of you ask the Father, in the name of Jesus, to manifest Himself to you through these powers and these gifts? Or do you go along day by day like a door turning on its hinges, without having any feeling upon the subject, without exercising any faith whatever; content to be baptized and be members of the Church, and to rest there, thinking that your salvation is secure because you have done this? I say to you, in the name of the Lord, as one of His servants, that you have need to repent of this. You have need to repent of your hardness of heart, of your indifference, and of your carelessness. There is not that diligence, there is not that faith, there is not that seeking for the power of God that there should be among a people who have

---

[202] The claim is that the apostles received all of Joseph's keys in the last charge meeting. The keys to the sealing power are never passed from a man to a man in scripture. As an illustration of the process, consider Elisha's request for Elijah to give him all of his keys. Elijah states that is a hard thing, and describes a sign that would come if it was God's will. After Elijah dies, Elisha sees the sign, indicating it was God's will. Even Elijah, among the mightiest in the priesthood, could not pass the sealing power to Elisha. God had to do it.

received the precious promises we have....I say to you that it is our duty to avail ourselves of the privileges which God has placed within our reach. If we have done wrong, repent of our wrong and feel after God, and not be satisfied till we have found Him, and He hears and answers us, and He speaks by His divine power in our hearts, bearing testimony to us in such a manner as cannot be doubted that He hears us, that He is near to us, and that He is watching over us and ready to bestow upon us all the blessings that are necessary for our happiness here and hereafter.....Let us seek for these gifts. Let us be exhorted this day in this Tabernacle, and bear in mind that these gifts are for us; and let us seek for them with all our might, mind and strength. (Elder George Q Cannon, Millennial Star, Apr. 1894, pp. 260–61.)

Conclusion

Though the church was designed to be a tool to help save men, it never was and still isn't the arbiter of salvation. Christ still employs no servant at the gate of salvation. The blessings are available to all who come to him, independent of church status. The danger of assuming his role has been replaced with a church is that, should the church modify the ordinances or mix scripture with the philosophies of men, those who put their trust in the church will be prevented from coming unto Christ.

President Lee once taught:

Much of what we do organizationally, then, is scaffolding, as we seek to build the individual, and we must not mistake the scaffolding for the soul. (Harold B. Lee, Conference Report, Oct. 1967, p. 107.)

When the scaffold builders ignore the architect's blueprint, and instead design scaffolding according to their own imaginations,[203] they will inevitably block the path of the building.[204] God is still in control, and still offers every

---

[203] "But what could I have done more in my vineyard? Have I slackened mine hand, that I have not nourished it? Nay, I have nourished it, and I have digged about it, and I have pruned it, and I have dunged it; and I have stretched forth mine hand almost all the day long, and the end draweth nigh. And it grieveth me that I should hew down all the trees of my vineyard, and cast them into the fire that they should be burned. Who is it that has corrupted my vineyard? And it came to pass that the servant said unto his master: Is it not the loftiness of thy vineyard—have not the branches thereof overcome the roots which are good? And because the branches have overcome the roots thereof, behold they grew faster than the strength of the roots, taking strength unto themselves. Behold, I say, is not this the cause that the trees of thy vineyard have become corrupted?" (Jacob 5:47-48.)

[204] As Jesus put it, "Woe unto you, lawyers! for ye have taken away the key of knowledge: ye entered not in yourselves, and them that were entering in ye hindered." (Luke 11:52.)

blessing to the faithful who, like Abraham, realize there are greater blessings available for any who will seek God directly.

Almost every aspect of the doctrine of Christ has been replaced, modified, or removed in modern Mormonism. However, institutional deviation from the gospel has never prevented an individual from obeying the doctrine of Christ.[205] Our day is no different. Each aspect of the gospel of Jesus Christ existed or has existed outside of an institution.

Because no aspect of the doctrine of Christ is controlled by the Church of Jesus Christ of Latter-day Saints, no changes to the doctrine of Christ made by the Church of Jesus Christ of Latter-day Saints need prevent a disciple of Christ from obtaining all the blessings available to any of God's children at any time.

---

[205] Almost every person who encountered the approval of God in the scriptures did so in an environment where the status quo was in opposition to God. Moses, Joseph Smith, Abraham, and even Jesus Christ were all justified before God despite having been born in a time where no institution was practicing the doctrine of Christ as revealed from heaven.

Apostasy

The meaning of words can be very important. Words can convey a lot of meaning. They can influence thought or stop it.[206] In modern Mormonism, once a person or belief has been defined as apostate, loyal members will avoid interacting with that person or thinking about the beliefs they hold. While scripture prescribes the identification of and treatment of apostates, scripture also shows that the mislabeling of true messengers as apostates has been a common occurrence that carries a heavy penalty. With such high stakes, an effort to understand the various definitions of apostasy is worthwhile.

The LDS church has defined apostasy in several public venues. Apostasy is defined on LDS.org as follows: "When individuals or groups of people turn away from the principles of the gospel, they are in a state of apostasy."[207] "True to the Faith," a book of short topical entries published by the church has the following definition for apostasy: "When individuals or groups of people turn away from the principles of the gospel, they are in a state of apostasy."

Interestingly, the church has a very different private definition. The church's private handbook distributed only to leaders states:
As used here apostasy refers to members who: Repeatedly act in clear, open and deliberate public opposition to the Church or its leaders. Persist in teaching as Church doctrine information that is not Church doctrine after they have been corrected by their bishop or a higher authority. Continue to

---

[206] It has been said that some phrases or words serve as an excuse for not thinking. Mormonism has many such words and phrases. Actually pinning a definition on these words and phrases is a revealing exercise. Some to consider are priesthood, keys, sustain, and church doctrine. The church has become so engrained in the use of words that have both a simple surface meaning and an expansive (and sometimes pernicious) subliminal meaning that it takes great effort to peel away the layers of ingrained automatic emotive response to become able to actually think freely on a topic. This is one reason why reading the scriptures and actually understanding what they say is so difficult for one raised in the Mormon tradition: the words on the page, through consistent alternative use, have come to mean something very different to the reader than they did to the author. "The purpose of Newspeak was not only to provide a medium of expression for the world-view and mental habits proper to the devotees of [the party], but to make all other modes of thought impossible." (George Orwell, 1984.)
[207] https://www.lds.org/topics/apostasy, retrieved 30 Oct 2015.

follow the teachings of apostate sects (such as those that advocate plural marriage) after being corrected by their bishop or a higher authority. Formally join another church and advocate its teachings. (Handbook 1: 2010.)

It is troubling that the private definition is the one that is used to charge and convict members of apostasy. Absent this description is any mention of Christ or his gospel. Instead, the charge is that of opposing the church, church leaders, or church doctrine, all of which have been shown in past instances to have been out of harmony with Christ and/or his gospel.

The Oxford English Dictionary defines apostasy as the "abandonment or renunciation of one's religious faith or moral allegiance." If the church prosecutes members as apostate whose only crime is to have opposed the church, church leaders, or church doctrine, doesn't this mean that the church has defined their moral allegiance to the church and/or the brethren, and not to God?

Scriptural Examples of Apostasy

Because the church offers two contradictory definitions of apostasy, perhaps the question of which is correct can be settled by an appeal to scripture. After all, Joseph Smith said,

> I told the brethren that the Book of Mormon was the most correct of any book on earth, and the keystone of our religion, and a man would get nearer to God by abiding by its precepts, than by any other book. (HC 4:461.)

Here are two examples from the Book of Mormon about apostates who are excommunicated: Sherem and Korihor. In both cases, the crime of these individuals was to preach that there would be no Christ. They preached against "the doctrine of Christ," which Nephi taught was faith, repentance, baptism, Holy Ghost, and seeking the face of Christ until you obtain it (see 2 Nephi 32). Sherem flattered the people by telling them that sin did not exist. He claimed to be living the law of Moses, but he was actually living something that had been drastically changed from the law of Moses as given by God. Korihor, meanwhile, preached "unto the people against the prophecies which had been spoken by the prophets..." (Alma 30:6.) He preached that there was no Christ and no atonement. He said that you could do as you please independent of God's law,[208] and he preached contrary to what the scriptures said. He spoke against visions and revelation. In the cases of these men, apostasy was not defined as daring to disagree with tradition, the commandments of the elders, or pointing out the error of the elders.

---

[208] The apostasy of both Korihor and Sherem consisted in replacing God's commandments with the teachings of uninspired men claiming that what was once considered sin was now acceptable.

Instead, it was defined as preaching against the gospel of Christ in favor of the traditions of men. The Book of Mormon clearly supports the church's public definition of apostasy.

There is another type for excommunication in the scriptures. This is the false type of excommunication, otherwise known as the stoning of the prophets. Many righteous men were subjected to this treatment, so many that Joseph Smith said:

> The world always mistook false prophets for true ones, and those that were sent of God, they considered to be false prophets, and hence they killed, stoned, punished and imprisoned the true prophets, and these had to hide themselves 'in deserts and dens, and caves of the earth' [see Hebrews 11:38], and though the most honorable men of the earth, they banished them from their society as vagabonds, whilst they cherished, honored and supported knaves, vagabonds, hypocrites, impostors, and the basest of men. (History of the Church 4:574.)

Consider the following examples of the excommunication of righteous individuals, and which definition of apostasy was used to condemn them.

Christ. Jesus' crime was that he preached the original law of Moses, which was very different from the adulterated version taught by the Pharisees. He publicly pointed out the hypocrisy and error of the church leadership. He went out of his way to teach against their traditions, proving from scripture that they deviated from God's word.[209] He told them they considered the commandments of men from their leaders to be greater than revealed commandments, and were thus wicked. Those who crucified God were the children of the devil, yet they truly believed they were doing God service. The church leaders cast him out for blasphemy and had him crucified—the highest ecclesiastical punishment they could render.

Abinadi. He publicly preached against his church leaders, quoting scripture to show that their actions and teachings deviated from God. Unlike Korihor or Sherem, Abinadi was not put on trial for the benefit of the people, but because Noah and his wicked priests were offended at his words[210] and

---

209 "Full well ye reject the commandment of God, that ye may keep your own tradition." (Mark 7:9.)

210 "And it came to pass that they were angry with him; and they took him and carried him bound before the king, and said unto the king: Behold, we have brought a man before thee who has prophesied evil concerning thy people, and saith that God will destroy them. And he also prophesieth evil concerning thy life, and saith that thy life shall be as a garment in a furnace of fire. And again, he saith that thou shalt be as a stalk, even as a dry stalk of the field, which is run over by the beasts and trodden under foot. And again, he saith thou shalt be as the blossoms of a thistle, which, when it is fully ripe, if the wind bloweth, it is driven forth upon the face of the land.

feared the response of the people if they, too, saw their wickedness, which they had till then successfully hidden. The leaders sought to cover their sins,[211] gratify their pride and their vain ambition, and exercise control and dominion upon the children of men (see D&C 121:37). He pointed out their wickedness, and the wicked take the truth to be hard. Were the charges against Abinadi justified? Is quoting God's word apostasy? If quoting scripture implicates leadership, is it the reader of scripture who has committed apostasy, or the leadership whose actions fit the sins described in scripture? Is not the punishment of someone for reading scripture at least as great a witness of the apostasy of a leader as anything else could be? Does truth cease to be truth when it implicates leadership? Abinadi did not commit apostasy. It was Noah and his priests who had deviated from God's word, not Abinadi. <u>One can never be righteously charged with apostasy for quoting God's word, no matter who it implicates.</u>

Abinadi was given a way to avoid punishment. Noah told him he would be killed "unless thou wilt recall all the words which thou hast spoken evil concerning me and my people." (Mosiah 17:8). Gratify my pride or suffer the full extent of my power! Abinadi's response is the response of the many righteous who find themselves in this common situation:[212] "Now Abinadi said unto him: I say unto you, I will not recall the words which I have spoken

---

And he pretendeth the Lord hath spoken it. And he saith all this shall come upon thee except thou repent, and this because of thine iniquities. And now, O king, what great evil hast thou done, or what great sins have thy people committed, that we should be condemned of God or judged of this man? And now, O king, behold, we are guiltless, and thou, O king, hast not sinned; therefore, this man has lied concerning you, and he has prophesied in vain." (Mosiah 12:9-14)

[211] The priests' defense is interesting: "And it came to pass that one of them said unto him: What meaneth the words which are written, and which have been taught by our fathers, saying: How beautiful upon the mountains are the feet of him that bringeth good tidings; that publisheth peace; that bringeth good tidings of good; that publisheth salvation; that saith unto Zion, Thy God reigneth; Thy watchmen shall lift up the voice; with the voice together shall they sing; for they shall see eye to eye when the Lord shall bring again Zion" (Mosiah 12:20-22). They seem to be saying: "the scriptures say our feet are beautiful upon the mountain so we can't be corrupt. how do you explain that Abinadi?" False priests always have an inflated view of their roles and use that to justify any wickedness they commit in their office.

[212] Orders of cease and desist under penalty of violence are the only reaction for those whose positions defy scriptural basis. After pointing out the scriptural contradictions of the Catholic Church, Martin Luther was told to recant or be punished. He responded: "Unless I am convinced by the testimony of the Scriptures or by clear reason (for I do not trust either in the pope or in councils alone, since it is well known that they have often erred and contradicted themselves), I am bound by the Scriptures I have quoted and my conscience is captive to the Word of God. I cannot and will not recant anything..."

unto you concerning this people, for they are true..." (Mosiah 17:9.) Abinadi simply says, "what I have said is true, and I will not recant." For Noah, and for all children of the devil, the question is whether or not his words are offensive. For Abinadi, and all servants of God, the question is whether or not what they say is true.

We could likewise analyze Stephen, Paul, Jeremiah, Zacharias, Isaiah, and many others who were cast out by the religious leaders of their day for "apostasy." In the case of each of these men, the charges of apostasy exactly match the church's second (secret) definition of apostasy. There isn't a single example in scripture of that definition being used righteously, only to condemn true messengers from God.

Conflicting Standards

The 11th Article of Faith states:

> We claim the privilege of worshiping Almighty God according to the dictates of our own conscience, and allow all men the same privilege, let them worship how, where, or what they may.

In the Book of Mormon "there was no law against a man's belief..." (Alma 30:7.) These perspectives match with our accounts of Joseph's treatment of church members. For example, when one man was disciplined for a difference in doctrine, Joseph argued in his favor, saying:

> I did not like the old man being called up for erring in doctrine. It looks too much like the Methodist, and not like the Latter-day Saints. Methodists have creeds which a man must believe or be asked out of their church. I want the liberty of thinking and believing as I please. It feels so good not to be trammeled. It does not prove that a man is not a good man because he errs in doctrine. (HC 5:340.)

There are plenty of statements from subsequent church leaders that seem to reinforce the same principle of freedom of belief and expression in the church. For instance, President Joseph F. Smith explained:

> [Latter Day Saints]are given the largest possible latitude of their convictions, and if a man rejects a message that I may give to him but is still moral and believes in the main principles of the gospel and desires to continue in his membership in the Church, he is permitted to remain...Members of the Mormon Church are not all united on every principle. Every man is entitled to his own opinion and his own views and his own conceptions of right and wrong so long as they do not come in conflict with the standard principles of the Church... But so long as a man believes in God and has a little faith in the Church organization, we nurture and aid that person to continue faithfully as a member of the Church though he may not believe all that is

revealed. (Joseph F. Smith U.S. Congress, Senate, 1904-1907, Vol. I, pp. 97-98.)

More recently, President Gordon B. Hinckley stated:

> We must work harder to build mutual respect, an attitude of forbearance, with tolerance one for another regardless of the doctrines and philosophies which we may espouse. Concerning these you and I may disagree. But we can do so with respect and civility. (Teachings of Gordon B. Hinckley [1997], 661, 665.)

And yet, the Handbook of Instructions states that members who publicly disagree with church leaders should be excommunicated from the church.

Is it Right to Publicly Disagree with Church Leaders?

The scriptural record unanimously provides support for publicly disagreeing with church doctrine or leaders when either is in error. The quintessential example is given in the opening pages of the Book of Mormon, where Lehi— a man without any office or authority in the Jewish realm—begins to preach against the wickedness of the church and its leaders:

> Therefore, I would that ye should know, that after the Lord had shown so many marvelous things unto my father, Lehi, yea, concerning the destruction of Jerusalem, behold he went forth among the people, and began to prophesy and to declare unto them concerning the things which he had both seen and heard. And it came to pass that the Jews did mock him because of the things which he testified of them; for he truly testified of their wickedness and their abominations; and he testified that the things which he saw and heard, and also the things which he read in the book, manifested plainly of the coming of a Messiah, and also the redemption of the world. And when the Jews heard these things they were angry with him; yea, even as with the prophets of old, whom they had cast out, and stoned, and slain; and they also sought his life, that they might take it away. (1 Nephi 1.)

With Lehi, the question was not whether Lehi had standing in the church he criticized, but whether or not his criticism was true.[213]

---

[213] Notably, Lehi was not actively searching for fault. Rather, he was a faithful member of the church who humbly considered that criticisms he had heard, and prayed to ask God if they were true. When God revealed that they were not only true, but that the truth was much worse than what he had heard, he took to warning others of what God had revealed. This is a righteous pattern. Had Lehi's actions been different, he would have been destroyed. Ignoring observed wickedness is not a righteous pattern.

Another lengthy but illustrative example is found in the book of Jeremiah. Not only does it provide one of very many scriptural examples of a righteous man criticizing his religious leaders' errors, it also provides Jeremiah's recalling to his subjects' memories the example of a few exceptional leaders past who, instead of prosecuting those who criticized them, heeded their words and were blessed for it:

> ...ye have not hearkened; Then will I make this house like Shiloh, and will make this city a curse to all the nations of the earth. So the priests and the prophets and all the people heard Jeremiah speaking these words in the house of the Lord. Now it came to pass, when Jeremiah had made an end of speaking all that the Lord had commanded him to speak unto all the people, that the priests and the prophets and all the people took him, saying, Thou shalt surely die. Why hast thou prophesied in the name of the Lord, saying, This house shall be like Shiloh, and this city shall be desolate without an inhabitant? And all the people were gathered against Jeremiah in the house of the Lord. When the princes of Judah heard these things, then they came up from the king's house unto the house of the Lord, and sat down in the entry of the new gate of the Lord's house. Then spake the priests and the prophets unto the princes and to all the people, saying, This man is worthy to die; for he hath prophesied against this city, as ye have heard with your ears. Then spake Jeremiah unto all the princes and to all the people, saying, The Lord sent me to prophesy against this house and against this city all the words that ye have heard. Therefore now amend your ways and your doings, and obey the voice of the Lord your God; and the Lord will repent him of the evil that he hath pronounced against you. As for me, behold, I am in your hand: do with me as seemeth good and meet unto you. But know ye for certain, that if ye put me to death, ye shall surely bring innocent blood upon yourselves, and upon this city, and upon the inhabitants thereof: for of a truth the Lord hath sent me unto you to speak all these words in your ears. Then said the princes and all the people unto the priests and to the prophets; This man is not worthy to die: for he hath spoken to us in the name of the Lord our God. Then rose up certain of the elders of the land, and spake to all the assembly of the people, saying, Micah the Morasthite prophesied in the days of Hezekiah king of Judah, and spake to all the people of Judah, saying, Thus saith the Lord of hosts; Zion shall be plowed like a field, and Jerusalem shall become heaps, and the mountain of the house as the high places of a forest. Did Hezekiah king of Judah and all Judah put him at all to death? did he not fear the Lord, and besought the Lord, and the Lord repented him of the evil which he had pronounced against them? Thus might we procure

great evil against our souls. And there was also a man that prophesied in the name of the Lord, Urijah the son of Shemaiah of Kirjath-jearim, who prophesied against this city and against this land according to all the words of Jeremiah: And when Jehoiakim the king, with all his mighty men, and all the princes, heard his words, the king sought to put him to death: but when Urijah heard it, he was afraid, and fled, and went into Egypt; And Jehoiakim the king sent men into Egypt, namely, Elnathan the son of Achbor, and certain men with him into Egypt. And they fetched forth Urijah out of Egypt, and brought him unto Jehoiakim the king; who slew him with the sword, and cast his dead body into the graves of the common people. Nevertheless the hand of Ahikam the son of Shaphan was with Jeremiah, that they should not give him into the hand of the people to put him to death. Jeremiah 26:5-24.)

Another example is provided by the high priest Eli and the child Samuel. Eli, despite his wickedness, was humble and honest enough to admit his folly even when God chose a non-priest child of no authority before the high priest to tell him that God would punish him for his sins.

And the Lord came, and stood, and called as at other times, Samuel, Samuel. Then Samuel answered, Speak; for thy servant heareth. And the Lord said to Samuel, Behold, I will do a thing in Israel, at which both the ears of every one that heareth it shall tingle. In that day I will perform against Eli all things which I have spoken concerning his house: when I begin, I will also make an end. For I have told him that I will judge his house for ever for the iniquity which he knoweth; because his sons made themselves vile, and he restrained them not. And therefore I have sworn unto the house of Eli, that the iniquity of Eli's house shall not be purged with sacrifice nor offering for ever. And Samuel lay until the morning, and opened the doors of the house of the Lord. And Samuel feared to shew Eli the vision. Then Eli called Samuel, and said, Samuel, my son. And he answered, Here am I. And he said, What is the thing that the Lord hath said unto thee? I pray thee hide it not from me: God do so to thee, and more also, if thou hide any thing from me of all the things that he said unto thee. And Samuel told him every whit, and hid nothing from him. And he said, It is the Lord: let him do what seemeth him good. (1 Samuel 3:10-18.)

In every case, the criteria held to modern Mormons would have convicted as apostate nearly every righteous man in the scriptures. If we know that these men were not apostate, but in fact righteous, should we not consider that modern men quoting the same scriptures with the same message of repentance might actually be on the Lord's errand, and not raging enemies of God?

Pharisaical priests—whose authorities recons not from God's voice to them, but rather through the inheritance of supposed authority from their predecessors—struggle to hear such challenges to their doctrine from people whose only authority is that they have heard God's word.[214] To them, it was not enough for him to say that God had told him to say those things.

Early leaders' statements teach plainly that public disagreement with church doctrines or church leaders is not apostasy. Joseph Smith said,

> We deem it a just principle, and it is one the force of which we believe ought to be duly considered by every individual, that all men are created equal, and that all have the privilege of thinking for themselves upon all matters relative to conscience. Consequently, then, we are not disposed, had we the power, to deprive any one of exercising that free independence of mind which heaven has so graciously bestowed upon the human family as one of its choicest gifts (Teachings of the Presidents of the Church: Joseph Smith, 2007, pp. 344-345.)

Modern leaders would claim that they agree with this statement, provided members keep their beliefs to themselves. However, Joseph made it clear that this was not just an internal freedom. He never once punished a member for differing in doctrine. Instead, he supported those who disagreed with him. He said,

> I want the liberty of believing as I please, it feels good not to be trammeled. It don't prove that a man is not a good man, because he errs in doctrine. (Joseph Smith, HC 5: 340.)

He explicitly taught that we should *not* obey leaders or agree with them simply because they preside over the church:

> We have heard men who hold the priesthood remark that they would do anything they were told to do by those who preside over them— even if they knew it was wrong. But such obedience as this is worse than folly to us. It is slavery in the extreme. The man who would thus willingly degrade himself should not claim a rank among intelligent beings until he turns from his folly. A man of God would despise this idea. Others, in the extreme exercise of their almighty authority have taught that such obedience was necessary...When Elders of Israel will so far indulge in these extreme notions of obedience as to teach them to the people, it is generally because they have it in their hearts to do

---

[214] For example, Jesus was confronted by the Pharisees who said, "By what authority doest thou these things? and who gave thee this authority?" (Matthew 21:23.)

wrong themselves. (Joseph Smith, Millennial Star, 14:38, pp. 593-595.)

Brigham Young echoed Joseph's positions on this issue.

I will tell you who the real fanatics are: they are they who adopt false principles and ideas as facts, and try to establish a superstructure upon a false foundation...If our religion is of this character we want to know it; we would like to find a philosopher who can prove it to us. (JD, 13:270.)

Elder Orson Pratt invited normal members to question what the brethren taught, stating that he would be grateful to have his errors pointed out:

Convince us of our errors of Doctrine, if we have any, by reason, by logical arguments, or by the Word of God and we will ever be grateful for the information and you will ever have the pleasing reflections that you have been instruments in the hands of God of redeeming your fellow beings. (Orson Pratt, The Seer (1853). p. 15.)

Elder James E. Talmage explained that we should all be open to criticism of our positions. He said,

[t]he man who cannot listen to an argument which opposes his views either has a weak position or is a weak defender of it. No opinion that cannot stand discussion or criticism is worth holding. And it has been wisely said that the man who knows only half of any question is worse off than the man who knows nothing of it. He is not only one-sided but his partisanship soon turns him into an intolerant and a fanatic. In general it is true that nothing which cannot stand up under discussion or criticism is worth defending. (James E. Talmage Improvement Era, Jan 1920, p. 204.)

President Hugh B. Brown held a similar position. He taught,

Only error fears freedom of expression....Neither fear of consequence nor any kind of coercion should ever be used to secure uniformity of thought in the church....we should also be unafraid to dissent—if we are informed. Thoughts and expressions compete in the marketplace of thought, and in that competition truth emerges triumphant. (Hugh B. Brown (1988) The Abundant Life: The Memoirs of Hugh B. Brown, ed. Edwin B. Firmage (Salt Lake City: Signature Books). pp. 137-139.)

President J. Reuben Clark, Jr. stated succinctly:

If we have the truth, it cannot be harmed by investigation. If we have not the truth, it ought to be harmed. (J. Reuben Clark quoted in "J. Reuben Clark: The Church Years," Quinn, D. M. (1983). Provo, Utah: Brigham Young University Press. p. 24.)

Clearly, the modern church's positions have shifted from what these men stated.

If God were to raise up a prophet from outside the hierarchy to call the church to repentance, as he did with Jeremiah, Lehi, Isaiah, Hosea, Samuel, Abinadi, Christ, etc., they would be excommunicated: not for disobeying the gospel, but for preaching in favor of it, to the church's condemnation:

For behold, have I testified against your law? Ye do not understand; ye say that I have spoken against your law; but I have not, but I have spoken in favor of your law, to your condemnation. (Alma 10:26.)

The words uttered many hundreds of years ago by a prophet of God are just as fitting today at they were then:

Yea, wo unto this people, because of this time which has arrived, that ye do cast out the prophets, and do mock them, and cast stones at them, and do slay them, and do all manner of iniquity unto them, even as they did of old time. And now when ye talk, ye say: If our days had been in the days of our fathers of old, we would not have slain the prophets; we would not have stoned them, and cast them out. Behold ye are worse than they; for as the Lord liveth, if a prophet come among you and declareth unto you the word of the Lord, which testifieth of your sins and iniquities, ye are angry with him, and cast him out and seek all manner of ways to destroy him; yea, you will say that he is a false prophet, and that he is a sinner, and of the devil, because he testifieth that your deeds are evil. But behold, if a man shall come among you and shall say: Do this, and there is no iniquity; do that and ye shall not suffer; yea, he will say: Walk after the pride of your own hearts; yea, walk after the pride of your eyes, and do whatsoever your heart desireth—and if a man shall come among you and say this, ye will receive him, and say that he is a prophet. Yea, ye will lift him up, and ye will give unto him of your substance; ye will give unto him of your gold, and of your silver, and ye will clothe him with costly apparel; and because he speaketh flattering words unto you, and he saith that all is well, then ye will not find fault with him. (Helaman 13:24-28.)

Breaking the Rules of Scripture in Church Trials:

The canonized instructions for church trials are provided in D&C 102 and D&C 42.[215] Here we will briefly compare the execution of church trials in modern Mormonism to the scriptural instructions provided.[216]

D&C 102 describes the roles of the Stake President (the judge) and the high councilors, who are split into defense and prosecution of the defendant.

> Whenever a high council of the church of Christ is regularly organized, according to the foregoing pattern, it shall be the duty of the twelve councilors to cast lots by numbers, and thereby ascertain who of the twelve shall speak first, commencing with number one and so in succession to number twelve. Whenever this council convenes to act upon any case, the twelve councilors shall consider whether it is a difficult one or not; if it is not, two only of the councilors shall speak upon it, according to the form above written. But if it is thought to be difficult, four shall be appointed; and if more difficult, six; but in no case shall more than six be appointed to speak. The accused, in all cases, has a right to one-half of the council, to prevent insult or injustice. And the councilors appointed to speak before the council are to present the case, after the evidence is examined, in its true light before the council; and every man is to speak according to equity and justice. Those councilors who draw even numbers, that is, 2, 4, 6, 8, 10, and 12, are the individuals who are to stand up in behalf of the accused, and prevent insult and injustice. (D&C 102:12-17.)

Current church trials have a very different form. The handbook reads:

> After hearing any additional comments from the high council, the stake presidency withdraws from the council room to confer in private. After consultation and prayer, the stake president makes the decision and invites his counselors to sustain it. The stake presidency then returns and announces the decision to the high council. The stake president asks the high councilors as a group to sustain his decision. The high council cannot veto the decision; it is binding even if it is not sustained unanimously. (Church Handbook of Instructions.)

---

[215] Discussion of the Elder's Council trial as described in D&C 42 is omitted, as the church no longer holds these councils.

[216] A great scripture study on this topic is provided here: https://ldsanarchy.wordpress.com/2013/09/04/the-doctrine-against-dissent/

Elder Oaks described that a church court today is not actually a court at all:

> In a stake disciplinary council, the stake president is assisted by twelve high councilors. Their role is easily misunderstood. Uninformed persons are tempted to liken the high council to a jury. In view of the not well understood instructions in section 102 of the Doctrine and Covenants, there is also a tendency to view individual high councilors as prosecutors or defenders. Neither of these comparisons is appropriate. Members of the high council are present to "stand up in behalf of the accused, and prevent insult and injustice" (Doc. & Cov 102:17). In other words, they are to give added assurance that the evidence is examined in its true light and that the procedures and treatment of the accused are consistent with equity and justice. Their roles are illumination and persuasion, not advocacy or decision. (Elder Dallin H. Oaks, "The Lord's Way," pp. 233-34, 1991.)

Elder Oaks mistakenly claims half the council does not advocate for the defendant. Behalf is defined as defense, support, or vindication. The sample sentence provided by the 1828 Webster's is "the advocate pleads in behalf of the prisoner." A literal reading of the scripture matches trials as they were held in Joseph's day, but contradicts the current implementation.

The church has also removed the veto power of the high council. In D&C 102, there are two veto mechanisms provided the high council. The first is to demand a retrial, a right of each member of the high council. Second, a "majority of the council" has to agree[217] with the decision in order for the Stake President's decision to stand.

> After the evidences are heard, the councilors, accuser and accused have spoken, the president shall give a decision according to the understanding which he shall have of the case, and call upon the twelve councilors to sanction the same by their vote. But should the remaining councilors, who have not spoken, or any one of them, after hearing the evidences and pleadings impartially, discover an error in the decision of the president, they can manifest it, and the case shall have a re-hearing. And if, after a careful re-hearing, any additional light is shown upon the case, the decision shall be altered accordingly. But in case no additional light is given, the first decision shall stand, the majority of the council having power to determine the same. (D&C 102:19-22.)

The church has recently claimed "[Disciplinary] Decisions are made

---

[217] Sanction means "to ratify; to confirm; to give validity or authority to." (Webster's 1828 Dictionary.)

by local leaders and not directed or coordinated by Church headquarters."[218] This is not true. A string of recent communications have been initiated by General Authorities. Recent excommunicant Denver Snuffer wrote:

> In my case the news came directly from Elder Russell M. Nelson of the twelve, who presides over the Strengthening the Members Committee. Usually the news comes through Elder Whitney Clayton, one of the seven presidents. He was also involved in my case, but the original pressure came through Elder Nelson directly. (http://denversnuffer.com/2014/06/church-discipline-top-down/)

The New York Times reported that, in the case of Rock Waterman,

> If he did not resign he would face excommunication, he said the bishop told him, on orders from another official higher up — one of the church's leaders known as an Area Seventy.[219]

The same article reported that Keith Kloosterman had his temple recommend removed at request of a Seventy for posting a pro-gay marriage twitter post. There are plenty of other examples.[220]

In defense of Jesus, a dissenting Pharisee attempted to correct the High Priest for unrighteously condemning Jesus without the requirement of hearing the defendant plead his case: "Doth our law judge any man, before it hear him, and know what he doeth?" (John 7:51.)[221] Likewise, D&C 102 requires that the councilors hear "the evidences and pleadings impartially" (D&C 102:20). They cannot do so if they are under the understanding that the defendant is guilty before the trial has even begun, or if they do not understand that their duty is to independently decide the matter and vote according to their own understanding, not merely agree with the Stake President.

Ironically, Elder Holland recently made this statement:

> In this Church there is an enormous amount of room—and scriptural commandment—for studying and learning, for comparing and considering, for discussion and awaiting further revelation. We all learn 'line upon line, precept upon precept,' with the goal being authentic religious faith informing genuine Christlike living. In this

---

[218] http://www.mormonnewsroom.org/article/church-responds-to-church-discipline-questions

[219] http://www.nytimes.com/2014/06/19/us/critical-online-comments-put-church-status-at-risk-mormons-say.html (retrieved 31 October 2015).

[220] A friend of mine serving as a Bishop has received instructions to discipline a member from a Seventy on two occasions.

[221] See also Proverbs 18:13: "He that answereth a matter before he heareth it, it is folly and shame unto him."

there is no place for coercion or manipulation, no place for intimidation or hypocrisy. (Jeffrey R. Holland, "A Prayer for the Children," Ensign, May 2003.)

There have been others like it.[222] And yet, the recent excommunication of Rock Waterman, Denver Snuffer, and many other less-known individuals followed a generic pattern: Charges of apostasy for pointing out church doctrines that contradicted scripture, coercion in threats to cease writing or suffer consequence, lack of attempts to reason with the individual and show error in their positions, and an anti-scriptural pre-decided court outcome.

If there are no charges against the gospel, then why hold a court?

And when he had thus spoken, one of the officers which stood by struck Jesus with the palm of his hand, saying, Answerest thou the high priest so? Jesus answered him, If I have spoken evil, bear witness of the evil: but if well, why smitest thou me? (John 18:22-23.)

Since there are no charges, there is nothing to persuade the member of. There is no need to continue ministering to the individual, because their facts are not the problem: their lack of allegiance to the brethren in spite of the facts is. Thus the suspicious absence of the mandated continual ministry to the excommunicant in modern apostasy excommunications.

Nevertheless, ye shall not cast him out of your synagogues, or your places of worship, for unto such shall ye continue to minister; (3 Nephi 18:32.)

Joseph taught that the way to minister to those in error is to teach them truth, not to shun them:

...If I esteem mankind to be in error, shall I bear down on them? No. I will lift them up, and in their own way too, if I cannot persuade them my way is better. I will not seek to compel any man to believe as I do, only by force or reasoning, for truth will cut its own way. Do you believe Jesus Christ and the gospel of salvation which he revealed? So do I. Christians should cease wrangling and contending with each other, and cultivate the principles of union and friendship. I am just as ready to die defending the rights of a Presbyterian, a Baptist, or a good man of any other denomination. (Joseph Smith, HC, 5:498–99.)

---

[222] "Neither fear of consequence or any kind of coercion should ever be used to secure uniformity of thought in the church. People should express their problems and opinions and be unafraid to think without fear of ill consequences...We should be dauntless in our pursuit of truth and resist all demands for unthinking conformity." (The Memoirs of Hugh B. Brown: An Abundant Life, Signature Books, Salt Lake City, 1988, pg. 135-140).

Church courts in modern Mormonism are vastly different from those described in the revelations. If the church's current practices bear no resemblance to what God revealed, how can they be binding in heaven? After all, God said, "I, the Lord, am bound when ye do what I say; but when ye do not what I say, ye have no promise." (D&C 82:10.) They are courts of men, operating under the commandments of men.

In these types of proceedings, men are judged for their allegiance to the commandments of men instead of the commandments of God. This is a Pharisaical condition. As the Pharisees taught:

> even if they tell us that what we think is our right hand is our left hand and what we think is our left hand is our right hand, we should accept their teaching. (Sifrei)

And again:

> According to the teaching that they will teach you and according to the judgment they will say to you, shall you do; you shall not deviate from the word they will tell you, right or left. (Devorim 17:11.)

Just as in the days of Jesus, righteous men are prosecuted not because they have broken God's word as revealed in scripture, [223] but because they have broken the man-made traditions of the elders, that in many cases contradict the scriptures.

> Therefore said some of the Pharisees, This man is not of God, because he keepeth not the sabbath day. Others said, How can a man that is a sinner do such miracles? And there was a division among them. (John 9:16.)

Nephi made a prophesy about our time and the consequences of men who hold these unjustified councils:

> For assuredly as the Lord liveth they shall see that the terrible one is brought to naught, and the scorner is consumed, and all that watch for iniquity are cut off; And they that make a man an offender for a word, and lay a snare for him that reproveth in the gate, and turn aside the just for a thing of naught. (2 Nephi 27:21-32.)

The only doctrine that matters in modern Mormonism is "believe anything

---

[223] You can break many of the commandments and still go without a disciplinary council. "A disciplinary council should not be held to discipline or threaten members who do not comply with the Word of Wisdom, who are struggling with pornography or self-abuse, or whose transgressions consist of omissions, such as failure to pay tithing, inactivity in the Church, or inattention to Church duties." ("Determining Whether a Disciplinary Council is Necessary," Church Handbook of Instructions.) Sins go unpunished, unless you are speaking against the brethren.

the brethren say."[224] As with all organizations led be man, "The price of maintaining membership in the establishment is unquestioning acceptance of authority."

---

[224] Postman and Weingartner, "Teaching as a Subversive Activity", p. 36.

The Leaven of the Pharisees

Much of the four gospels consist of Jesus attempting to counter the teachings of the Pharisees—the governing council of Jews whose traditions had in large part replaced God's commandments. Several of Jesus' parables targeted the Pharisees, such as the parable of the leaven:

> Then Jesus said unto them, Take heed and beware of the leaven of the Pharisees and of the Sadducees....Then understood they how that he bade them not beware of the leaven of bread, but of the doctrine of the Pharisees and of the Sadducees. (Matthew 16:6,12.)

Leaven is a foreign substance that, when added to a much more plentiful substrate, changes the properties of the substrate far beyond what the miniscule quantity of foreign impurity would suggest. Had Jesus been preaching in our day, he probably would have used the analogy of a virus, which takes over the host cell and converts it to its own purposes. Such was Jesus' view of the doctrine of the Pharisees, which taught wickedness under the pretense of the revelations of God to Moses. The scriptures teach plainly that men's words are not to be mingled into scripture:

> Ye shall not add unto the word which I command you, neither shall ye diminish ought from it, that ye may keep the commandments of the Lord your God which I command you. (Deuteronomy 4:2.)

> What thing soever I command you, observe to do it: thou shalt not add thereto, nor diminish from it. (Deuteronomy 12:32.)

> Every word of God is pure: he is a shield unto them that put their trust in him. Add thou not unto his words, lest he reprove thee, and thou be found a liar. (Proverbs 30:6.)

The role of the Pharisees transitioned over time. At first, the Pharisees' role was to interpret the scripture given to Moses. To back this claim, they referenced an unbroken chain of authorized appointments to office from Moses' day to present. By degrees, the Rabbis' focus shifted from preserving the original meaning of Moses to adding to God's commandments by creating new traditions.[225] In other words, while the early Rabbis assumed

---

[225] "As for my people, babes subject them; women wield authority over them.

the role of interpreting Moses, the latter Rabbis assumed the far greater role of innovating Moses. While the former had at least the pretense of maintaining the word of God to Moses, the latter were free to create ad-hoc commandments detached from any literal connection to God's word to Moses. [226] By the advent of the Savior's mortal ministry, the Pharisees' modifications had poisoned the religion of the Jews to such a degree that Jesus was identified as an apostate for preaching the law of Moses in its original form. The people rejected Jesus because they judged him against their apostate religion— the result of hundreds of years of innovative non-revelatory tradition—which they mistakenly understood to be the law of Moses.

Jesus came to fulfill the law of Moses, and he kept it through deliberate and careful effort despite the Pharisees constant attempts to get him to break it.[227] On the other hand, he went out of his way to break the traditions of the elders, which added to, removed from, or replaced the commandment of God. To the people, who were blind to the difference between God's command and man's tradition, he overtly broke the law. He

---

O my people, your leaders mislead you, abolishing your traditional ways. Jehovah will take a stand and contend with them..." (Isaiah 3:12-13, Gileadi Translation.)

[226] Degenerate religion always starts under the auspices of the power of the founder, but ends with a consideration that successors hold as great or greater authority in the absence of God's presence than did the founder who enjoyed God's presence.

[227] Jesus constantly outsmarted the Pharisees' attempts to prey on his mercy to entrap him in breaking the law of Moses. In every case he found a way to both keep the law and exercise mercy. For example, when brought the women caught in adultery, he did not immediately tell her she was forgiven, as that would be a violation of the law of Moses, which commanded her to be stoned. Instead, he charged the crowd that the man without sin could cast the first stone. The crowd departed, leaving the woman without the witnesses required by law to condemn her, allowing Jesus to forgive her without breaking the law of Moses.

healed on the Sabbath,[228] did not wash his hands before eating,[229] ate with sinners,[230] and plucked and ate wheat on the Sabbath.[231]

The Savior is our best example of why we need to distinguish between God's word and man's word. He clearly explained the dangers of accepting man's commandments as if they were God's commandments.

One danger of accepting men's commandments as God's commandments is that the former shift the focus from one's internal relationship with and attitude towards God and others to external, measurable practices. These practices are much like a hamster wheel, absorbing an infinite quantity of effort without bringing about any difference in the position of the person with God. They are vain practices that conflate effort with progress. Modern Mormons chronically fall into the same mistake, with endless checklists and "key indicators" that can be executed with perfection without ever bringing the performer closer to Christ. Consider, for example, monthly home and visiting teaching. The insistence of managerial oversight requires externally measured statistics, which fail to capture what is actually of importance: the immeasurable relationship of the person being ministered to with Christ.

The Pharisees overemphasized the outward commandments and significantly added to them with invented traditions. Their focus on tithing, fasting, and ritualistic rules distracted them from the weightier commandments that mattered much more: judgment, mercy, and faith:

> Woe unto you, scribes and Pharisees, hypocrites! for ye pay tithe of mint and anise and cummin, and have omitted the weightier matters

---

[228] "And it came to pass, as he went into the house of one of the chief Pharisees to eat bread on the sabbath day, that they watched him. And, behold, there was a certain man before him which had the dropsy. And Jesus answering spake unto the lawyers and Pharisees, saying, Is it lawful to heal on the sabbath day? And they held their peace. And he took him, and healed him, and let him go;" (Luke 14:1-4.)

[229] "And as he spake, a certain Pharisee besought him to dine with him: and he went in, and sat down to meat. And when the Pharisee saw it, he marvelled that he had not first washed before dinner. And the Lord said unto him, Now do ye Pharisees make clean the outside of the cup and the platter; but your inward part is full of ravening and wickedness. Ye fools, did not he that made that which is without make that which is within also? But rather give alms of such things as ye have; and, behold, all things are clean unto you." (Luke 11:38-41.)

[230] "And when the scribes and Pharisees saw him eat with publicans and sinners, they said unto his disciples, How is it that he eateth and drinketh with publicans and sinners?" (Mark 2:16.)

[231] "And it came to pass on the second sabbath after the first, that he went through the corn fields; and his disciples plucked the ears of corn, and did eat, rubbing them in their hands. And certain of the Pharisees said unto them, Why do ye that which is not lawful to do on the sabbath days?" (Luke 6:1-2.)

of the law, judgment, mercy, and faith: these ought ye to have done, and not to leave the other undone. Ye blind guides, which strain at a gnat, and swallow a camel. (Matthew 23:23-24.)

Modern Mormons have replaced the immeasurable process of re-entering the presence of God with many measurable commandments of men, such as the Word of Wisdom, whose modern interpretation would be completely unrecognizable to a contemporary of Joseph Smith (see "Church History" for more information).

Modern Mormons overemphasize outward commandments like tithing and temple worship just as the Pharisees did, with ambivalence toward the purpose of tithing and forgetting the purpose of the temple. They focus on the paying of tithing, not the spending of it. They focus on "doing" ordinances instead of rising up to the invitation they provide. They focus on providing these ordinances for the dead without being able to describe what benefit they themselves have received from them. They operate like cogs in a machine, endlessly writing checks and sitting through sessions without ever coming   any   closer   to   God.

These distractions matter. There is no such thing as a neutral act. If something does not bring us closer to God, it occupies precious time that could be spent in that pursuit, and thus takes us further away from him. Joseph said, "While our hearts are filled with evil, and we are studying evil, there is no room in our hearts for good, or for studying good." (Joseph Smith, TPJS 217.)

The over focus on the external not only crowds out God's commandments, but also provides a false standard for evaluating God's true messengers. Jesus and his disciples were rejected by the Pharisees in part because they drank too much, fasted too little, omitted hand washing, and failed to live the adulterated Sabbath rules. Yet, in their perceived iniquity, they were actually aligned with God while their judges were not.

> Woe unto you, scribes and Pharisees, hypocrites! for ye make clean the outside of the cup and of the platter, but within they are full of extortion and excess. Thou blind Pharisee, cleanse first that which is within the cup and platter, that the outside of them may be clean also. Woe unto you, scribes and Pharisees, hypocrites! for ye are like unto whited sepulchres, which indeed appear beautiful outward, but are within full of dead men's bones, and of all uncleanness. Even so ye also outwardly appear righteous unto men, but within ye are full of hypocrisy and iniquity. (Matthew 23:25-28.)

Would modern Mormons do any better? What if a preacher came drinking alcohol, not paying a "full tithe," not wearing a white shirt, outside of the hierarchy, not being clean shaven, etc.? Would a modern Mormon believe that this person could possibly be a messenger of God? In much the same way as the Pharisees were exacting in their obedience to outward commandments and traditions, but were unbridled in their inward disobedience to God's commandments, modern Mormons bristle at someone who breaks the traditional mold and will deny them a temple recommend for breaking the commandments of men, but will allow those who are internally addicted to lust, greedy, or judgmental, against which there are no temple recommend questions. We would do well to remember Jesus' comparison of the Pharisee and Publican. The former checked all the outward boxes. He said he was more righteous than others, that he fasted twice a week and was a full tithe payer (Luke 18:11-12). Yet, it was the humble Publican, a self-ascribed sinner, that Jesus said was the worthier of the two. Ironically, the temple recommend interview not only focuses on outward performances, but also requires one to certify their own worthiness. It is hard to imagine a process that could more diametrically oppose Jesus' teachings.

A real and present danger of measuring inward righteousness by outward practice of tradition is that it provides incentive to game the system by devoting one's attention to self-righteousness. Instead of calling individuals to private repentance, leaders are tempted to draw attention to the acts in which they can demonstrate their own progress. As the Pharisees,

> ...all their works they do for to be seen of men: they make broad their phylacteries, and enlarge the borders of their garments. (Matthew 23:5.)

Phylacteries—boxes worn containing written copies of scripture—and the borders of garments were both tangible symbols prescribed by Moses during prayer. Making broad phylacteries and enlarging the borders of their garments describes a visible over-emphasis of prescribed ritual—counterfeit righteousness. Of course, such self-aggrandizement doesn't pay much of a dividend from heaven, as God knows their hearts.

> And he said unto them, Ye are they which justify yourselves before men; but God knoweth your hearts: for that which is highly esteemed among men is abomination in the sight of God. (Luke 16:15.)

At the end of the day, it doesn't matter at all how many baptisms we've conducted, how much tithing we are bringing in, how many temples we've built, or how many ordinances we've performed. As a church or as individuals, the only metric that matters is whether we have obtained Zion and been redeemed from the fall and brought into God's presence.

Jesus taught that the traditions of the elders not only distract men from seeking after and following God's commandments, but also invariably come to replace and contradict God's commandments. For instance, when the Pharisees challenged Jesus for not submitting to the man-made commandment of washing his hands, "he answered and said unto them, Why do ye also transgress the commandment of God by your tradition?" (Matthew 15:3.) He went on to give an example of the tradition of Corban, which was used by the Pharisees as an excuse to break the commandment of taking care of one's parents by claiming they would instead donate the money to the church.[232] Pharisees invariably claim the authority to make such changes. However, in the absence of revelation, no man can contradict God.[233]

Jesus taught that any who followed the Pharisees were doomed to their same fate:

> For I say unto you, That except your righteousness shall exceed the righteousness of the scribes and Pharisees, ye shall in no case enter into the kingdom of heaven. (Matthew 5:20.)

Because their teachings led away from God (despite being understood to be the true form of worship), he taught that the Pharisees:

> shut up the kingdom of heaven against men: for ye neither go in yourselves, neither suffer ye them that are entering to go in...Woe unto you, scribes and Pharisees, hypocrites! for ye compass sea and land to make one proselyte, and when he is made, ye make him twofold more the child of hell than yourselves. (Matthew 23:13,15.)

It is difficult for us to imagine how it could be that the teachings of our leaders could actually make us worse off than having never heard them. It is difficult for us to imagine God being angry with our leaders that are so revered by men. Although most of us would be quick to quip that "we talk of Christ, we rejoice in Christ, we preach of Christ, we prophesy of Christ..." (2 Nephi 25:26) the question is not one of what we say but rather of what we do. The difference between our words and our intentions can often be found in our actions (or the lack thereof). James taught clearly that omission of

---

[232] This is also the practice in modern Mormonism, where an incorrect definition of tithing is used to excuse members from obeying the commandment to care for family members or neighbors in need by instead donating their money to the church. Under the scriptural definition of tithing, only net income is subject to tithing, thus local need charitable giving does not compete with tithing, as the latter comes after the former. (See "No Poor Among Them.")

[233] The priests duty is to teach the word of God, not replace it. "For the priest's lips should keep knowledge, and they should seek the law at his mouth: for he is the messenger of the Lord of hosts. But ye are departed out of the way; ye have caused many to stumble at the law; ye have corrupted the covenant of Levi, saith the Lord of hosts. Therefore have I also made you contemptible and base before all the people, according as ye have not kept my ways, but have been partial in the law. Have we not all one father? hath not one God created us? why do we deal treacherously every man against his brother, by profaning the covenant of our fathers?" (Malachi 2:7-10)

action is sin: "Therefore to him that knoweth to do good, and doeth it not, to him it is sin." (James 4:17.)

Joseph Smith knew the importance of living one's professed beliefs. He was very familiar with those contemporaries and ancients who assumed the pretense of religion. In his normal illustrative manner, he taught

> I love that man better who swears a stream as long as my arm, yet deals justice to his neighbors and mercifully deals his substance to the poor, than the smooth-faced hypocrite. (Joseph Smith, DHC, 5:401).

Often, measurable outward practices are placed at a higher level of importance than internal charity.[234]

Without works, no man can say that he has faith. This, talking of Christ, rejoicing in Christ, preaching of Christ, etc. is all of no worth unless we are acting in Christ to bring to pass those things we are talking about. When it comes to the principles of the gospel, talking the talk without walking the walk is as contemptible to God as it is common to man. In James 1 we read:

> But be ye doers of the word, and not hearers only, deceiving your own selves. For if any be a hearer of the word, and not a doer, he is like unto a man beholding his natural face in a glass: For he beholdeth himself, and goeth his way, and straightway forgetteth what manner of man he was. (James 1:22-24.)

Joseph frequently taught this principle by example. For instance, one day:

> ...a man came up and said that a poor brother who lived out some distance from town had had his house burned down the night before. Nearly all of the men said they felt sorry for the man. Joseph put his hand in his pocket, took out five dollars and said, 'I feel sorry for this brother to the amount of five dollars; how much do you all feel sorry?' (Andrew J. Workman, in "Recollections of the Prophet Joseph Smith," Juvenile Instructor, Oct. 15, 1892, p. 641.)

God described the priests in Ezekiel's time as having

> ...taken the treasure and precious things; they have made her many widows in the midst thereof. Her priests have violated my law, and

---

[234] As Hugh Nibley put it, "The worst sinners, according to Jesus, are not the harlots and publicans, but the religious leaders with their insistence on proper dress and grooming, their careful observance of all the rules, their precious concern for status symbols, their strict legality, their pious patriotism... the haircut becomes the test of virtue in a world where Satan deceives and rules by appearances." (Hugh Nibley "Approaching Zion." The Collected Works of Hugh Nibley, Vol 9. Deseret Book Co. 1998. Page 54, 57.)

have profaned mine holy things: they have put no difference between the holy and profane, neither have they shewed difference between the unclean and the clean, and have hid their eyes from my sabbaths, and I am profaned among them. Her princes in the midst thereof are like wolves ravening the prey, to shed blood, and to destroy souls, to get dishonest gain. (Ezekiel 22:25-27.)

Yet, were they widely recognized as wicked? Did they think of themselves as wicked? Or did they think they were honestly serving God in the way he had told them to, because they were fooled by the false traditions of their fathers? Recall that Jesus said that the men who killed him and his disciples thought they were doing God a service.[235] Ezekiel's priests would probably say that they were teaching the law of tithing, and that it was a blessing for the widows to choose to pay their tithing as taught by the priests, even if it meant they would starve, because the Lord would bless them for it.[236] And yet, their willful ignorance of the truth does not excuse them from being abominable in God's eyes.

Isaiah 58 contains a lament toward the house of Israel because they practice the forms of religion yet their hearts are far from God.

> Proclaim it aloud without restraint; raise your voice like a trumpet! Declare to my people their transgressions, to the house of Jacob its sins. Yet they importune me daily, eager to learn my ways, like a nation practicing righteousness and not forsaking the precepts of its God. They inquire of me concerning correct ordinances, desiring to draw nearer to God: (Isaiah 58:1-2.)

Despite being sinful in God's eyes, the Israelites still practiced religion as if they were righteous and as if they were hearkening to the precepts of God. Paul described this blindness as having:

> ...a zeal of God, but not according to knowledge. For they being ignorant of God's righteousness, and going about to establish their own righteousness, have not submitted themselves unto the righteousness of God. (Romans 10:2-3.)

Such deception is only possible when the people fully believe that their vain forms of worship are in fact from God. They are daily praying to him, eager to learn his ways, yet they are abominable to him. Why? Because they ignore the commandments he gave through his prophet, and instead follow the traditions given of men that have replaced revealed religion. Their vain

---

[235] "...the time cometh, that whosoever killeth you will think that he doeth God service." (John 16:2.)
[236] See "No Poor Among Them."

religion is of no effect, because you cannot receive blessings for following false commandments.

God's rejection of those who practice abominations despite being very religious and ignorant of what they do is common throughout scripture. Amos criticizes the pious hypocrisy of the people, who worship but seemingly unknowingly are doing it wrong:

> Come to Beth-el, and transgress; at Gilgal multiply transgression; and bring your sacrifices every morning, and your tithes after three years: And offer a sacrifice of thanksgiving with leaven, and proclaim and publish the free offerings: for this liketh you, O ye children of Israel, saith the Lord God. (Amos 4:4-5.)

These people were making sacrifices daily and paying tithing at regular intervals, yet they were abominable before God because they were practicing their religion in ways that he had not appointed.[237] It is not enough for men to simply keep commandments. They must be *God's* commandments.

Isaiah focuses on the Israelites false practice of fasting. The apostate Israelites fasted regularly, yet because the revealed reasons for the fast (caring for the poor) had been forgotten and replaced by a man-made focus on the practice itself, it ceased to bring about the promised blessing of answer to prayer. Thus, the Israelites complained, "Why, when we fast, do you not notice? We afflict our bodies and you remain indifferent!" (Isaiah 58:3.) God spends the balance of the chapter reteaching them that fasting is not about the affliction of being without food and water, but about teaching the faster to be more merciful towards his fellows, "to share your food with the hungry, to bring home the wretchedly poor, and when you see men underclad to clothe them, and not to neglect your own kin?" (Isaiah 58:7.) Only by living the commandment as originally revealed can the participant receive the promised blessing: "Then, should you call, Jehovah will respond; should you cry, he will say, I am here." (Isaiah 58:9.)

---

[237] Beth-el and Gilgal were not appointed places to sacrifice, but were used by the people. Individuals were not meant to sacrifice every day. Likewise, the "three year" tithe (mistranslated from "three days") was also a modification of the requirement to bring them annually (Deuteronomy 14:28, 26:12). They had modified the ordinances to be more aggressive than God had intended, and in doing so offended God. The inclusion of leavened bread is notable. Under the law of Moses, leavened bread was almost entirely excluded from sacrifice. The only time it was prescribed was in a thanksgiving offering (see Leviticus 7:13 and 23:17). This may indicate that the people in Amos' day were under the impression that they were in an exultant state, when in reality they were under condemnation. All was NOT well for them, and they should have reduced themselves to sackcloth and ashes instead of being in a celebratory mood.

The Israelites' failure to receive the promised blessings of the true fast through living an adulterated version of the commandment illustrates how false traditions damage faith in God. Those who believe the commandment of men falsely attributed to God will find that they do not received the blessings promised in scripture for obedience to the law. Instead of attributing their unbelief to those who taught them false tradition, they (believing their teachers are of God) misplace their unbelief to Christ, causing them to lose faith in the gospel and become atheists. Because of this, Satan can make great progress by convincing men and women that everything goes together in one: either everything church leaders teach is true, or everything they teach is false. Thus, he can overcome the positive witnesses received from living the as yet undefiled true commandments by focusing the person's attention on the undeniable falsehood of man made commandments while persisting the illusion that the philosophies of men are from the same source as the scripture with which they are mingled.

One challenge we have in seeing our own behavior in the behavior of wicked people in the scriptures is that the accounts were written by those who saw things as they really are. When Ezekiel writes that the priests "devoured souls" by taking the treasure and precious things, that is surely not the way the priests would have described it. For instance, King Noah's priests give us an account in their own words against which we can compare the account of Abinadi. [238] Similarly, Laman and Lemuel described their counterparts in Jerusalem as good people doing good things. [239]

We frequently see leaders in modern Mormonism justifying their actions in ways that indicate they see themselves as serving God, even when they are in the act of breaking his commandments. For example, Elder Oaks explained how he believes God would rather have the church spend hundreds of millions of dollars on multiplying temples rather than helping the poor. [240]

---

[238] "And now, O king, what great evil hast thou done, or what great sins have thy people committed, that we should be condemned of God or judged of this man? And now, O king, behold, we are guiltless, and thou, O king, hast not sinned; therefore, this man has lied concerning you, and he has prophesied in vain." (Mosiah 12:13-14.)

[239] "And we know that the people who were in the land of Jerusalem were a righteous people; for they kept the statutes and judgments of the Lord, and all his commandments, according to the law of Moses; wherefore, we know that they are a righteous people; and our father hath judged them, and hath led us away because we would hearken unto his words; yea, and our brother is like unto him. And after this manner of language did my brethren murmur and complain against us." (1 Nephi 17:22.)

[240] "The preeminence of the spiritual over the temporal, which Jesus taught, has many applications in our own day. For example, it explains why our church spends great sums preaching the restored gospel and building temples to perform the ordinances of eternity rather than (as some advocate) devoting these same resources to temporal concerns already being pursued by others, such as preserving the environment,

As with King Noah and Laman and Lemuel, modern leaders' descriptions do not necessarily convey things as they really are. Rather, leaders' words simply describe things as they see them. A better standard for judgment is found in God's word, particularly as found in the scriptures.

The commandments of men are falsehood. By following them, we by necessity forget God, because we are overwriting his commandments with the commandments of men. We can choose to ignore the scriptural standard and examples of deviation from that standard, but that does not change reality. When our wickedness is finally brought to our attention, it will come as a great surprise. The shock will be as one who thinks they are the epitome of piety, only to discover in an instant their skirts on their face as a harlot in the act.[241] The people do not realize their wickedness, and therefore will not understand God's punishment when it comes upon them.[242]

> Run ye to and fro through the streets of Jerusalem, and see now, and know, and seek in the broad places thereof, if ye can find a man, if there be any that executeth judgment, that seeketh the truth; and I will pardon it. And though they say, The Lord liveth; surely they swear falsely. O Lord, are not thine eyes upon the truth? thou hast stricken them, but they have not grieved; thou hast consumed them, but they have refused to receive correction: they have made their faces harder than a rock; they have refused to return. Therefore I said, Surely these are poor; they are foolish: for they know not the way of the Lord, nor the judgment of their God. (Jeremiah 5:1-4.)

As Isaiah quoted, "Therefore are my people exiled without knowing why;" (Isaiah 5:13, Gileadi Translation.) They are so busy with the practice of their vain religion that it is outside their realm of possibilities to believe that God might find what they are doing abominable.

Why is it so difficult to see? One problem is they no doubt have positive experiences in their lives that they attribute to following the false traditions of their fathers. Few religions can maintain followers without some semblance of positive experiences. No doubt "faithful" Israelites had many

---

researching cures for diseases, or administering to other physical needs that can be accomplished without priesthood power or direction." ("The Lord's Way," Dallin H. Oaks, p.111.)

[241] "This is thy lot, the portion of thy measures from me, saith the Lord; because thou hast forgotten me, and trusted in falsehood. Therefore will I discover thy skirts upon thy face, that thy shame may appear." (Jeremiah 13:25-26.)

[242] One example: "And that they had altered and trampled under their feet the laws of Mosiah, or that which the Lord commanded him to give unto the people; and they saw that their laws had become corrupted, and that they had become a wicked people, insomuch that they were wicked even like unto the Lamanites." (Helaman 4:22.)

positive experiences they attributed to following the Pharisees. Yet, those who followed Jesus recognized that the signs that accompanied his ministry were superior to those they previously received. Abraham probably could have been satisfied with the fruits of the apostate religion of his father, which was sufficient to occupy the intentions of an entire nation, but instead he read the scriptures and realized that the religion of Noah and Shem had greater blessings than the religion of his father could offer.

Satan's followers succeed in ensnaring others by mixing truth with falsehood. It is the true portions of their mixture that generate the positive experiences that allow others to be ensnared into believing the false portions. There is nothing wrong with identifying things that are true and produce fruits. The danger lies in incorrectly attributing these fruits to the false traditions mingled with scripture. Positive experiences in an adulterous religion do not preclude greater positive experiences in a true one. The failure to understand this is one reason that so many Israelites, Abraham's peers, and so many today are ignorant of their situation. Those who are in a religion that consists primarily of commandments of men distance themselves from God with every precept they are taught, every ritual practiced, and every tradition kept because, despite any portion of truth they may be exposed to, the overwhelming false traditions that come with it are sufficient to damn the individual to a far greater extent than any good that comes with the system.

Followers of Pharisees become "twofold more the child of hell" then those who were teaching them, meaning they are worse off for having met them—despite any minority truths imparted in the process—than if they had never met them: "...you prophets in Jerusalem...lead others to sin instead of helping them turn back to me." (Jeremiah 23:14 CEV.)

The reason their truths are not worth their false traditions is because a pre-requisite to entering into a Pharisaical religion is swearing allegiance to leaders. This is, in effect, to cut oneself off from God's word through scripture and personal revelation as the source of all truth in favor of the commandments of men. Such an act damns the follower to a Telestial glory.[243] Followers of Pharisees seek them for truth instead of seeking God directly. They are blinded to the true meaning of scriptures by the incessant false interpretations from the Pharisees. They fill their lives with vain

---

[243] It is impossible to receive one's calling and election and the everlasting covenant while following a man. Instead, it is required to follow only Christ. "And the glory of the terrestrial is one, even as the glory of the moon is one. For these are they who are of Paul, and of Apollos, and of Cephas. These are they who say they are some of one and some of another—some of Christ and some of John, and some of Moses, and some of Elias, and some of Esaias, and some of Isaiah, and some of Enoch; But received not the gospel, neither the testimony of Jesus, neither the prophets, neither the everlasting covenant." (D&C 76:97,99-101)

pretenses that do not draw them closer to God, and crowd[244] out and contradict the commandments that would draw them closer. As long as they seek Pharisee leaders for truth, they will never wake up from their delusion.

> I was available to those who did not inquire of me; I was accessible to those who did not seek me. I said, Here am I; I am here, to a nation that did not invoke my name. I held out my hands all the day to a defiant people, who walk in ways that are not good, following their own imagination—a people who constantly provoke me to my face, sacrificing in parks, making smoke upon bricks, who sit in sepulchres, spend nights in hideouts, who eat swine's flesh, their bowls full of polluted broth, who think, Keep your distance, don't come near me; I am holier than you! Such are a smoke to my nostrils, a fire smoldering all day long. (Isaiah 65:1-5.)

Jesus knew how to discern between God's commandments and man's commandments. He was intimately acquainted with the content of the scriptures and used his knowledge to detect discrepancies between the Pharisee's teachings and scripture.[245] Joseph Smith taught that this strategy is just as valid in our day as in Jesus':

---

[244] Church doctrine leads members to believe that when they are carrying out their prescribed assignments, they are doing God's work. They are oblivious to the missed opportunities that come as a result of having no free time and no capacity to register an invitation from the Spirit of God. President Monson spoke of one occasion when this happened to him: "One night, during a stake priesthood leadership meeting, he had the distinct impression that he should leave the building and drive to the veterans' hospital on the north end of Salt Lake City....Sensing that leaving at that moment would be clumsy and disrespectful, he anxiously awaited the conclusion of his remarks. At the end of the stake president's message, Bishop Monson hurried out the door and rushed to the hospital. Running the full length of the corridor on the fourth floor, he saw a flurry of activity outside the designated room. A nurse stopped him and asked, 'Are you Bishop Monson?' When he responded, 'Yes,' the young lady continued, "I'm sorry. The patient was calling your name just before he died." (https://www.lds.org/media-library/video/2012-05-1607-teachings-of-thomas-s-monson-following-the-promptings-of-the-spirit). How many members make a point to visit neighbors who are not on their home or visit teaching list? How many members make significant efforts to care for the poor outside of tithing and fast offerings? How many members spend more time each week in meetings associated with their calling than with their wives and children? How many are too busy to study their scriptures, but never miss a meeting? How many spend more time sitting in silence across a temple room from their spouse than they do in meaningful conversation with their spouse?

[245] For example, "have ye not read in the law, how that on the sabbath days the priests in the temple profane the sabbath, and are blameless?" (Matthew 12:5.)

If any man writes to you, or preaches to you, doctrines contrary to the Bible, the Book of Mormon, or the Book of Doctrine and Covenants, set him down as an imposter. (Joseph Smith, Times & Seasons, April 1, 1844.)

Scriptural comparisons contradict Pharisaical authority claims. Pharisees are renown for quoting scripture out of historical or textual context (otherwise known as proof-texting). However, because their appeals to scripture do not hold up to scrutiny, their principle claim to authority is that of continuous succession. Though early Pharisees no doubt recognized the difference in power and authority between Moses and the elders of Israel that succeeded him, later Pharisees considered themselves equal with Moses, able to not only interpret the revelations received by Moses, but also to give additional council and even commandments that contradicted those given by Moses. In modern Mormonism, this passable authority that makes successors equal to the predecessors is known as "keys."

Keys do not prevent leaders from leading a church into apostasy. The Pharisees[246] at the time of Jesus had a valid chain of authorized appointments to church office from their founder Moses.[247] Yet, they were woefully apostate.

Jesus' interactions with the Pharisees provide sufficient evidence that keys are insufficient to imply God's authority. Jesus did not recognize the continuous appointment of leaders in the church as authoritative. Speaking of the Pharisees he said, "Every plant, which my heavenly Father hath not planted, shall be rooted up." (Matthew 15:13.) He did not recognize the Sanhedrin as planted by Heavenly Father despite their legal appointment. He openly rejected their pronouncements and pointed out their deviations from Moses' revelations. Jesus showed that the traditions or commandments created by key holders are not the same as God commandments. As Joseph Smith taught, the pronouncements of men have no authority, even if those men and their followers claim authority:

---

[246] The Catholics are another example. Though modern Mormons are taught that the Catholics' claim is invalid because their authority reckons from a legally appointed bishop, Brigham Young's succession claim rests upon the validity of a higher priesthood office (church president) being attainable from the keys of a subordinate priesthood office.

[247] Joseph Smith taught that John's father, Zacharias, possessed the keys of the Aaronic priesthood: "The priesthood was given to Aron and his posterity throughout all generations We can trace the leanage down to Zachariah he being the only lawfull administrator in his day and the jews knew it well for they always acknowledge the priesthood" (James Burgess Notebook, 23 July 1843, original spelling.)

> ...we never can comprehend the things of God and of heaven but by revelation. We may spiritualize and express opinions to all eternity but that is no authority. (Joseph Smith, WOJS 8 Apr 1843.)

Charles Penrose, counselor to Brigham Young, stated:

> God is the author or revealer of true religion. Men may invent and arrange methods of worship, imagine and think out doctrines, and formulate and enforce creeds; but they are of no value as a means of salvation. God must be approached and served in the way which He ordains, or the worship and service will not be accepted. (Charles W. Penrose, "Mormon Doctrine, Plain and Simple", pp. 9-10.)

Jesus distinguished between God's commandments and the traditions of the elders and showed that teachings of key holders, if contradictory to God's word as given through a dispensation head, will lead the followers down to hell.

> But woe unto you, scribes and Pharisees, hypocrites! for ye shut up the kingdom of heaven against men: for ye neither go in yourselves, neither suffer ye them that are entering to go in. (Matthew 23:13.)

If keys were sufficient, why would heaven be shut to the rightful key holders? Why would the key holders' teachings prevent their followers from entering into the kingdom of heaven? Can someone who is barred from heaven lead you to heaven? Can one who is not sealed up to eternal life seal you up to eternal life? The leaders of such religions truly are the blind leading the blind:

> Let them alone: they be blind leaders of the blind. And if the blind lead the blind, both shall fall into the ditch. (Matthew 15:14.)

They are blind because they have never seen the promised blessings of obedience to God. Their followers are blind because they choose to emulate guides expecting outcomes that their guides themselves have never obtained.

Of course, informing Pharisees of their error is nearly impossible, as the more faithful they are to their profession, the less willing they are to consider that they may be wrong. This is because they believe they already know everything needed for salvation, and that there is no true knowledge that they do not already possess.[248] This allows them to dismiss anyone who contradicts their position as a sinner.

> [The healed blind man said:] If this man were not of God, he could do nothing. They answered and said unto him, Thou wast altogether

---

[248] "Yea, wo be unto him that saith: We have received, and we need no more!" (2 Nephi 28:27.)

born in sins, and dost thou teach us? And they cast him out. (John 9:33-34.)

Pharisees have an inflated view of their own righteousness, and do not realize that they fit the historical pattern of previous apostate groups. They overestimate the authority they possess, and use it as an excuse to ignore "subordinates" who identify contradictions to the scriptures in their teachings.[249] The Pharisees speak highly of prophets past while their deeds witness that they, too, would have rejected them, as they presently reject their teachings.

> Woe unto you, scribes and Pharisees, hypocrites! because ye build the tombs of the prophets, and garnish the sepulchres of the righteous, And say, If we had been in the days of our fathers, we would not have been partakers with them in the blood of the prophets. Wherefore ye be witnesses unto yourselves, that ye are the children of them which killed the prophets. Fill ye up then the measure of your fathers. (Matthew 23:29-32.)

The Pharisees in Jesus' day admitted they were the children of those who had rejected the prophets. Jesus made the point that they had not deviated from their parents' ways. Modern Mormons hold two mutually exclusive positions: they whiten both the sepulchers of Joseph Smith and their parents, who rejected him and were responsible for his death. [250]

Jesus made the point that the Pharisees had not only inherited the traditions of their fathers—which opposed the teachings of the prophets— but also their behavior:

> Ye serpents, ye generation of vipers, how can ye escape the damnation of hell? Wherefore, behold, I send unto you prophets, and

---

[249] Joseph said, "I will inform you that it is contrary to the economy of God for any member of the church, or any one, to receive instruction for those in authority, higher than themselves, therefore you will see the impropriety of giving heed to them: but if any have a vision or a visitation from a heavenly messenger, it must be for their own benefit and instruction, for the fundamental principles, government, and doctrine of the church is vested in the keys of the kingdom." (History of the Church, 1:338.) Church leaders frequently use this passage to claim that no one in the church can receive revelations contradicting policies or doctrines espoused by the brethren. The same brethren that quote this passage teach that Joseph Smith's successors, have the ability to modify, ignore, or replace the revelations given to Joseph Smith, despite the fact that Brigham Young was never "legally constituted and ordained to" be president of the church. Rather than support the ignoring of God's word quoted by other-than-leaders, this passage condemns the leaders themselves.

[250] "Faith of our fathers, holy faith, we will be true to thee till death!" (LDS Hymns 84). Members of the church ought not celebrate the example of their fathers. Their fathers failed to build Zion. Idolizing them cannot lead to any but the same result.

wise men, and scribes: and some of them ye shall kill and crucify; and some of them shall ye scourge in your synagogues, and persecute them from city to city: That upon you may come all the righteous blood shed upon the earth, from the blood of righteous Abel unto the blood of Zacharias son of Barachias, whom ye slew between the temple and the altar. (Matthew 23:33-35.)

They were actively rejecting the present messengers of God (Zecharias was John Baptists' father), just as their fathers had rejected the former prophets.

Modern Mormons not only descend in tradition from their fathers who rejected Joseph Smith's teachings, but when God sends messengers who preach the gospel of Joseph, they cast them out of their churches and communities. Modern Mormons feign honor towards Joseph by recognizing him as the head of this dispensation and claim his calling as the source of their authority,[251] all while rejecting his teachings in the same ways as their fathers.

Because God does not honor the authority of the Pharisees, they must cite things other than miracles and appearances of God and angels as evidence of their divine approbation.

Therefore, as Aaron entered into one of their synagogues to preach unto the people, and as he was speaking unto them, behold there arose an Amalekite and began to contend with him, saying: What is that thou hast testified? Hast thou seen an angel? Why do not angels appear unto us? Behold are not this people as good as thy people? Thou also sayest, except we repent we shall perish. How knowest thou the thought and intent of our hearts? How knowest thou that we have cause to repent? How knowest thou that we are not a righteous people? Behold, we have built sanctuaries, and we do assemble ourselves together to worship God. We do believe that God will save all men. (Alma 21:5-6.)

The Amalekite was saying: You couldn't have seen an angel, because we are righteous, and we don't see them, and you are less than us, therefore you couldn't have seen one. We don't need to repent, because we are righteous. Look at the chapels and temples we built![252] Plus, we meet every Sunday to worship God. How could he be displeased with us?

---

[251] The Pharisees said "we are Moses' disciples" (John 9:28) and were understood to "sit in Moses' seat" (Matthew 23:2), yet their teaching contradicted Moses'.

[252] "The pattern is for some false prophet to claim that the spirit has revealed to him or her that the established leaders of the church are in error in some way and that he or she is to be the Lord's agent to correct them....Here's the temple, the great symbol and manifestation of our faith. There are now more than 140 operating temples, just

Pharisees think they are chosen by virtue of their pedigree, independent of their own righteousness or lack thereof.

> But when he saw many of the Pharisees and Sadducees come to his baptism, he said unto them, O generation of vipers, who hath warned you to flee from the wrath to come? Bring forth therefore fruits meet for repentance: And think not to say within yourselves, We have Abraham to our father: for I say unto you, that God is able of these stones to raise up children unto Abraham. And now also the axe is laid unto the root of the trees: therefore every tree which bringeth not forth good fruit is hewn down, and cast into the fire. (Matthew 3:7-10.)

Modern Mormons commit the same error by considering themselves a chosen people despite having failed to attain Zion or several of the easier commandments, such as caring for the poor.

Pharisees do not accept truth from anyone outside their leadership.[253] They believe that they already know of all things that are true, and that nothing that they don't already believe can be of worth. They preach that any who believe differently than they do so out of wickedness[254] or ignorance of

---

one fruit of the restored gospel and of our prophetic leadership." (Elder Oaks, Boise, Idaho, June 17, 2105.)

[253] "They are a rebellious people, sons who break faith, children unwilling to obey the law of Jehovah, who say to the seers, See not! and to those with visions, Predict not what is right for us: flatter us; foresee a farce! Get out of the way; move aside, off the path! Cease confronting us with the Holy One of Israel! Therefore, thus says the Holy One of Israel: Because you have rejected this word, and rely on manipulation and double dealing, and on them are dependent, this iniquity will be to you as a perilous breach exposed in a high wall which suddenly and unexpectedly collapses." (Isaiah 30:9-13, Gileadi Translation)

[254] "Studying the Church...through the eyes of its defectors is like interviewing Judas to understand Jesus. Defectors always tell us more about themselves than about that from which they have departed." (Elder Neal A. Maxwell, "All Hell Is Moved," Brigham Young University devotional, Nov. 8, 1977.) This is a relatively recent position. For example, Brigham Young invited correction from those who disagreed with him: "I will tell you who the real fanatics are: they are they who adopt false principles and ideas as facts, and try to establish a superstructure upon a false foundation...If our religion is of this character we want to know it; we would like to find a philosopher who can prove it to us." (JD 13:270.) Orson Pratt expressed the same position: "Convince us of our errors of Doctrine, if we have any, by reason, by logical arguments, or by the Word of God and we will ever be grateful for the information and you will ever have the pleasing reflections that you have been instruments in the hands of God of redeeming your fellow beings." (Orson Pratt, The Seer, 1853, p. 15.)

the scriptures, ignoring any scriptures that controvert their position. [255] Pharisees believe that they alone possess the ability to correctly interpret scripture or know the will of God pertaining to doctrine. This is a very dangerous position, because it allows Pharisees to dismiss any scripture that contradicts them as being misinterpreted.[256]

> Then answered them the Pharisees, Are ye also deceived? Have any of the rulers or of the Pharisees believed on him? But this people who knoweth not the law are cursed. (John 7:47-49.)

In modern Mormonism, this idea is expressed with the phrase "revelation for the church," though, ironically, the position of leaders hasn't been informed by revelation since the death of Joseph Smith.[257] Instead, Pharisees cite traditional precedent—the commandments of men created by their predecessors—as the source of their positions. This reductive process takes the doctrine of the church further and further away from the doctrine of Christ as revealed by the dispensation head much in the same way as successive photocopies are less and less true to the original document. The succession chain features no more of the dispensation head's revelations than the last leader had, with some portion removed or replaced by innovated tradition in each instance. The further along the process is, the easier it is for a man to exceed the spiritual knowledge of the Pharisees, obtaining greater power in the priesthood and obtaining experiences with God and angels by hearkening to the original revelations of the dispensation head instead of the repetitive and reductive philosophies of men mingled by scripture taught by the Pharisees.[258]

---

[255] "Nicodemus saith unto them, (he that came to Jesus by night, being one of them,) Doth our law judge any man, before it hear him, and know what he doeth? They answered and said unto him, Art thou also of Galilee? Search, and look: for out of Galilee ariseth no prophet." (John 7:50-52) The Pharisees ignored Nicodemus' pointing out that they were violating the scriptural law, and instead misapplied tradition to justify their action. A modern rendition of their answer would be, "if God calls a prophet it will be through the normal church channels." However, a man doesn't need to be a prophet in order to quote scripture or in order for quoted scripture to be valid. Joseph Smith called the Book of Mormon "the most correct of any book on earth" and said "a man would get nearer to God by abiding by its precepts, than by any other book." (HC 4:461.) If a man's teachings or actions are contrary to the precepts in the Book of Mormon, then correcting them will bring them nearer to God.

[256] "…the Pharisees and lawyers rejected the counsel of God against themselves…" (Luke 7:30.)

[257] See "Prophet: Title or Description?"

[258] This is exactly the process followed by Abraham to overcome the false traditions of his fathers and actually encounter the God of Shem, a fruit that the traditions of

> But my Lord says, Because these people approach me with the mouth and pay me homage with their lips, while their heart remains far from me—their piety toward me consisting of commandments of men learned by rote—therefore it is that I shall again astound these people with wonder upon wonder, rendering void the knowledge of their sages and the intelligence of their wise men insignificant. (Isaiah 29:13-14, Gileadi Translation.)

Isaiah's quoting the Lord's use of the word "rote" is not coincidental. Repetition as a teaching technique of false priests is a theme throughout the Book of Isaiah.

> For it is but precept upon precept, precept upon precept, measure by measure, measure by measure; a trifle here, a trifle there. Therefore, by incomprehensible speech and a strange tongue must he speak to these people, to whom he said, This is rest; let the weary rest! This is a respite! But they would not listen. So to them the word of Jehovah remained: Precept upon precept, precept upon precept, measure by measure, measure by measure; a trifle here, a trifle there, that, persisting, they might lapse into stumbling and break themselves, become ensnared and be taken captive. Therefore hear the word of Jehovah, you scoffers who preside over these people in Jerusalem... (Isaiah 28:10-14.)

The Pharisees must endlessly repeat the stories and sermons of their predecessor Pharisees, unable to expound the scriptures either for lack of revelation or for fear of exposing the error of their innovative traditions.

The doctrine of the Pharisees is a fluid one. It shifts when leaders respond to social trends, presuming they understand doctrine better than the dispensation head whose authority they claim without any of the associated revelations.[259] It is not principle-based and it is not based on God's word. Instead, it can be represented as one simple commandment: whatever the Pharisees say, that do.

The inconsistency of the doctrines of the Pharisees was well known. Paul jabbed at them when he said:

---

his fathers had failed to produce in his all his peers despite making a full-time job of the pursuit (See Abraham 1).

[259] This book is filled with examples of this. For example, when Wilford Woodruff removed the doctrine of the law of adoption created by Joseph because it didn't make sense to him (see "Temples"), or when a committee of scholar apostles removed the canonized "Lectures on Faith" from the D&C because they thought Joseph had made a mistake regarding the nature of the Holy Ghost, or when the brethren decided that substantial portions of the endowment that had been flagged by surveys as offensive were not essential content and were removed (see "Temples").

> That we henceforth be no more children, tossed to and fro, and carried about with every wind of doctrine, by the sleight of men, and cunning craftiness, whereby they lie in wait to deceive; (Ephesians 4:14.)

The doctrine of the Pharisees does indeed toss its believers to and fro from one position to the opposite and back again like a flag in the wind. This is why Jesus was able to describe the Pharisees as

> ...children sitting in the marketplace, and calling one to another, and saying, We have piped unto you, and ye have not danced; we have mourned to you, and ye have not wept. For John the Baptist came neither eating bread nor drinking wine; and ye say, He hath a devil. The Son of man is come eating and drinking; and ye say, Behold a gluttonous man, and a winebibber, a friend of publicans and sinners! (Luke 7:32-33.)

Within the space of just a few years, the Pharisees were able to criticize John for fasting and abstaining from liquor and Jesus for not fasting and drinking. Modern Mormonism is likewise plagued by commandments that flip 180 degrees within short spans of time, the most recent being the church's position on homosexuality, which has gone from being strictly sinful to being publicly admissible in less than ten years.[260]

---

[260] The Pew Research Group pointed out that Mormons are the fastest changing religious group when it comes to homosexuality. In the 7 year period between 2007 and 2014, the percentage of Mormons who believed that society should accept gay marriage doubled (see http://janariess.religionnews.com/2015/11/03/mormons-50-more-likely-to-accept-homosexuality-than-in-2007-says-new-pew-study/). There were only 7 years from Proposition 8 in 2008, where members were encouraged to spend their time and money lobbying against homosexual marriage as an immoral threat to families, to Elder Christofferson's March 2015 statement that supporting homosexual marriage was merely an issue, not a doctrine, and that the church would not discipline those who advocated for it. "We have individual members in the church with a variety of different opinions, beliefs and positions on these issues...In our view, it doesn't really become a problem unless someone is out attacking the church and its leaders...trying to pull people, if you will, out of the church or away from its teachings and doctrines.' In the KUTV interview, Christofferson further acknowledged that LDS leaders have evolved in their thinking about homosexuality...'This is not a doctrinal evolution or change, as far as the church is concerned,' the apostle said. 'It's how things are approached.'" (http://www.huffingtonpost.com/2015/03/17/d-todd-christofferson-gay-marriage_n_6887730.html, retrieved 28 Oct 2015.) Not even one year prior, the New York Times ran a story about church members disciplined for their online comments, including "advocacy for same-sex marriage." Keith Kloosterman had his temple recommend removed at the request of a Seventy for a twitter post congratulating the first gay marriage in Utah. (http://www.nytimes.com/2014/06/19/us/critical-online-

Pharisees will trump up religious reasons to dismiss justified challenges to their doctrine and authority. Although Jesus had committed no charge worthy of death, the Pharisees conspired to kill him for fear that his popularity would cause the Romans to deprive them of their power.[261] Unable to prosecute him according to the law of Moses, they broke their own laws in trying Jesus.[262] There have been many examples of late church proceedings that broke God's instructions for both the grounds for excommunication and the manner of holding a trial for membership.[263]

---

comments-put-church-status-at-risk-mormons-say.html). Interestingly, Elder Christofferson here admits that fighting what is clearly against God's doctrine is no problem as long as someone isn't publicly attacking the church or its leaders. In other words, the only doctrine is: "whatsoever the leaders say, do."

[261] "But some of them went their ways to the Pharisees, and told them what things Jesus had done. Then gathered the chief priests and the Pharisees a council, and said, What do we? for this man doeth many miracles. If we let him thus alone, all men will believe on him: and the Romans shall come and take away both our place and nation....Then from that day forth they took counsel together for to put him to death." (John 11:46-48,53.)

[262] "Now the chief priests, and elders, and all the council, sought false witness against Jesus, to put him to death; But found none: yea, though many false witnesses came, yet found they none. At the last came two false witnesses, And said, This fellow said, I am able to destroy the temple of God, and to build it in three days. And the high priest arose, and said unto him, Answerest thou nothing? what is it which these witness against thee? But Jesus held his peace. And the high priest answered and said unto him, I adjure thee by the living God, that thou tell us whether thou be the Christ, the Son of God. Jesus saith unto him, Thou hast said: nevertheless I say unto you, Hereafter shall ye see the Son of man sitting on the right hand of power, and coming in the clouds of heaven. Then the high priest rent his clothes, saying, He hath spoken blasphemy; what further need have we of witnesses? behold, now ye have heard his blasphemy. What think ye? They answered and said, He is guilty of death. Then did they spit in his face, and buffeted him; and others smote him with the palms of their hands..." (Matthew 26:59-67.)

[263] Two typical examples: Rock Waterman and Denver Snuffer. Both were excommunicated for teaching false doctrine without any specific examples of what they taught that was false. In both cases, their stake presidents were instructed by General Authorities to prosecute them. A friend of mine, who is a sitting Bishop, has twice received instructions from a General Authority to prosecute members, once via phone call and once via letter. Though the offenses are allegedly public, the trials are not, preventing the public from knowing exactly what was said and done in the meetings. It is left to the reader to compare these situations to the scriptures and find whether they more closely match the instructions given in the D&C, or the behavior of the Pharisees toward Jesus.

Pharisees break God's commandments through their traditions.[264] Modern Mormons do the same. The example of tithing has already been discussed. Another example is obedience to the handbook of instructions instead of scripture. Modern Mormons consider the handbook to be the most relevant source of instruction in our day,[265] and filter personal revelation that does not agree with it.[266] Today's handbooks expand broadly beyond scripture and contradict scripture in many instances. The handbook takes precedence despite modern Mormons' temple covenant to obey "the law of the gospel as

---

[264] "Then came to Jesus scribes and Pharisees, which were of Jerusalem, saying, Why do thy disciples transgress the tradition of the elders? for they wash not their hands when they eat bread. But he answered and said unto them, Why do ye also transgress the commandment of God by your tradition? For God commanded, saying, Honour thy father and mother: and, He that curseth father or mother, let him die the death. But ye say, Whosoever shall say to his father or his mother, It is a gift, by whatsoever thou mightest be profited by me; And honour not his father or his mother, he shall be free. Thus have ye made the commandment of God of none effect by your tradition." (Matthew 15:1-6)

[265] "While [the] handbooks do not have the same standing as the scriptures, they do represent the most current interpretations and procedural directions of the Church's highest authorities." (Elder Dallin H. Oaks, "Overview of the New Handbooks," 2010 Worldwide Leadership Training Meeting, 2010.)

[266] I was once a ward mission leader. The Bishop informed me that he had explicit revelation from God that I was to be the mission leader. We coalesced on a ward mission plan that we both felt was God's word. The goal was to bring individuals to Christ. Instead of focusing on programs and statistics, we simply went about trying to teach members of the second great commandment. We taught them that love of one's neighbors crosses the bounds of church assignments. We simply taught them to take a vested interest in actually caring about those around them. In a few short months, the progress was notable. Any night brought the sight of neighbors visiting other neighbors for dinner or activities. The neighborhood felt a lot closer. During this time, I found that the requirements of work, school, and family restricted my available time for meetings. While Sunday morning meetings were easy to accommodate, the Wednesday night meeting where the Stake's ward mission leaders would report to the High Councilman were not. I asked God if I should go to it, and he told me that it would be better for me to spend the time visiting a family or with my own family. The High Councilor reported to my Bishop that I was not attending. He said the handbook said I was supposed to attend that meeting. I told him that the Lord had told me otherwise. I asked him if he felt that our weekly encounters at PEC kept him informed. He said they did. I asked him if he delivered a report to the Stake President in their meetings about missionary work. He said he did. He said he felt the Spirit confirm to him that I should omit the meeting, but that he was conflicted because the handbook said otherwise. After a week of consideration, he said I either would have to follow the handbook or be released. I told him that I could not disobey God, and was released. Ironically, my bishop routinely denied that prescribed church assignments could preclude the instructions of the Holy Ghost. His own vindication of my point did not seem to register.

contained in the Book of Mormon and the Bible." There have been 27 versions of church handbooks since 1899.[267] The principles taught vary vastly between editions. [268] Church leaders admit the frequent changes, but erroneously characterize the changes as limited to programs and policy.[269]

Pharisees love positive attention that comes by reason of their office. They love preferential treatment over those who do not hold their office. They love special titles. Jesus says we should not treat one man different than another. We should only show deference to God, who is the only one who can save us. If God's servants are to be different than others, it should be through their abasement and service to others, not through positive preferential treatment.

> And love the uppermost rooms at feasts, and the chief seats in the synagogues, And greetings in the markets, and to be called of men, Rabbi, Rabbi. But be not ye called Rabbi: for one is your Master, even Christ; and all ye are brethren. And call no man your father

---

[267] https://en.wikipedia.org/wiki/Handbook_(LDS_Church)

[268] An analysis of this issue is beyond the scope of this book, and apparently has not yet been undertaken, probably due to the church's prosecution of those who post the contents of the CHI online. However, the following changes to the 2010 CHI provide a case study of changing doctrines. The previous version is reproduced below, with italics representing additions to the 2010 edition, and strikethroughs identifying removals in the 2010 edition. The doctrinal significance is left to the reader. "Homosexual behavior violates the commandments of God, is contrary to the purposes of human sexuality, distorts loving relationships, and deprives people of the blessings that can be found in family life and in the saving ordinances of the gospel. Those who persist in such behavior or who influence others to do so are subject to Church discipline. Homosexual behavior can be forgiven through sincere repentance. If members have homosexual thoughts or feelings or engage in homosexual behavior, Church leaders should help them have a clear understanding of faith in Jesus Christ, the process of repentance, and the purpose of life on earth. Leaders also should help them accept responsibility for their thoughts and actions and apply gospel principles in their lives. While opposing homosexual behavior, the Church reaches out to understanding and respect to individuals who are attracted to those of the same gender. In addition to the inspired assistance of Church leaders, members may need professional counseling. When appropriate, bishops should contact LDS Social Services to identify resources to provide such counseling in harmony with gospel principles. If members feel same-gender attraction but do not engage in any homosexual behavior, leaders should support and encourage them in their resolve to live the law of chastity and to control unrighteous thoughts. These members may receive Church callings. If they are worthy and qualified in every other way, they may also hold temple recommends and receive temple ordinances."

[269] "Procedures, programs, the administrative policies, even some matters of organization are subject to change. We are quite free, indeed quite obliged to alter them from time to time. But the principles, the doctrines, never change." (Boyd K. Packer, "Principles," Ensign Mar 1985, 8).

upon the earth: for one is your Father, which is in heaven. Neither be ye called masters: for one is your Master, even Christ. But he that is greatest among you shall be your servant. And whosoever shall exalt himself shall be abased; and he that shall humble himself shall be exalted. (Matthew 23:6-12.)

Pharisees are obsessed with money and exacting with debts. Pharisees find the principle that you cannot serve two masters to be a hard one, for they love the money they control by virtue of their office, the power it buys, and the feeling of security it provides.

And he said also unto his disciples, There was a certain rich man, which had a steward; and the same was accused unto him that he had wasted his goods. And he called him, and said unto him, How is it that I hear this of thee? give an account of thy stewardship; for thou mayest be no longer steward. Then the steward said within himself, What shall I do? for my lord taketh away from me the stewardship: I cannot dig; to beg I am ashamed. I am resolved what to do, that, when I am put out of the stewardship, they may receive me into their houses. So he called every one of his lord's debtors unto him, and said unto the first, How much owest thou unto my lord? And he said, An hundred measures of oil. And he said unto him, Take thy bill, and sit down quickly, and write fifty. Then said he to another, And how much owest thou? And he said, An hundred measures of wheat. And he said unto him, Take thy bill, and write fourscore. And the lord commended the unjust steward, because he had done wisely: for the children of this world are in their generation wiser than the children of light. And I say unto you, Make to yourselves friends of the mammon of unrighteousness; that, when ye fail, they may receive you into everlasting habitations....No servant can serve two masters: for either he will hate the one, and love the other; or else he will hold to the one, and despise the other. Ye cannot serve God and mammon. And the Pharisees also, who were covetous, heard all these things: and they derided him. (Luke 16:1-9,13-14.)

In one application of the parable, the church leaders are the steward, the rich man is God. Jesus was saying that all men, including leaders, commit sin and fall short. He was suggesting that they should pardon those who owe money to them, knowing their master will be as exacting on them as they were to others. The Pharisees knew both exactly who he was talking about and what he was implying about their performance.

Modern Mormonism places significant emphasis on the modern version of the law of tithing, which exacts 10% of one's gross income whether rich or poor. Failure to pay a full 10% of one's gross income to the church strips a member of temple entrance rights. The application of Jesus' parable to today would mean that leaders who require perfection of the law of tithing to enter the symbolic presence of the Lord will be held to the same standard of perfection in all things to enter into the actual presence of the Lord.

Pharisees seek to punish any who question their authority, claims, or beliefs.

> And many of the people believed on him, and said, When Christ cometh, will he do more miracles than these which this man hath done? The Pharisees heard that the people murmured such things concerning him; and the Pharisees and the chief priests sent officers to take him. (John 7:31-32.)

In modern Mormonism, this persecution comes through the order of the Strengthening the Members Committee, an organization that searches out members who publicly disagree with church leaders and asks their stake presidents to discipline them.

Although Pharisees claim their persecution is because men are breaking God's commandments, some are—like Jesus—only breaking the tradition of the elders. The Pharisees judge unrighteously, rejecting true messengers using false standards.

> They brought to the Pharisees him that aforetime was blind. And it was the sabbath day when Jesus made the clay, and opened his eyes. Then again the Pharisees also asked him how he had received his sight. He said unto them, He put clay upon mine eyes, and I washed, and do see. Therefore said some of the Pharisees, This man is not of God, because he keepeth not the sabbath day. (John 9:13-16.)

Individuals who oppose the traditions of men are investigated by the Pharisees, not in order to evaluate whether their position is true, but in order to entrap the individual in charges of apostasy (see, for example John 8:1-6, Matthew 22:15-17, Matthew 19:3, Luke 11:53-54, and Mark 10:2.) In the mind of the Pharisees, there is no possibility that they are out of alignment with God, therefore any dissenter from their tradition is necessarily an apostate.

Even those faithful to the Pharisees would likely see the error in such accusations, therefore Pharisees conspire in secret to avoid negative public reactions to their evil designs. The Pharisees discussed in private councils how they could entrap Jesus, and they interrogated him in the middle of the night.[270] In modern Mormonism, dissenters from the traditions of the elders are targeted in private leadership meetings. Investigations triggered by the

---

[270] "Then the Pharisees went out, and held a council against him, how they might destroy him." (Matthew 12:14.) "Then went the Pharisees, and took counsel how they might entangle him in his talk." (Matthew 22:15) See also Matthew 21:45-46.

Strengthening the Members Committee are done via private letters or phone calls to stake presidents and bishops. The body of the membership is only notified after disciplinary decisions have been made.

The Pharisees disbelieve miracles by their dissenters.[271]

> for behold there is no God today, for the Lord and the Redeemer hath done his work, and he hath given his power unto men; Behold, hearken ye unto my precept; if they shall say there is a miracle wrought by the hand of the Lord, believe it not; for this day he is not a God of miracles; (2 Nephi 28:5-6.)

They do not accept miracles as witnesses of true messengers.

> They brought to the Pharisees him that aforetime was blind. And it was the sabbath day when Jesus made the clay, and opened his eyes....But the Jews did not believe concerning him, that he had been blind, and received his sight. (John 9:13-14,18.)

While the miracles Jesus performed were sufficient to convince Nicodemus that he was sent by God,[272] they were insufficient to convince any of his fellows in the Sanhedrin. If the Pharisees witness the miracles with their own eyes, they ascribe the miracle to the devil.

> Then was brought unto him one possessed with a devil, blind, and dumb: and he healed him, insomuch that the blind and dumb both spake and saw. And all the people were amazed, and said, Is not this the son of David? But when the Pharisees heard it, they said, This fellow doth not cast out devils, but by Beelzebub the prince of the devils. (Matthew 12:22-24; See also Matthew 9:34.)

Jesus said of the Pharisees: "But in vain they do worship me, teaching for doctrines the commandments of men." (Matthew 15:9.) What does it mean to worship in vain? It means to worship without any of the desired or expected effects. When your religion consists of the commandments of men, God does not recognize it. At best, it will produce none of the desired effects.

---

[271] "Show me Latter-day Saints who have to feed upon miracles, signs and visions in order to keep them steadfast in the Church, and I will show you members of the Church who are not in good standing before God, and who are walking in slippery paths. It is not by marvelous manifestations unto us that we shall be established in the truth, but it is by humility and faithful obedience to the commandments and laws of God." (Joseph F. Smith, Gospel Doctrine)

[272] "There was a man of the Pharisees, named Nicodemus, a ruler of the Jews: The same came to Jesus by night, and said unto him, Rabbi, we know that thou art a teacher come from God: for no man can do these miracles that thou doest, except God be with him." (John 3:1-2.)

More likely, your religion offends God and will result in cursings instead of blessings.

Sincerity, piousness, sacrifice and ritual are not hallmarks of the righteous. They are at least as popular among the misguided as they are among the righteous. We should be very concerned about our own status before God. We should revisit the scriptures, particularly the prophecies for our time. We should ask ourselves, "Lord, is it I?"

Whether our doctrine comes from men or comes from Christ matters. It is of especial importance in our day, when we face the fulfillment of the prophecies of what is to come before Christ's return.

> For the time speedily cometh that the Lord God shall cause a great division among the people, and the wicked will he destroy; and he will spare his people, yea, even if it so be that he must destroy the wicked by fire. (2 Nephi 30:10.)

What will this division be? It will be those who listen to God against those who listen to men. Those who listen to men will resist the true messengers God sends to renew to pure gospel of Christ by direct commission from him.

> Therefore it shall come to pass that whosoever will not believe in my words, who am Jesus Christ, which the Father shall cause him to bring forth unto the Gentiles, and shall give unto him power that he shall bring them forth unto the Gentiles, (it shall be done even as Moses said) they shall be cut off from among my people who are of the covenant....Yea, wo be unto the Gentiles except they repent; for it shall come to pass in that day, saith the Father, that I will cut off thy horses out of the midst of thee, and I will destroy thy chariots; And I will cut off the cities of thy land, and throw down all thy strongholds; And I will cut off witchcrafts out of thy land, and thou shalt have no more soothsayers; Thy graven images I will also cut off, and thy standing images out of the midst of thee, and thou shalt no more worship the works of thy hands; And I will pluck up thy groves out of the midst of thee; so will I destroy thy cities. And it shall come to pass that all lyings, and deceivings, and envyings, and strifes, and priestcrafts, and whoredoms, shall be done away. For it shall come to pass, saith the Father, that at that day whosoever will not repent and come unto my Beloved Son, them will I cut off from among my people, O house of Israel; And I will execute vengeance and fury upon them, even as upon the heathen, such as they have not heard. (3 Nephi 21:11,14-20.)

Modern Mormons will find themselves without their idols and soothsayers, without their Babylonian goods that provide carnal security, and the confidence they have placed in men will be shredded to taters, leaving them to curse God and wish for death in overwhelming fear for the shock of what has come upon them. When this promised destruction occurs, and Jesus will once again lament,

> O Jerusalem, Jerusalem, thou that killest the prophets, and stonest them which are sent unto thee, how often would I have gathered thy children together, even as a hen gathereth her chickens under her wings, and ye would not! Behold, your house is left unto you desolate. For I say unto you, Ye shall not see me henceforth, till ye shall say, Blessed is he that cometh in the name of the Lord. (Matthew 23:37-39.)

He will lament because those who do not recognize his voice, preferring the voice of the Pharisees, will not be gathered to places of safety, and will suffer through the destruction of the wicked. Before that day, there will be a bundling of the wicked and a gathering of the righteous:

> Let both grow together until the harvest: and in the time of harvest I will say to the reapers, Gather ye together first the tares, and bind them in bundles to burn them: but gather the wheat into my barn. (Matthew 13:30.)

How are they bundled?

> As, therefore, the tares are gathered and burned in the fire, so shall it be in the end of the world; that is, as the servants of God go forth warning the nations, both priests and people, and as they harden their hearts and reject the light of truth, these first being delivered over to the buffetings of Satan, and the law and the testimony being closed up, as it was in the case of the Jews, they are left in darkness, and delivered over unto the day of burning; thus being bound up by their creeds, and their bands being made strong by their priests, are prepared for the fulfilment of the saying of the Savior—'The Son of Man shall send forth His angels, and gather out of His Kingdom all things that offend, and them which do iniquity, and shall cast them into a furnace of fire, there shall be wailing and gnashing of teeth.' We understand that the work of gathering together of the wheat into barns, or garners, is to take place while the tares are being bound over, and preparing for the day of burning; that after the day of burnings, the righteous shall shine forth like the sun, in the Kingdom of their Father. Who hath ears to hear, let him hear. (Joseph Smith, TPJS, p. 69.)

The false traditions of the priests not only condemn them, but they make their bands strong because their ability to connect to God has been cut off. They have been taught to disregard personal revelation that contradicts the

216

Pharisees. They have been taught to superimpose the traditions of the Pharisees onto the scriptures, preventing a literal interpretation of what they say. They have been taught that feelings are revelation, thus clogging the revelatory channel with false signals. They truly are blinded by the traditions of their fathers.

In our day, we can recognize the destruction as a herald that we are in the time prophesied by the Book of Mormon prophets.[273] We can find in our present situation every quality of the last days they describe:

---

[273] These warnings are not new. Ezekiel prophesied in his day what could very well be a dual prophecy applying both then and now. "I am the LORD God, and I have made Jerusalem the most important place in the world, and all other nations admire it. But the people of Jerusalem rebelled and refuse to obey me. They ignored my laws and have become even more sinful than the nations around them. So tell the people of Jerusalem: I am the LORD God! You have refused to obey my laws and teachings, and instead you have obeyed the laws of the surrounding nations. You have become more rebellious than any of them! Now all those nations will watch as I turn against you and punish you 9for your sins. Your punishment will be more horrible than anything I've ever done or will ever do again. Parents will be so desperate for food that they will eat their own children, and children will eat their parents. Those who survive this horror will be scattered in every direction. Your sins have disgusted me and made my temple unfit as a place to worship me. So I swear by my own life that I will cut you down[u] and show you no pity. A third of you will die here in Jerusalem from disease or starvation. Another third will be killed in war. And I will scatter the last third of you in every direction, then track you down and kill you. You will feel my fierce anger until I have finished taking revenge. Then you will know that I, the LORD, was furious because of your disobedience. Every passerby will laugh at your destruction. Foreign nations will insult you and make fun of you, but they will also be shocked and terrified at what I did in my anger. I will destroy your crops until you starve to death, and disasters will strike you like arrows. Starvation and wild animals will kill your children. I'll punish you with horrible diseases, and your enemies will strike you down with their swords. I, the LORD, have spoken. (Ezekiel 5:5-17, CEV) Note that despite being a chosen people, God said all these terrible things about Israel. He also said that later, when they realize their contemptible state, "they will realize that they disgraced me" and "will hate themselves for the evil things they did" (Ezekiel 6:9, CEV) Despite Israel being a chosen people, God promised that they would be "killed by enemy troops, or they will die from starvation and disease." (Ezekiel 6:11, CEV) "The LORD God said: Ezekiel, son of man, tell the people of Israel that I am saying: Israel will soon come to an end! Your whole country is about to be destroyed as punishment for your disgusting sins. I, the LORD, am so angry that I will show no pity. I will punish you for the evil you've done, and you will know that I am the LORD. There's never been anything like the coming disaster. And when it comes, your life will be over. You people of Israel are doomed! Soon there will be panic on the mountaintops instead of celebration. I will let loose my anger and punish you for the evil things you've done. You'll get what you deserve. Your sins are so terrible, that you'll get no mercy from me. Then you will know that I, the LORD, have punished you. Disaster is near! Injustice and arrogance are everywhere, and

And behold, their prayers were also in behalf of him that the Lord should suffer to bring these things forth. And no one need say they shall not come, for they surely shall, for the Lord hath spoken it; for out of the earth shall they come, by the hand of the Lord, and none can stay it; and it shall come in a day when it shall be said that miracles are done away; and it shall come even as if one should speak from the dead. And it shall come in a day when the blood of saints shall cry unto the Lord, because of secret combinations and the works of darkness. Yea, it shall come in a day when the power of God shall be denied, and churches become defiled and be lifted up in the pride of their hearts; yea, even in a day when leaders of churches and teachers shall rise in the pride of their hearts, even to the envying of them who belong to their churches. Yea, it shall come in a day when there shall be heard of fires, and tempests, and vapors of smoke in foreign lands; And there shall also be heard of wars, rumors of wars, and earthquakes in divers places. Yea, it shall come in a day

---

violent criminals run free. None of you will survive the disaster, and everything you own and value will be shattered. The time is coming when everyone will be ruined. Buying and selling will stop, and people who sell property will never get it back, because all of you must be punished for your sins. And I won't change my mind! A signal has been blown on the trumpet, and weapons are prepared for battle. But no one goes to war, because in my anger I will strike down everyone in Israel. The LORD said to the people of Israel: War, disease, and starvation are everywhere! People who live in the countryside will be killed in battle, and those who live in towns will die from starvation or deadly diseases. Anyone who survives will escape into the hills, like doves who leave the valleys to find safety. All of you will moan because of your sins. Your hands will tremble, and your knees go limp. You will put on sackcloth to show your sorrow, but terror will overpower you. Shame will be written all over your faces, and you will shave your heads in despair. Your silver and gold will be thrown into the streets like garbage, because those are the two things that led you into sin, and now they cannot save you from my anger. They are not even worth enough to buy food. You took great pride in using your beautiful jewelry to make disgusting idols of foreign gods. So I will make your jewelry worthless. Wicked foreigners will rob and disgrace you. They will break into my temple and leave it unfit as a place to worship me, but I will look away and let it happen. Your whole country is in confusion! Murder and violence are everywhere in Israel, so I will tell the most wicked nations to come and take over your homes. They will put an end to the pride you have in your strong army, and they will make your places of worship unfit to use. You will be terrified and will desperately look for peace—but there will be no peace. One tragedy will follow another, and you'll hear only bad news. People will beg prophets to give them a message from me. Priests will stop teaching my Law, and wise leaders won't be able to give advice. Even your king and his officials will lose hope and cry in despair. Your hands will tremble with fear. I will punish you for your sins and treat you the same way you have treated others. Then you will know that I am the LORD. (Ezekiel 7, CEV)

when there shall be great pollutions upon the face of the earth; there shall be murders, and robbing, and lying, and deceivings, and whoredoms, and all manner of abominations; when there shall be many who will say, Do this, or do that, and it mattereth not, for the Lord will uphold such at the last day. But wo unto such, for they are in the gall of bitterness and in the bonds of iniquity. Yea, it shall come in a day when there shall be churches built up that shall say: Come unto me, and for your money you shall be forgiven of your sins. O ye wicked and perverse and stiffnecked people, why have ye built up churches unto yourselves to get gain? Why have ye transfigured the holy word of God, that ye might bring damnation upon your souls? Behold, look ye unto the revelations of God; for behold, the time cometh at that day when all these things must be fulfilled. Behold, the Lord hath shown unto me great and marvelous things concerning that which must shortly come, at that day when these things shall come forth among you. Behold, I speak unto you as if ye were present, and yet ye are not. But behold, Jesus Christ hath shown you unto me, and I know your doing. And I know that ye do walk in the pride of your hearts; and there are none save a few only who do not lift themselves up in the pride of their hearts, unto the wearing of very fine apparel, unto envying, and strifes, and malice, and persecutions, and all manner of iniquities; and your churches, yea, even every one, have become polluted because of the pride of your hearts. For behold, ye do love money, and your substance, and your fine apparel, and the adorning of your churches, more than ye love the poor and the needy, the sick and the afflicted. O ye pollutions, ye hypocrites, ye teachers, who sell yourselves for that which will canker, why have ye polluted the holy church of God? Why are ye ashamed to take upon you the name of Christ? Why do ye not think that greater is the value of an endless happiness than that misery which never dies—because of the praise of the world? Why do ye adorn yourselves with that which hath no life, and yet suffer the hungry, and the needy, and the naked, and the sick and the afflicted to pass by you, and notice them not? Yea, why do ye build up your secret abominations to get gain, and cause that widows should mourn before the Lord, and also orphans to mourn before the Lord, and also the blood of their fathers and their husbands to cry unto the Lord from the ground, for vengeance upon your heads? Behold, the sword of vengeance hangeth over you; and the time soon cometh that he avengeth the blood of the saints upon you, for he will not suffer their cries any longer. (Mormon 8:25-41.)

Prophets have described our day with precise clarity, and yet we ignore their call to repentance. We are surrounded by plain and abundant evidence that we are repeating the sins of the Pharisees, but we ignore it. We do so at the peril of our physical and spiritual wellbeing.

Similar to the claims of modern Mormons, the Jews believe that the rabbis today have authority from an unbroken line of rabbis going back to the establishment of the Pharisees. They have an unbroken line of authorized appointments from the Sanhedrin of Jesus' day until today. They believe that their council has authority from Moses, given to Moses from God. Yet, their teachings contradict Moses on almost every issue. In Hebrew, Matthew 23:2-3 says something very different from the KJV (which is based on a later Greek text):

> The Pharisees and sages sit upon the seat of Moses. Therefore, all that he [Moses] says to you, diligently do, but according to their reforms and their precedents do not do, because they [teach what they call God's word] but they do not do [what Moses said].

The brethren sit in Joseph's seat. They invoke Joseph's authority, but teach innovations and traditions that contradict Joseph's words. Therefore, do according to what Joseph taught, not what they teach.

Prophet: Title or Description?

Joseph Smith taught that the attainment of knowledge and intelligence in this life is a factor of the diligence and obedience exerted by the individual. He taught that blessings come commensurate with obedience to God's law.[274] In contrast to this idea there is a notion that the receipt of a church calling automatically entitles an individual to spiritual gifts not previously obtained. Members would like to think that church leaders either receive some special gift upon selection, or that God specifically chooses men for leadership callings who already possess certain spiritual gifts. Bruce R. McConkie taught that the former assertion is false:

> The idea is prevalent that with the call to the prophetic office comes an endowment of spiritual ability, understanding, and power that was not previously experienced and that exceeds that which is enjoyed generally by righteous men. Challenging that conclusion, Elder Bruce R. McConkie has written that a call to positions of leadership 'adds little knowledge or power of discernment to an individual, although every person called to a position in the Church does grow in grace, knowledge, and power by magnifying the calling given him.'(Joseph Fielding McConkie, "Seeking_the_Spirit," p. 33.)

The falseness of the second assertion is by the fact that, according to President Joseph F. Smith, apostles since Joseph Smith's death have been called by men and not by God.[275]

---

[274] "And if a person gains more knowledge and intelligence in this life through his diligence and obedience than another, he will have so much the advantage in the world to come. There is a law, irrevocably decreed in heaven before the foundations of this world, upon which all blessings are predicated—And when we obtain any blessing from God, it is by obedience to that law upon which it is predicated." (D&C 130:19-21.)

[275] Joseph F. Smith gave the following testimony under oath to Congress during the Reed Smoot hearings: "In the first place [the Apostles] were chosen by revelation. The council of the apostles have had a voice ever since in the selection of their successors....[They are] Chosen by the body, the twelve themselves, by and with the consent and approval of the first presidency." When asked if there was any revelation in regard to the subsequent ones he replied, "No, sir; it has been the choice of the body." The Senator then asked "Then the apostles are perpetuated in succession by their own act and the approval of the first presidency?" President Smith replied,

The Lord said that it is the duty for the President of the church to be a seer, a prophet, a translator, and a prophet, just like Moses.

> And again, the duty of the President of the office of the High Priesthood is to preside over the whole church, and to be like unto Moses—Behold, here is wisdom; yea, to be a seer, a revelator, a translator, and a prophet, having all the gifts of God which he bestows upon the head of the church....Wherefore, now let every man learn his duty, and to act in the office in which he is appointed, in all diligence. He that is slothful shall not be counted worthy to stand, and he that learns not his duty and shows himself not approved shall not be counted worthy to stand. Even so. Amen. (D&C 107:91-92,99-100.)

Note that God did *not* say that these gifts would be given automatically to the person deemed by the hierarchy to be the next president of the church (or, as the case may be, the next apostle). He said it was the duty of the individual thus selected to obtain those gifts. This is a description of a responsibility to obtain, not of a gift bestowed.

Though God charges the president of the church to *become* a prophet, seer, and revelator, and though history suggests the wisdom in voting for a man who already possesses these gifts, the concept that a man will be given the gifts of prophecy, seership, and revelation simply because he is ordained president of the church is not supported in scripture or history.

Brigham Young distinguished between the right to administer the church and the ability to obtain God's word:

> Perhaps it may make some of you stumble, were I to ask you a question—Does a man's being a Prophet in this Church prove that he shall be the President of it? I answer, no! A man may be a Prophet, Seer, and Revelator, and it may have nothing to do with his being the President of the Church. Suffice it to say, that Joseph was the President of the Church, as long as he lived: the people chose to have it so. He always filled that responsible station, by the voice of the people. Can you find any appointing him the President of the Church? The keys of the Priesthood were committed to Joseph, to build up the Kingdom of God on the earth, and were not to be taken from him in time or in eternity; but when he was called to preside over the Church, it was by the voice of the people; though he held the keys of the Priesthood, independent of their voice. (Brigham Young, JD 1:133.)

"That is right." The inescapable conclusion is that either the apostles (and subsequently, the church president) are not chosen by revelation, or a church president lied while under oath to Congress.

A seer is someone to whom God communicates through the use of "Urim and Thummim"—physical media into which a seer gazes. [276] Urim and Thummim can mean the specific glasses used by Joseph Smith and ancient seers, but properly refers more generally to other objects used for the same purpose, such as Joseph's seer stones and Joseph of Egypt's goblet. Joseph Smith used both the Urim and Thummim and several seer stones. Though the church possesses several of Joseph Smith's seer stones, none have been used since his death. [277] Orson Pratt lamented the lack of the gift of seership in post-Joseph church leaders:

> This failure to realize all the blessings and powers of the Priesthood does not apply to the elders and lesser Priesthood only; but it applies to the higher quorums, and comes home to ourselves, who are Apostles of Jesus Christ. We are presented before the Church, and sustained as prophets, seers and revelators, and we have received oftentimes the gift of prophecy and revelation, and have received many great and glorious gifts. But have we received the fullness of the blessings to which we are entitled? No, we have not. Who, among the Apostles have become seers, and enjoy all the gifts and powers pertaining to that calling? (Orson Pratt, JD 25:145.)

Joseph Smith taught that "a prophet is a prophet only when he was acting as such." (Joseph Smith, DHC-5: 265.) In other words, one who prophesies can be called a prophet. One who does not, cannot. There is no such thing as a true prophet who does not prophecy. "There is no calling of God to man on earth but what brings with it the evidences of its authenticity." (Brigham Young, JD 9:27.)

Do our leaders receive prophecy or receive revelation? Joseph F. Smith stated:

> I have never pretended nor do I profess to have received revelations. I never said I had a revelation except so far as God has shown to me

---

[276] "And now he translated them by the means of those two stones which were fastened into the two rims of a bow. Now these things were prepared from the beginning, and were handed down from generation to generation, for the purpose of interpreting languages; And they have been kept and preserved by the hand of the Lord, that he should discover to every creature who should possess the land the iniquities and abominations of his people; And whosoever has these things is called seer, after the manner of old times." (Mosiah 28:13-16.)

[277] First Presidency counselor Hugh B. Brown stated, "I do not know of any Urim and Thummim used in the Church today." (Oct. 10, 1969, University of Utah Institute of Religion) Modern Mormonism has fulfilled Isaiah's prophecy: "Jehovah has poured out on you a spirit of deep sleep: he has shut your eyes, the prophets; he has covered your heads, the seers." (Isaiah 29:10, Gileadi Translation.)

that so called Mormonism is God's divine truth; that is all. (Reed Smoot Hearings Vol.1, p. 483, 1904.)

But is President Joseph F. Smith's experience general among church leaders? There have been four canonized revelations to the successors of Joseph Smith: D&C 136, D&C 138, and Official Declarations 1 and 2. Brigham Young received D&C 136 on Jan. 14, 1847, nearly a year before he was sustained as President of the Church on Dec 27th, 1847. According to church doctrine, he did not have the authority to receive revelation for the church at the time. D&C 138 was received by Joseph F. Smith on October 3rd, 1918. He read the words in the section as a conference talk the next day. A few weeks later, it was "accepted" by his counselors, the Twelve, and the Patriarch. However, the section was not sustained by the church for another 57 years. The first official declaration is the manifesto of Wilford Woodruff, which was meant as a deceitful appeasement to the U.S. government, as it did not actually end plural marriage.[278] The second official declaration is a report of President Kimball lifting the priesthood ban. Most members assume that President Kimball received a revelation where God stated to lift the ban. Instead, President Kimball decided to lift the ban, and prayed that God would speak to him if that was not his will.[279] In absence of a message from God, he lifted the ban.[280] The claim of only four revelations over more than 150 years does not make a strong case for the persistence of modern prophecy. The substance and circumstances of the four revelations weaken the argument further. More than half the current church membership has joined or been born since 1978, meaning that, even if the lifting of the priesthood ban was a bona fide revelation, most modern Mormons find themselves in the awkward position of preaching the need for modern revelation without ever having witnessed an example of it.

---

[278] This issue is discussed further in the chapter entitled "Church History."

[279] "He had reached a decision after great struggle, and he wanted the Lord's confirmation, if it would come. They surrounded the altar in a prayer circle. President Kimball told the Lord at length that if extending the priesthood was not right, if the Lord did not want this change to come in the Church, he would fight the world's opposition." (Spencer W. Kimball and the Revelation on the Priesthood, BYU Studies 47:2 (2008) pp. 54-56.)

[280] It is ironic that most members view the 1978 declaration to be a witness that God speaks through the president of the church. In reality, this was one of the most auspicious occasions of God *not* having spoken to the president of the church, as it is hard to imagine a situation more worthy of his interest. Most members realize that presidents of the church for many decades had debated the cessation of the priesthood ban. Where they err is in their estimation that President Kimball differed from his predecessors in that he received an answer from God. In reality, the only difference between President Kimball and his predecessors was that, while they were not willing to remove the ban without God's voice on the matter, he was.

For fear of the implications, Modern Mormons rationalize away the lack of revelation by redefining the term to mean emotional impressions, supposing that the same God who dictated hundreds of pages written of revelation in less than 20 years of Joseph's ministry now only communicates through feelings. The brethren do not think "something is wrong with or lacking in [them]" if "they do not receive frequent, miraculous, or strong" revelations from God. In fact, expecting such is "look[ing] beyond the mark." Instead, it is "quite normal" to only experience God's "customary pattern" of communication as "small an incremental impressions…over time."[281] These are not revelations, but opinions. Joseph Smith taught of opinions:

> We all form opinions on spiritual matters. Every man has a right to believe whatever his conscience will bear; but, we must seek that straight and narrow path which leads into the kingdom of God and offers the opportunity to be resurrected in the celestial glory. 'Because strait is the gate, and narrow is the way, which leadeth unto life, and few there be that find it.' (Matthew 7) Opinions, where we have the word of the Lord, are worth nothing. Since the days of the Savior, they have strangely divided men into almost as many sects, as the number of the name of the beast that John saw. All men have a right to their opinions, but to adopt them for rules of faith and worship, is wrong, and may finally leave the souls of them that receive them for spiritual guides, in the telestial kingdom. (Evening and Morning Star, Vol. 1, p. 69.)

In the lack of prophecy from leaders today, we see the fulfillment of this prophecy from Isaiah:

> All you wild beasts, you animals of the forest, come and devour! Their watchmen are altogether blind and unaware; all of them are but dumb watchdogs unable to bark, lolling seers fond of slumber.

---

[281] "We as members of the Church tend to emphasize marvelous and dramatic spiritual manifestations so much that we may fail to appreciate and may even overlook the customary pattern by which the Holy Ghost accomplishes His work. The very 'simpleness of the way' (1 Nephi 17:41) of receiving small and incremental spiritual impressions that over time and in totality constitute a desired answer or the direction we need may cause us to look 'beyond the mark' (Jacob 4:14). I have talked with many individuals who question the strength of their personal testimony and underestimate their spiritual capacity because they do not receive frequent, miraculous, or strong impressions. Perhaps as we consider the experiences of Joseph in the Sacred Grove, of Saul on the road to Damascus, and of Alma the Younger, we come to believe something is wrong with or lacking in us if we fall short in our lives of these well-known and spiritually striking examples. If you have had similar thoughts or doubts, please know that you are quite normal." (Elder David A. Bednar, "The Spirit of Revelation," April 2011 General Conference.)

Gluttonous dogs, and insatiable, such indeed are insensible shepherds. They are all diverted to their own way, every one after his own advantage. Come, they say, let us get wine and have our fill of liquor. For tomorrow will be like today, only far better! (Isaiah 56:9-12, Gileadi Translation.)

Modern Mormons would here object by claiming that everything church leaders say is revelation from God. It is a mistake to assume this. The Lord said that the words of leaders are only his word when given by the Holy Ghost:

> And this is the ensample unto them, that they shall speak as they are moved upon by the Holy Ghost. And whatsoever they shall speak when moved upon by the Holy Ghost shall be scripture, shall be the will of the Lord, shall be the mind of the Lord, shall be the word of the Lord, shall be the voice of the Lord, and the power of God unto salvation. (D&C 68:3-4.)

That this is not always the case is readily apparent. President Harold B. Lee said,

> It is not to be thought that every word spoken by the General Authorities is inspired, or that they are moved upon by the Holy Ghost in everything they write. (Harold B. Lee, "Stand Ye In Holy Places" p. 162-163.)

Elder B.H. Roberts taught similarly:

> Sometimes, the servants of God stand on planes infinitely lower than the one here described. Sometimes they speak merely from their human knowledge, influenced by passions; influenced by the interests of men, and by anger, and vexation, and all those things that surge in upon the minds of even servants of God. When they so speak, then that is not Scripture, that is not the word of God, nor the power of God unto salvation; but when they speak as moved upon by the Holy Ghost, their voice then becomes the voice of God. So that men, even some of high station in the Church, sometimes speak from merely human wisdom; or from prejudice or passion; and when they do so, that is not likely to be the word of God....In any event it must be allowed by us that many unwise things were said in times past, even by prominent elders of the Church; things that were not in harmony with the doctrines of the Church; and that did not possess the value of Scripture, or anything like it; and it was not revelation. (B.H. Roberts, "Defense of the Faith and the Saints" [Salt Lake City: Deseret News Press, 1912], 2:455-61.)

Some claim that impressions are the same as revelation.[282] Modern Mormon leaders consider any impression they receive to be just as good as God's transcribable voice:

> Most of the revelation that comes to leaders and members of the Church comes by the 'still small voice' or by a feeling rather than by a vision or a voice that speaks specific words to our hearing. (Dallin Oaks, "In His Own Time, in His Own Way," New Mission Presidents' Seminar, June 27, 2001.)

Yet, President Joseph F. Smith would not consider Elder Oaks' experiences as revelation:

> ...I am susceptible, I think, of the impressions of the spirit of the Lord upon my mind at any time, just as any good Methodist or any other good church member might be. And so far as that is concerned, I say yes; I have had impressions of the spirit upon my mind very frequently, but they are not revelations. (Reed Smoot Hearings Vol.1, p. 483, 1904.)

Promoting one's impressions to the status of revelation is indeed dangerous. Joseph Smith taught:

> ...nothing is a greater injury to the children of men than to be under the influence of a false spirit when they think they have the Spirit of God. Thousands have felt the influence of its terrible power and baneful effects. Long pilgramages have been undertaken, penances endured, and pain, misery and ruin have followed in their train; nations have been convulsed, kingdoms overthrown, provinces laid waste, and blood, carnage and desolation are habiliments in which it has been clothed. (Joseph Smith, TPJS 205.)

George Cannon said:

> There is one thing that we have all got to be very careful about, and that is this: I have seen Elders in my experience that when they got their own spirit moved very much they imagined that it was the Spirit of God, and it was difficult in some instances to tell the difference between the suggestions of their own spirit and the voice of the spirit of God. This is a gift of itself, to be able to distinguish that which suggests itself to our own hearts and that which comes from God. (George Q Cannon JD 22:104.)

What are the implications of no revelation among leaders of the church after Joseph Smith? Joseph said,

---

[282] See "Revelation" chapter for more on this topic.

All men are liars who say they are of the true Church without the revelations of Jesus Christ and the Priesthood of Melchizedek, which is after the order of the Son of God. (Joseph Smith, TPJS, p. 375-376.)

Orson Pratt said about revelation:

In all ages and dispensations, when the Church of God has been on the earth, the gift of revelation has been one of the most important gifts of the Spirit. It is essential to the very existence of the Church; for without it, the Church would become as lifeless as the human body without food, drink, or air. As the mortal body would die and become disorganized without these necessary elements, so the body of Christ---the Church---would die, become disorganized, and cease to exist on the earth, if this essential spiritual gift were taken from it. The gift of revelation is the spiritual food, and drink, and the very life of the Church. Without it, God never has accepted nor ever will recognize any Church, as His own, in any age or generation, or among any people, nation, or tongue. (Orson Pratt, "Spiritual Gifts".)

If God does not change, and the restoration's purpose was to bring Zion, and Zion is not yet here, shouldn't we expect just as many revelations today as in Joseph's day? Joseph described the reason for religious leaders' lack of revelation:

What is the reason that the Priests of the day do not get revelation? They ask only to consume it upon their lusts. Their hearts are corrupt, and they cloak their iniquity by saying there are no more revelations. But if any revelations are given of God, they are universally opposed by the priests and Christendom at large; for they reveal their wickedness and abominations. (Joseph Smith, April 10, 1842. DHC 4:588.)

What about visions? God said "If there be a prophet among you, I the Lord will make myself known unto him in a vision, and will speak unto him in a dream." (Numbers 12:6.) Sidney Rigdon preached that visions were "one of the most important parts (of the Spirit's work) in the salvation of men." He said it was a necessary quality of any people of God, and that the lack thereof always signaled apostasy from God:

There is no society of which we have an account in the revelations of God, that he acknowledged as his own, except they had visions among them, and that as long as they continued to walk according to the directions of the Holy Spirit...We readily admit that a corrupt religion can exist, and false prophecies exist, and sectarian dogmas abound; men-made worshipers increase, and the world abound in a religion that the Lord was not the author of, and yet no visions be among them; but wherever the truth of heaven abounds, there will visions abound also; for it is a part of heaven's scheme to save men, and without it, we are not authorized to say there is salvation (Sidney Rigdon, "Faith of the Church," Latter Day Saints' Messenger and Advocate 1:9.)

Lehi, Ezekiel, Isaiah, and other prophets of the scriptures were capable of teaching others how to come back into the presence of God because they had been there themselves and thus knew the way. In Lehi's vision of the tree of life, it is not until after he reaches the tree of life that he attempts to lead his family there. Yet, none of Joseph's successors have publicly claimed to have been in the Lord's presence (see "Witnesses"). For instance, Brigham Young said:

> I have flattered myself, if I am as faithful as I know how to be to my God, and my brethren, and to all my covenants, and faithful in the discharge of my duty, when I have lived to be as old as was Moses when the Lord appeared to him, that perhaps I then may hold communion with the Lord, as did Moses [it was believed Moses spoke to God face-to-face at age 80]...I am not now in that position, though I know much more than I did twenty, ten, of five years ago...If I am faithful until I am eighty years of age, perhaps the Lord will appear to me and personally dictate me in the management of his Church and people. (JD 7:243.)

Leaders' lack of obtaining God's presence does not imply that being in God's presence is not important, as certain leaders have recently taught. God does not change. If it was important for men to be restored into God's presence in the scriptures and during Joseph's life, it is important now. Instead, the lack of experience in these men is a witness that they do not know the way.

> And by this you may know they are under the bondage of sin, because they come not unto me. For whoso cometh not unto me is under the bondage of sin. And whoso receiveth not my voice is not acquainted with my voice, and is not of me. And by this you may know the righteous from the wicked, and that the whole world groaneth under sin and darkness even now. (D&C 84:50-53.)

Modern Mormons follow men who purport to lead them to a place they have never been themselves.

> O ye wicked and ye perverse generation; ye hardened and ye stiffnecked people, how long will ye suppose that the Lord will suffer you? Yea, how long will ye suffer yourselves to be led by foolish and

blind guides? Yea, how long will ye choose darkness rather than light? (Helaman 13:29.)

What is a blind guide, if not he who has never been to where he claims to lead others? There is only one outcome for blind leaders and their followers.

> Then came his disciples, and said unto him, Knowest thou that the Pharisees were offended, after they heard this saying? But he answered and said, Every plant, which my heavenly Father hath not planted, shall be rooted up. Let them alone: they be blind leaders of the blind. And if the blind lead the blind, both shall fall into the ditch. (Matthew 15:12-14.)

Our present condition is well described by the prophets of the Old Testament. Isaiah 59 describes in detail the reasons why a people would cease to receive institutional revelation. Isaiah proclaims, "surely Jehovah's hand has not become too short to save, nor his ear dull of hearing!" No, it is not a changing God that has caused the silence, but a rebellious people. Isaiah says that it is our iniquities that have caused God to stop speaking to us. He says our "palms are defiled with blood" because we do works of evil. Our "lips speak guile" and our "tongue utters duplicity." Instead of preaching the gospel, we repeat platitudes and self-praise. We "rely on empty words, deceitfully spoken." These empty teachings are like "vipers' eggs and...spiders' webs" that bear no fruit and do not stand up to investigation: "whoever eats of their eggs dies, and if any is smashed, there emerges a serpent." The teachings are hypocritical, preaching one thing and doing another "their cobwebs are useless as clothing; their fabrications are worthless for covering themselves." "Their works consist of wrongdoing; they manipulate injurious dealings." They have modified God's word and therefore do not encounter God's peace: "willfully denying Jehovah, backing away from following our God." "They have made crooked their paths; none who treads them knows peace." Having abandoned God's word, we are left with ignorance and the consequences thereof: "havoc and disaster follow in their wake....They are unacquainted with the way of perfection; integrity is not within their bounds. We look for light, but there prevails darkness; for a glimmer of hope, but we walk amid gloom." In place of wisdom we receive the philosophies of men. "We grope along the borders like the blind; we flounder like those without eyes. We stumble at noon as in the dark of night; in the prime of life we resemble the dead." Instead of all this, we ought to be fighting for the cause of the poor and the oppressed: "None call for righteousness; no one sues for an honest cause."

In Amos 8 we find another apt description of our present situation:

> Behold, the days come, saith the Lord God, that I will send a famine in the land, not a famine of bread, nor a thirst for water, but of

> hearing the words of the Lord: And they shall wander from sea to sea, and from the north even to the east, they shall run to and fro to seek the word of the Lord, and shall not find it. In that day shall the fair virgins and young men faint for thirst. (Amos 8:11-13.)

Not only do we find ourselves in a famine of the word of God, but the damage from the want of revelation seems disproportionately levied against our "fair virgins and young men." Tech-savvy youth, who are more likely to find historical misrepresentations and fabrications, are among those leaving the church in highest numbers, with many losing all faith in God through having lost all faith in the church.

Throughout history, God's silence has been interpreted as divine disfavor—an invitation to repent and request forgiveness in order to restore communication from heaven. The scriptures are replete with examples of people who, finding themselves in heavenly silence, assumed they had retained their standing with God, forcing the promotion of their own thoughts as God's word in order to cover the consequence of their sins. In reality, the obvious thing to do was and is to ask God why he has asked speaking, with the assumption that something is gravely wrong. Instead, "the people do not turn back to him who smites them, nor will they inquire of Jehovah of Hosts." The penalty is that God ratifies his separation from the leaders:

> Therefore Jehovah will cut off from Israel head and tail, palm top and reed, in a single day; the elders or notables are the head, the prophets who teach falsehoods, the tail. The leaders of these people have misled them, and those who are led are confused. (Isaiah 9:13-16, Gileadi Translation.)

Brigham Young erroneously taught that God's silence in response to a question is not a sign of divine disfavor, but a witness that he trusts and will own any decision you make without his word.

> If I do not know the will of my Father, and what He requires of me in a certain transaction, if I ask Him to give me wisdom concerning any requirement in my life, or in regard to my own course, or that of my friends, my family, my children, or those that I preside over, and get no answer from Him, and then do the very best that my judgement will teach me, He is bound to own and honor that transaction, and He will do so to all intents and purposes. (Brigham Young, JD 3:205.)

Unfortunately, this principle guides those in the leading councils of the church today.

What about those times when we seek revelation and do not receive it? We do not always receive inspiration or revelation when we request it. Sometimes we are delayed in the receipt of revelation, and sometimes we are left to our own judgment. We cannot force spiritual things....Even in decisions we think very important, we sometimes receive no answers to our prayers. This does not mean that our prayers have not been heard. It only means that we have prayed about a decision which, for one reason or another, we should make without guidance by revelation. (Oaks, "Revelation", Sep 29, 1981 BYU devotional)

We should study things out in our minds, using the reasoning powers our Creator has placed within us. Then we should pray for guidance and act upon it if we receive it, and upon our best judgment if we do not. (Dallin Oaks, "Our Strengths Can Become Our Downfall," BYU Speeches June 7, 1992.)

The Doctrine and Covenants demonstrates that questions of church administration occur with regularity. In the absence of revelation, the ideas of the leaders, usually with debate, are substituted as the word and will of God. First Presidency councilor Hugh B. Brown described how decisions are made by the brethren:

When a question arises today, we work over the details and come up with an idea. It is submitted to the First Presidency and Twelve, thrashed out, discussed and rediscussed until it seems right. Then, kneeling together in a circle in the temple, they seek divine guidance and the president says, 'I feel to say this is the will of the Lord.' That becomes a revelation. It is usually not thought necessary to publish or proclaim it as such, but this is the way it happens. (Hugh B. Brown, quoted in: Firmage, "An Abundant Life", p. 125.)

Feelings are used as if they were God's voice. They need not be particularly notable feelings, just impressions or hunches.[283] This is seen as just as valid as the actual voice of God. When God speaking is seen as a rare occurrence,[284]

---

[283] "I have met persons who told me they have never had a witness from the Holy Ghost because they have never felt their bosom 'burn within' them. What does a 'burning in the bosom' mean? Does it need to be a feeling of caloric heat, like the burning produced by combustion? If that is the meaning, then I have never had a burning in the bosom." (Elder Oaks, "Teaching and Learning by the Spirit," Ensign, March 1997.)

[284] "Some have been misled by expecting revelations too frequently. I have learned that strong, impressive spiritual experiences do not come to us very frequently. Revelations from God—the teachings and directions of the Spirit—are not constant. We believe in continuing revelation, not continuous revelation. We are often left to

and when leaders don't think they need much revelation,[285] deviate from God's gospel[286] is certain to follow; "without [revelation] we can neither know nor understand anything of God." (TPJS, p. 205)

The understanding that the lack of revelation is a signal that God desires you to act on your own creates the perfect environment for deviating from God's will and from God's word as already received. This is the exact environment that enabled the great apostasy: men refusing to heed the revelations that had already been received, thinking they understood more about God than those preceding men who actually spoke with him. Seeking to obtain revelation to support a system that deviates from what God has already revealed will never lead to God speaking.

> What is the reason that Priests of the day do not get revelation? They ask only to consume it upon their lusts. Their hearts are corrupt, and they cloak their iniquity by saying there are no more revelations. But if any revelations are given of God, they are universally opposed by the priests and Christendom at large; for they reveal their wickedness and abominations. (Joseph Smith, TPJS 217.)

No man is entitled to fabricate God's word in the absence of his giving it:

> Everything that God gives us is lawful and right; and it is proper that we should enjoy His gifts and blessings whenever and wherever He is disposed to bestow; but if we should seize upon those same blessings and enjoyments without law, without revelation, without commandment, those blessings and enjoyments would prove

---

work out problems without the dictation or specific direction of the Spirit. That is part of the experience we must have in mortality. The people I have found most confused in this Church are those who seek personal revelations on everything." (Elder Packer, "Teaching and Learning by the Spirit," Ensign, March 1997.)

[285] "Let me say first that we have a great body of revelation, the vast majority of which came from the prophet Joseph Smith. We don't need much revelation. We need to pay more attention to the revelation we've already received." (President Gordon B. Hinckley, "Sunday Interview—Musings of the Main Mormon," Don Lattin, Chronicle Religion Writer, April 13, 1997.) It is interesting that President Hinckley stated that the lack of revelation was due to the preeminence of Joseph Smith's revelations given how often the church has contradicted them without claiming new revelation (see "The Preeminence of Joseph Smith's Teachings").

[286] "What constitutes the kingdom of God? Where there is a prophet, a priest, or a righteous man unto whom God gives His oracles, there is the kingdom of God; and where the oracles of God are not, there the kingdom of God is not....The plea of many in this day is, that we have no right to receive revelations; but if we do not get revelations, we do not have the oracles of God; and if they have not the oracles of God, they are not the people of God." (Joseph Smith, TPJS, p. 272)

cursings and vexations in the end, and we should have to lie down in sorrow and wailings of everlasting regret. (Joseph Smith, TPJS, p. 256.)

The results of acting under the auspices of God's command without his having spoken are demonstrated in 1 Samuel 13. Here, king Saul—distressed with many Philistine armies threatening his meager forces—called for Samuel, who said he would come in 7 days, but didn't. With his army deserting, Saul offered a burnt offering himself. Samuel announced that God would remove the kingdom from Saul as a result (see 1 Samuel 13).

Modern Mormonism offers many examples of acting without God's word. The first occurred during the succession crisis. Without acknowledging the possibility of Joseph's death as a sign of divine disapproval, the Saints assumed that one of the several leaders campaigning to take over church leadership was divinely appointed to do so. Instead of inquiring of the Lord on the topic, they listened to speeches from each candidate and then took a vote, with the Quorum of the Twelve winning a majority. Since then, history provides a constant chain of decisions and changes made by man's judgment without God's word on the matter.

Because God's word is not being dispensed, those in leadership must claim some other mechanism for the authority of their words. Nephi, foreseeing this, explained it as follows:

> For it shall come to pass in that day that the churches which are built up, and not unto the Lord, when the one shall say unto the other: Behold, I, I am the Lord's...and their priests shall...teach with their learning, and deny the Holy Ghost, which giveth utterance. And they deny the power of God, the Holy One of Israel; and they say unto the people: Hearken unto us, and hear ye our precept; for behold there is no God today, for the Lord and the Redeemer hath done his work, and he hath given his power unto men; Behold, hearken ye unto my precept...Yea, and there shall be many which shall teach after this manner, false and vain and foolish doctrines....Yea, they have all gone out of the way; they have become corrupted. (2 Nephi 28:3-11.)

Today we see the claim to authority in terms of claims to keys or callings or unanimity of those in callings. One way church leaders justify making decisions without God's word is through the understanding that God has given his authority to them to act without his speaking to them. In other words, "and the Redeemer hath done his work, and he hath given his power unto men; Behold, hearken ye unto my precept." (2 Nephi 28:5-6.) The leaders refer to this paradigm with a repurposed term from the scriptures: "keys."[287]

> The divine nature of the limitations put upon the exercise of priesthood keys explains an essential contrast between decisions on matters of Church administration and decisions affecting the priesthood. The First Presidency and the Council of the First Presidency and Quorum of the Twelve, who preside over the Church, are empowered to make many decisions affecting Church policies and procedures—matters such as the location of Church buildings and the ages for missionary service. (Dallin Oaks, April 2014 General Conference.)

Not even one true messenger in the scriptures ever claimed keys as a source of their authority. For example, Jesus came without any pretense to church calling or keys. Instead, when given the opportunity, he listed examples of miracles performed as evidence of his divine role:

> Now when John had heard in the prison the works of Christ, he sent two of his disciples, And said unto him, Art thou he that should come, or do we look for another? Jesus answered and said unto them, Go and shew John again those things which ye do hear and see: The blind receive their sight, and the lame walk, the lepers are cleansed, and the deaf hear, the dead are raised up, and the poor have the gospel preached to them. (Matthew 11:2-5.)

In modern Mormonism, keys are incorrectly taught as the catalyst of the great apostasy.[288] Less than 100 years ago, apostle James E. Talmage and others claimed that, instead, the great apostasy came not from the loss of ephemeral "keys," but because the ancient church supplanted scripture with council decisions and other worldly wisdom. The great apostasy was not the result of

---

[287] The choice of the word "keys" to convey the authority to make decisions in the absence of God's word is ironic, given that Joseph used the word to describe the right to obtain real revelation from God in response to questions posed by the bearer.
[288] "After the death of Jesus Christ, wicked people persecuted the Apostles and Church members and killed many of them. With the death of the Apostles, priesthood keys and the presiding priesthood authority were taken from the earth. The Apostles had kept the doctrines of the gospel pure and maintained the order and standard of worthiness for Church members. Without the Apostles, over time the doctrines were corrupted, and unauthorized changes were made in Church organization and priesthood ordinances, such as baptism and conferring the gift of the Holy Ghost. Without revelation and priesthood authority, people relied on human wisdom to interpret the scriptures and the principles and ordinances of the gospel of Jesus Christ. False ideas were taught as truth." ("Preach My Gospel," Lesson One.)

a loss of authority, but a loss of power. Ordinations still occurred. Offices continued. Vacancies were filled. However, even before the death of the apostles, the doctrine had become corrupted through the false teachings of duly appointed leaders (see "The Great Apostasy" by James Talmage).

The Catholics' claim to authority seems to be vindicated by history. They can trace their authority in an unbroken chain to a bishop who appears to have been legitimately ordained by the church established by Christ. Priesthood lineage is not enough. When the membership of the church appointed men to declare what was doctrine who trusted in their own wisdom rather than obtaining the word of God (or leaving the word of God as it has already been revealed), apostasy followed. These men conducted councils where they decided what doctrine was and wasn't with their own learning. It is likely that they may have prayed about things, but God did not give them his word. They were left to assume that their feelings and impressions were God's revelation to them. Yet—in a telltale sign of false revelation—councils were still necessary to settle the differing views. God's revelation is self-consistent. Arguments are not necessary when men are led by God's voice. Thus the church of God was severed from the true vine and became nothing more than a shadow of the philosophies of men mingled with scripture.

True messengers do not charge those they serve to follow them. They, like Nephi, teach their people to seek God's word—not theirs—in order to avoid being led astray:

> And I said unto them that it was the word of God; and whoso would hearken unto the word of God, and would hold fast unto it, they would never perish; neither could the temptations and the fiery darts of the adversary overpower them unto blindness, to lead them away to destruction. (1 Nephi 15:24.)

Confide in God, and do what he says. That will protect you from doctrines of devils and commandments of men:

> But ye are commanded in all things to ask of God, who giveth liberally; and that which the Spirit testifies unto you even so I would that ye should do in all holiness of heart, walking uprightly before me, considering the end of your salvation, doing all things with prayer and thanksgiving, that ye may not be seduced by evil spirits, or doctrines of devils, or the commandments of men; for some are of men, and others of devils. (D&C 46:7.)

If church leaders had the word of God, concepts proclaimed as essential for salvation by one leader would not be called unnecessary by another.[289] What one leader called immutable doctrine from God would not be dismissed by later leaders as policy. [290]

If church leaders had the word of God, quoting it would carry far more weight than justifying their decisions based on keys. Instead, keys are considered sufficient to promote leaders' opinions over scripture—the same mistake made by the church leaders that precipitated the great apostasy.

> ...never follow those who think they know more about how to administer the affairs of the Church than...the priesthood leaders who have the keys to preside... (M. Russell Ballard, October 2014 General Conference.)

Using this reasoning, a normal member citing revelation through Joseph Smith can be overruled by the contrary opinion of a leader simply by virtue of keys.

Another way church leaders justify making decisions without God's word is through promoting the unanimous decision of their councils to be equal to God's revealed word.[291] The church has repeatedly insisted that the

---

[289] For several decades, many leaders publicly preached that plural marriage was an essential ordinance required for exaltation. For example, Orson Pratt said that plural marriage was "an ordinance pertaining to this mortal life—to this world—this probation, just the same as baptism and the laying on of hands." (JD 17:229.)

[290] According to David O McKay's first presidency's official statement, the church's restriction on blacks receiving the priesthood "is not a matter of the declaration of policy but of direct commandment from the Lord." (Aug 17,1951, First Presidency statement) However, President McKay changed from his earlier position and that of his predecessors as early as 1954, and repeatedly after that, "There is no doctrine in this church and there never was a doctrine in this church to the effect that the Negroes are under any kind of a divine curse." He also said: "As a matter of fact, there is no doctrine in this church whatsoever that pertains to the Negroes." He also said: "It is a practice, not a doctrine and the practice will some day be changed. And that's all there is to it." ("Educator Cites McKay Statement of No Negro Bias in LDS Tenants", SL Tribune, Thursday, January 15, 1970) Today the church says the priesthood ban was a policy, controverting the first presidency letter of Aug 17, 1951: "In two speeches delivered before the Utah territorial legislature in January and February 1852, Brigham Young announced a *policy* restricting men of black African descent from priesthood ordination." ("Race and the Priesthood," https://www.lds.org/topics/race-and-the-priesthood, retrieved 7 Oct 2015.) Brigham Young elevated his own policy to a commandment from God, and temple blessings were withheld from approximately one third of the world's population because several subsequent presidents automatically considered it to be one, despite none of them having seen an actual revelation on the subject.

[291] "Doctrinal exposition may also come through the combined council of the First Presidency and Quorum of the Twelve Apostles (see, for example, Official Declaration 2). Council deliberations will often include a weighing of canonized

leading councils of the church have authority to "establish doctrine" without revelation.

> With divine inspiration, the First Presidency (the prophet and his two counselors) and the Quorum of the Twelve Apostles (the second-highest governing body of the Church) counsel together to establish doctrine that is consistently proclaimed in official Church publications. (Official Statement, The Church of Jesus Christ of Latter-day Saints, "Approaching Mormon Doctrine" May 4, 2007.)

> ...when the First Presidency and the Quorum of the Twelve speak with a united voice, it is the voice of the Lord for that time. (M. Russell Ballard, October 2014 General Conference.)

The church teaches that unanimity implies God's revealed will, as if a group of men couldn't agree without God's intervention:

> The calling of 15 men to the holy apostleship provides great protection for us as members of the Church. Why? Because decisions of these leaders must be unanimous.13 Can you imagine how the Spirit needs to move upon 15 men to bring about unanimity?... Trust me! These 15 men—prophets, seers, and revelators—know what the will of the Lord is when unanimity is reached! (Elder Russell M. Nelson, "Sustaining the Prophets," April 2014 General Conference.)

Unanimity does not equate to God's word. Consider how many times King Noah's priests were in unanimous support of Noah's wicked doctrines. Similarly, God's word can be spoken even if only one speaks it. Consider that Alma was right even though he was the only voice on the council of King Noah's priests.

What is quite remarkable about the assertion that unanimity equates God's word is the frequency with which the brethren are not unanimous, and can only gain unanimity through sideways means. The minutes of the meetings of the brethren reveal unexpected tactics to achieve "unanimity." These include dissenting members' abstinence from voting, sending dissenting members abroad, and exerting seniority in order to facilitate a unanimous vote.[292]

In any case, to assume that the prevailing opinion of a group of men mirrors God's will without his having spoken is to assume that the mind of

---

scriptures, the teachings of Church leaders, and past practice." (Elder D. Todd Christofferson, April 2012 General Conference.)

[292] D. Michael Quinn's book "Mormon Heirarchy: Extensions of Power" examines several case studies of disagreement in the Quorums of the Church, each heavily footnoted from the minutes of the meetings taken from the Church Archives.

man is equal to the mind of God, an assumption clearly disputed in scripture. Such an assumption guarantees that the laws of the church will follow the ever sliding moorings of society. Hence, that which is decided by a council of men in one generation will be replaced by that which is decided by a council of men in the next, with the small lag between the world's standards and the church's standards due to the previous generation status quo embedded in the aging brethren, rather than the undeviating standard of God's word.

Attributing to God what came from a committee or your own mind is taking strength unto yourself. This was prophesied to happen in the latter days in Jacob 5.

> And it came to pass that the servant said unto his master: Is it not the loftiness of thy vineyard? have not the branches thereof overcome the roots which are good? And because the branches have overcome the roots thereof, behold they grew faster than the strength of the roots, taking strength unto themselves. Behold, I say, is not this the cause that the trees of thy vineyard have become corrupted? (Jacob 5:48.)

Because we are "taught by the precepts of men," "in many instances" we err in doctrine. (2 Nephi 28:14.) To assume that God does not give revelation today like he always has is to deny the power of God and the gift of the Holy Ghost. To listen to men who claim they have the authority to declare the word of God without God speaking it to them is to hearken to the precepts of men. This is exactly what Nephi was talking about when he said,

> Yea, wo be unto him that hearkeneth unto the precepts of men, and denieth the power of God, and the gift of the Holy Ghost!....Cursed is he that putteth his trust in man, or maketh flesh his arm, or shall hearken unto the precepts of men, save their precepts shall be given by the power of the Holy Ghost. (2 Nephi 28:26,31.)

Without any new revelation, and with apparent disdain for the words of God through Joseph Smith, prescribed conferences and publications are filled instead with platitudes, gimmicks, and self-help advice. Recent conference talks feature less than 2 verses of scripture on average. Instead of turning to revelation, scripture, or the teachings of Joseph Smith, leaders instead quote each other in a reductive cycle.[293] This repetition, predicted by

---

[293] This seemingly inflammatory point is quickly affirmed by anyone who has read Ensigns more than a few decades old, or the Journal of Discourses. Historic context plots an unmistakable reduction in doctrine, a systemic dumbing down corresponding to the rise of correlation.

Isaiah,[294] is explained away by faithful members who notice it,[295] and actually celebrated by leaders:

> When the words of prophets seem repetitive, that should rivet our attention and fill our hearts with gratitude to live in such a blessed time. (Elder Henry B. Eyring, "Finding Safety in Counsel," April 1997 General Conference.)

How can we approach Zion if our current teachings have not brought us there, and our future teachings will simply repeat our current teachings? If "a man is saved no faster than he gets knowledge,"[296] as Joseph taught, how can we become saved if we receive less of God's worth with each passing generation of General Authorities, less versed in Joseph's doctrines and the scriptures than the last?

Though church leaders have made valiant public assertions of the independence of God's will from public opinion,[297] the LDS church has been

---

[294] The repetition of our leaders, the "drunkards of Ephraim," is a curse brought about by ceasing to heed the word of God through Joseph Smith, and instead substituting the philosophies of men mingled with scripture. "Woe to the garlands of glory of the drunkards of Ephraim! Their crowning splendor has become as fading wreaths on the heads of the opulent a overcome with wine. 7 These too have indulged in wine and are giddy with strong drink: priests and prophets have gone astray through liquor. They are intoxicated with wine and stagger because of strong drink; they err as seers, they blunder in their decisions. 8 For all tables are filled with vomit; no spot is without excrement. 9 Whom shall he give instruction? Whom shall he enlighten with revelation? Weanlings weaned from milk, 10 For it is but precept upon precept, precept upon precept, measure by measure, measure by measure; a trifle here, a trifle there. 11 Therefore, by incomprehensible speech and a strange tongue must he speak to these people, 12 to whom he said, This is rest; let the weary rest! This is a respite! But they would not listen. 13 So to them the word of Jehovah remained: Precept upon precept, precept upon precept, measure by measure, measure by measure; a trifle here, a trifle there, that, persisting, they might lapse into stumbling and break themselves, become ensnared and be taken captive." (Isaiah 28: 1,7-13, Gileadi Translation)

[295] Every active member has no doubt heard the opinion that and if people would actually listen and put into practice the things taught in conference, then we could move on to other messages.

[296] Joseph Smith, TPJS, p. 217.

[297] "It is impossible to stand upright when one plants his roots in the shifting sands of popular opinion and approval. Needed is the courage of a Daniel, an Abinadi, a Moroni, or a Joseph Smith in order for us to hold strong and fast to that which we know is right. They had the courage to do not that which was easy but that which was right. We will all face fear, experience ridicule, and meet opposition. Let us—all of us—have the courage to defy the consensus, the courage to stand for principle. Courage, not compromise, brings the smile of God's approval." (Pres. Thomas S, Monson, "Be Strong and of a Good Courage", April 2014 General Conference.)

heavily influenced by public opinion through surveys, focus groups, and outside public relations consulting for decades.[298] Many changes in the last few decades were catalyzed by public opinion polling, including the church's logo, the subtitle to the Book of Mormon, the "I'm a Mormon" campaign, the change of missionary age, and the decision to remain in the Boy Scouts despite the latter's pro-homosexual posture. Public opinion polling has catalyzed more than superficial changes. Societal pressure was the onus for the 1990 changes to the endowment ceremony[299] and the recent litany of concessions to feminist progressives.[300] This is not a new pattern, with history dotted with other similar examples such as the lifting of the priesthood ban, the repeated modifications to garments, and the cessation of plural marriage.[301] Most recently, the church has changed its position on homosexual marriage as a result of public opinion polling,[302] and continues to survey members to reflect changing sentiments in leaders' statements, doctrine, and policy.

The will of the Lord is not obtained through public polling or public relations consulting. Relying on PR firms and surveys as a surrogate for God's word is at least a partial fulfillment of scriptural prophecies that speak of

---

"…the Lord's truth is not altered by fads, popularity, or public opinion polls" (Elder David A. Bednar, April 2013 General Conference.) "The scribes and the Pharisees sit in Moses' seat: All therefore whatsoever they bid you observe, that observe and do; but do not ye after their works: for they say, and do not." (Matthew 23:2-3.) "For behold, have I testified against your law? Ye do not understand; ye say that I have spoken against your law; but I have not, but I have spoken in favor of your law, to your condemnation." (Alma 10:26)

[298] "The church has a very progressive research and information division, with tremendous public opinion surveyors. And the church is constantly running surveys, and employing consultants that do focus groups on a variety of topics, but especially on the ones that we are talking about right now, that are so sensitive to the faith of members." (Elder Marlin Jensen, Q&A at Utah State University)

[299] http://www.lds-mormon.com/whytemplechanges.shtml

[300] "LDS leaders are listening to women and responding. The recent changes you have seen, most notably the lowering of missionary age for sisters, serve as examples and were facilitated by the input of many extraordinary LDS women around the world." (LDS Church: Aims of 'Ordain Women' Detract from Dialogue, Deseret News 17 March 2014). These changes would include making the Relief Society broadcast into "women's conference," making "women's conference" the first session of General conference, and adding women to the governing councils of the church.

[301] "When we pursue any course which results in numerous letters being written to the Presidency critical of our work, it should be some evidence we should change our course." (Henry D. Moyle, second counselor in First Presidency, to J.D. Williams, January 9, 1963, Quoted in David O McKay and Rise of Modern Mormonism, p. 290.)

[302] http://imgur.com/a/RtLtB

relying on mystics, soothsayers, and spiritists—experts sought after in ancient days as a more accessible avenue of obtaining advice than inquiring of the Lord.[303] Just as ancient Israel relied on the arm of the flesh in the form of militarily mighty Egypt, the church is allying itself with the world—not only through the methods employed to survey the feelings of the people, but in the act of using popular will to supplant God's commandments.[304] What is right for God's people is given by his word, not the opinion of the people. The dispensation of God's word should not depend on whether a critical majority of church members will favorably accept it or not.[305] Moses did not dispatch Aaron to poll focus groups to see how they would react to the Ten Commandments, and once delivering them, he surely did not repeal them because the Canaanites found them offensive.

While some rightly point out that popularity with a fallen world can only be achieved by jettisoning foundational doctrines of the restoration,[306]

---

[303] "For you, O Jehovah, have forsaken your people, the house of Jacob, because, like the Philistines, they provide themselves with mystics from the East and are content with the infantile heathen. Their land is full of silver and gold and there is no end to their wealth; their land is full of horses and there is no end to their chariots. Their land is full of idols: Mankind is brought low when men thus debase themselves. Forbear them not!" (Isaiah 2:6-9, Gileadi Translation) "When men tell you to inquire of mediums and spiritists who huddle together and mutter, say to them, Should not a people inquire of their God? Should one inquire of the dead on behalf of the living for doctrine and for a testimony? Surely, while they utter such words devoid of light, they roam about embittered by hunger; and when they are hungry, they become enraged and, gazing upward, curse their king and their God. They will look to the land, but there shall be a depressing scene of anguish and gloom; and thus are they banished into outer darkness." (Isaiah 8:19-22, Gileadi Translation)

[304] "Woe to you, rebellious sons, says Jehovah, for drawing up plans, but not by me, for making alliances without my approval, only adding sin to sin! They are bent on going down to Egypt—but have not inquired at my mouth—on seeking protection in Pharaoh's forces, on taking shelter in Egypt's shadow. But Pharaoh's protection shall turn to your shame, shelter in Egypt's shadow to embarrassment." (Isaiah 30:1-3, Gileadi Translation)

"When you saw the city of David increasingly breached, you conserved water in the Lower Reservoir. You took a census of the buildings in Jerusalem, tearing down buildings to fortify your wall. You built cisterns between the walls for the water from the Old Reservoir, but you did not look to its Maker, nor have regard for the One who designed it long ago." (Isaiah 22:9-11, Gileadi Translation.)

[305] "Though hand join in hand, the wicked shall not be unpunished: but the seed of the righteous shall be delivered." (Proverbs 11:21.)

[306] "It has become somewhat of a commonplace to observe that modern Mormonism tends to reduce itself to another Protestant sect, another Christian heresy, while the religion of Joseph Smith, Brigham Young, Parley and Orson Pratt and other leading early Mormons was a far more radical swerve away from Protestant tradition."

some hail the lack of persecution in modern Mormonism as a blessing and a sign of divine favor.[307]

What is more important: the church's public image in a fallen society, or the transmission of saving (but unpopular) truths? Some would contend that popularity is necessary for preaching the gospel. Earlier church leaders would vehemently disagree.[308]

(Harold Bloom, The Annual David P. Gardner Lecture, Kingsbury Hall, University of Utah, November 15, 1990.)

"If the Latter-day Saints do not desist from running after the things of this world, and begin to reform and do the work the Father has given them to do, they will be found wanting, and they, too, will be swept away and counted as unprofitable servants" (Brigham Young, Journal of Discourses, 18:262).

"Our failure to be a "peculiar" people in maintaining our standards, despite the jeers and the criticisms of the crowd, will be our failure to be chosen for that calling to which we are called. The Lord has told us, 'Behold, there are many called, but few are chosen' (D&C 121:34), and then in the same revelation points out two reasons why men fail of their blessings. The first reason he gives is that their hearts are set so much upon the things of this world, and the second is that they aspire so much to the honors of men. So then as Church members let us beware lest we set our hearts upon the things of this world and lest we aspire so much to the honors of men that we compromise our standards. If we do so, we will be cut off in the Day of Judgment and will lose our blessings. Our reward for daring to live the gospel despite the oppositions from the outside world will be to have blessings added upon our heads forever and forever." (President Harold B. Lee, "Our Responsibility before God and Men," General Conference October 1945.)

[307] "Ours is the blessing to live in a better season [than the early saints]. The terrible persecutions of the past are behind us. Today we are looked upon with respect by people across the world." (Gordon B. Hinckley, Ensign, Conference Report, November, 1996.)

[308] "It always has been when a man was sent of god with the priesthood and he began to preach the fulness of the gospel. That he was thrust out by his friends, who are ready to butcher him if he teaches things which they imagine to be wrong: and Jesus was crucified upon this principal." (Joseph Smith, DHC 5:425.) "And when the spirit of persecution, the spirit of hatred, of wrath, and malice ceases in the world against this people, it will be the time that this people have apostatized and joined hands with the wicked, and never until then; which I pray may never come." (JD 4:326-327.) "There is nothing that would so soon weaken my hope and discourage me as to see this people in full fellowship with the world, and receive no more persecution from them because they are one with them. In such an event, we might bid farewell to the Holy Priesthood with all its blessings, privileges and aids to exaltations, principalities and powers in the eternities of the Gods." (Brigham Young, JD 10:32.)

"When we see the time that we can willingly strike hands and have full fellowship with those who despise the Kingdom of God, know ye then that the Priesthood of the Son of God is out of your possession. Let us be careful how we make friends with and fellowship unrighteousness, lest the curse of God descends heavily upon us." (Brigham Young, JD 10:273.) When "Mormonism" finds favor with the wicked

Since 1890, leaders have contorted doctrine, misrepresented history, and wrested scripture to whittle the peculiarity of the saints into something appeasing to ever-changing societal sensibilities. This continuing chain has been and will continue to be ineffective to stem the negative rewards of abandoning God's standards—like all deals with the devil, the outcome is never as rosy as promised.[309]

> O ye pollutions, ye hypocrites, ye teachers, who sell yourselves for that which will canker, why have ye polluted the holy church of God? Why are ye ashamed to take upon you the name of Christ? Why do ye not think that greater is the value of an endless happiness than that

---

in this land, it will have gone into the shade; but until the power of the Priesthood is gone, "Mormonism" will never become popular with the wicked. (Brigham Young, JD 4:38.) "They would come now by thousands and thousands, if the Latter day Saints were only popular. 'What, these honorable men?' Yes, they would say, 'I want to be baptized. I admire your industry, and your skill in governing. You have a system of governing that is not to be found anywhere else. You know how to govern cities, territories, or the world, and I would like to join you.' But take care if you join this people without the love of God in your soul it will do you no good. If they were to do this, they would bring in their sophistry, and introduce that which would poison the innocent and honest and lead them astray. I look at this, and I am satisfied that it will not do for the Lord to make this people popular. Why? Because all hell would want to be in the Church. The people must be kept where the finger of scorn can be pointed at them. Although it is admitted that we are honest, industrious, truthful, virtuous, self denying, and, as a community, possess every moral excellence, yet we must be looked upon as ignorant and unworthy, and as the offscouring of society, and be hated by the world. What is the reason of this? Christ and Baal can not become friends. When I see this people grow and spread and prosper, I feel that there is more danger than when they are in poverty. Being driven from city to city or into the mountains is nothing compared to the danger of our becoming rich and being hailed by outsiders as a first class community. I am afraid of only one thing. What is that? That we will not live our religion, and that we will partially slide a little from the path of rectitude, and go part of the way to meet our friends. (Brigham Young, JD 12:272.) "And when the spirit of persecution, the spirit of hatred, of wrath, and malice ceases in the world against this people, it will be the time that this people have apostatized and joined hands with the wicked, and never until then; which I pray may never come." (Brigham Young, JD 4:326 327.) "Both Alma and Helaman told the church in their day. They warned about fast growth, the desire to be accepted by the world, to be popular, and particularly they warned about prosperity. Each time those conditions existed in combination, the church has drifted off course. All of those conditions are present in the church today." (President Boyd K. Packer, "Let Them Govern Themselves," Reg. Rep. Seminar, March 30, 1990.)

[309] "Therefore, thus says the Holy One of Israel: Because you have rejected this word, and rely on manipulation and double dealing, and on them are dependent, this iniquity will be to you as a perilous breach exposed in a high wall which suddenly and unexpectedly collapses." (Isaiah 30:12-13, Gileadi Translation.)

misery which never dies—because of the praise of the world?
(Mormon 8:38.)

Protection from the world is given by God, not men. It is wrong to strategize in anticipation of societal pressure, making accommodations to the world even before they are demanded.[310] Abandoning God's standards to gain perceived protection from earthly threats is uniformly decried in scripture and likened unto whoredom (see, for example Ezekiel 23:1-21, Hosea 4:1-19, Hosea 7:1-16, and Hosea 9:1.) Some would define this as apostasy.[311]

We ought to fear God, and not manipulate the gospel in a bid to buy protection from persecution.[312] Isaiah predicted the outcome of allying with the world, and we see its fulfillment unrolling today:

> As for my people, babes subject them; women wield authority over them. O my people, your leaders mislead you, abolishing your traditional ways. Jehovah will take a stand and contend with them; he has arisen to judge the nations. He will bring to trial the elders of his people and their rulers....Jehovah says, moreover, Because the women of Zion are haughty and put on airs, painting their eyes, ever flirting when they walk and clacking with their feet, my Lord will afflict the scalps of the women of Zion with baldness; Jehovah will expose their private parts. (Isaiah 3:12-14,16-17, Gileadi Translation.)

This pattern will continue as the church continues to allow society to dictate doctrine.

The scriptures tell us how God feels about attributing his name to the words of men. They say God has not sent the men who do so: "For thus saith the Lord of hosts, the God of Israel; Let not your prophets and your diviners, that be in the midst of you, deceive you...For they prophesy falsely unto you in my name: I have not sent them, saith the Lord." (Jeremiah 29:8-9.) They say God is against these men:

---

[310] "The wicked flee when no man pursueth: but the righteous are bold as a lion." (Proverbs 28:1.)

[311] "Lowering the Lord's standards to the level of a society's inappropriate behavior is—apostasy." (Elder Lynn G. Robbins, "Which way do you face?", Oct 2014 Gen Conference.)

[312] "And behold, how oft you have transgressed the commandments and the laws of God, and have gone on in the persuasions of men. For, behold, you should not have feared man more than God. Although men set at naught the counsels of God, and despise his words—Yet you should have been faithful; and he would have extended his arm and supported you against all the fiery darts of the adversary; and he would have been with you in every time of trouble." (D&C 3:6-8.) "To have respect of persons is not good: for for a piece of bread that man will transgress." (Proverbs 28:21.)

Therefore, behold, I am against the prophets, saith the Lord, that steal my words every one from his neighbour. Behold, I am against the prophets, saith the Lord, that use their tongues, and say, He saith. Behold, I am against them that prophesy false dreams, saith the Lord, and do tell them, and cause my people to err by their lies, and by their lightness; yet I sent them not, nor commanded them: therefore they shall not profit this people at all, saith the Lord. (Jeremiah 23:30-32.)

They say God will reprove those who do so. "Every word of God is pure: he is a shield unto them that put their trust in him. Add thou not unto his words, lest he reprove thee, and thou be found a liar." (Proverbs 20:5-6.) They say how God will reprove them, by calling real prophets to speak against them:

And the word of the Lord came unto me, saying, Son of man, prophesy against the prophets of Israel that prophesy, and say thou unto them that prophesy out of their own hearts, Hear ye the word of the Lord; Thus saith the Lord God; Woe unto the foolish prophets, that follow their own spirit, and have seen nothing!...They have seen vanity and lying divination, saying, The Lord saith: and the Lord hath not sent them...whereas ye say, The Lord saith it; albeit I have not spoken? Therefore thus saith the Lord God; Because ye have spoken vanity, and seen lies, therefore, behold, I am against you, saith the Lord God. (Ezekiel 13:1-8.)

They say how words spoken in God's name in vain have no strength, and should be expected to fall apart in due time:

And her prophets have daubed them with untempered mortar, seeing vanity, and divining lies unto them, saying, Thus saith the Lord God, when the Lord hath not spoken. (Ezekiel 22:28.)

They say we should not listen to these vain messages:

Thus saith the Lord of hosts, Hearken not unto the words of the prophets that prophesy unto you: they make you vain: they speak a vision of their own heart, and not out of the mouth of the Lord. (Jeremiah 23:16.)

The nature and disposition of all men, including leaders, is fallen. Revelation is needed to elevate our thoughts to God's thoughts. Joseph called the Holy Ghost "the mind of the Lord". Without revelation, a leader's opinion is almost certainly wrong.[313] Countering God's revealed word should

---

[313] "Every way of a man is right in his own eyes: but the Lord pondereth the hearts." (Proverbs 21:2.) "There is a way that seemeth right unto a man, but the end thereof are the ways of death." (Proverbs 16:25.)

only be considered with great trepidation and absolute certainty of new revelation.[314] Supplanting God's word with a man's opinion is folly. "Be not wise in thine own eyes: fear the Lord, and depart from evil." (Proverbs 3:5-7.)

Modern church leaders have received honors from world leaders, medals from U.S. presidents, honorary degrees from universities, have buildings and camps named after them, own multiple homes, and receive new luxury cars yearly. They are revered by their subordinates, take the chief seats in the synagogues,[315] receive hero's welcomes by members in their travels, and are treated to lavish birthday celebrations. None of this behavior is seen in the prophets of the scriptures. Joseph Smith was hated by at least as many members as he was beloved, and even among those who claimed to sustain him, the word of God delivered through him was difficult enough to accept that it was largely ignored.

Is this the pattern provided in scripture? Joseph Smith wrote:

> The world always mistook false prophets for true ones, and those that were sent of God, they considered to be false prophets, and hence they killed, stoned, punished and imprisoned the true prophets, and these had to hide themselves 'in deserts and dens, and caves of the earth,' and though the most honorable men of the earth, they banished them from their society as vagabonds, whilst they cherished, honored and supported knaves, vagabonds, hypocrites, impostors, and the basest of men. (Joseph Smith, HC 4:574.)

True prophets have to hide from society or face pain or death as a result of their hatred of the message they bear. True prophets do not preach easy messages that are compliant with modern sensibilities.[316] They do not use

---

[314] "He that trusteth in his own heart is a fool: but whoso walketh wisely, he shall be delivered." (Proverbs 28:26.) Nephi provided an example of the type of caution that ought to be exercised when he debated with the Lord over killing Laban.

[315] "Saying, The scribes and the Pharisees sit in Moses' seat: All therefore whatsoever they bid you observe, that observe and do; but do not ye after their works: for they say, and do not. For they bind heavy burdens and grievous to be borne, and lay them on men's shoulders; but they themselves will not move them with one of their fingers. But all their works they do for to be seen of men: they make broad their phylacteries, and enlarge the borders of their garments, And love the uppermost rooms at feasts, and the chief seats in the synagogues, And greetings in the markets, and to be called of men, Rabbi, Rabbi." (Matthew 23:2-7.)

[316] "For the time will come when they will not endure sound doctrine; but after their own lusts shall they heap to themselves teachers, having itching ears;" (2 Timothy 4:3.) "And now when ye talk, ye say: If our days had been in the days of our fathers of old, we would not have slain the prophets; we would not have stoned them, and cast them out. Behold ye are worse than they; for as the Lord liveth, if a prophet come among you and declareth unto you the word of the Lord, which testifieth of your sins and iniquities, ye are angry with him, and cast him out and seek all manner

popular gimmicks. They do not cry that all is well[317] or that what we are doing is good enough.[318] True prophets are not hypocrites.[319] The Lord's watchmen do not cry "tomorrow will be like today, only far better!"[320] [321] The Lord's

---

of ways to destroy him; yea, you will say that he is a false prophet, and that he is a sinner, and of the devil, because he testifieth that your deeds are evil. But behold, if a man shall come among you and shall say: Do this, and there is no iniquity; do that and ye shall not suffer; yea, he will say: Walk after the pride of your own hearts; yea, walk after the pride of your eyes, and do whatsoever your heart desireth—and if a man shall come among you and say this, ye will receive him, and say that he is a prophet. Yea, ye will lift him up, and ye will give unto him of your substance; ye will give unto him of your gold, and of your silver, and ye will clothe him with costly apparel; and because he speaketh flattering words unto you, and he saith that all is well, then ye will not find fault with him. (Helaman 13:25-28.)

[317] "The Church is doing very well. We are far from that state of perfection for which we work, but we are trying—and we are making substantial progress. We are growing consistently and remarkably...there is growing faith and faithfulness among the Latter-day Saints. I am encouraged by what I see. Things are getting consistently better....I have served as a stake or general officer of this church for more than half a century, and I am confident that never, during all of that time, has a larger percentage of our people been actively engaged in Church responsibility. I submit that this is one of the great success stories of all time." (Gordon B. Hinckley, "State of the Church," April 1991 General Conference.) Also, see "All is Well," July 2015 First Presidency Message.

[318] "Yea, and there shall be many which shall say: Eat, drink, and be merry, for tomorrow we die; and it shall be well with us. And there shall also be many which shall say: Eat, drink, and be merry; nevertheless, fear God—he will justify in committing a little sin; yea, lie a little, take the advantage of one because of his words, dig a pit for thy neighbor; there is no harm in this; and do all these things, for tomorrow we die; and if it so be that we are guilty, God will beat us with a few stripes, and at last we shall be saved in the kingdom of God. Yea, and there shall be many which shall teach after this manner, false and vain and foolish doctrines....Yea, they have all gone out of the way; they have become corrupted...they have all gone astray save it be a few, who are the humble followers of Christ; nevertheless, they are led, that in many instances they do err because they are taught by the precepts of men....they will say: All is well in Zion; yea, Zion prospereth, all is well—and thus the devil cheateth their souls, and leadeth them away carefully down to hell....Therefore, wo be unto him that is at ease in Zion! (2 Nephi 28:7-24)

[319] Jesus taught to be on the watch for church leaders who teach good things, but whose private actions do not match their teachings "Beware of false prophets, which come to you in sheep's clothing, but inwardly they are ravening wolves." (Matthew 7:15) For an example of hypocrisy in the LDS church, see "Are We Not All Beggars," from Oct. 2014 General Conference where Elder Holland admonishes members to do all they can to help the poor, and compare with the "No Poor Among Them."

[320] "Their watchmen are altogether blind and unaware; all of them are but dumb watchdogs unable to bark, lolling seers fond of slumber. Gluttonous dogs, and insatiable, such indeed are insensible shepherds. They are all diverted to their own

watchmen do not ignore the prophecies he has given of destruction[322] by crying "peace,"[323] [324] erroneously assuming that the Lord is with them and will protect them.[325] [326] They do not say that the Lord delays his coming.[327] [328]

---

way, every one after his own advantage. Come, they say, let us get wine and have our fill of liquor. For tomorrow will be like today, only far better!" (Isaiah 56:10-12, Gileadi Translation.)

[321] "I reassure you that things have been worse and they will always get better—especially when we live the gospel of Jesus Christ and give it a chance to flourish in our lives." (President Howard W. Hunter, "Why Try?" Jan. 1994 Ensign.)

[322] An extensive but incomplete list of all scriptures prophesying the destruction precede the second coming of Christ is provided at www.latterdaydestruction.blogspot.com.

[323] "For from the least of them even unto the greatest of them every one is given to covetousness; and from the prophet even unto the priest every one dealeth falsely. They have healed also the hurt of the daughter of my people slightly, saying, Peace, peace; when there is no peace. Were they ashamed when they had committed abomination? nay, they were not at all ashamed, neither could they blush: therefore they shall fall among them that fall: at the time that I visit them they shall be cast down, saith the Lord." (Jeremiah 6:13-15.)
"They have belied the Lord, and said, It is not he; neither shall evil come upon us; neither shall we see sword nor famine: And the prophets shall become wind, and the word is not in them: thus shall it be done unto them." (Jeremiah 5:12-13) "They say still unto them that despise me, The Lord hath said, Ye shall have peace; and they say unto every one that walketh after the imagination of his own heart, No evil shall come upon you." (Jeremiah 23:17.)

[324] "...this nation, founded on principles laid down by men whom God raised up, will never fail....This is the favored land in all the world. Yes, I repeat, men may fail, but this nation won't fail." President Lee then beckoned: "I plead with you not to preach pessimism. Preach that this is the greatest country in all the world. This is the favored land. This is the land of our forefathers. It is the location that will stand despite whatever trials or crises it may have to pass through" (Harold B. Lee Quoted in "Ye Are the Light of the World," Deseret Book, 1974, 350-51).

[325] "Thus saith the Lord concerning the prophets that make my people err, that bite with their teeth, and cry, Peace; and he that putteth not into their mouths, they even prepare war against him. Therefore night shall be unto you, that ye shall not have a vision; and it shall be dark unto you, that ye shall not divine; and the sun shall go down over the prophets, and the day shall be dark over them. Then shall the seers be ashamed, and the diviners confounded: yea, they shall all cover their lips; for there is no answer of God....The heads thereof judge for reward, and the priests thereof teach for hire, and the prophets thereof divine for money: yet will they lean upon the Lord, and say, Is not the Lord among us? none evil can come upon us. Therefore shall Zion for your sake be plowed as a field, and Jerusalem shall become heaps, and the mountain of the house as the high places of the forest." (Micah 3:5-12.)

[326] "The Lord has power over his Saints and will always prepare places of peace, defense and safety for his people." (President Howard W. Hunter, "Why Try?" Ensign, January 1994.)

True prophets do not teach for money.[329] [330] True prophets do not neglect the poor.[331] True prophets do not feel threatened by others who are receiving revelations from God or visitations from God. [332] False prophets [333] do,

---

[327] "But if that evil servant shall say in his heart: My lord delayeth his coming, And shall begin to smite his fellow-servants, and to eat and drink with the drunken, The lord of that servant shall come in a day when he looketh not for him, and in an hour that he is not aware of, And shall cut him asunder, and shall appoint him his portion with the hypocrites; there shall be weeping and gnashing of teeth. And thus cometh the end of the wicked, according to the prophecy of Moses, saying: They shall be cut off from among the people; but the end of the earth is not yet, but by and by. (JST Matthew 1:51-54.)

[328] "Sometimes you might be tempted to think as I did from time to time in my youth: "The way things are going, the world's going to be over with. The end of the world is going to come before I get to where I should be." Not so! You can look forward to doing it right—getting married, having a family, seeing your children and grandchildren, maybe even great-grandchildren." (Elder Boyd K. Packer, "Counsel to Youth," Oct. 2011 General Conference.) This talk was quoted by Elder David A. Bednar in the same conference.

[329] "Her leaders judge for a bribe, her priests teach for a price, and her prophets tell fortunes for money. Yet they look for the LORD's support and say, 'Is not the LORD among us? No disaster will come upon us.'"(Micah 3:11.)

[330] President Gordon B. Hinckley said General Authorities receive a "living allowance." (see "Questions and Answers," Ensign, November 1985.)

[331] "And I said, Hear, I pray you, O heads of Jacob, and ye princes of the house of Israel; Is it not for you to know judgment? Who hate the good, and love the evil; who pluck off their skin from off them, and their flesh from off their bones; Who also eat the flesh of my people, and flay their skin from off them; and they break their bones, and chop them in pieces, as for the pot, and as flesh within the caldron. Then shall they cry unto the Lord, but he will not hear them: he will even hide his face from them at that time, as they have behaved themselves ill in their doings." (Micah 3:1-4.)

[332] Moses said, "Would God that all the Lord's people were prophets, and that the Lord would put his spirit upon them!" (Num. 11:26-29.) Joseph explained that "no man is a minister of Jesus Christ without being a Prophet. No man can be a minister of Jesus Christ except he has the testimony of Jesus; and this is the spirit of prophecy." (Joseph Smith, TPJS, p. 110.)

[333] "Then said the Lord unto me, Pray not for this people for their good. When they fast, I will not hear their cry; and when they offer burnt offering and an oblation, I will not accept them: but I will consume them by the sword, and by the famine, and by the pestilence. Then said I, Ah, Lord God! behold, the prophets say unto them, Ye shall not see the sword, neither shall ye have famine; but I will give you assured peace in this place. Then the Lord said unto me, The prophets prophesy lies in my name: I sent them not, neither have I commanded them, neither spake unto them: they prophesy unto you a false vision and divination, and a thing of nought, and the deceit of their heart. Therefore thus saith the Lord concerning the prophets that prophesy in my name, and I sent them not, yet they say, Sword and famine shall not be in this land; By sword and famine shall those prophets be consumed. And the people to

because their competitors, like Jeremiah, Elijah, Isaiah, and Amos, receive true revelations and bear tangible fruits of being true messengers, and pose a threat to their priestcraft.

> They are a rebellious people, sons who break faith, children unwilling to obey the law of Jehovah, who say to the seers, See not! and to those with visions, Predict not what is right for us: flatter us; foresee a farce! Get out of the way; move aside, off the path! Cease confronting us with the Holy One of Israel! Therefore, thus says the Holy One of Israel: Because you have rejected this word, and rely on manipulation and double dealing, and on them are dependent, this iniquity will be to you as a perilous breach exposed in a high wall which suddenly and unexpectedly collapses. (Isaiah 30:9-13, Gileadi Translation.)

Those who stand as prophets have an obligation to point out sin, and will be held accountable by God to the extent that they do not.[334]

Conclusion

Ezekiel saw a day when the people would "seek a vision of the prophet; but the law shall perish from the priest, and counsel from the ancients." (Ezekiel 7:26, KJV). Do people seek visions from the prophet today? Does President Monson give it? Do we receive the word of the Lord from our "ancients" (Elders)? Do priests speak the law? Or are we instead nourished on ever-changing PR-firm-written policy?

> They are a rebellious people, sons who break faith, children unwilling to obey the law of Jehovah, who say to the seers, See not! and to

---

whom they prophesy shall be cast out in the streets of Jerusalem because of the famine and the sword; and they shall have none to bury them, them, their wives, nor their sons, nor their daughters: for I will pour their wickedness upon them." (Jeremiah 14:11-16.)

[334] "Son of man, I have made thee a watchman unto the house of Israel: therefore hear the word at my mouth, and give them warning from me. When I say unto the wicked, Thou shalt surely die; and thou givest him not warning, nor speakest to warn the wicked from his wicked way, to save his life; the same wicked man shall die in his iniquity; but his blood will I require at thine hand. Yet if thou warn the wicked, and he turn not from his wickedness, nor from his wicked way, he shall die in his iniquity; but thou hast delivered thy soul. Again, When a righteous man doth turn from his righteousness, and commit iniquity, and I lay a stumblingblock before him, he shall die: because thou hast not given him warning, he shall die in his sin, and his righteousness which he hath done shall not be remembered; but his blood will I require at thine hand. Nevertheless if thou warn the righteous man, that the righteous sin not, and he doth not sin, he shall surely live, because he is warned; also thou hast delivered thy soul." (Ezekiel 3:17-21.) See also Ezekiel 33:1-12.

those with visions, Predict not what is right for us: flatter us; foresee a farce! Get out of the way; move aside, off the path! Cease confronting us with the Holy One of Israel! Therefore, thus says the Holy One of Israel: Because you have rejected this word, and rely on manipulation and double dealing, and on them are dependent, this iniquity will be to you as a perilous breach exposed in a high wall which suddenly and unexpectedly collapses. (Isaiah 30:9-13, Gileadi Translation.)

The word "prophet" is not a title, but a description. It is a term defined repeatedly and clearly in the scriptures, as is it's opposite, "false prophet." Modern Mormons are in the uncomfortable position of having to reconcile their tradition of equating the 15 governing men in the church to the description of prophet when it not only does not apply in any case, but when the observations can be found in their behavior to fit every scriptural property of false prophets.

LDS leaders after Joseph Smith have taught their own ideas and feelings as the word of God. They have promoted their own words and the decisions of their councils as equal to God's word, and used this to rationalize a systemic turn away from the revelations given through Joseph Smith.

Church History

Although modern Mormonism deemphasizes the value of what Joseph Smith received from God in favor of what is taught by successors to Joseph Smith,[335] God considered Joseph's revelations important enough to preserve that he routinely appointed scribes to record the revelations and history of the restoration.[336] We cannot live the doctrines of the restoration without knowing history. We cannot compare present teachings to what Joseph taught without knowing history. Our acceptance of Joseph's teachings requires knowledge of church history.

Nevertheless, modern LDS leaders do not appreciate the importance of church history. Church leaders rose up in the ranks from lay positions. Like the body of normal members they were chosen from, church leaders do not know church history.[337] Any expectation we may have for them to know more about church history than normal members do would come from some sense of obligation we would expect them to have in relation to their office. Yet, with frequent comments deprecating the value of church history,[338] it is clear that, to today's leaders, knowing church history is not a priority.

Church history ironically presents a record of not caring very much about the history of the church. Joseph Fielding Smith, who served as church historian from 1921 to 1970, found that many important historical documents had not been collected and archived prior to his tenure, and built up an impressive collection that was donated to the church at the time of his death. Why didn't any of his predecessors do so? Hyrum Andrus reported opening crates of church archive documents around 1965 that had been sealed since Nauvoo.[339] Why did it take ten decades and the instigation of historians outside the church hierarchy to think that historic records from Nauvoo

---

[335] This entire book lays out this argument in detail.

[336] See D&C 47:1-3, 69:3, 85:1.

[337] In a recent Q&A, LDS history author Richard Bushman explained that the brethren were not informed about the issues "for many years, but recently they have had to get up to speed." (http://www.wheatandtares.org/17915/richard-bushman-on-mormonism/, retrieved 27 Sept 2015.)

[338] For example, Elder M. Russell Ballard recently quipped, "the Lord does not require His Saints to have advanced degrees in history and Church doctrine." https://www.lds.org/prophets-and-apostles/unto-all-the-world/to-the-saints-in-the-utah-south-area

[339] Recollection of Paul Toscano in private correspondence to author.

might be worth reading, or at least uncrating? Leonard Arrington—the church's first historian chosen for his professional talent rather than church rank—was the first to open the church archives, something that one would assume would have been done much earlier. The Joseph Smith papers are a landmark project to collect and publish every document created by Joseph Smith. It is the first historic project undertaken by the LDS church with an unbiased approach in mind.[340] Still, it is perplexing why a church who celebrates Joseph Smith as a prophet would have waited 160 years after his death to undertake to collect and publish his writings and speeches. Even then, the impetus for the project came largely not from the church, but from a private member who contributed substantial funding for the project.[341]

In recent years, church leaders have taken an increased interest in church history in direct proportion to how much bad press has been garnered from omissions, alterations, and fabrications brought to light by ease of access due to the internet.[342] Though the church has responded with a flood of historic materials, including essays on troubling topics, the persistence of omissions, alterations, and fabrications suggest that the new initiative is more about convincing members they need not investigate church history than it is about a clean, honest approach to the past.

---

[340] See later comments in this chapter.

[341] The late Larry H. Miller provided an undisclosed amount to finance the Joseph Smith Papers Project. "The Family and Church History Department of the church and BYU's Joseph Fielding Smith Institute for Latter-day Saint History haver [sic] provided space, resources and manpower, but funding comes from the Millers." (http://www.deseretnews.com/article/600123721/Miller-funding-Joseph-Smith-project.html?pg=all, retrieved 24 Sept 2015)

[342] Q: What do you think is spurring this change in focus for including the more controversial aspects of the history when it has previously not been a priority?
Bushman: Doubtless the blast of information on the internet changed the situation drastically. The Church had to face that fact that information of all kinds was now in the public realm...
Q: Is there a consensus among the brethren about the history of the church? Are they usually fairly informed about the issues?
Bushman: They were not for many years, but recently they have had to get up to speed. The recent Church historians have done a great job of informing the Brethren. The gospel topics were a surprise to many. They are often charged with concealing the truth. I think the fact is the old narrative was all they knew. I don't think that all believe we have to tell the whole story. Why bring all that up they are wont to say. But those on the side of transparency are prevailing.
(Richard Bushman, http://www.wheatandtares.org/17915/richard-bushman-on-mormonism/, retrieved 27 Sept 2015.)

Suppressing History

In recent years, the church has determined through extensive surveys that unfiltered church history available online is a driving force in the loss of members in the tithing-crucial first world, particularly among younger members, who tend to be tech savvy.[343] In response, the church recently quickly built a sophisticated search engine optimization (SEO) program. Search engines are designed to show users the websites most likely to contain what they are searching for. SEO is a business strategy to manipulate the search engine results from what the user wants to see to what the business wants them to see. From the church's point of view, a search on "LDS finances" should link to LDS-owned websites that offer only church-positive information, not to Wikipedia or other objective discussions. The church has exerted great effort on ensuring that the first few results of a Google search return church-owned websites that contain only a church-positive relation of events.[344]

SEO is only the most recent tool in a long-standing effort to withhold true history that challenges present traditions or suggests that church leaders past or present have made mistakes.

Elder Oaks has taught that facts that portray church leaders in a negative light should be omitted from church materials.[345] He also taught:

---

[343] "It's a different generation. Everything's out there for them to consume if they want to Google it....maybe since Kirtland, we never have had a period of, I'll call it apostasy, like we're having right now; largely over these issues.....The church has a very progressive research and information division, with tremendous public opinion surveyors. And the church is constantly running surveys, and employing consultants that do focus groups on a variety of topics, but especially on the ones that we are talking about right now, that are so sensitive to the faith of members.... We are suffering a loss; both in terms of our new converts that come in that don't get really established in the church, as well as very faithful members who because of things we're talking about, as well as others, are losing their faith in the process. It is one of our biggest concerns right now." (Elder Marlin Jenson, Utah State University Q&A)

[344] "We have hired someone that's in charge of search engine optimization. We realize that people get their information basically from Google. They don't come to LDS.org. If they get there, it's through Google." (Elder Marlin Jensen, Utah State University Q&A) See also https://www.washingtonpost.com/lifestyle/style/mormons-using-the-web-to-control-their-own-image/2011/08/11/gIQA1J6BMJ_print.html, retrieved 4 Oct. 2015.

[345] "It is one thing to depreciate a person who exercises corporate power or even government power. It is quite another thing to criticize or depreciate a person for the performance of an office to which he or she has been called of God. It does not matter that the criticism is true....This reality should be part of the spiritual evaluation that LDS readers and viewers apply to those things written about our history and

My duty as a member of the Council of the Twelve is to protect what is most unique about the LDS church, namely the authority of priesthood, testimony regarding the restoration of the gospel, and the divine mission of the Savior. Everything may be sacrificed in order to maintain the integrity of those essential facts. Thus, if Mormon Enigma reveals information that is detrimental to the reputation of Joseph Smith, then it is necessary to try to limit its influence and that of its authors. (Dallin Oaks, footnote 28, Inside the Mind of Joseph Smith: Psychobiography and the Book of Mormon, Introduction p. xliii.)

On another occasion, Elder Oaks taught that:

Truth surely exists as an absolute, but our use of truth should be disciplined by other values....When truth is constrained by other virtues, the outcome is not falsehood but silence for a season. As the scriptures say, there is "a time to keep silence, and a time to speak." (Apostle Dallin H. Oaks, "Criticism," Ensign, Feb. 1987, page 68.)

Elder Oaks is not alone in his views. Elder Nelson has taught: "Indeed, in some instances, the merciful companion to truth is silence. Some truths are best left unsaid."[346] President Boyd K. Packer was an outspoken critic of objective history. He wrote,

There is a temptation for the writer or the teacher of Church history to want to tell everything, whether it is worthy or faith promoting or not. Some things that are true are not very useful. (Apostle Boyd K. Packer, "The Mantle is Far,Far Greater Than the Intellect," 1981 CES Talk.)

The policy of intentionally withholding history that contradicts church tradition has led to many examples of true history that was actively suppressed. For example, by the time correlation took over church curricula, plural marriage was something for which the church received only negative attention. You will not find mention of anything regarding Joseph Smith's polygamy in church materials during the decades between correlation's inception and the recent admissions in the church topics essays on LDS.org. In every location where you would expect some mention of topic, it is omitted. This blackout continued even into recent years. The D&C manual covers only verses 4-33 of D&C 132, conveniently skipping over the many verses that describe Abraham's polygamy and lack of sin in practice thereof, David, Solomon, and Moses' polygamy, Joseph's authority to give women to

---

those who made it." (Dallin H. Oaks, "Reading Church History," CES Doctrine and Covenants Symposium, Brigham Young University, 16 Aug. 1985, p25.)

[346] Russell M. Nelson, "Truth—and More," Ensign, Jan. 1986, p. 69.

other men, and the command for Joseph to practice polygamy. The manual never mentions Joseph's polygamy, and only mentions plural marriage at all as a minor bullet point at the end of the lesson, with the instructions, "The following information is provided to help you if class members have questions about the practice of plural marriage. It should not be the focus of the lesson." Similarly, the "Teachings of the Presidents of the Church: Joseph Smith" manual's introduction states:

> This book also does not discuss plural marriage. The doctrines and principles relating to plural marriage were revealed to Joseph Smith as early as 1831. The Prophet taught the doctrine of plural marriage, and a number of such marriages were performed during his lifetime.

Surely, even if the manual does not include quotes on plural marriage, this disclosure should say "taught and practiced" plural marriage? The perpetual avoidance of this topic has led to a condition where a surprising number of fully active, lifelong members were broadsided by the recent gospel topics essays that discussed Joseph Smith's polygamy. These are members who attended seminary, attended BYU, served a mission, and still had never been told that Joseph Smith practiced plural marriage.

The open archives of the 1970s provided ample historical research material for graduate students at BYU. This period produced two works analyzing changes to the text of canonized scripture: "Study of Some Textual Variations in the Book of Mormon, Comparing the Original and Printer's MSS., and Comparing the 1830, 1837, and 1840 Editions," and "Historical Development of the Doctrine and Covenants." The board authorized both theses on condition that they remain unpublished and inaccessible to all except those cleared by church leadership. This policy was lifted after a threat to accreditation some years later over the access restrictions.[347] "Historical Development of the Doctrine and Covenants" was briefly available by purchase on CD-ROM, but continues today to be accessible only in person at the BYU library, where 2 copies of the set are available for public view. Woodford's "Historical Development of the Doctrine and Covenants"[348] includes thousands of modifications to the text of the D&C—enough to occupy 3 massive volumes. Among these changes were a modification to the wording of the baptismal prayer, which originally took the form found in the Book of Mormon:[349] This is a significant change that might impact every

---

347 See "Brigham Young University: A House of Faith" by Gary James Bergera and Ronald Priddis.

348 "The historical development of the Doctrine and Covenants", 3 vol set. Woodford, Robert J. Thesis (Ph.D.) Brigham Young University. Dept. of Ancient Scripture, 1974.

349 See "The Gospel of Christ" for more details surrounding this change.

baptized member of the church, yet there is no mention of this change in any official publication of the church.

As detailed elsewhere in this book, the LDS temple garment has been dramatically modified multiple times since it was revealed to Joseph. The church has had Hyrum Smith's temple garment in possession since Joseph Fielding Smith was president, yet no access to or reports of the original pattern or symbols have been given. We know from accounts given that nearly everything about the garment has been changed, and any sort of access to the original would reveal that immediately. Likewise, the temple ceremony itself is vastly different from the 1877 transcript,[350] purportedly the first time the ceremony was recorded. The original transcript survived an attempted purge in the 1920s by apostle George Richards, thanks to a defiant St. George Temple President. The church still has this copy, yet it is not accessible to any outside of top leadership.

The policy of withholding history is not just a part of traditions among the brethren. It is codified in the "Handbook of Instructions." The handbook includes under the definition of apostasy criticizing the brethren, with an automatic penalty of excommunication. This means that anyone who teaches church history without withholding history that incriminates current church practices or past or present leaders is considered an apostate and will be excommunicated. This was illustrated recently when Denver Snuffer was excommunicated for refusing to remove "Passing the Heavenly Gift" from publication. The book contains scriptures and quotes from church leaders that suggest a version of history that differs from LDS claims. The stake president who charged Snuffer with apostasy did not attempt to outline or correct any errors in the book, but merely maintained that the history presented was "in direct conflict with church doctrine" and "placed the church in a negative light."[351] Denver Snuffer was not the first member to be excommunicated for publishing true history, and he will not be the last.

As George Orwell said, "The most powerful form of lie is the omission." Withholding true information assists only the perpetuation of disinformation, not the cause of truth. As the church historian that oversaw the window of open church archives put it:

> My own impression is that an intensive study of church history, while it will dispel certain myths or half-myths sometimes perpetuated in

---

[350] See "Temples" for more about changes to temple ordinances.

[351] A copy of the letter from Snuffer's stake president is available at http://denversnuffer.blogspot.com/2013/08/dont-call-me-yes-that-means-you-too_23.html, retrieved 27 Sept. 2015.

Sunday school (and other) classes, builds faith rather than weakens it.[352]

Only truth can lead us closer to Christ. Faith cannot be had on false principles. Therefore, as Joseph stated "we should waste and wear out our lives in bringing to light all the hidden things of darkness, wherein we know them;" (D&C 123:13.)

Misrepresenting History

A quintessential example of misrepresented history is found in the story of Thomas Marsh. Thomas Marsh was excommunicated for providing an affidavit that stated:

> A company of about eighty of the Mormons, commanded by a man fictitiously named Captain Fearnot [David W. Patten], marched to Gallatin. They returned and said they had run off from Gallatin twenty or thirty men and had taken Gallatin, had taken one prisoner and another had joined the company. I afterwards learned from the Mormons that they had burned Gallatin, and that it was done by the aforesaid company that marched there. The Mormons informed me that they had hauled away all the goods from the store in Gallatin, and deposited them at the Bishop's storehouses at Adam-on-diahmon.

History supports the factually accuracy of this statement. As such, it is unclear why he was excommunicated. From other documents, it seems that Joseph Smith may not have been aware of the actions of or existence of the Danites at this time.

Most members will not recognize that Thomas B. Marsh was excommunicated for swearing out an affidavit correctly describing the pillaging conducted by the Missouri Mormons. Instead, they have been told that he was excommunicated over a dispute between his wife and another sister regarding milk strippings.

The first telling of the milk stripping story was in 1864 when George A. Smith. There is no contemporary evidence supporting this story. Furthermore, there is no mention of the issue in the Far West High Council minutes, despite Smith having said that Thomas Marsh "immediately took an appeal to the High Council, who investigated the question with much patience."

---

[352] Leonard Arrington, "The Search for Truth and Meaning in Mormon History," Dialogue: A Journal of Mormon Thought 3/2 (Summer 1968): 61; reprinted in D. Michael Quinn, ed., New Mormon History: Revisionist Essays on the Past (Salt Lake City: Signature Books, 1992), 6.

Marsh requested rebaptism on September 6, 1857, addressing a large gathering in the Salt Lake City Bowery. The event was a critical one in the history of the succession of leaders in the LDS church. Prior to this time, in each case where an apostle had been excommunicated, they resumed their ranking at the time of reinstatement. At the time of his excommunication, Marsh was the president of the quorum. Following precedent, his reinstatement would make him the president of the church.[353] In a public reply to Marsh's request to be rebaptized, Brigham Young gave him a severe dressing down. Though rebaptized, he was not reinstated to the Quorum of the Twelve.[354] The misrepresentation of Marsh's excommunication has been perpetuated ever since, including by President Monson,[355] and is even contained in the church's history article on him.[356]

Another perpetuated myth is that of Brigham Young appearing or sounding like Joseph Smith during his campaigning in the succession crisis.[357] Like the milk strippings, there is no contemporary evidence that this event actually occurred. The first accounts occurred much after the fact in a time

---

[353] Interestingly, had it not been for a subsequent demotion of Orson Pratt, he would have been the 3rd president of the church. See Gary James Bergera, "Seniority in the Twelve: The 1875 Realignment of Orson Pratt," Journal of Mormon History 18:1 (1992).

[354] "I presume that Brother Marsh will take no offen[s]e if I talk a little about him. We have manifested our feelings towards him, and we know his situation. With regard to this Church's being reconciled to him, I can say that this Church and people were never dissatisfied with him; for when men and women apostatize and go from us, we have nothing to do with them. If they do that which is evil, they will suffer for it. Brother Marsh has suffered....He has told you that he is an old man. Do you think that I am an old man? I could prove to this congregation that I am young; for I could find more girls who would choose me for a husband than can any of the young men. Brother Thomas considers himself very aged and infirm, and you can see that he is, brethren and sisters. What is the cause of it? He left the Gospel of salvation. What do you think the difference is between his age and mine? One year and seven months to a day; and he is one year, seven months, and fourteen days older than brother Heber C. Kimball. "Mormonism" keeps men and women young and handsome; and when they are full of the Spirit of God, there are none of them but what will have a glow upon their countenances; and that is what makes you and me young; for the Spirit of God is with us and within us. When Brother Thomas thought of returning to the Church, the plurality of wives troubled him a good deal. Look at him. Do you think it need to? I do not; for I doubt whether he could get one wife. Why it should have troubled an infirm old man like him is not for me to say." (Brigham Young, JD 5: 210)

[355] https://www.youtube.com/watch?v=oZWY3r5EV3Y

[356] https://history.lds.org/article/revelations-in-context-doctrine-and-covenants-thomas-marsh?lang=eng

[357] See Richard S. Van Wagoner, "The Making of a Mormon Myth: The 1844 Transfiguration of Brigham Young," Dialogue 28:4, Winter 1995.

when there were significant reasons to justify Brigham's succession claims. In both cases, the perpetuated accounts distract from a factual discussion of whether Brigham Young's succession claims were justified.[358]

Some quotes from Joseph Smith are published and republished despite the lack of any firsthand contemporary accounts. For example, the History of the Church states that Joseph said,

> I will give you one of the Keys of the mysteries of the Kingdom. It is an eternal principle, that has existed with God from all eternity: That man who rises up to condemn others, finding fault with the Church, saying that they are out of the way, while he himself is righteous, then know assuredly, that that man is in the high road to apostasy; and if he does not repent, will apostatize, as God lives. (HC 3:385.)

The doctrinal importance of this quote is significant, as it is the only source in Joseph's words or in scripture of which I am aware that states that one who criticizes the church is committing or will soon commit apostasy. The History of the Church takes the quote from a discourse given by Joseph Smith on July 2, 1839, in Montrose, Iowa; reported by Wilford Woodruff and Willard Richards. The problem is that, although Wilford Woodruff was present at and recorded this sermon, his account does not contain this quote. Willard Richard's Pocket Companion is the only source for this quote. Importantly, Richards was in England at the time, and therefore copied his account from somewhere else. There are many other examples of quotes attributed to Joseph Smith that have no contemporary support. For example, the church recently reprinted the following in a Priesthood/Relief Society manual:

> Joseph the Prophet... said, 'Brethren, remember that the majority of this people will never go astray; and as long as you keep with the majority you are sure to enter the celestial kingdom.' (Orson Hyde, Deseret News: Semi-Weekly, June 21, 1870, p. 3.)

The problem is that there is no contemporary source of this quote. Orson Hyde's was an extemporaneous recollection[359] at least 27 years after the fact. Various versions of this quote exist, all given decades after the fact, with no contemporary recording of the quote despite all or nearly all of Joseph's

---

[358] For a much more objective discussion of the succession, see Andrew Ehat's BYU Master's Thesis, "Joseph Smith's Introduction of Temple Ordinances and the 1844 Mormon Succession Question" available at https://onewhoiswatching.files.wordpress.com/2014/09/ehat-succession.pdf at the time of writing.

[359] This quote was from a General Conference sermon. At this time, sermons were not written or even assigned ahead of time. Speakers were expected to speak without prior notice or preparation.

Nauvoo sermons having been recorded.[360] Because the church has repeatedly engaged in citation obfuscation,[361] it is not easy to tell what quotes ascribed to Joseph were witnessed firsthand and recorded contemporarily, no quote from Joseph ought to be trusted unless it can be traced to the original source. The Joseph Smith papers, which has a free online portal, is the best resource at this point. Anything less than a firsthand contemporary account is not historical record, but uncorroborated hearsay from a leaders proven to have engaged in intentional historical fabrication for church-promoting purposes.

In the case of another misrepresented historical topic—plural marriage—the driving factor seems to be a desire to avoid negative public opinion rather than strengthen otherwise weak authority claims.

From the first public teaching of plural marriage on August 29, 1852, until the so-called "Second Manifesto" in 1904 that marked the end of church-sanctioned polygamy, the doctrine occupied preeminence among the LDS faith.[362] It is important to understand that to Latter-day Saints between 1852 and 1904, plural marriage was just as central a tenant of the gospel as

---

[360] For more, see http://www.totheremnant.com/2014/07/history-hearsay-and-heresy-part-1-is.html.

[361] Almost all quotes from the early brethren in church materials originate from the Journal of Discourses. However, to allow plausible deniability for content that contradicts current doctrines and policy, the church avoids quoting from JD and instead finds republication sources to quote, no matter how obscure. The church attempts to hold two mutually exclusive positions: that modern General Conference is worth studying as doctrine, while former General Conferences are not. The most curious example of this is the "Teachings of the Church Presidents" series, which consists of cherry-picked quotes from former leaders presented as a summary of their teachings. Yet, former church leaders' teachings almost never overlapped with the current positions and topic preference of the modern church, meaning that entire topics germane to the ministry of the leader are completely omitted. For example, calling and election and the Second Comforter are missing from Joseph Smith's manual, blood atonement and Adam God are missing from Brigham Young's manual, and communism is missing from Ezra Taft Benson's manual. Yet, a considerable portion of each man's ministry was spent on these topics. A more accurate title for the series would be "Teachings of the Correlation Committee, featuring quotes from Church Presidents."

[362] There are many, many quotes from this period where church leaders taught that polygamy was essential to salvation. For instance, "The only men who become Gods, even the Sons of God, are those who enter into polygamy. Others attain unto a glory and may even be permitted to come into the presence of the Father and the Son; but they cannot reign as kings in glory, because they had blessings offered unto them, and they refused to accept them." (Brigham Young, JD 11:268-269.)

baptism.[363] The church's treatment of plural marriage is an example of how any central tenant could be handled in the future.

The official position has been and continues to be that no church sanctioned plural marriages after 1890 or that the only sanctioned ones took place in Mexico where it was legal. Both statements are untrue. Hundreds of plural marriages occurred with the sanction of the First Presidency in the United States and Mexico after 1890, with some even occurring after 1904.[364]

Faced with significant public opinion ramifications,[365] the church misrepresented plural marriage for generations after the 1890 manifesto, at first continuing plural marriages in secret despite public denials, then (after 1904) misrepresenting plural marriage as having ended in 1890 so as to vindicate leaders who said one thing and practiced another. Leaders from 1890-1904 and beyond had personal knowledge of hundreds of post-manifesto plural marriages, having been personally involved in many. For example, President Joseph F. Smith—a strong proponent of post-manifesto plural marriages—stated under oath in the Reed Smoot hearings, "There never has been a plural marriage by the consent or sanction or knowledge or approval of the church since the manifesto." Apostle John Widstoe wrote in 1936: "Since that day [6 October 1890] no plural marriage has been performed with the sanction or authority of the Church."[366] After these first-hand witnesses of post-manifesto plural marriage had been replaced by the next generation, it is unclear to what degree leaders were aware that their statements were incorrect. BYU Historian Gustive O. Larson taught in 1958:

---

[363] Orson Pratt said that plural marriage was "an ordinance pertaining to this mortal life—to this world—this probation, just the same as baptism and the laying on of hands." (JD 17:229.)

[364] Although the official story attempts to pin all post-manifesto plural marriages to apostles Cowley and Taylor, who were excommunicated for the same, at a minimum Wilford Woodruff (as church President), George Q. Cannon (as First Presidency Councilor), Joseph F. Smith (as First Presidency Councilor and then church President) all personally sanctioned many post-manifesto plural marriages. Apostles Cowley and Taylor were authorized by these men in at least some of the post-manifesto plural marriages they performed. (See Quinn, "LDS Authority and New Plural Marriages, 1890-1904")

[365] The financial implications of the recent seizure of church properties, the resulting high interest mortgages, and tenuous statehood decisions were all very recent and very painful events in the wake of the 1890 manifesto. Financial and political ramifications gave way to leader image and missionary work implications: Admitting the truth was tantamount to ceding that Wilford Woodruff, Joseph F. Smith, and other top leaders were liars, while the national and (later) international growth of the church relied in part upon a modern, more socially acceptable Mormonism that had no place for plural marriage.

[366] Quinn, LDS Church Authority and New Plural Marriages, 1890—1904, "Dialogue", Spring 1985

"While Presidents Woodruff, Snow, and Smith maintained monogamous integrity of the Church, plural marriages were being performed secretly by two members of the Apostles' Quorum."[366] Stephen L Richards (First Presidency counselor) stated in 1961: "Since that time [1890], entering into plural marriage has been construed to be an offense against the laws of the Church."[366] Apostle Gordon B. Hinckley stated in 1969: "Since that time [September 1890] the Church has neither practiced nor sanctioned such marriage."[366] Apostle Mark E. Petersen wrote in 1974 that "the Manifesto put an end to all legal plural marriages."[366] Whether or not leaders after 1905 were aware of the falsehood of their statements, whatever ignorance church leaders had should have ended with the publication of Quinn's 1985 report on the topic. This report was hand delivered to President Gordon B. Hinckley, who gave the author his permission to publish the document.[367] Yet, years later, Hinckley made the following statement:

> I condemn it [polygamy], yes, as a practice, because I think it is not doctrinal. It is not legal. And this church takes the position that we will abide by the law. We believe in being subject to kings, presidents, rulers, magistrates in honoring, obeying and sustaining the law. (Gordon B. Hinckley, Interview with Larry King, September 1998.)

This statement is misleading at best, given the evidence that church leaders have not only openly broken the law with regards to plural marriage, but also committed perjury in denying doing so under oath.[368]

Church leaders have not corrected the facts regarding plural marriage in statements since then. The recent essay "The Manifesto and the end of Plural Marriage"[369] continues many of the falsehoods, among them that the manifesto ended plural marriage, that the manifesto was a revelation,[370] that

---

[367] Quinn was a BYU professor of history at the time of the 1985 publication, and realized that the essay, while objective, would be seen as non-faith promoting. Permission was granted.

[368] After the manifesto, there were no less than 24 denials by the First Presidency or its members that any church sanction plural marriages had occurred, culminating with Joseph F. Smith's second manifesto in 1904 where he stated, "Joseph F. Smith, President of the Church of Jesus Christ of Latter-day Saints, hereby affirm and declare that no such marriages have been solemnized with the sanction, consent or knowledge of the Church of Jesus Christ of Latter-day Saints." (See Quinn, "LDS Authority and New Plural Marriages, 1890-1904")

[369] https://www.lds.org/topics/the-manifesto-and-the-end-of-plural-marriage

[370] The first draft of the manifesto was written by Woodruff. This draft was revised three times, first by George Reynolds, Charles W. Penrose, and John R. Winder, then by George Q. Cannon, then by Franklin D. Richards, Moses Thatcher, and Marriner W. Merrill. The original draft of 510 words was modified to one of 365 words, with many changes, including carefully modifying incorrect statements of the First Presidency's involvement in recent plural marriages, to make them less false. As

only a "smaller number of new plural marriages" were performed between 1890 and 1904, and that these did not have church sanction. The church has published many articles stating that the 1890 manifesto ended plural marriage.[371] The statement is made in at least four current church manuals.[372] President Gordon B. Hinckley, on national television, stated "In 1890, that practice was discontinued."[373] He made a similar statement in conference that same year.[374] Even the timeline in the *Presidents of the Church: Joseph F. Smith* manual, which includes an entry stating Smith issued a "second manifesto on plural marriage (without describing what it was) states that Woodruff's manifesto ended plural marriage.[375]

What does it mean that church leaders were willing to abandon what they believed was a commandment from God essential for salvation in order to gain worldly power? If modern Mormons can call a commandment of God

---

Quinn commented, "the revised Manifesto was a curious document because most of its retrospective statements were untrue." (See Quinn, "LDS Authority and New Plural Marriages, 1890-1904") If the manifesto is a revelation, why was it heavily edited by a non-prophetic committee, why was almost every statement it made false, and why did church leaders continue to sanction plural marriages after it was received?

[371] "Polygamy, a limited practice in the early pioneer days of the Church, was discontinued in 1890, some 117 years ago." (Elder M. Russell Ballard, "Faith, Family, Facts, and Fruits," Oct 2007 General Conference.) "An example is plural marriage. This ended in the Church as an official practice in 1890. It's now 2010. Why are we still talking about it? It was a practice. It ended. We moved on." (Elder M. Russell Ballard, ""Sharing the Gospel with Confidence," Ensign July 2010.) See also Lavina Anderson, "Church Publishes First LDS Edition of the Bible," Ensign Oct 1979; Sheri Dew, "Something Extraordinary," March 1992 Ensign; Glen Leonard, "The Gathering to Nauvoo, 1839–45," Ensign, April 1979; Gracia Jones, "My Great-Great-Grandmother, Emma Hale Smith," Ensign, Aug. 1992; "Times of the Prophets," New Era, Jan. 2005;

[372] Doctrine and Covenants and Church History Class Member Study Guide, (1999), 27–28; Book of Mormon Seminary Teacher Manual, Lesson 44: Jacob 2:12–35, 2012; The Eternal Family Teacher Manual, Lesson 15: Eternal Marriage, 2015; Foundations of the Restoration Teacher Manual, Lesson 20: Plural Marriage, 2015;

[373] Larry King Live, "Gordon Hinckley: Distinguished Religious Leader of the Mormons", Aired September 8, 1998 - 9:00 p.m. ET. President Hinckley was well aware that this statement was not true, given that Quinn had provided him with an advanced copy of his work on post-manifesto plural marriages seeking permission to publish it years earlier.

[374] "More than a century ago God clearly revealed unto His prophet Wilford Woodruff that the practice of plural marriage should be discontinued, which means that it is now against the law of God." ("What are People Asking About Us?" General Conference Oct. 1998.)

[375] Presidents of the Church Student Manual, (2012), 94–111.

considered essential to salvation[376] in 1890 "not doctrinal" 100 years later, are there any doctrines that are protected from modern sensibilities? Furthermore, none of the information in the essay is new. Why did it take over 100 years for the church to finally report the truth about polygamy? Even without any effort on the part of the church, Quinn published his searching report of post-manifesto sanctioned polygamy in 1985. Why did it take 30 years for the church to make a statement on the topic, and then only making some half-truth concessions towards the truth?[377]

Publicly expressed reasons for substituting water for wine in the sacrament is another example of historical misrepresentation. In modern Mormonism, water is used exclusively for the sacrament instead of wine. D&C 27 is usually cited for this change. The heading for D&C 27 says:

> In preparation for a religious service at which the sacrament of bread and wine was to be administered, Joseph set out to procure wine. He was met by a heavenly messenger and received this revelation, a portion of which was written at the time and the remainder in the September following. Water is now used instead of wine in the sacramental services of the Church.

Although the last line in the heading gives the impression that this section is the reason water is used instead of wine in the sacrament, this is simply not

---

[376] "Where did this commandment come from in relation to polygamy? It also came from God. It was a revelation given unto Joseph Smith from God, and was made binding upon His servants. When this system was first introduced among this people, it was one of the greatest crosses that ever was taken up by any set of men since the world stood. Joseph Smith told others; he told me, and I can bear witness of it, 'that if this principle was not introduced, this Church and kingdom could not proceed.' When this commandment was given, it was so far religious, and so far binding upon the Elders of this Church that it was told them if they were not prepared to enter into it, and to stem the torrent of opposition that would come in consequence of it, the keys of the kingdom would be taken from them. When I see any of our people, men or women, opposing a principle of this kind, I have years ago set them down as on the high road to apostasy, and I do to-day; I consider them apostates, and not interested in this Church and kingdom." (John Taylor, Journal of Discourses, Vol.11, p. 221.)

[377] The article makes very impressionable statements in the text that support the official story, while the footnotes tell a different story. For example, the essay gives a gross underrepresentation of the number of post-manifesto plural marriages, stating that the paltry 25 recorded instances from one ledger provides "a rough sense of scale," when the footnote indicates that the ledger does not include any of the marriages performed by those known to have performed the majority of plural sealings during that time. It also states that 8 of the 19 brethren serving during that time took plural wives, probably including President Wilford Woodruff. Is this really the most honest way to present this information?

true. The church continued to use wine for the sacrament until well after 1900. Sometimes the Word of Wisdom is cited as the reason for the change from wine to water. Yet, the change was not made until long after the Word of Wisdom revelation was received. The Word of Wisdom actually explicitly states that wine is acceptable to drink for the sacrament.[378] The change came not because of D&C 27, or because of the Word of Wisdom, but in deference to the personal opinions of certain leading brethren, fans of the increasingly popular prohibition movement.[379] In this case, the misappropriation of the change to revelation shields church leaders from the charge that they changed a revealed ordinance to accord with social pressure.

The telling of the history of the Nauvoo temple is another example of how history in modern Mormonism is warped to avoid negative implications. The original Nauvoo temple has a rich history.[380] At the time of the martyrdom, the temple was far from complete, with walls only about halfway to their final height and most interior construction not yet started. It took almost another year to finish the walls, with the attic still not framed and the roof not yet shingled. The Saints used the incomplete temple for Oct. 1845 general conference, despite the need for temporary floors to be installed in order to do so. At this time, the first dedication of the incomplete temple took place. In Nov. 1845, the unfurnished attic level was dedicated and repurposed for endowments until February 1846, when no more ordinances were performed in the temple. At this time, the Saints began moving west, with members of the 12 praying in the temple that the Lord would "bless their move to the west and asked Him to enable them to complete the temple and have it formally dedicated" as it was not yet "formally dedicated." The day after this, the roof caught fire. Later, the floor cracked under weight, some smash windows to make it out of the building. In April 1846, a general conference was held in the basement of the temple, as the other floors were still under construction. Mob persecution was so great that a secret dedication was held. After holding a public dedication (with $1 cover charge), Orson

---

[378] "That inasmuch as any man drinketh wine or strong drink among you, behold it is not good, neither meet in the sight of your Father, only in assembling yourselves together to offer up your sacraments before him" (D&C 89:5).

[379] "George F. Richards preferred the technique of interviewing and urging compliance rather than insisting on lack of toleration. In keeping with the change in emphasis, the First Presidency and Twelve substituted water for wine in the sacrament in their temple meetings, apparently beginning July 5, 1906." ("The Word of Wisdom: From Principle To Requirement," Thomas G. Alexander, p. 79) See below for more on the shift from the Word of Wisdom as revealed to the Word of Wisdom as practiced today.

[380] The facts in this paragraph can be found in "Nauvoo Temple History" by David R. Crockett.

Hyde and Wilford Woodruff, the last apostles in Nauvoo, headed west. Unable to sell the temple as intended, they abandon it to the mob, who destroy the interior the following month (June 1846). In Sept. 1846, the steeple was struck by lightning. In Oct. of 1848, much of the temple was destroyed by fire. Finally, the church was able to sell the temple in March 1849. Ten years later it is knocked to the ground by cyclone. The stones of the building were used to build other buildings, resulting in not one stone being left upon another.

While the temple was dedicated many times, it is a stretch to say that it was ever completed. The temple was indeed used for ordinances long before the building was completed, but even these required the rigging of canvas to repurpose the attic, which had not been designed for endowments. Lack of sufficient donations for construction, settling floors, fires, and general lags in construction created a constant block to completion of the temple until it was finally "formally dedicated" long after the Saints had left Nauvoo. Still, the impression given in modern mentions are quite different from the reality. Elder Cook's recent account is typical, giving no mention of the delays or complications of building the temple, and featuring an ordering that gives the false impression that the temple was completed prior to the endowments being given:

> After the Prophet's martyrdom, the Saints completed the Nauvoo Temple, and the sealing power was used to bless thousands of faithful members before the exodus to the Mountain West. (Elder Quentin Cook, "Roots and Branches," April 2014 General Conference.)

President Monson glosses over the delays and gives the impression that the temple was in fact finished before they left. In reality, they were driven from their homes before the temple was anything close to completed.

> Persecutions raged, however, and with the Nauvoo Temple barely completed, they were driven from their homes once again, seeking refuge in a desert. (President Thomas Monson, "The Holy Temple— a Beacon to the World," April 2011 General Conference.)

Why aren't leaders more straightforward in their accounts of the Nauvoo temple? As with many other examples of misrepresented church history, plain recitation of the facts raises undesired negative implications. The Lord gave specific promises to accompany the completion of the Nauvoo temple, and curses to accompany the lack of completing it by the appointed time.[381] The leaders of the time knew this well. Orson Hyde stated:

---

[381] "But I command you, all ye my saints, to build a house unto me; and I grant unto you a sufficient time to build a house unto me; and during this time your baptisms

If we moved forward and finished this house we should be received and accepted as a church with our dead, but if not we should be rejected with our dead. These things have inspired and stimulated us to action in the finishing of it which through the blessing of God we have been enabled to accomplish and prepared it for dedication. In doing this we have only been saved as it were by the skin of our teeth. (Wilford Woodruff's Journal, 3:46-47; May 8, 1846.)

Leaders today know that an admission that the Saints fled Nauvoo prior to the completion of the temple would draw attention to the possibility that the martyrdom marked something other than a routine succession of church leadership. The fulfillment of the curses promised in D&C 124[382] for failure

---

shall be acceptable unto me. But behold, at the end of this appointment your baptisms for your dead shall not be acceptable unto me; and if you do not these things at the end of the appointment ye shall be rejected as a church, with your dead, saith the Lord your God." (D&C 124:31-32.) Joseph Smith occupied much time in Nauvoo preaching that the Saints should repent of taking lightly the instruction to build the temple, emphasizing that if they failed to do so, the Lord would abandon them. For example, "I will now ask this assembly and all the Saints if you will now build this house and receive the ordinances and blessings which God has in store for you; or will you not build unto the Lord this house, and let Him pass by and bestow these blessings upon another people? I pause for a reply." (DHC, June 11, 1843.) The people of Nauvoo were spending their money on brick homes, a masonic lodge, and other endeavors, delaying the construction of the temple. One convert recalled "I never shall forget the words he spoke on the first Sunday after I came to Nauvoo. The temple was built a few feet above the ground. While preaching he pointed towards it and said, 'The Lord has commanded us to build that temple. We want to build it, but we have not the means. There are people in this city who have the means, but they will not let us have them. What shall we do with such people? I say damn them!' and then he sat down." (Elder William E. Jones, "Recollections of the Prophet Joseph Smith," The Juvenile Instructor 27, 1892.)

[382] "If ye labor with all your might, I will consecrate that spot that it shall be made holy. And if my people will hearken unto my voice, and unto the voice of my servants whom I have appointed to lead my people, behold, verily I say unto you, they shall not be moved out of their place. But if they will not hearken to my voice, nor unto the voice of these men whom I have appointed, they shall not be blest, because they pollute mine holy grounds, and mine holy ordinances, and charters, and my holy words which I give unto them. And it shall come to pass that if you build a house unto my name, and do not do the things that I say, I will not perform the oath which I make unto you, neither fulfil the promises which ye expect at my hands, saith the Lord. For instead of blessings, ye, by your own works, bring cursings, wrath, indignation, and judgments upon your own heads, by your follies, and by all your abominations, which you practice before me, saith the Lord." Were the Nauvoo Saints "moved out of their place"? Did God "perform the oath" whereby he promised to send Elijah to the Nauvoo temple to restore the priesthood? Did any heavenly messenger visit the Nauvoo temple? What does this signify, other than that

to heed God's commandments regarding the Nauvoo temple are not simply a historical chastisement—there are contemporary implications, and they are significant.[383]

The evidence of deliberate and substantial omission, alteration, and fabrication of elements of church history beginning with the death of Joseph Smith is undeniable. One writer wrote:

> The official History of the Church of Jesus Christ of Latter-day Saints was published in book form under the direction of the First Presidency in 1902. The introductory assurance that 'no historical or doctrinal statement has been changed' is demonstrably wrong. Overshadowed by editorial censorship, hundreds of deletions, additions, and alterations, these seven volumes are not always reliable....Commenting on the many changes made in the historical work as it was being serialized in the Deseret News, Wandell [an assistant church historian] noted in his diary: ' I notice the interpolations because having been employed in the Historian's office at Nauvoo by Doctor Richards, and employed, too, in 1845, in compiling this very autobiography, I know that after Joseph's death his memoir was 'doctored' to suit the new order of things, and this, too, by the direct order of Brigham Young to Doctor Richards and systematically by Richards.' (Richard S. Van Wagoner, "Sidney Rigdon: A Portrait of Religious Excess," Signature Books (Salt Lake City, 1994), p. 322.)

Joseph's use of a seer stone to translate the Book of Mormon has long been an accusation against the official story. Images in church materials show Joseph reading directly from the uncovered plates. In response to the allegations, Joseph Fielding Smith wrote:

> ...there is no authentic statement in the history of the Church which states that the use of such a stone was made in that translation. The information is all hearsay, and personally, I do not believe that this stone was used for this purpose. (Joseph Fielding Smith, Doctrines of Salvation 3:225-226.)

---

the actions of the Nauvoo saints were viewed by God as "follies" and "abominations"?

[383] "I grant unto you a sufficient time to build a house unto me; and during this time your baptisms shall be acceptable unto me. But behold, at the end of this appointment your baptisms for your dead shall not be acceptable unto me; and if you do not these things at the end of the appointment ye shall be rejected as a church, with your dead, saith the Lord your God. (D&C 124:31-32.)

Joseph Fielding Smith dismissed this as anti-Mormon propaganda. Yet, the modern church has changed the narrative, admitting that the "anti" materials were actually correct:

> In fact, historical evidence shows that in addition to the two seer stones known as 'interpreters,' Joseph Smith used at least one other seer stone in translating the Book of Mormon, often placing it into a hat in order to block out light. (Ensign, Oct 2015.)

Joseph Fielding Smith, as the church historian for decades, had full access to church archives. There is nothing that modern church historians have access to that Joseph Fielding Smith didn't have access to, if he was willing to look. How is it that this information was only admitted recently?

A modest number of honest mistakes are reasonable in a church composed of lay local membership. However, when General Authorities have stated that their duty is to purposefully manipulate history[384] to preserve the reputation of leaders[385] and make the story of the restoration more palatable to the public, all while maintaining the accuracy[386] and transparency[387] of

---

[384] "My duty as a member of the Council of the Twelve is to protect what is most unique about the LDS church, namely the authority of priesthood, testimony regarding the restoration of the gospel, and the divine mission of the Savior. Everything may be sacrificed in order to maintain the integrity of those essential facts. Thus, if Mormon Enigma reveals information that is detrimental to the reputation of Joseph Smith, then it is necessary to try to limit its influence and that of its authors."(Elder Dallin Oaks, footnote 28, "Inside the Mind of Joseph Smith: Psychobiography and the Book of Mormon," Introduction p. xliii.)

[385] "It is one thing to depreciate a person who exercises corporate power or even government power. It is quite another thing to criticize or depreciate a person for the performance of an office to which he or she has been called of God. It does not matter that the criticism is true. As Elder George F. Richards, President of the Council of the Twelve, said in a conference address in April 1947, 'when we say anything bad about the leaders of the Church, whether true or false, we tend to impair their influence and their usefulness and are thus working against the Lord and his cause.'" (Elder Dallin H. Oaks, "Reading Church History," CES Doctrine and Covenants Symposium, Brigham Young University, 16 Aug. 1985, page 25. also see Dallin H. Oaks, "Elder Decries Criticism of LDS Leaders," quoted in The Salt Lake Tribune, Sunday August 18, 1985, p. 2B.)

[386] "The Church publishes reliable information on topics of current interest…in the Gospel Topics section of the Church's website, at lds.org/topics. The purpose of the Gospel Topics section is to provide accurate and transparent information on Church history and doctrine within the framework of faith." (Letter to Bishops and Stake Presidents, Sept 9, 2014.)

[387] "Our history is an open book. They may find what they are looking for, but the fact is the history of the church is clear and open and leads to faith and strength and virtues." (Gordon B. Hinkley, Deseret News Dec 25, 2005

church-produced history, the fine line between presentation and dishonesty is crossed.

Deference to Biased Professionals

Church leaders rely on church historians for their history. [388] Church historians have been continually warned to only present church-positive narratives and evidences at penalty of their jobs.

> That historian or scholar who delights in pointing out the weaknesses and frailties of present or past leaders destroys faith. A destroyer of faith—particularly one within the Church, and more particularly one who is employed specifically to build faith—places himself in great spiritual jeopardy. He is serving the wrong master, and unless he repents, he will not be among the faithful in the eternities....Do not spread disease germs! (President Boyd K. Packer, "The Mantle is Far, Far Greater Than the Intellect", 1981, BYU Studies, Vol. 21, No. 3, pp. 259-271.)

And again,

> Any who are tempted to rake through the annals of history, to use truth unrighteously, or to dig up facts with the intent to defame or destroy, should hearken to this warning of scripture: 'The wrath of God is...against all...who hold the truth in unrighteousness.' To anyone who, because of truth, may be tempted to become a dissenter against the Lord and his anointed, weigh carefully your action... (Elder Russell M. Nelson, "Truth—and More," Ensign, Jan. 1986, p. 69.)

---

http://www.deseretnews.com/article/635171604/Pres-Hinckley-answers-myriad-questions-about-the-LDS-Church.html).

[388] "When I have a question that I cannot answer, I turn to those who can help me. The Church is blessed with trained scholars and those who have devoted a lifetime of study, who have come to know our history and the scriptures. These thoughtful men and women provide context and background so we can better understand our sacred past and our current practices." (Elder M. Russell Ballard, Southern Utah Conference, Sept. 2015) "The fifteen men really do know, and they really do care. And they realize that maybe since Kirtland, we never have had a period of, I'll call it apostasy, like we're having right now; largely over these issues. We do have another initiative that we have called, "Answers to Gospel Questions". We are trying to figure out exactly what channels to deliver it in and exactly what format to put it in....we are trying to create an offering that will address these issues and be available for the public at large *and to the church leaders, because many of them don't have answers either.* It can be very disappointing to church members." (Church historian Elder Marlin Jensen, Q&A at Utah State University.)

Two public examples of the enforcement of this long-standing policy are that of Leonard Arrington and Randy Bott. Arrington was called as the church historian in the early 1970s. He presided over a decade of unprecedented open access to church records and objectivity in church history. He was rewarded with a non-public release and replacement. More recently, Bott, an award winning religion professor at BYU, was pressured to retire after providing a quote accurately representing the church's historical view on the priesthood ban during a time when the church was going to great measures to distance themselves from that history.

The reticence of church historians to provide correct information to church leaders is apparent in official teachings. For example, in the October 2014 General Conference, Elder Nelson stated, "No Prophet has ever been elected." Brigham Young himself said, "I was unanimously elected President of the Church of Jesus Christ of Latter-day Saints." (Winter Quarters, Dec 27, 1847, Complete Discourses of Brigham Young, Signature Books, 2009, page 267.) Every church historian should know the basic details of the succession crisis in order to know that Brigham Young was elected president of the church, let alone that the practice of voting on candidates for leadership began before Brigham Young and continued long after him.[389] Yet, no one on

---

[389] An example of how sustaining operated in Joseph's day: "[Sidney Rigdon as the Moderator of the meeting] nominated Joseph Smith jr. the first President of the whole Church, to preside over the same. All were requested to vote—who was unanimously chosen. He then made a few remarks, accepting the appointment requesting the prayers of the Church in his behalf. President Smith then nominated Prest. Sidney Rigdon to be one of his counselors—who was unanimously chosen. He then nominated Fredrick G Williams to be his next counsillor who was objected to by Elder Lyman Wight in a few remarks referring to a certain letter written to this place by the said Frederick G Williams Also Elder Marsh objected to Prest Williams Elder James Emmet also objected to Prest Williams. Bishop Edward Partridge said he seconded Prest. William's nomination and should vote for him; and as to said letter, he had heard it, and saw nothing so criminal in it. President David Whitmer also made a few remarks in Prest. Williams' favor. Elder Marsh made further remarks. Elder Thomas Grover also objected to Prest. Williams. Prest. S. Rigdon then nominated Prest. Hyrum Smith to take Prest. Williams' place. He then called for a vote in favor of Prest. Williams' who was rejected. He then called for a vote in favor of Prest Hyrum Smith, which was carried unanimously." (Minutes of the Far West High Council, November 7, 1837.) God provided for the voting process to be an opportunity to express disapproval: "And a commandment I give unto you, that you should fill all these offices and approve of those names which I have mentioned, or else disapprove of them at my general conference;" (D&C 124:144.) Common consent (see D&C 26:2) means much more than just accepting the provided candidates for office—God instructs us to vote for and against leaders: "No person is to be ordained to any office in this church, where there is a regularly organized branch of the same, without the vote of that church;" (D&C 20:65.) Modifying the

the correlation committee corrected Elder Nelson.[390] This is not an isolated occurrence. Historical errors riddle general conference talks and church manuals.

Church leaders perpetuate falsehoods in ignorance and will continue to do so until they view objective church history as valuable[391] or until they reverse the precedence of disciplining church employees who publicize true history that happens to contradict the official actions and policies of the modern church. A first step is to realize and admit the errors they have made.[392] Until active members value church history and stop relying upon church employees for their history,[393] they will be blind to perpetuated historical falsehoods and historically contraindicated contemporary church policies.

The Word of Wisdom: A Case Study in Fabricated Doctrine

The evolution of the word of wisdom is a wonderful case study in how doctrines can be created through historical ignorance. Abstinence from coffee, tea, tobacco, and alcohol is considered a hallmark of modern Mormons. The Bible dictionary defines peculiar as carrying "the meaning of the saints' being the Lord's own special people or treasure."

Leaders have indicated that these restrictions are what makes modern Mormons peculiar. Abstinence from these materials has come to be

---

idea of sustaining to only meaning supporting the candidate proposed is an innovation of modern Mormonism.

[390] The stated purpose of the correlation committee is to prevent doctrinal and historical mistakes in official church publications. They proofread all General Conference talks.

[391] "That historian or scholar who delights in pointing out the weaknesses and frailties of present or past leaders destroys faith....Do not spread disease germs!" (President Boyd K. Packer, "The Mantle is Far, Far Greater Than the Intellect", 1981, BYU Studies, Vol. 21, No. 3, pp. 259-271.)

[392] Despite many attempts to point out the mistakes church history contains, the church recently claimed that it "publishes reliable information on topics of current interest...in the Gospel Topics section of the Church's website, at lds.org/topics. The purpose of the Gospel Topics section is to provide accurate and transparent information on Church history and doctrine within the framework of faith." (Letter to Bishops and Stake Presidents, Sept 9, 2014.) The gospel topics section is ghost written by church historian employees, and thus riddled with omissions, alterations, and fabrications.

[393] Assistant church historian Richard Turley said at a recent meeting with historically-concerned Swedish members: "Much of what you get about history comes from historians; from the people like me who do the best they can under the circumstances of their time. And then somebody else comes along later, with new discoveries, new documents, and they rewrite it, okay? So it's—Don't put the responsibility on the prophet; put it on ordinary people like me who do the best we know how to do it."

understood as "the maintenance of an identity for the church separate from the world" (Edwin B. Firmage, "The Word of Wisdom: Mark of a Peculiar People," Oct 1972), the thing that makes Mormons more like God than the rest of the world. In other words, church leaders teach that abstinence from coffee, tea, tobacco, and alcohol makes the subject more special to God, or more holy. For example, President Joseph Fielding Smith explained:

> When we join the Church and receive the priesthood, we are expected to forsake many of the ways of the world and live as becometh saints....Many in the world use tea, coffee, tobacco, and liquor, and are involved in the use of drugs. Many profane and are vulgar and indecent, immoral and unclean in their lives, but all these things should be foreign to us. We are the saints of the Most High. We hold the holy priesthood. To ancient Israel, by the mouth of Moses, the Lord said: "... if ye will obey my voice indeed, and keep my covenant, then ye shall be a peculiar treasure unto me above all people: for all the earth is mine: And ye shall be unto me a kingdom of priests, and an holy nation." (Ex. 19:5–6.) This promise is ours also. If we will walk in paths of virtue and holiness, the Lord will pour out his blessings upon us to a degree we have never supposed possible. We shall be in very deed, as Peter expressed it, "a chosen generation, a royal priesthood, an holy nation, a peculiar people." (1 Pet. 2:9.) And we will be peculiar because we will not be like other people who do not live up to these standards. (Joseph Fielding Smith, "Our responsibilities as priesthood holders," April 1971 General Conference.)

President Smith implies that use of these materials is just as effectual in preventing one from becoming part of a holy nation as immoral and unclean behavior. This belief is a part of the traditions of modern Mormonism.

From where do these perceptions stem? In the context of history, the current understanding of the word of wisdom did not come into place until 1930, when the word of wisdom as a temple requirement was added to the General Handbook of Instructions.[394] Though pressures to make the word of wisdom a commandment existed even during Joseph Smith's life, these pressures were resisted over several successors. For example, Joseph Smith continued to drink coffee, tea, beer, and wine at times (including wine for the sacrament) throughout his life. He had a stocked bar in the Nauvoo house, and drank wine on the day he died.[395]

---

[394] See Joseph Fielding McConkie and Craig J. Ostler, "Revelations of the Restoration: A Commentary on the Doctrine and Covenants and Other Modern Revelations."

[395] See Diary of Joseph Smith, March 11, 1843 entry, History of the Church (January 1836), vol. 2, 369 ("Our hearts were made glad by the fruit of the vine."; History of

After Joseph's death, Brigham Young refused to endorse the idea of making the word of wisdom into a commandment. In 1861 he said,

> Some of the brethren are very strenuous upon the "Word of Wisdom", and would like to have me preach upon it, and urge it upon the brethren, and make it a test of fellowship. I do not think I shall do so. I have never done so. (Brigham Young, JD 9:35.)

In 1870 he said,

> The observance of the Word of Wisdom, or interpretation of God's requirements on this subject, must be left, partially, with the people. We cannot make laws like the Medes and Persians. We cannot say you shall never drink a cup of tea, or you shall never taste of this, or you shall never taste of that... (Brigham Young, JD 14:20.)

Brigham's successor John Taylor reiterated that the word of wisdom was not necessary for a temple recommend, but differed from his predecessors in suggesting that those who do not observe it ought to be ashamed of themselves.[396] President Woodruff said

> ...he regarded the Word of Wisdom in its entirety as given of the Lord for the Latter-day Saints to observe, but he did not think that Bishops should withhold recommends from persons who did not adhere strictly to it.[397]

---

the Church (May 2, 1843), vol. 5, p. 380, History of the Church (June 27, 1844), vol. 6, p. 616, History of the Church (June 27, 1844, vol. 7, p. 101), (Millennial Star, vol. 23, no. 45 p. 720 (9 November 1861).

[396] "The Word of Wisdom as originally given was sent not by commandment or constraint; but 'by revelation on the the [sic] Word of Wisdom, for the temporal salvation of all Saints in these days,' and no rule has been formulated, nor law proclaimed, nor counsel given since that time which makes its strict observance, necessary to receive ordinances of life and salvation in the temples. There are many cases where people may violate the strict letter of the Word of Wisdom, and yet be following its spirit in doing so.....and yet...we are opposed to the common use of these articles by Latter-day Saints. A man or a woman who disregards the Word of Wisdom and still profess to be a Latter-day Saint ought to be ashamed of their conduct. A judicious bishop will not give a recommend to such a person without first taking up a labor with him or her against the indulgence in the habits mentioned in the Word of Wisdom. No person who flagrantly violates that word should ask for a recommend." (John Taylor to John D.T. McAllister and David H. Cannon, Nov 30, 1886.)

[397] Minutes of First Presidency and Council of Twelve Meeting, Journal History of the Church of Jesus Christ of Latter-day Saints," May 5, 1898, LDS Church Archives; cited in Thomas G. Alexander, "The Word of Wisdom: From Principle to Requirement," Dialogue: A Journal of Mormon Thought 14:3 (Autumn 1981), 78–88.

In 1901, Apostles Brigham Young, Jr. and John Henry Smith argued that beer was not prohibited.[398]

The transition from advice to commandment essentially began during the administration of Joseph F. Smith. In 1902, Joseph F. Smith suggested that drunkards be denied recommends, but that older or more subtle users should not be penalized.[398] In making this change, President Smith did not cite any revelation. In fact, under oath to the U.S. Congress in 1904, President Smith indicated that he had never received a revelation as president of the church (see Reed Smoot hearings transcripts). In other words, President Smith elevated the word of wisdom from a principle explicitly indicated by God as a non-commandment to a commandment required for entrance into the temple. The next year, the commandment was expanded to prevent any man from holding a leadership position if they did not obey the word of wisdom.[398] Again, this change did not come via revelation, if we are to take President Smith at his word under oath to Congress. On 5 July 1906, the First Presidency and Council of the Twelve began using water instead of wine for their sacrament meetings.[399] President Smith speculated that "the reason undoubtedly why the Word of Wisdom was given as not by 'commandment or restraint' was that at that time, at least, if it had been given as a commandment it would have brought every man, addicted to the use of these noxious things, under condemnation; so the Lord was merciful and gave them a chance to overcome, before He brought them under the law."[400] Two years later, he made compliance with the word of wisdom a requirement for ordination to the priesthood.[398] Note that the brethren had used wine for the sacrament every Sunday in the temple until just 7 years prior.

It is clear from history that the word of wisdom was not a commandment until President Joseph F. Smith made it so without revelation. However, has the meaning of the word of wisdom always been the same? As previously cited, Joseph Smith's understanding did not seem to preclude the consumption of tea, wine, beer, or tobacco. He used all of these products from time to time from when the revelation was received until his death. In fact, the list of leaders just who consumed alcohol post-word of wisdom include (at a minimum) Joseph Smith (President of Church), Brigham Young (President of Church), John Taylor (President of Church), Brigham Young, Jr. (Apostle), John Henry Smith (Apostle), BH Roberts (President of 70), Anthon H. Lund (1st Presidency), Matthias F. Cowley (Apostle), Charles W. Penrose (1st Presidency), and George Albert Smith (President of Church). As already noted, wine was used for the sacrament until 1906, therefore all

---

[398] Alexander, "Principle to Requirement", pp. 78–88.

[399] Some have speculated that the timing of the change--just as the church ended the practice of plural marriage--indicates that the church was looking for something to replace the previously necessary for salvation law of plural marriage.

[400] Joseph F. Smith, Conference Report, October 1913, p. 14.

leaders who participated in the temple sacrament (at a minimum the 15) would be included in this list. The names listed are all documented as using alcohol outside of the sacrament.

It is clear that leaders prior to President Joseph F. Smith's change did not believe abstinence from alcohol was a commandment from God. What about tobacco, coffee, tea, or otherwise? It turns out that the interpretation of several elements of the word of wisdom was highly disputed from the start. From the start, many were willing to put forth their diverse opinions on the matter. Early on, Hyrum Smith indicated that "'hot drinks are not for the body, or belly;' there are many who wonder what this can mean; whether it refers to tea, or coffee, or not. I say it does refer to tea, and coffee."[401] Here, he both admits to the confusion about the meaning of the imprecise parts of the word of wisdom, and gives his opinion of the same. Although our modern day traditions blind us to the ambiguity of the original revelation, Hyrum Smith's documentation of the confusion surrounding the meaning of the revelation is understandable in a historical context. For example, when the revelation was given, the meaning of "hot drinks" was not necessarily a question of their temperature. The 1828 Webster's dictionary indicates that this phrase was regularly used as a synonym for liquor, as liquor burns the drinker's throat. In other words, it is completely possible that God did not mention tea and coffee at all in the word of wisdom. As another example, the most likely definition of the "mild drinks" made from barley[402] in the word of wisdom was beer, meaning that far from banning alcohol, the word of wisdom might actually endorse it!

The meaning of the word of wisdom was never canonized by vote of the church, or even cemented by proclamation of the 15. Latter leaders came up with a variety of items that were against the word of wisdom. For example, President Lorenzo Snow emphasized that not eating meat was central to the Word of Wisdom in 1900. In 1930, Apostle John A. Widtsoe claimed that refined flour was contrary to the word of wisdom.[398] Caffeine became another item that some said was against the word of wisdom, while others said it was not. Joseph Smith never received (and doesn't appear to have asked for) a clarifying revelation on the word of wisdom. None of his successors recorded a revelation on the subject.

With knowledge of history, these changes could have been avoided. Instead, we have a worthiness test that has nothing to do with morality that excludes countless numbers of people from baptism and the temple simply for drinking tea and coffee, when early leaders did both without any loss of spiritual blessings. Jesus clearly taught that "Not that which goeth into the

---

[401] "The Word of Wisdom," *Times and Seasons*, 1 June 1842, p. 800.

[402] "Nevertheless, wheat for man, and corn for the ox, and oats for the horse, and rye for the fowls and for swine, and for all beasts of the field, and barley for all useful animals, and for mild drinks, as also other grain."

mouth defileth a man; but that which cometh out of the mouth, this defileth the man." (Matthew 15:10, Inspired Version.) The modern version of the word of wisdom is not only *not* God's word, but teaches the *opposite* of God's word: that somehow tea, coffee, tobacco, and alcohol spiritually defile you.

The Second Comforter: A Case Study in Removed Doctrine

Historical knowledge prevents the loss of true doctrine. The doctrines of "calling and election" and "Second Comforter" are taught plainly in scripture and in the teachings of Joseph Smith, as detailed in the chapter "The Gospel of Christ." Joseph called obtaining your calling and election "among the first principles of the gospel" (Words of Joseph Smith, 27 June 1839) and frequently preached it among public crowds.

Seeking these experiences are not optional for a disciple of Christ. We are commanded to seek the face of the Lord:

> And seek the face of the Lord always, that in patience ye may possess your souls, and ye shall have eternal life. (D&C 101:38.)

To *know* Christ is required for eternal life. "And this is life eternal, that they might know thee the only true God, and Jesus Christ, whom thou hast sent." (John 17:3.) How can you *know* someone you have never met? Jesus said we must actually *receive* him in order to know him.

> But if ye receive me in the world, then shall ye know me, and shall receive your exaltation; that where I am ye shall be also. This is eternal lives—to know the only wise and true God, and Jesus Christ, whom he hath sent. I am he. Receive ye, therefore, my law. (D&C 132:23-24.)

Because one cannot have eternal life without obtaining these experiences, true messengers from God always commend others to seek Jesus:

> And now, I would commend you to seek this Jesus of whom the prophets and apostles have written, that the grace of God the Father, and also the Lord Jesus Christ, and the Holy Ghost, which beareth record of them, may be and abide in you forever. Amen. (Ether 12:41.)

You will not find mention of either of these doctrines in the teachings of modern Mormonism. When was the last time you heard a General Authority bear their witness of having their calling and election made sure or having received the Second Comforter? When was the last time you heard a General Conference talk that even referenced either of these topics? When have you seen them mentioned in church manuals? The "Gospel Topics" page on LDS.org does not list "Calling and Election" or "Second Comforter." Nevertheless, General Authorities used to bear their witness of having their calling and election made sure and having received the Second Comforter.[403] There used to be General Conference talks and Ensign articles on these topics. [404] They used to be described in church manuals.

What changed? Harold B. Lee's correlation program formalized doctrinal creation, modification, and deletion via an outline of permissible gospel topics. It is probable that "Second Comforter" and "calling and election" were not on the original list. As the brethren who had begun leadership callings pre-correlation passed away, so did these topics.

In contrast to God's word in the scriptures and through Joseph Smith, modern LDS leaders have not only neglected to teach the doctrines of the Second Comforter and calling and election made sure, but have actually preached against them.[405]

Conclusion

The church persists in omissions, alterations, and fabrications for several reasons. First, the leaders are ignorant of objective church history. Second, they rely on church employees, who have a vested interest in hiding and misrepresenting church history to present the church and its leaders in a positive light. When church leaders believe that the Holy Ghost testifies of all truth but only church-promoting truth,[406] it is not surprising that their policies

---

[403] Joseph Smith, Oliver Cowdery, Lyman Wight, and many other contemporaries of Joseph Smith openly claimed to have seen Jesus in waking vision.

[404] The last conference talk using the phrase "Second Comforter" was in 1963. The last conference talk referencing "calling and election" was in 1984. Each of the three references to the topic in the 1980s were from Elder Bruce R. McConkie, the last general authority to teach this doctrine.

[405] "I have never prayed to see the Savior, I know of men—Apostles—who have seen the Savior more than once. I have prayed to the Lord for the inspiration of his Spirit to guide me, and I have told him that I have seen so many men fall because of some great manifestation to them..." (Heber J. Grant Journal, 4 October 1942) "Of course, all of the righteous desire to see the face of our Savior, but the suggestions that this must happen in mortality is a familiar tactic of the adversary." (Dallin Oaks, Boise, Idaho, June 17, 2105.) In the newest LDS edition of the Bible, the footnotes to John 14:16, 18, and 23—previously referring to Christ—have been changed to refer to the Holy Ghost. It is clear that the former content was not only the position of the committee of apostles that created the footnotes, but also Joseph's position, as given in D&C 130:3: "John 14:23—The appearing of the Father and the Son, in that verse, is a personal appearance; and the idea that the Father and the Son dwell in a man's heart is an old sectarian notion, and is false." (D&C 130:3.)

[406] "It does not matter that the criticism is true....The Holy Ghost will not guide or confirm criticism of the Lord's anointed, or of Church leaders, local or general. This reality should be part of the spiritual evaluation that LDS readers and viewers apply to those things written about our history and those who made it." (Elder Dallin H. Oaks, "Reading Church History," CES Doctrine and Covenants Symposium,

of purposefully omitting, misrepresenting, and fabricating history to create a church-positive narrative continue.

These problems have no simple solution. To reverse the system now and interpret modern Mormonism within the context of true history would contraindicate many traditions in the church.

We should not fear true history. We must resist the pernicious tradition in the church that there is such a thing as non-faith-promoting history. *All* church history is faith promoting, no matter how disturbing, because the only thing it can displace is something that isn't true. Falsehoods can never save you. False traditions damn us. They prevent us from progressing towards God. You cannot have real faith in something that is false. Alma wrote, "If ye have faith ye hope for things which are not seen, which are true." (Alma 32:21.) Even when it is painful, true church history will bring you closer to Christ through freeing you from false tradition. The efficacy of truth is not dependent on its source or how it is presented. Truth "is knowledge of things as they are, and as they were, and as they are to come;" (D&C 93:24). It is *not* things as we wish they had been. The heading in a chapter from the Joseph Smith priesthood manual says, "The gospel of Jesus Christ embraces all truth; the faithful accept the truths God has revealed and put aside false traditions." Joseph taught "To become a joint heir of the heirship of the Son, one must put away all his false traditions." (Joseph Smith, HC 5:554.) It is not false tradition, but knowledge that leads us to eternal life. Saul was probably very disappointed to find out that all his pre-theophany Phariseeism was actually leading him away from God, despite his contemporary beliefs to the contrary. Still, he recognized that what Jesus had told him—the truth—would draw him closer to Christ than all that Phariseeism ever did. He said, "I count all things but loss for the excellency of the knowledge of Christ Jesus my Lord: for whom I have suffered the loss of all things, and do count them but dung, that I may win Christ." (Phillipians 3:8). Paul had no sacred cows, no false idols he wasn't willing to let go of when provided the opportunity to embrace mutually exclusive knowledge of God. Are you willing to embrace truth at all costs?

What Latter-day Saint can say that they are not interested in church history, when their very salvation depends on rooting out the many false traditions present in their understanding of the gospel, which can only occur through knowing church history? This attitude is opposite of what Joseph demonstrated. He said, "When things that are of the greatest importance are passed over by weak-minded men without even a thought, I want to see truth in all its bearings and hug it to my bosom." (HC 6:477.)

Brigham Young University, 16 Aug. 1985, page 25. also see Dallin H. Oaks, "Elder Decries Criticism of LDS Leaders," quoted in The Salt Lake Tribune, Sunday August 18, 1985, p. 2B)

Modern church history has for decades matched Napoleon Bonaparte's purported definition: "what is history but fables agreed upon?" He knew that "Whoever controls the image and information of the past determines what and how future generations will think; whoever controls the information and images of the present determines how those same people will view the past."[407] George Orwell said something similar but simpler: "He who controls the past controls the future. He who controls the present controls the past." Ignorance of the past invites mistaken ideas about the present. One who thinks his forebears were righteous will seek God very differently than one who knew his forebears were wicked. The Lamanites consistently suffered from a mistaken idea of the righteousness of Laman and Lemuel.

In the New Testament, Jesus told the Pharisees that they had strayed away from the gospel by substituting the commandments of men for God's word. These Pharisees spent a lot of time studying the gospel and practicing religious ceremony. It was not for lack of effort that they missed the mark, but lack of focus. Had they spent only a little of that time studying their church history, they never would have been swept away by the traditions of their elders, which were contrary to the gospel. If we do not know the gospel as given through Joseph, we are just as incapable of noticing deviations from the gospel restored through Joseph as the Pharisees were of noticing deviations from the law given to Moses.

Church history is vital to living the gospel of the restoration. Church history is the link to the gospel restored through Joseph Smith. Our familiarity with his teachings in the context in which they were given in a large part dictates at once the degree to which we can live the doctrines of the restoration and our capacity to detect deviations therefrom.

Without history we cannot know our religion, but only what it has become. With history, we can know what differences exist and where they came from. We can ascertain whether the spiritual fruits present today are different from those manifested in the past, and know what changes account for the difference in fruits. The purpose of church history is not to keep our testimonies strong, or in other words, reinforce our traditions. Rather, it is to seek the truth. The truth can and does disagree with our traditions. The descendants of Laman and Lemuel continued to believe that Nephi was a liar, that he stole governance, and that the people of Jerusalem were not wicked. All of these things could be disproved through accurate history. Apologetic history ("keeping our testimonies strong") is a sure-fire way to dwindle in unbelief because it disconnects our current perspective from what was actually restored in the past.

---

[407] Arnold Toynbee, "A Study of History."

As an institution, we need to repent of our ignorance and dishonesty, even if it requires a serious and reaching reevaluation of fundamental claims. God will not honor anything built on lies. "He that covereth his sins shall not prosper: but whoso confesseth and forsaketh them shall have mercy." (Proverbs 28:13.)

Temples

The book of Isaiah opens with a scathing rebuke of a people engrossed in blindness. They are spoken of as rebellious sons. He calls these people worse than dumb animals, totally incapable of an informed relationship with him. He calls them sinners, wrongdoers, perverts, and apostates. He says they are sick and diseased from their head to their heart to the soles of their feet, connoting that their gospel understanding, desires, and actions are wrong, from normal members to leaders. He says they are covered with bruises, wounds, and festering sores, intimating that despite the gravity of their condition, they aren't aware of it. He says they are as bad as Sodom and Gomorrah.[408]

Most Mormons shed off this condemnatory language as applying to some historical group, or some contemporary Christian sect. But the chapter continues, making the target of the rebuke more clear.

God continues with some very specific temple language:

> For what purpose are your abundant sacrifices to me? says Jehovah. I have had my fill of offerings of rams and fat of fatted beasts; the blood of bulls and sheep and he-goats I do not want. When you come to see me, who requires you to trample my courts so? Bring no more worthless offerings; they are as a loathsome incense to me. As for convening meetings at the New Month and on the Sabbath, wickedness with the solemn gathering I cannot approve. Your monthly and regular meetings my soul detests. They have become a burden on me; I am weary of putting up with them. When you spread forth your hands, I will conceal my eyes from you; though you

---

[408] "Hear, O heavens! Give heed, O earth! Jehovah has spoken: I have reared sons, brought them up, but they have revolted against me. The ox knows its owner, the ass its master's stall, but Israel does not know; my people are insensible. Alas, a nation astray, a people weighed down by sin, the offspring of wrongdoers, perverse children: they have forsaken Jehovah, they have spurned the Holy One of Israel, they have lapsed into apostasy. Why be smitten further by adding to your waywardness? The whole head is sick, the whole heart diseased. From the soles of the feet even to the head there is nothing sound, only wounds and bruises and festering sores; they have not been pressed out or bound up, nor soothed with ointment.....Hear the word of Jehovah, O leaders of Sodom; give heed to the law of our God, you people of Gomorrah!" (Isaiah 1:2-6,10 Gileadi Translation.)

pray at length, I will not hear—your hands are filled with blood. Wash yourselves clean: remove your wicked deeds from before my eyes; cease to do evil. (Isaiah 1:11-16, Gileadi Translation.)

What religious group today practices temple worship? What group emphasizes frequent temple worship while de-emphasizing the purpose of temple worship[409] to the point that they can be compared to dumb cattle who trample the court of the temple, unaware of the reason they are there? What group has special meetings on the first Sabbath of the "New Month"? What group "spreads forth" their hands in prayer in temple worship, pleading for the Lord to hear them? Only the Latter-day Saints.

Is it possible that modern LDS temple worship is viewed by God much differently than it is viewed by modern Mormons?

Experience vs. Ordinances

Anciently, there were two main purposes of the temple. The more common purpose, both in the number of occurrences and the number of people to whom it was available, was to participate in ordinances that typified re-entrance into the presence of God. The more important but less common experience was to actually re-enter the presence of God in the temple. Everything in the temple pointed to re-entering God's presence.

Over time, the wickedness of the priests caused a cessation of God's appearances in the temple. The inevitable outcome of such a transition is a reconstruction of the intent of the practice. In this case, the ordinances that taught one what to do to re-enter God's presence became the end instead of a means to an end. Thus, the ordinances that typified the appearance of God took precedence over the actual appearance of God, until finally the typifying symbolism was lost and the ordinances became practiced without a recognition of what they represented, let alone an attempt to actually obtain a visitation from God.

In Jesus' time, the Pentecost proved to be a restoration of the purpose of the temple, although the structure itself was dissociated from the event due to the apostate rulers' control of the actual temple. On that day,

> when the day of Pentecost was fully come, they were all with one accord in one place. And suddenly there came a sound from heaven as of a rushing mighty wind, and it filled all the house where they were sitting. And there appeared unto them cloven tongues like as of fire, and it sat upon each of them. And they were all filled with the Holy Ghost, and began to speak with other tongues, as the Spirit gave them utterance. And there were dwelling at Jerusalem Jews,

---

[409] As described later in this chapter, the purpose of the temple is to re-enter the presence of God.

devout men, out of every nation under heaven. Now when this was noised abroad, the multitude came together, and were confounded, because that every man heard them speak in his own language. (Acts 2:1-6.)

This, Joseph taught, was an endowment of power from on high, designed to give the disciples power in the priesthood, manifested by outward spiritual gifts, before they went out to preach the gospel to the world.[410] As First Presidency counselor Charles Penrose later taught, although the receipt of the gift of the Holy Ghost was an internal occurrence, it is always attended by outward manifestations of spiritual gifts.[411]

> [The gift of the Holy Ghost's] internal fruits are faith, knowledge, wisdom, joy, peace, patience, temperance, long suffering, brotherly kindness and charity. Its external gifts are manifested in prophecies, visions, discernments, healings, miracles, power over evil spirits, speaking in various tongues, interpretation of tongues, etc. (Charles W. Penrose, "Mormon Doctrine, Plain and Simple," p. 17.)

Jesus had commanded them to await this "endowment of power from on high" before leaving to preach the gospel.[412]

The pattern of endowment was renewed in our dispensation in 1831. On Jan 2, 1831 the Lord said,

---

[410] "Christ preached through Jerrusalem on the same ground whare John had preached & when the Apostles were raised up they worked in Jerrusalem & Jesus Commanded them to tarry thare untill they were endowed with power from on high 16 had they not work to do in Jerrusalem. they did work & prepared a people for the pentecost The Kingdom of God was with them before the day of pentecost as well as afterwards & it was also with John & he preached the same gospel & Baptism that Jesus & the Apostles preached after him The endowment was to prepare the desiples for their mission into the world." (WOJS, 22 Jan 1843)

[411] This was a common understanding at the time. Orson Pratt taught, "Spiritual gifts are those blessings given by the Holy Spirit to all who are made partakers of it. Whenever the Holy Ghost takes up its residence in a person, it not only cleanses, sanctifies, and purifies him, in proportion as he yields himself to its influence, but also imparts to him some gift, intended for the benefit of himself and others. No one who has been born of the Spirit, and who remains sufficiently faithful, is left destitute of a Spiritual Gift. A person who is without a Spiritual Gift, has not the Spirit of God dwelling in him, in a sufficient degree, to save him; he cannot be called a Saint, or a child of God ; for all Saints who constitute the Church of Christ, are baptized into the same Spirit; and each one, without any exception, is made a partaker of some Spiritual Gift."

[412] "And, behold, I send the promise of my Father upon you: but tarry ye in the city of Jerusalem, until ye be endued with power from on high." (Luke 24:49.)

> Wherefore, for this cause I gave unto you the commandment that ye should go to the Ohio; and there I will give unto you my law; and there you shall be endowed with power from on high; And from thence, whosoever I will shall go forth among all nations, and it shall be told them what they shall do; (D&C 38:32-33.)

In Feb 1831 he said,

> Again I say, hearken ye elders of my church, whom I have appointed: Ye are not sent forth to be taught, but to teach the children of men the things which I have put into your hands by the power of my Spirit; And ye are to be taught from on high. Sanctify yourselves and ye shall be endowed with power, that ye may give even as I have spoken. (D&C 43:15-16.)

In the same month he said,

> Behold, thus saith the Lord unto you my servants, it is expedient in me that the elders of my church should be called together, from the east and from the west, and from the north and from the south, by letter or some other way. And it shall come to pass, that inasmuch as they are faithful, and exercise faith in me, I will pour out my Spirit upon them in the day that they assemble themselves together. (D&C 44:1-2.)

This promise was fulfilled prior to the building of the Kirtland temple. On June 3, 1831, a conference began where many Elders experienced Pentecostal experiences. Here are several first hand accounts:

> It was clearly evident that the Lord gave us power in proportion to the work to be done, and strength according to the race set before us, and grace and help as our needs required. Great harmony prevailed; several were ordained; faith was strengthened; and humility, so necessary for the blessing of God to follow prayer, characterized the Saints. (Joseph Smith, HC, 1:176-177.)

> The spirit of the Lord fell upon Joseph in an unusual manner. And prophesied that John the Revelator was then among the ten tribes of Israel who had been led away by Salmaneser, king of Assyria, to prepare them for their return from their long dispersion, to again possess the land of their fathers. He prophesied many more things that I have not written. After he had prophesied he laid his hands upon Lyman Wight and ordained him to the High Priesthood, after the holy order of God. And the spirit fell upon Lyman, and he prophesied, concerning the coming of Christ, He said that there were some in the congregation that should live until the Savior should descend from heaven with a shout, with all the holy angels with him.

He said the coming of the Savior should be like the sun rising in the east, and will cover the whole earth....He saw the heavens opened and the Son of Man sitting on the right hand of the Father... (John Whitmer, HC 1:176.)

Some curious things took place. The same visionary and marvelous spirits, spoken of before, got hold of some elders; it threw one from his seat to the floor; it bound another, so that for some time he could not use his limbs nor speak; and some other curious effects were experienced, but, by a mighty exertion, in the name of the Lord, it was exposed and shown to be from an evil source. The Melchizedek Priesthood was then for the first time introduced, and conferred on several of the elders. In this chiefly consisted the endowment--it being a new order--and bestowed authority. (John Corrill, History of the Mormons (1839), p.18.)

In January 1833, the school of the Prophets at Kirtland opened with Joseph's washing of the Elders' feet. Fasting and prayer followed the ordinance, and the participants witnessed Pentecostal experiences. Zebedee Coltrin reported "many powerful manifestation [sic] of the holy spirit...the gift of tongues and the interpretation thereof."[413] In 1883, Coltrin reminisced that Jesus himself had appeared to the school of the Prophets.[414]

From the preceding examples, we can see abundant evidence that a temple is not actually necessary to obtain an endowment of power from on high. Yet, the Kirtland temple provides a wonderful example that they can co-occur.

On June 1, 1833, the Lord said to Joseph,

Yea verily I say unto you I gave unto you a commandment that you should build an house in the which house I design to endow those whom I have chosen with power from on high, for this is the promise of the Father unto you. Therefore, I commanded you to tarry even as mine Apostles at Jerusalem. (Kirtland Revelation Book, pp. 59-60.)

---

[413] Zebedee Coltrin Diary, 24 January 1833

[414] "At one of these meetings after the organization of the school... a personage walked through the room from east to west, and Joseph asked if we saw him. I saw him and suppose the others did and Joseph answered that is Jesus, the Son of God, our elder brother. Afterward Joseph told us to resume our former position in prayer, which we did. Another person came through; he was surrounded as with a flame of fire. He (Brother Coltrin) experienced a sensation that it might destroy the tabernacle as it was of consuming fire of great brightness. The Prophet Joseph said this was the Father of our Lord Jesus Christ. I saw Him." (Source: Minutes, Salt Lake City School of the Prophets, October 3, 1883.)

The construction of the Kirtland temple took 3 years. During that time the Lord repeated that the Elders would be "endowed with power from on high; for, behold, I have prepared a greater endowment and blessing to be poured out upon them..."[415] During this time, the twelve apostles were chosen. In Oliver Cowdery's charge, he told them that although they were meant to go to all nations to preach, "you are not to go to other nations, till you receive your endowment. Tarry at Kirtland until you are endowed with power from on high."[416]

Before the ordinances began, Cowdery prayed, "O may we be prepared for the endowment,--being sanctified and cleansed from all sin."[417] A few days later the brethren washed their bodies and anointed their heads with oil. Joseph then experienced the vision of the celestial kingdom recorded in D&C 137. Two days later, they sealed the anointings. These ordinances continued through the winter for all priesthood brethren (all ranks from deacons up). The ordinances themselves were not the endowment, but were tools to help the brethren prepare themselves through repentance so that the endowment could come. The understanding of the brethren that the endowment (not the ordinances) would bring power to perform miracles is captured in an article in the local paper: "They assure you, with the utmost confidence, that they shall soon be able to raise the dead, to heal the sick, the deaf, the dumb, and the blind..."[418] Joseph Smith was teaching that those who followed the gospel would receive the promised spiritual manifestations:

> If you will obey the Gospel with honest hearts, I promise you, in the name of the Lord, that the gifts as promised by our Saviour will follow you, and by this you may prove me to be a true servant of God. (Joseph Smith, Journal History, October 16, 1834.)

Those going to preach this gospel would first have to obtain the spiritual manifestations before promising them to others.

The endowment came at the dedication services, when outwardly manifested signs were given in abundance to witness the internal dispensation of power through the Holy Ghost. The dedication came with reports of all sorts of Pentecostal activity: people spoke in tongues, angels were seen, prophecies were made, etc.. "The Savior made his appearance to some, while angels ministered unto others, and it was a penticost and enduement indeed, long to be remembered..."[419] One man said he "saw the Spirit in the form of cloven tongues as fire descend in thousands, and rest upon the heads of the

---

[415] Kirtland Revelation Book, 97-98, 22 June 1834.
[416] Kirtland Council Minute Book, 14 Feb 1835.
[417] Oliver Cowdery's Kirtland, Ohio Sketch Book, 17 Jan 1836.
[418] Ohio Atlas, 16 March 1836.
[419] Joseph Smith diary, March 30, 1836, as written.

Elders..."[420] David Patten said "the heavens Was opened unto them. Angels & Jesus Christ was seen of them sitting at the right hand of the Father."[421] Erastus Snow reported seeing angels. [422] These types of experiences reoccurred at each of the subsequent rededications necessary for lack of available seating.

Since the Kirtland temple, not one Pentecostal event has been recorded in church history, despite over 150 years and nearly 150 dedicated temples.

On November 12, 1835, Joseph gave his own explanation of what the endowment was:

> You need an Endowment brethren in order that you may be prepared and able to over come all things. Those that reject your testimony will be damned. The sick will be healed, the lame made to walk, the deaf to hear and the blind to see through your instrumentality....But when you are endowed and prepared to preach the gospel to all nations, kindred and toungs in there own languages you must faithfully warn all and bind up the testimony and seal up the law. (Joseph Smith Diary, 12 Nov 1835, as recorded).

How is the endowment defined today? Instead of using Joseph's definition, the modern church uses Brigham Young's definition:

> Your endowment is, to receive all those ordinances in the house of the Lord, which are necessary for you, after you have departed this life, to enable you to walk back to the presence of the Father, passing the angels who stand as sentinels, being enabled to give them the key words, the signs and tokens, pertaining to the holy Priesthood, and gain your eternal exaltation in spite of earth and hell. (Brigham Young, JD 2:31 Apr 6, 1853.)

In the Encyclopedia of Mormonism, we read

> The endowment of 'power from on high' in modern temples has four main aspects. First is the preparatory ordinance, a ceremonial washing and anointing, after which the temple patron dons the sacred clothing of the temple. Second is a course of instruction by lectures and representations...Third is making covenants...Fourth is a sense of divine presence... (Alma P. Burton, "Endowment," Encyclopedia of Mormonism, ed. Daniel H. Ludlow 1992 2:455.)

Under this definition, the actual divine presence is replaced by a "sense" of divine presence (or feelings instead of actual experience), and even that is

---

[420] Autobiography of Milo Andrus, 1814-1875.
[421] Recorded as accounted by Patten to Wilford Woodruff, 19 Apr 1836.
[422] Erastus Snow Sketch Book.

relegated to the final part of the endowment, instead of the whole of it. In its place are informational ceremony and ritual.[423] Just as in ancient times, we have repeated the pattern: Originally, the purpose of temples was to re-enter God's presence. Now, ordinances given as a means to that end have become the entire focus of temple worship, with few if any remembering the original purpose of temple worship, let alone attempting to re-enter God's presence.

Ordinances were not a part of any endowment in church history or scripture. The only time they are mentioned, as detailed above, is as part of the preparation of the individual for the endowment, not as the endowment itself.

Endowments are not about knowledge—they are about power. If you go to the temple to obtain knowledge, you are not obtaining anything that can't be had without a temple. Of course, power can also be had outside of a temple, as it was given in the Pentecostal experiences of the meridian apostles and early saints.

While Joseph Smith's endowment, like Jesus' and all those who came before, was about power and experience with God, modern Mormonism's endowment is about information. It is unclear how learning signs and tokens empower someone to teach the gospel by the Spirit in foreign lands. But this is no longer the stated purpose of the endowment. According to modern Mormonism, the things you are told and the things you are shown give you the ability to return to God's presence after this life. There are no gifts, no angels, no tongues, and no manifestations of Jesus or the Father in this latter endowment. The word "endowment" seems to be the only commonality.

Ordinances Have Changed

Joseph taught,

> Now the purpose in Himself in the winding up scene of the last dispensation is that all things pertaining to that dispensation should be conducted precisely in accordance with the preceding

---

[423] One interesting side effect of changing the meaning of endowment from a spiritual outpouring with an informational ceremony is that temple ceremony, whose open attendance without recommends did not preclude spiritual outpourings, had to become limited in access. If the endowment gives you spiritual power manifested by outward spiritual manifestations, then the draw to participate is to experience these things. If, on the other hand, the endowment merely gives you information, it can be pilfered by anyone who reads the transcript of the ceremony. Most modern Mormons would balk at that comment and respond that the modern endowment gives covenants which can only be obtained in the temple. Yet, the covenants given in the modern endowment hold promises no different than those offered to anyone who is baptized or reads the scriptures. They are all conditional, meaning that those who live the required law outside of the temple will obtain the blessing proffered, whether they experienced the modern endowment or not.

dispensations....He set the temple ordinances to be the same forever and ever and set Adam to watch over them, to reveal them from heaven to man, or to send angels to reveal them. (Joseph Smith, HC 4:208.)

From the preceding we see that: 1) the ordinances of this dispensation must remain the same as those in prior dispensations,[424] 2) the temple ordinances are to be "the same forever and ever," and 3) when God gives these ordinances, he does so by sending Adam or other angels to reveal them to men. Furthermore, we can conclude that the temple ordinances prescribed by Joseph were received from angels—perhaps even Adam himself—with precisely the same format and content of prior dispensations.

Although these expressions by Joseph may seem contradictory to understandings today, it should be noted that Joseph's positions were echoed by church leaders over the years. Over 50 years after Joseph's death, apostle Reed Smoot reported to Congress that "...the endowments have never changed and can never change; as I understand it; it has been so testified, and that Joseph Smith Jr., himself was the founder of the endowments."[425] The idea that Joseph was "the founder of the endowments" is enshrined in our scriptures. The Lord told Joseph that "all things pertaining" to the temple would be shown him.[426]

Since Elder Smoot's comment in 1905, there have been significant changes to the temple ceremonies in the 1920s and again in 1990, with many minor changes before, during, and after that interval. The task of listing all changes since Joseph's death is impossible since not all changes have been recorded.[427] Still, the publicly documented changes would necessitate an entire book.[428] Instead of listing out every documented change to temple

---

[424] On another occasion, Joseph taught "Ordinances instituted in the heavens before the foundation of the world, in the priesthood, for the salvation of men, are not to be altered or changed. All must be saved on the same principles." (Teachings of the Presidents of the Church: Joseph Smith, pp412-422)

[425] Senator Reed Smoot, Reed Smoot Case, vol. 3, p. 185.

[426] See D&C 124.

[427] Every change has *not* been recorded. According to the church, Brigham Young's 1877 transcript of the endowment was the first time it was written down. In the over 30 years between Joseph's endowment and Brigham's transcript, temple presidents in Salt Lake City and St. George conducted the endowment according to their memory without extensive communication. Given the embellishments documented by Wilford Woodruff (the St. George temple president) and the two months it took for Young and Woodruff to write up the endowment, it is clear that the endowments of each temple were different, though to what degree we cannot say.

[428] An incomplete listing can be found in "Development of LDS Temple Worship" by Devery Scott Anderson. The book does not contain the author's commentary, but merely provides a repository for every available communication concerning changes

ordinances, we will here highlight only a few to demonstrate the degree of changes made to the temple ordinances and the process by which these changes have occurred.

Of principle interest are the following questions: What portions of the ceremonies have been changed? Were these segments superficial, or did they concern the core of the ceremony (such as the covenants)? On what authority were the changes made? Did the changes come as a result of revelation, opinions from the brethren, or social pressure? If revelation, of what degree? Joseph taught that the manner in which God reveals the temple ordinances is through visitation of angels under the supervision (or participation) of Adam. Did an angelic visitation precede *each* change to the temple? If not, did an angelic visitation precede *any* of the changes?

The changes encompass almost every aspect of temple worship. For example, the gradations of the priesthood, robe dressing order, fashion, and timing, wording of the ordinances, and wording of the lecture were all changed in the 1920s changes.[429] Before, during, and after those changes, covenants have been added,[430] removed,[431] and modified.[432]

---

to the temple. To date that I am aware, this chapter is the first attempt at an even partially listing of all changes.

[429] 1922, May 31-June 3: Apostle George F. Richards makes the first significant changes to ceremony since 1877. Among them "the robes should be placed on the left shoulder first and then changed to the right shoulder once only before entering the Terrestrial room; also that Aaronic and Melchizedek be used instead of lower order of the Melchizedek and higher order of the Aaronic...This on my own suggestion." (Elder George F. Richards diary, June 3, 1922.) "I presented the suggestions of a change in the order of robing and in the wording of the ordinances and lecture which were by vote approved. This order is to place the robe on the left shoulder at that point in the Terrestrial room when formerly it was placed on the right shoulder, and change onto the right shoulder at that point in the ceremony in the Telestial room where at present it is changed onto the left shoulder—there will be no other changing of the robes [previously there was an additional switch back to the right shoulder]. The ceremonies and Lecture will be changed to conform..." (Elder George F. Richards diary, June 7, 1922.) "I represented having discussed with associates in the temple the advisability of instituting a change in the procedure of placing the Endowment Robes on the individuals receiving endowments the present method being to first place the robe on the right shoulder, subsequently change it to the left shoulder, and later again back to the right shoulder. The proposed change would be to place the robe first on the Left shoulder, ...then to change it to the Right shoulder,...thus obviating one of the changes heretofore made, and more effectively indicating transition from the lower to the higher orders of the Priesthood. After considering carefully the proposed change, the [1st] Presidency decided unanimously that from that time on the Robe should first be placed on the Left shoulder, and then be changed to the Right shoulder..." (Elder George F. Richards memorandum, June 7 1922.) His changes are announced to all temple workers on Aug 14. In September, 1922, George F. Richards "spent the day at the Temple where I read carefully all the

Although changes to the temple ceremonies began immediately upon Joseph's death and have continued thereafter, the scope and frequency of changes did not increase substantially until the passing of the generation that knew Joseph. Contemporaries of Joseph attributed the temple ceremonies to God. It was seen as a one-time dictation, never to be changed. Although Brigham Young's changes to the temple no doubt deviated the ceremonies from their original form, it is important to note that they were presented as corrections—reversals of men's innovations that had crept in—to bring the ceremonies into accordance with what Joseph had received. [433] Wilford Woodruff said,

> I consider that if there ever was any man who thoroughly understood the principle of the Endowments it was Brigham Young. He had been with Joseph Smith from the beginning of the Endowments to the end; and he understood it if any man did. And before his death he required me to write in a book every Ordinance in the Church and

---

ordinances used in the temples as changed and corrected and noted 18 times which I think need changing." (Ibid, Oct 5 1922.) He reports his changes were accepted and adopted. Until this time, the covenants and the instructions regarding the prayer circle and veil were unscripted. Richards' work included writing a script for these portions.

[430] The so-called oath of vengeance was a covenant inserted into the endowment by Brigham Young for participants to "pray to Almighty God to avenge the blood of the prophets [Joseph and Hyrum] upon this nation, and that you will teach the same to your children and to your children's children unto the third and fourth generation."

[431] The oath of vengeance was seen as unpatriotic. After attracting sufficient negative attention, it was removed and replaced by a covenant of patriotism. This covenant was subsequently removed as well.

[432] Elder George Richards, the architect of the 1920s changes, wrote in his journal that his modifications changed the ordinances in at least 18 places (see Oct 5, 1922 entry). Later, President Grant changed the law of chastity to allow for marriages outside of the covenant, a practice that violated the law of chastity as previously worded: "As you are aware, a few years ago the Temple Covenant of chastity was modified so as to permit faithful, worthy women of the Church whose husbands have not received the Endowment to go to the Temple for their own endowments and not be violating their covenant by living with their husbands thereafter, to whom they have not been given of the Lord in the authority of the Holy Priesthood. Young unmarried women are also affected by the foregoing named action, so, if they marry outside the Temple after receiving their endowment they will not be violating their covenants." (George F. Richards letter to Heber J. Grant, March 13, 1939)

[433] St. George temple president David H. Cannon said, "Pres. Young had 20 men revise the ceremonies of the ordinances. Pres Young said 'we are going to give endowments for the dead for the first time and we want to give you the ceremonies as they were given by the Prophet Joseph Smith in the Nauvoo Temple.' These endowments were received from the Lord by the Prophet Jos Smith in the Nauvoo Temple." (St George Temple Presidency Meeting Minutes, June 19, 1924.)

Kingdom of God, from the first to the last...and President Young corrected it all until he got through. Then he said to me, 'Now, there you have a pattern of all the Ordinances and Endowments for every Temple we shall build, until the coming of the Son of Man.' Now if I ever have anything to do, or to say, in any Temple on the earth, concerning Endowments, I would say: follow the pattern that President Young has set us; and not deviate from it one iota....While on the other hand, if every man...introduces his own form and ceremonies, our Temple work would be as diverse as the sectarian world and God would not appro[ve] it. (Wilford Woodruff, June 8, 1887.)

In time, the reasoning for ongoing changes detached from any connection to their original form, and shifted to changes that brought the material into closer alignment with doctrines and sensibilities, which had shifted from Joseph's time. Ironically, it was President Woodruff—the same who earlier testified of President Young's revisions having brought the material into alignment with Joseph's instructions—who later made perhaps the first significant change to the temple ordinances dissociated from Joseph's original instructions. By changing the sealing process from a link between living Saints and the exalted fathers (Abraham, Isaac, Jacob, and others known to be saved) to links to genealogical fathers (father, grandfather, etc.), Woodruff obliterated the original doctrinal significance of sealing—a process that was intended to provide access for living members to the covenants made to the exalted fathers.

In his provided reasoning, we have a case study for how subsequent changes have and do come into play. In General Conference on April 8, 1894, President Woodruff stated:

I have not felt satisfied, nor has any man since the Prophet Joseph Smith who has attended to the ordinance of adoption in the temples of our God. We have felt there was more to be revealed on this subject than we have received...and the duty that I want every man who presides over a Temple to see performed from this day henceforth, unless the Lord Almighty commands otherwise, is let every man be adopted to his father.

There was no "thus saith the Lord" and no claim of angelic visitation.[434] The motive was that he thought it didn't seem right to seal a person to the fathers.

---

[434] Woodruff claimed that this change was given to him by God. However, the Saints of the time had a much different opinion of Woodruff and supposed revelations than we do today. Through reading the addresses of his contemporaries in General Conference, it is apparent that they believed President Woodruff was prone to exaggeration in his attribution of revelation. On one occasion, Apostle Charles

His willingness to change the ordinance without even a minor attempt to review his own diary containing Joseph's words on the subject[435] suggests a shift from the opinion that Joseph was the authority on the subject of the temple ceremonies. Had he bothered to review Joseph's teachings, he would have seen that sealing an individual to a father who does not possess the covenant of eternal life is as effectual as a freefalling man grabbing another who does not possess a parachute.

Like President Woodruff's changes to sealing, subsequent changes (as far as documented) came as the result of individual ideas and council votes without deference to Joseph's teachings. When historical transcripts of the endowment disagreed with modern innovations, concerns were addressed with claims to authority, not with claims to revelation, and without one reference to angelic ministration.[436]

Penrose stated, Apostle Charles W. Penrose, who would later serve as counselor to President Smith, declared: "President Wilford Woodruff is a man of wisdom and experience, and we respect him, but we do not believe his personal views or utterances are revelations from God; and when 'Thus saith the Lord', comes from him, the saints investigate it: they do not shut their eyes and take it down like a pill." (Millennial Star 54:191.) One example that seems to support this opinion is Woodruff's insistence, many years after the fact, that the founding fathers attended him in the St. George temple, begging for their ordinance work to be done. Woodruff was a stalwart journal keeper, yet somehow omitted any mention of this visit in his journal. Furthermore, records of the endowment house in Salt Lake indicate that at the time he claimed they had visited him, the work had been done for those brethren not once but several times.

[435] Joseph taught clearly that what saves the descendants is the covenant given to the fathers. "When a seal is put upon the father and mother it secures their posterity so that they cannot be lost but will be saved by virtue of the covenant of their father." (Words of Joseph Smith, 13 August 1843) "If you have power to seal on earth & in heaven then we should be Crafty, the first thing you do go & seal on earth your sons & daughters unto yourself, & yourself unto your fathers in eternal glory, & go ahead and not go back, but use a little Craftiness & seal all you can; & when you get to heaven tell your father that what you seal on earth should be sealed in heaven 31 I will walk through the gate of heaven and Claim what I seal & those that follow me & my Council" (Words of Joseph Smith, 10 March 1844)

[436] When the St. George temple president Cannon was presented with Elder Richards' extensively modified temple ceremonies, he argued that Brigham Young had said that the 1877 transcript presented the endowment as it was given to Joseph in Nauvoo. He "referred to the President's book which contained all the ceremonies of the Temple ordinances...President Richards...said 'you must either conform to our method or we to yours.' Said Prest Richards told him that the Presidency of the Church and the twelve Apostles were the presiding authorities of in [sic] the Church at present, and they must stand at the head and be responsible for the direction of the affairs of the Church, and the parts in the ordinances of the Temples must be rendered as they have directed. Said Prest Richards instructed him to gather up all the

Temple changes seem to have been motivated by a limited set of factors. Many temple changes came because the brethren felt the changed material did not make sense. The temple ordinances written by Brigham Young and featuring an hour long lecture at the veil on Adam God doctrine were not in accordance with the more recent changes to the doctrine of the Godhead. [437] Perhaps motivated by this inconsistency, Elder George F. Richards spent years of the 1920s revising the temple ceremonies. He made clear that the changes were his "own suggestion"[438] as a result of careful study identifying areas that he thought needed changing.[439] This was not a case of carefully studying historic manuscripts to detect deviations from Joseph's endowment. As with President Woodruff's changes, this was wholesale revision. After changes were suggested, they were discussed as a council, and unanimously approved. The pattern continued. Years later, President McKay indicated that he thought his own modifications would make the temple easier to understand:

> [The endowment] is seldom, if ever, really comprehended by our young folks when they first go through the Temple. I think the ceremony can be presented more effectively, but before any changes are made they will be presented to the members of the Temple Committee. (David O McKay Diary, Oct 6, 1957.)

President McKay made no mention of angelic visitation or revelation. By his time, the pattern of changing the temple ceremonies to accord with the wisdom of men was well established.

Other changes were proposed to ease administrative burden. For example, on Jan 1, 1965, the church announced that patrons would no longer each be given a new name by revelation, but that the new name would be the same for each individual attending the temple that day in order "to facilitate record keeping."[440] In another example, it was proposed that ceremonies for the dead be shortened to decrease the time needed for an endowment.[441] In

---

old rulings and instructions and burn them up..." (St George Temple Presidency Meeting Minutes, June 19, 1924.) Luckily, president Cannon did not burn up what was the only surviving copy of the 1877 manuscript. The church has it to this day.

[437] The new doctrine of the Godhead was at odds with many staples in the church. Beyond the endowment, Joseph Smith's description of the Godhead in "Lectures on Faith" was at odds with the new doctrine, and therefore was removed from the canon at this time. See "The Reconstruction of Mormon Doctrine" by Thomas Alexander, Sunstone 5:4 (July-August 1980) pp. 24-33.

[438] George F. Richards diary, June 3, 1922.

[439] Ibid, Oct 5 1922.

[440] Development of LDS Temple Worship, p 389.

[441] "President [N. Eldon] Tanner said the suggestion has been made that the temple ceremonies for the dead be shortened to do away with repetition. This would not

1989, the church stopped recording the names of proxies, witnesses, and officiators of ordinances to ease record storage requirements.[442]

Still other changes have come as a result of surveys of member opinions. The most substantial of these were the 1990 changes to the endowment. In 1987, the church issued a survey to 3,000 members to ascertain their opinion on the endowment ceremony. As a result, in 1990 the ceremonies of the temple were overhauled. Large swaths of the ceremony that were offensive to modern sensibilities were removed, such as a Protestant minister who is paid by Lucifer to preach false doctrine and the penalties associated with revealing the things patrons promise to keep secret. Covenants were changed, such as that made by women to their husbands. Elements of the ceremony, such as the physical exchange at the veil, and the words used in the true order of prayer, were changed. In 2005, the initiatory was further modified to remove any touching of the body of the patron by the worker, except on the head. The most recent set of films further de-emphasize the transgression of Eve.

In no case, it seems, were changes motivated by the suspicion that perhaps the ceremony had somehow deviated from the first written record from 1877 (which the church still possesses). In no case, it seems, were decisions made based on an assumption that the historical endowment was revealed by God. Changes were made without historical study or reference to the 1877 temple book. For example, President McKay observed that when considering whether

> the procedure which has been followed over the years as to the manner in which the garment should be placed on the individual, one leg at a time, etc., is a part of the ceremony. The brethren did not feel

---

pertain to the living but only the dead. The brethren who have considered the matter say that it would not in any way detract from the importance of the covenants, promises and ceremonies. President Tanner said that if I felt that the suggestion is worthy of consideration there could be arranged a condensed version of these ceremonies for presentation to me for my approval. President Tanner said that Elders Howard W. Hunter, Gordon B. Hinckley and Theodore M. Burton think it could be done very well and he believed that Brother Richard L. Evans felt the same way. President [Hugh B.] Brown suggested that these brethren be asked to bring a copy of the present ceremony and also a copy of the proposed ceremony so that comparisons could be made. I said this might be done." (David O McKay Diary, Feb 19, 1969.)

[442] "There is pressing need for less complex temple procedures and reduced personnel requirements. Accordingly, we have prayerfully determined that it is no longer necessary to permanently record the names of proxies, witnesses, or officiators for any temple ordinances for the deceased....The implementation of this decision will substantially reduce the complexity of temple operation and simplify record storage. However, temples will no longer be able to provide stakes and wards with patron attendance information." (First Presidency letter, Sept 20, 1989.)

that this is a part of the ritual. It was agreed to announce this new policy regarding the garments to the General Authorities in their meeting on Thursday, March 27th. (David O McKay diary, Mar 18, 1969).

Instead of obtaining God's word on the subject, or withholding changes until an angel visited to indicate the way to proceed, the brethren have made changes based on their own feelings and wisdom.

Through frequent small changes, tremendous differences have accumulated in the ceremonies. For example, it was by small changes that the initiatory washing was changed from the literal bathing of a participant in a bathtub[443] as done in the Old Testament and Nauvoo to what is done today, where the patron receives merely a reference to the real thing. If it is sufficient to symbolically summarize multiple rites into one gesture, why not condense the whole endowment into one symbolic gesture? Would any member consider that valid? Would God?

These small changes seemed like a good idea to those who made them, without God's voice and without deference to history, especially to Joseph Smith's revelations. There is no historical evidence that suggests that the brethren responsible for the changes thought they were doing anything but God's work. Ironically, among the men responsible for the changes, we see many interesting statements about the need for the ordinances and ceremonies to remain unchanged. It is unclear how the brethren who made the changes did not feel they were usurping God's authority or committing apostasy. The same Wilford Woodruff who replaced sealing to the fathers with sealing to genealogical fathers wrote

> I consider that if there ever was any man who thoroughly understood the principle of the Endowments it was Brigham Young. He had been with Joseph Smith from the beginning of the Endowments to the end; and he understood it if any man did. And before his death he required me to write in a book every Ordinance in the Church and Kingdom of God, from the first to the last...and President Young corrected it all until he got through. Then he said to me, 'Now, there you have a pattern of all the Ordinances and Endowments for every Temple we shall build, until the coming of the Son of Man.' Now if I ever have anything to do, or to say, in any Temple on the earth,

---

[443] "The earliest accounts of the Nauvoo temple endowment indicate that initiatory washings followed a literal Old Testament model of actual bathing. Large tubs of water are specified in the separate men's and women's rooms. The anointing was performed by liberally pouring consecrated oil from a horn over the head and allowing it to run over the whole body." (The Mysteries of Godliness: A History of Mormon Temple Worship, p 81.)

concerning Endowments, I would say: follow the pattern that President Young has set us; and not deviate from it one iota....While on the other hand, if every man...introduces his own form and ceremonies, our Temple work would be as diverse as the sectarian world and God would not appro[ve] it. (Wilford Woodruff, June 8, 1887.)

The same Elder Richards who spent two entire years transfiguring nearly every aspect of the temple ceremonies railed against Catholics' changing baptism from immersion to sprinkling:

For a century we have tried to show to the world from the scriptures that baptism is necessary to man's salvation; that baptism signifies immersion and that immersion was the only form of baptism known and practiced in the primitive Church until several centuries A. D., and that the changing of the mode of baptism from immersion to pouring or sprinkling is apostasy and fulfils the prediction of Isaiah with respect to the last times, "The earth, also, is defiled under the inhabitants thereof, because they have transgressed the laws, changed the ordinance, broken the everlasting covenant." (George F. Richards, Conference Report, April 1930, p.76.)

The same President David O. McKay who made many changes to temple ceremonies through his "personal convictions" said:

...God is unchangeable, the same yesterday, today and forever... The great mistake made down through the ages by teachers of Christianity, is that they have supposed they could place their own private interpretation upon scriptures, allow their own personal convenience to become a controlling factor, and change the basis of Christian law and practice to suit themselves. This is apostasy. (President David O. McKay, The Prophet's Message, Church News, June 5, 1965.)

Through these means we have come to the point today that a temple patron from 1877 would not recognize the ceremonies as we have them today. The would not recognize the wording of the initiatory or the symbolic rituals. They would not recognize the garment. They would not recognize the wording, covenants, and symbols of the endowment. They would not recognize the sealing ordinance. In fact, it is hard to imagine just how foreign today's temple would be to them. They would not even recognize the white clothing (an innovation of Wilford Woodruff begun on February 1, 1877).

The question is, does God recognize these changed ordinances? Apparently, Presidents Joseph Smith, David O. McKay, Wilford Woodruff, and Elder Richards would all say that he cannot, because the ordinances and ceremonies have been modified from what God gave to Joseph through

Adam. Perhaps these brethren would quote Mormon 8:33, which asks "Why have ye transfigured the holy word of God, that ye might bring damnation upon your souls?" The Lord has been very clear that unauthorized ordinances are an abomination to him. For instance, in Malachi 1, the Lord equates turning away from the ordinances he has revealed to despising his name. He clearly states he will not accept modified ordinances:

> A son honoureth his father, and a servant his master: if then I be a father, where is mine honour? and if I be a master, where is my fear? saith the Lord of hosts unto you, O priests, that despise my name. And ye say, Wherein have we despised thy name? Ye offer polluted bread upon mine altar; and ye say, Wherein have we polluted thee? In that ye say, The table of the Lord is contemptible. And if ye offer the blind for sacrifice, is it not evil? and if ye offer the lame and sick, is it not evil? offer it now unto thy governor; will he be pleased with thee, or accept thy person? saith the Lord of hosts. And now, I pray you, beseech God that he will be gracious unto us: this hath been by your means: will he regard your persons? saith the Lord of hosts. Who is there even among you that would shut the doors for nought? neither do ye kindle fire on mine altar for nought. I have no pleasure in you, saith the Lord of hosts, neither will I accept an offering at your hand. For from the rising of the sun even unto the going down of the same my name shall be great among the Gentiles; and in every place incense shall be offered unto my name, and a pure offering: for my name shall be great among the heathen, saith the Lord of hosts. But ye have profaned it, in that ye say, The table of the Lord is polluted; and the fruit thereof, even his meat, is contemptible. Ye said also, Behold, what a weariness is it! and ye have snuffed at it, saith the Lord of hosts; and ye brought that which was torn, and the lame, and the sick; thus ye brought an offering: should I accept this of your hand? saith the Lord. But cursed be the deceiver, which hath in his flock a male, and voweth, and sacrificeth unto the Lord a corrupt thing: for I am a great King, saith the Lord of hosts, and my name is dreadful among the heathen. (Malachi 1:6-14.)

The Lord makes clear that when men defile his temple by changing his ordinances

> Wherefore, as I live, saith the Lord God; Surely, because thou hast defiled my sanctuary with all thy detestable things, and with all thine abominations, therefore will I also diminish thee; neither shall mine eye spare, neither will I have any pity. (Ezekiel 5:11.)

If temples today are meant to be a continuation of what the Lord restored through Joseph, the contents of the ordinances must remain as they were revealed to him. If they have changed, there are only two possibilities: either they are a product of man's invention and not revelation from God, or Joseph was wrong not only in teaching that ordinances never change and temple ordinances must be revealed from an angel, but also in his original instructions regarding the temple. If the first option is true, it must be concluded that the temple work of modern Mormons is not accepted by God, for, as apostle Charles Penrose said, "Christ will not accept the devices and ordinances and ceremonies ordained of men." (Charles W. Penrose, "Mormon Doctrine, Plain and Simple," p. 24) If the later option is true, it would indicate not only that Joseph made a tremendous mistake in what he said on the topic, but also that he had given a false revelation when he said that God said that the Lord would show him all things pertaining to the temple.

"Saving Ordinances"

Modern church leaders counsel members to "fix our focus on the temple. There we receive the highest blessings that God has in store for His faithful children."[444] According to them, exaltation is dependent, at least in part, upon obtaining and "remaining faithful to the ordinances and covenants of the temple." This focus creates a lot of discomfort in members when analyzing the historical basis for such faith in modern temples. After all, one's salvation and family is at stake. But *is* exaltation dependent upon the ordinances and covenants of the modern temples? *Is* the eternal integrity of one's family at stake?

The scriptural basis for this focus is unclear. Perhaps most obvious is the point that if the temple ordinances are, in fact, the key to eternal life, *which* temple ordinances? Those that Joseph revealed, those that Brigham wrote in 1877, the very much different ordinances we have today, or any version in between? If one is right, the others are not. From a different perspective, we note the absence of any requirement for temple ordinances in the scriptures.

In support of their position, the leaders of the church quote the following from Joseph Smith:

> If a man gets a fullness of the priesthood of God he has to get it in the same way that Jesus Christ obtained it, and that was by keeping all the commandments and obeying all the ordinances of the house of the Lord. (Teachings of the Prophet Joseph Smith, p. 308.)

But does this quote support the modern endowment? First, the ordinances of the Israelite temple at the time of Jesus were completely dissimilar to the modern endowment. If the Israelite temple ceremonies are

---

[444] Elder Russell M. Nelson, "Salvation and Exaltation," April 2008 General Conference.

"the ordinances of the house of the Lord," then the LDS endowment is not, and vice versa. Second, the Israelites had long ago lost the fullness of the gospel by Jesus' time. We know that Melchizedek keys are required for temple ordinances. Joseph taught that the Israelites in Jesus' time no longer had even Aaronic priesthood keys.[445] Thus, if Jesus' exalted status came from his mortal reception of apostate temple ordinances from priests without keys, why would God need to affect a restoration? Why couldn't mankind be saved through receiving apostate ordinances from Catholic priests without keys?

If Jesus did not receive the fullness of the priesthood by obeying the religious ceremonies of the Israelite temple, how did he get it? It turns out the answer lies in the quote from Joseph. The original quote reads much shorter than the elaborated version reprinted above and found in TPJS. The original quote is found in Wilford Woodruff's diary from 11 June 1843: "if a man gets the fulness of God he has to get [it] in the same way that Jesus Christ obtain it & that was by keeping all the ordinances of the house of the Lord." (See WOJS). In the doctored quote, the list for getting the fullness includes two things: keeping all the commandments and obeying the ordinances of the house of the Lord. A distinction is made between keeping God's commandments and making and keeping temple covenants made in modern temples. Yet, the original quote has only one requirement: "keeping all the ordinances of the house of the Lord." Although the word "ordinance" can mean religious rite or ceremony (how it is used in the church today), the 1828 Webster's dictionary lists this as the last possible definition. The first is a permanent rule of action established by authority; In other words, God's commandments. The word "house" is commonly understood to mean the temple. Though the Lord does use this meaning in the D&C (see D&C 124:23, for example), he also uses the meaning "family."[446] The house of the Lord can mean a building, or it can mean a group of people. Since Jesus received the fullness of the priesthood through "keeping all the ordinances of the house of the Lord," and since that cannot refer to the apostate and limited Israelite temple ordinances, "the ordinances of the house of the Lord" has to mean something other than "receiving the ordinances of the temple." For instance, Jesus could have received whatever this refers to on the Mount

---

[445] "John, at that time, was the only legal administrator in the affairs of the kingdom there was then on the earth, and holding the keys of power. The Jews had to obey his instructions or be damned, by their own law; and Christ Himself fulfilled all righteousness in becoming obedient to the law which He had given to Moses on the mount, and thereby magnified it and made it honorable, instead of destroying it. The son of Zacharias wrested the keys, the kingdom, the power, the glory from the Jews, by the holy anointing and decree of heaven, and these three reasons constitute him the greatest prophet born of a woman." (Joseph Smith, HC5:260-261.)

[446] "…mine house is a house of order" (D&C 132:8)

of Transfiguration. Alternatively, "the ordinances of the house of the Lord" could simply mean, "the commandments of those in the family of God."[447]

When preaching against the priests of King Noah, Abinadi asked them if it was obedience to the law of Moses that brought salvation. The priests believed it was. Abinadi explained:

> And now ye have said that salvation cometh by the law of Moses. I say unto you that it is expedient that ye should keep the law of Moses as yet; but I say unto you, that the time shall come when it shall no more be expedient to keep the law of Moses. And moreover, I say unto you, that salvation doth not come by the law alone; and were it not for the atonement, which God himself shall make for the sins and iniquities of his people, that they must unavoidably perish, notwithstanding the law of Moses. (Mosiah 13:27-28.)

Although the law of Moses was a tool that could assist in obtaining what (or who) actually saves, it was not necessary or sufficient in and of itself. The same can be accurately said of temples. The temple itself can save no one. The ordinances in the temple do not save, either. It is Jesus, and only Jesus, that can save.

> O then, my beloved brethren, come unto the Lord, the Holy One. Remember that his paths are righteous. Behold, the way for man is narrow, but it lieth in a straight course before him, and the keeper of the gate is the Holy One of Israel; and he employeth no servant there; and there is none other way save it be by the gate; for he cannot be deceived, for the Lord God is his name. (2 Nephi 9:41.)

Though the temple can teach us how to come back to Christ, it cannot take us there. Nor can it be said that it is necessary to have access to the temple in order to make the journey. Jesus showed through his own mortal life that salvation is attainable without a temple.

Temples are a useful tool to help individuals come closer to Christ, but when they are adulterated in their ceremonies or become an end in and of themselves, they actually make the participants less likely to re-enter God's presence than they would be without a temple. This is because, in addition to all the challenges of overcoming the natural man organic to this life, they must also overcome false traditions instilled in them through adulterated temple worship.

As for individuals, so for families. The spousal sealing ordinance is widely regarded as the means by which a couple becomes sealed for eternity.

---

[447] It is my personal opinion that Joseph said it as he did to distinguish between the general laws of the gospel, which are associated with a terrestrial degree of glory, and those associated with a celestial (or god-like) degree of glory. God's family (Zion, the city of Enoch, etc.) resides in celestial glory.

However, both in the wording of the ordinance itself and in leaders' description of it, it is obvious that the modern temple sealing is conditional on the faithfulness of the couple to God.[448] Thus, in order to obtain the unconditional sealing described in D&C 132:19, something more is required. Would the same process still required of a couple after temple sealing to obtain heavenly sealing yield the same result in a couple that had not been sealed in a temple? Upon receiving a temple sealing, the couple possesses nothing more upon exiting the temple than they had upon entering: an invitation (already in the scriptures) to remain true and faithful with the promise that if they do so, eventually God will seal them together eternally.[449]

Given that modern temples are not essential for salvation and do not provide anything unobtainable outside them, it is somewhat surprising that they are given pre-imminence in modern Mormonism. God gave Isaiah a vision of a time when men would cease to focus on dead ordinances, and remember that it is Jesus, and not temples, that saves.

In that day men will have regard to their Maker, and their eyes look to the Holy One of Israel, and regard not the altars, the works of

---

[448] The sealer announces a chain of blessings upon bride and groom but makes clear that they are only attained "through your faithfulness." Many leaders have explained that a couple is not actually sealed when they leave the temple, but rather can attain to that blessing through faithfulness. This, then, is a different sealing than that described in D&C 132, where the only condition that can break that seal is the sin of murder by those sealed: "And again, verily I say unto you, if a man marry a wife by my word, which is my law, and by the new and everlasting covenant, and it is sealed unto them by the Holy Spirit of promise, by him who is anointed, unto whom I have appointed this power and the keys of this priesthood; and it shall be said unto them—Ye shall come forth in the first resurrection; and if it be after the first resurrection, in the next resurrection; and shall inherit thrones, kingdoms, principalities, and powers, dominions, all heights and depths—then shall it be written in the Lamb's Book of Life, that he shall commit no murder whereby to shed innocent blood, and if ye abide in my covenant, and commit no murder whereby to shed innocent blood, it shall be done unto them in all things whatsoever my servant hath put upon them, in time, and through all eternity; and shall be of full force when they are out of the world; and they shall pass by the angels, and the gods, which are set there, to their exaltation and glory in all things, as hath been sealed upon their heads, which glory shall be a fulness and a continuation of the seeds forever and ever." (D&C 132:19.) It is curious, then, why the temple sealers need the sealing power, since they do not exercise it. Rather, they merely invite the couple to obtain the sealing at the hands of the "Holy Spirit of promise, by him who is anointed," which apparently is someone else.

[449] Church leaders would disagree with this description. They believe either that the ratifying sealing comes through the Holy Ghost, or is conducted by an apostle during the second anointing ordinance (see "The Gospel of Christ" for more about the second anointing).

their hands, nor look to things their fingers have made—the idols of prosperity and the shining images. (Isaiah 17, Gileadi Translation.)

Perhaps that day is soon upon us.

Prayer Circles

Endowments after the Kirtland temple did not feature an endowment of the Holy Ghost as witnessed by outward manifestations. However, one item patrons *did* receive post-Kirtland was a knowledge of the true order of prayer.

There was special power in this form of prayer, over and above normal prayer. This type of prayer is seen practiced by Jesus in 3 Nephi. Joseph called this the key by which you could ask and receive answers.[450] Modern Mormons do not attribute much weight to the true order of prayer, as witnessed by its limited mention as a semi-prescribed single prayer towards the end of the current endowment. It is not mentioned in talks about the temple as temple covenants and ordinances are, suggesting the possibility that modern Mormons understand it to be an unimportant piece of window dressing. Yet, despite the scope of changes to the temple, it is still illustrated in today's endowment as the penultimate step in the dramatized return to God's presence. Even in its current relegated form, it really ought to get more attention than it does.

In former days, the true order of prayer was a focal point of the temple ceremonies. It was one of only three pieces of temple worship that extended beyond the temple (the others being the garment and a portion of the second anointing ordinance). Not only did temples once have dedicated altars in private rooms where individuals could go and engage in the true order of prayer, but chapels did as well.[451] Some even had dedicated altars in their homes.[451] Patrons, not temple workers, were the voice of the prayer over the altar in the endowment until at least September 1965.[452] They prayed according to what the Spirit told them to pray for, not a rote repetition of roughly the same prayer. There were multiple opportunities for normal members to voice a prayer in the true order.

---

[450] Joseph Smith was commanded to teach others the "keys by which they could ask and receive" (D&C 124:95, 97). It was believed by early leaders including Orson Pratt and Charles C. Rich that the true order of prayer was these keys (see 1879 edition of D&C and JD 19:250). Rich taught that the key word in D&C 130:10-11 used to unlock God's response to our prayerful questions was the new name received in the temple (see Journal of Discourses, 19:250). Prohibition of practicing the true order of prayer and removal of the receipt of a new name by revelation effectively remove one of the main purposes for the endowment—learning the way ordained by God for men to receive revelation on demand.

[451] See, for example, Quinn's "Latter-day Prayer Circles."

[452] Personal correspondence from Rex Lowe detailing this occurrence at several temples in the 1960s.

Now, however, the altar rooms have been repurposed, patrons are not allowed to even kneel in prayer anywhere in the temple,[453] temple workers offer up a repetitive prayer at the altar, and practice of the true order of prayer has been prohibited outside of temples.[454]

For those who dare exercise the key of asking and receiving in their own homes, they will find some difficulty in that what they have been taught varies significantly with what was revealed to Joseph. First, they will find themselves dressed differently than their forebears. [455] They will find themselves using different words than their forebears.[456] Although the fact that the current form is different from the original is well documented, the oldest known documented form is absconded in the 1877 transcript, nestled in the First Presidency's vault.

Proxy Work

The modern narrative suggests that one of the main reasons the church builds temples is to perform necessary ordinances vicariously for the dead, enabling them to progress onward. However, Joseph's described pattern was not for endowment ordinances to be performed for the dead, as we perform baptisms for the dead, but for the living to obtain election, and then seal their kindred dead to themselves. What good does it do to seal yourself to ancestors who themselves are not saved? What good does it do to seal them to you when you yourself have not been redeemed? This is like having a group of 10 people jump off a cliff without parachutes. They can link to each other as many ways as they choose, but unless they can tie themselves to someone who is still on the cliff, they will all likewise perish.[457]

Joseph Smith never performed an ordinance for the dead outside of baptism. He did, on <u>one</u> occasion that I've found, state that the ordinances

---

[453] "No special arrangements are made for members to pray privately in the temples. However, members may remain briefly in the celestial room and meditate in silent prayer." (General Handbook of Instructions, 1985.)

[454] A First Presidency letter dated May 3, 1978 made the practice of private prayer circles prohibited.

[455] Among the changes made by George Richards is that the robe is placed on the opposite shoulder. There used to be one more change prior to the end of the ceremony. Of course, the garments are significantly different as well.

[456] Prior to the 1990 changes, the participants said, "Pay Lay Ale" three times instead of "Oh God, hear the words of my mouth."

[457] Joseph taught that we ought to seal ourselves to our "fathers in eternal glory," that is, the patriarchs, not to our genealogical fathers. "Again the doctrin or sealing power of Elijah is as follows if you have power to seal on earth & in heaven then we should be Crafty, the first thing you do go & seal on earth your sons & daughters unto yourself, & yourself unto your fathers in eternal glory, & go ahead and not go back, but use a little Craftiness & seal all you can; & when you get to heaven tell your father that what you seal on earth should be sealed in heaven" (WOJS 10 March 1844.)

for the living would have to be done for the dead, but he did not describe the mechanism for how this was to be done.[458] Joseph did, however, explicitly describe exactly who the work could be done for. He said,

> A man may act as proxy for his own relatives; the ordinances of the Gospel which were laid out before the foundations of the world have thus been fulfilled by them, and we may be baptized for those whom we have much friendship for; but it must first be revealed to the man of God, lest we should run too far. (Joseph Smith, HC, 6:366.)

Brigham Young, whose only claim of authority in temple ordinances came from his implementing what Joseph had given, began the practice of initiatories, endowments, and sealings for the dead. From the opening of the Endowment House in 1855 until Wilford Woodruff began proxy endowments in 1876, only living ordinances were allowed for all ordinances except baptisms, which resumed in 1856 after a 20 year pause. The pause began when the Lord said baptisms for the dead would no longer be acceptable without a temple to perform them in. In 1856, without a temple to perform them in, they were resumed.

Instead of building the Nauvoo temple, as God had commanded, and receiving further light and truth through Joseph on the nature and form of proxy temple work, the Saints were cast out of Nauvoo and made their best guess as to how it would work. They multiplied temple "offerings" in the form of vicarious ordinances, with over 150 million endowments performed since 1876.[459]

Innovation of ordinances was not unknown in ancient Israel, but it was routinely condemned. God once said,

---

[458] "Then you must not only be baptized for them but they must receive the Holy Ghost by Proxy and be sealed by it unto the day of their redemption as all the other ordinances by proxy." (WOJS 12 May 1844.) It is amazing that so much of modern Mormon doctrine, so much time, and so much money is dedicated to proxy ordinances when the entire doctrinal basis for it rests in two concise quotes from one sermon immediately before Joseph's death. To put this into context, Joseph referred to the need to restore animal sacrifice many times in his Nauvoo sermons. It would be quite a stretch for modern Mormons to suppose that was sufficient instruction and authority to flesh out all the particulars of animal sacrifice and build hundreds of temples to perform it. Yet, that is exactly what they have done with proxy ordinances beyond baptism, and that with much less information than Joseph provided regarding animal sacrifice.

[459] In 1996 Richard Cowan estimated that 150 million endowments had been performed. If this number was accurate, adding those performed since and subtracting all living ordinances, it is safe to say at least 150 million endowments for the dead have been performed.

> For I desired…the knowledge of God more than burnt offerings. But they like men have transgressed the covenant: there have they dealt treacherously against me. Gilead is a city of them that work iniquity, and is polluted with blood. (Hosea 6:6-8.)

How applicable this scripture is to the current situation. The purpose of the temple—obtaining knowledge of God through re-entering his presence—has been replaced with multiplying "burnt offerings," strange incense that God has not commanded. As Gileadi described,

> [Isaiah 1:12 reads] 'When you come to see me, who requires you to trample my courts so?' The question asked at the beginning of verse 11 is answered at the beginning of verse 12: God's people go to the temple to SEE GOD. If they aren't there for that purpose, then all else doesn't count for much. This reveals an appalling paradox: instead of going to see God, his people resemble the dumb animals that were anciently brought for sacrifice, which were unaware of their reason for being there. Instead of making an offering of their whole souls to God—as symbolized by burnt offerings and the shedding of the animals' blood—his people trudge about the temple's courts defiling it. (Avraham Gileadi, http://www.isaiahexplained.com/isaiah_ch_01.html)

The focus on multiplying ordinances is not an issue of actually completing work for the approximately 70 billion dead who have never received them as much as it is a mechanism of providing ample opportunity for patrons to return to the temple.[460] Name shortages have been a staple ever since proxy work was changed from a mechanism for "saving" individuals known by the patron to a mechanism for getting the patron back into the temple.[461] To alleviate the problem, the church has employed many means such as limiting ordinances,[462] allowing work to be done for those of known sinful life,[463] and

---

[460] In 1961, President McKay took means to keep patrons visiting the temple despite "almost daily" shortages of names. (George Fudge oral history, Jan 29-30 1976, pp 15, 17, 19, Buerger Papers).

[461] During Brigham Young's life, church members would attend the temple perhaps four times in their lives: once for themselves, and once for each dead relatives that: 1) they personally knew, 2) whose character they could vouch for, and 3) who had not had the opportunity to join the church.

[462] In April 1962 the Salt Lake Temple reduced the endowment sessions to "five each day Monday through Friday….Furthermore, sisters will be permitted to perform not more than one endowment each day." ("Special Salt Lake Temple Notice," Messenger)

[463] On August 30, 1966, the policy of only doing work for those who have not murdered, committed suicide, or been excommunicated was rescinded. All names

employing teams to scrape historical records for names. The vast majority of names come from this final source (76% according to George Fudge's 1976 report).

If the ordinances of the modern temple are essential to salvation, what of the billions upon billions who never received them? Several decades ago, the brethren were informed that temple ordinances were not even keeping pace with the current birthrate, let alone putting a dent in the estimated 70 billion people who have ever lived.[464] Every member of the church would have to do 466 endowments over the course of their lives just to break even with the number of people alive today. But because active membership is about 1/3 of reported membership, that number is actually tripled. Some contend the work will be completed in the millennium. Even if the work were conducted around the clock without any breaks for eating, sleeping, drinking, or any other work, it would require 17.5 million people to complete the endowment.

If the point of the modern temples isn't to complete ordinances for the 70 billion dead (an impossibility due to time and information limitations), and it isn't to see God in the temple (something not taught by the hierarchy in over 100 years), and if temple attendance does not provide an interaction with the Holy Ghost manifested by the outward signs that always follow, then what is their purpose? That only leaves the memorization of the lectures given, which simply does not require many trips to memorize and can easily be done at home. In reality, the point of attending for most people is either for service to the dead (which is not supported by scripture or Joseph's teachings) or to receive emotional validation after being told how important it is to attend.

God Hasn't Commanded Temple Construction

When God wanted the Kirtland Temple built, he told Joseph:

> ...build a house to my name, for the Most High to dwell therein. For there is not a place found on earth that he may come to and restore again that which was lost unto you, or which he hath taken away, even the fullness of the priesthood....And verily I say unto you, let this house be built unto my name, that I may reveal mine ordinances therein... For I deign to reveal unto my church things which have been kept hid from before the foundation of the world, things that pertain to the dispensation of the fullness of times. And I will show unto my servant Joseph all things pertaining to this house, and the

---

were cleared for vicarious work "except those of known Negro blood." (First Presidency Letter.)
[464] See Gary Carlson Oral History Jan 15, 1980 pp 8, 10, 25 from Buerger Papers.

priesthood thereof, and the place whereon it shall be built. (D&C 124:27-28, 40-42.)

Since Nauvoo, no revelation has been published where God commanded a temple to be built. Instead, according to the church architect, "the Church looks for sites 'that would have prominence, be in an attractive neighborhood, a neighborhood that would withstand the test of time.'"[465] Since Nauvoo, God has not specified the architecture of temples. Instead,

> After the temple site is selected and the Church determines how large the building should be (based on the number of members in the area), a team of Church architects creates potential exterior and interior designs. [The architect] 'want[s] to create something unique, something that has its own personality, and [Church leaders] allow us to do that' with temples. He adds that much can be done to make a temple unique, including 'the decorative motifs, the kind of furniture, the interior accouterments, how articulate it is. It could be anything from the modern look that you see in the Washington D.C. Temple to something like the gothic, neoclassical look that you find in the Salt Lake Temple.' To create a look and feel that is just right for a specific temple, architects solicit a number of sources. For example, as the Church has designed its future temple in the Democratic Republic of Congo, Williams says his team met with locals to 'understand the nature of the people, the country that they live in, the Mormons that are there and how we can better fit the temple' to them. A critical aspect of the planning process is "sustainable design," a concept…seeks to reduce a temple's long-term operational cost. 'Whatever we can do to make the environmental systems, the mechanical systems energy efficient, to make the interior materials have longevity so that they don't wear out straightaway, anything we can do to conserve water, it's great for us as the owner because it makes that long-term cost less. That's what it means to be sustainable.'[44]

Instead of God revealing the design in a moment, it is designed through architectural research, sustainable building, and unique design—a process that "can take up to two years."[44] Although "the First Presidency is involved and provides final approvals," the process is bottom up, instead of top down, and no mention of revelation is provided.[44]

The pattern of God specifying the location and layout of each temple he's ever commanded built ended when Joseph died. Perhaps the most illustrative comparison is provided in the modern Nauvoo temple and the

---

[465]   http://www.mormonnewsroom.org/article/mormon-temple-building-process, retrieved 21 Jun 2015.

former Nauvoo temple, which was destroyed shortly after the Saints abandoned and attempted to sell it. While the modern temple is build in the same style as other modern temples, the original Nauvoo temple "contained two assembly halls, one on the first floor and one on the second, called the lower and upper courts." It "had classrooms and offices in the attic."[466]

"Observers might have difficulty detecting differences between the" current and former Nauvoo temple exteriors.[467] Every effort was made to create a façade that would be indistinguishable to most laypeople: "The stone on the outside of the new temple was carefully chosen to have, as nearly as possible, the same color and texture as the limestone of the original temple,"[44] although it was from quarries states away from the original. "The new temple was not built with stone piled on stone and cemented, as was the original."[44] Instead, the stone is a façade attached to concrete walls. Every effort and expense was taken to ensure that the temple looked the same from the outside, even if it was completely different. "The interior of the temple, however, is a different story,"[44] because it features a completely different floor plan than the one revealed to Joseph.

It is reasonable to wonder what the Lord thinks of temples built without his commandment, in forms he has not provided, with great aims employed to lead those who don't know any better to assume that all is as it was revealed to Joseph. Because this is a pattern that appeared with great frequency in the Old Testament, there is no need to speculate.

> Come to Beth-el, and transgress; at Gilgal multiply transgression; and bring your sacrifices every morning, and your tithes after three years: And offer a sacrifice of thanksgiving with leaven, and proclaim and publish the free offerings: for this liketh you, O ye children of Israel, saith the Lord God. (Amos 4:4-5.)

Beth-el and Gilgal were not appointed places to sacrifice. Despite having the same form as worship at God's authorized temple, God considered it a transgression. God shows us that when his people do not hearken to his words or his law, even though they engage in temple worship, it is not acceptable to him.

> Hear, O earth: behold, I will bring evil upon this people, even the fruit of their thoughts, because they have not hearkened unto my words, nor to my law, but rejected it…your burnt offerings are not acceptable, nor your sacrifices sweet unto me. (Jeremiah 6:19-20.)

---

[466] https://en.wikipedia.org/wiki/Nauvoo_Temple, retrieved 20 Sept 2015.
[467] Don Searle, Nauvoo: A Temple Reborn, July 2002 Ensign.

Unless temples are commanded by God, they cannot be his. Instead of worshipping him, temples built by the designs and commandments of men mock him and raise his ire.

Garments

Most members believe that wearing the garment entitles them to some sort of protection, as is promised during the initiatory. The question is whether the promise provided applies to any particular garment, or only the garment revealed to Joseph.[468] If the garment has undergone similar changes as the temple ceremonies under similar circumstances, can we really expect God to fulfill the promises recited in the initiatory?

The original garment was a one piece, full body (to the wrist and ankle[469]) textile made of only white cotton, flax, or wool. It required being stepped into from the neck. It had tie strings to take out the slack. In 1894, the brethren decided to end the practice of cutting the marks into the garment through the shirt, reversing an instruction from Brigham Young, because "we think this unnecessary" (Wilford Woodruff, George Q. Cannon, and Joseph F. Smith to Lorenzo Snow, Aug 31 1894). At that time, they also moved the garment marking from the veil portion of the ceremonies to the initiatory. [470] During John Taylor's administration the original garment material was replaced with a knitted fabric. In 1923, the collar was removed and the tie strings were replaced with buttons. The women's garments were shortened to the elbows and knees. These changes came "after careful and prayerful consideration,"[471]—not from the voice of God, but because "the living authority said we might."[472] Erroneously, the First Presidency claimed that "no fixed pattern of Temple garment has ever been given," and concluded that they could change it without regards to Joseph's garment. Ironically, the commissioned author of the temple instruction pamphlet wrote that same year that

> When Joseph Smith received the endowments and revelation from the Lord to be given to his peope by authority, he also received instructions as to how to make this garment. None had ever seen anything like it and the sisters who made it were under his direction

---

[468] "I, the Lord, am bound when ye do what I say; but when ye do not what I say, ye have no promise." (D&C 82:10.)

[469] "This garment had a collar and it had strings to tie it and sleeves that came to the wrist, not to the hand, but about an inch above, and the leg came down to the ankle joint. (Zina Y. Card, "Garments", Temple Instructions, 1923.)

[470] Originally, the garment marks were cut into the garment as part of the ceremony. The patron had to sew the marks closed at home.

[471] First Presidency Letter to Bishops, June 1923.

[472] Zina Y. Card, "Garments", Temple Instructions, 1923.

and when it was submitted to him, he said that it was right and the way it had looked to him [in his mind] and he accepted it. (Zina Y. Card, "Garments", Temple Instructions.)

Just eleven years earlier, President Joseph F. Smith had said,

The Saints should know that the pattern of endowment garments was revealed from heaven, and that the blessings promised in connection with wearing them will not be realized if any unauthorized change is made in their form, or in the manner of wearing them.

He reiterated in a joint First Presidency statement in 1915, "The pattern of the temple garment was given by revelation to the Prophet Joseph Smith." (Joseph F. Smith, Anthon H. Lund, and Charles W. Penrose to Arthur C. Smith.)

Apparently, there was some resistance to the idea of changing the garment. The temple instruction pamphlet recognized the changes from what God had revealed to Joseph, but assuaged concerns by citing the change as a valid use of authority by the brethren:

Thus the Kingdom of God rolls on and the living authorit[ies] are the ones who can make changes in the revealed work of the Lord to answer the purposes of the day in which they live. (Zina Y. Card, "Garments", Temple Instructions, 1923.)

The "modified" garment, as it was called, was only permitted to be used outside the temple. Somehow in the minds of the people, it was wrong for a private member to fashion their own garment pattern, because it would "not [be] approved of nor accepted by the authority of God." (Ibid.) At the same time, the modified garment, which came from men and not God, was somehow valid. In 1934, apostle John Widstoe dealt with the issue differently, at once admitting the garment was revealed to Joseph, but claiming that no changes had been made: "The temple ordinances were revealed as many other things have been revealed to the Prophet....There have been no changes in the garment. Fundamentally it is like it was in the beginning. Lengthening or shortening of the sleeve is not a change really. It is just a minor thing, in line with our needs, especially in the summer time; but that does not make any difference to the garment itself." (John A. Widstoe, "Answers to Seminary Teachers' Questions," 1934 pp. 32-33.)

Widstoe contended, as many do with all temple changes, that the changes made do not affect the vital parts. After all, he reasoned, "It is [still] a covering for my body, representing covenants I have made. We make entirely too much of the so-called changes. There have been no changes to the ideas." (Ibid). People using this line of reasoning are surprisingly unable to enumerate the parts that *are* vital. The cognitive dissonance increases as these same people who contend that as long as the garment is a covering for one's body (no matter how much or how little of the body) and represents covenants (no matter if those covenants change or not) it is still valid, also claim that any garment that covers the body and represents the covenants but is not prayerfully considered and unanimously approved by the brethren "desecrates the marks of the priesthood." (Zina Card, Temple Instructions, 1923.) Thus, both the most different design to God's revealed design and God's revealed design itself can be either approved or abominable depending not on God's word on the subject, but on whether the current brethren are currently favorable towards it or not. A telling example of dissent is found in then President of the Quorum of the Twelve Joseph Fielding Smith. One member wrote how on his 21 February 1964 visit,

> I asked President [Joseph Fielding] Smith, 'Is it wrong to wear the string tie garments outside the temple?' President Smith looked at me for several moments and then unbuttoning the third button in his shirt, brought out one of the ties on a pair of old style temple garments and said, 'This is what we should be wearing---the Lord gave them to us, and so this is what I wear.' I said, 'I have worn the old style garments for two years now and some of the ignorant brethren have accused me, so now I wear a tee shirt over them.' President Smith then said, 'When the Lord gave the garments to us they had strings. I have never worn a button pair; however, I don't say those with buttons are not garments.' (W. Cleon Anderson, notarized statement, in Buerger Papers.)

Joseph Fielding Smith had inherited Hyrum Smith's original garment, and thus knew firsthand what the differences were between modern and the original garments.[473]

In 1936, the garments were modified again to include a sleeveless pattern.[474] The brethren expressed reluctance to the change, but agreed to it "only because we have convinced ourselves that it will tend to bring" more adherence to the instruction to wear the garment day and night without rolling up the sleeves.[474] As with previous changes, it seems to have been instigated by the women of the church who wanted to accommodate current styles. [474] The brethren insisted that "we have not been able to see that we are yielding any vital thing in this slight change."[474] At this time the committee also recommended providing an explanation for the symbols on the garment, something not then provided. The brethren wrote:

---

[473] Upon his death, the garment remained the property of the First Presidency.
[474] George F. Richards, Joseph Fielding Smith, Stephen L. Richards, and Melvin J. Ballard, Committee Report to the First Presidency and Council of the Twelve Apostles, Apr 22 1936.

The best interpretation which has come to us up to this time has been supplied by President McKay. It is as follows: A. The square: Honor, integrity, loyalty, trustworthiness. B. The compass: An undeviating course in relation to truth. Desires should be kept within proper bounds. C. The navel: That spiritual life needs constant sustenance. D. The kness: Revernce [sic] for God, the source of divine guidance and inspiration.[474]

In 1965, the older garment used in temples was updated from strings to buttons, but not fully updated to the outside of temple garment.[475] The full update to bring them into parity was subsequently made.

Over time, the garment marking process was changed. By 1979, all symbolism of the marking of the garment was lost. Instead of placing the garment on the patron and cutting marks into the garment, the garments were manufactured already containing the marks, which had ceased to be cuts and become mere embroidery.[476] A December 1979 First Presidency letter announced the two piece garment, citing "due consideration" as the means of the change.

Like the 1877 transcript of the endowment, the church possesses an original temple garment (that belonging to Hyrum Smith). It could duplicate that garment to revert the modern garment back to the one that God revealed to Joseph. However, it defers to the opinions of Joseph's successors, who never once claimed revelation in their changes, and the requirements of modern style and comfort, rather than trusting that God knew what he was talking about when he revealed the garment to Joseph. Those, like President Joseph Fielding Smith, who would prefer to wear the garment revealed to Joseph are prevented from doing so. They are not given the pattern, and even if they had it, they would be disciplined for creating and wearing the original garment.

If we are to accept that God honors the promises he offered with the garment revealed to Joseph with the current garment, we should also expect he will honor them with *any* set of underclothing, as the cut, cloth, manner of marking, and meaning of the garment have all changed. You would be hard pressed to change the garment more than it has been changed. Can the modern garment be viewed as anything but a mockery of God?

---

[475] David O. McKay Diary, May 14, 1965.

[476] "Many of the garments (with the exception of the cotton garments) are being marked electronically. As a result, the material is not cut, nor is there a need for backing. This procedure has been approved by the First Presidency, and members, when inquiring, should be assured that the marking is proper and that they have no need to communicate with the Relief Society Distribution Center." (Washington, D.C. Temple Presidency to All Stake and District Presidents in the DC Temple District, June 1, 1979.)

Multiplying Temples

Modern Mormonism asserts that temple work for the living and the dead is the principle mission of the church to which all other ends and means are subordinate. Therefore, it is reasoned, we must build temples all over the world to facilitate access. History shows, however, that rather than having originated with Joseph Smith, this position emerged gradually as Joseph's temple doctrine was forgotten.

To understand the development of multiplying temples, you have to understand temples not in their modern context, but how they were revealed in Joseph's day. Then, temples were commanded to be constructed one at a time, with specific purposes in mind. There was no general program for ordinances for the dead, except baptism. There was no endowment as we have it today. The purpose of the Kirtland temple was not to expose members to a symbolic lecture or to make promises to God. It was to provide a Pentecostal experience for leaving missionaries. Similarly, the purpose of the Nauvoo temple was to provide a place for Elijah to return and restore the high priesthood and sealing powers.[477] Temples were not spaces dedicated for repetitive experiences, but places set apart for an explicit one-time event.[478] After all, the purpose of these events was to dispense knowledge that would empower the people to come into the consistent presence of God in the normal course of their lives. In contrast to the modern temple experience, this did not necessitate numerous buildings or numerous visits to buildings. In Joseph's day, this experience was extended to members through the physical gathering, not the building of many temples. With Joseph's death, the purpose of the Nauvoo temple was lost. Brigham Young did not know or understand what had been revealed to Joseph about its purpose. He repurposed the attic of that temple to reveal the original version of the endowment we practice today. That endowment, which was carried to Utah, was not an event. It was a repetitive experience.

Where Joseph gathered the saints and brought them into access to revelatory events for which a temple had been constructed, Brigham sent out the saints to establish colonies to which temples could be brought to provide repetitive experiences. Even still, the tradition of gathering was strong enough that all saints were commanded to gather to and around Utah. Therefore, the idea of building a temple outside of Utah did not emerge for decades after the Nauvoo exodus. This changed with the Hawaii, Cardston, Mesa, and Idaho

---

[477] Joseph additionally taught that the Nauvoo temple would continue after that event to be a place where people would come to be baptized for the dead.

[478] After the dedication of the Kirtland temple, which brought the fulfillment of the purpose of the building in the Pentecostal experiences of those who attended, the temple was used for normal meetings. The church did not build a single chapel during Joseph's life.

Falls temples, all overseen under the radical administration of Heber J. Grant, the first president of the church who had not known Joseph.[479]

At the onset of President McKay's administration, the idea of building temples outside of Utah-Zion[480] was foreign. However, in an attempt to bolster flat conversions to the church, President McKay revoked the commandment to physically gather. International missionary areas had been burned over, with anyone willing to accept the gospel having already been converted and exported to Utah. As with many dramatic experimental changes during President McKay's administration, building temples around the world was not about bringing temple blessings to global saints, but about increasing the number of converts, in this case by keeping strong members in their country of origin.

Lavish Materials

Years ago, I attended the Draper, Utah temple dedication. The tour guide led us through the ornate building, describing various elements of the temple. The lavish wood panels, doors, and moldings are imported African cherry wood. The limestone coverings on the floor are imported from France. The white granite covering the exterior of the building is from China.[481] In modern Mormonism it is understood that expensive and ornate finishings are required in order for a temple to be acceptable to God. Church members were taught in the October 2012 General Conference that no expense is spared in ensuring that every aspect of the building—visible or not—is as perfect as possible with the example of an entire expensive stained glass panel that was replaced because a single small square was off by an eighth of an inch.[482]

Perhaps to the surprise of many members, this perspective is very much an innovation. In 2015 dollars, the Kirtland temple cost $68 per sqft.,[483] the St. George temple cost $165 per sqft.,[484] the Manti temple cost $247 per

---

[479] The pace and magnitude of changes to LDS doctrine increased remarkably once saints born in Utah, and therefore only knowing the restoration second-hand, became the majority of the 15. For one perspective, read the essay, "The Reconstruction of Mormon Doctrine" by Thomas Alexander (available online).

[480] By this time, the Nauvoo era Mormon's concept of someday returning to Jackson County had been replaced by their children's concept that Utah was the permanent gathering place appointed for the Saints.

[481] http://www.deseretnews.com/article/705276337/New-LDS-temple-unlike-others-in-the-area.html, retrieved 20 Sept 2015.

[482] https://www.lds.org/general-conference/2012/10/temple-standard, retrieved 20 Sept 2015.

[483] https://en.wikipedia.org/wiki/Kirtland_Temple, retrieved 20 Sept 2015.

[484] http://historytogo.utah.gov/places/stgeorge.html, retrieved 20 Sept 2015.

sqft.,[485] and the Salt Lake temple cost $364 per sqft.[486] Meanwhile, modern temples cost at least $1,400 per square foot.[487] Clearly, there has been a change. When and how did it occur?

David O. McKay, who began the modern temple building program, was very intent on building inexpensive buildings. He wrote in his diary,

> It is not contemplated that an expensive edifice would be erected but that temples be built that would accommodate the people under a new plan whereby temple ceremonies can be presented in one room without moving from one room to another....It is felt that such a building could be erected and adequately equipped for about the cost of one of our present meeting houses, namely, two hundred or two hundred fifty thousand dollars. (Diary of David O. McKay, April 17, 1952.)

The change to expensive temples did not occur in the McKay administration. As near as can be seen, it did not happen all at once. The DC temple (1974 at $507 per sqft. in 2015 dollars[488]) and the San Diego temple (1993 at $553 per sqft. in 2015 dollars[489]) serve as trend points along the march to current temple costs. This tradition developed slowly over time. There was no one point where the church suddenly jumped from temples with the same cost of chapels (David O. McKay's ideal) to what they cost today. Instead, it seems that the gradual building of more expensive temples predicated the development of a tradition that they had to be expensive. And as that tradition developed, temples necessarily became more expensive. Thus we can contrast the inexpensive fake marble on the outside of the D.C. temple with the imported granite façade of the Draper temple.

With all this in mind, there are two problems with modern temple construction. First, there is absolutely no justified reason for such expensive construction materials and methods. If LDS temples from an equally wealthy

---

[485] https://www.lds.org/ensign/1978/03/the-manti-temple?lang=eng, retrieved 20 Sept 2015.

[486] http://utah.com/mormon/temples/salt-lake, retrieved 20 Sept 2015.

[487] Before removing the unusually transparent post, the church posted that the 10,700 sqft. Brisbane Australia temple cost $11.5 million to build in 2003, a figure that probably does not include the grounds or the furnishings. The Brisbane temple is the same design as the small temples built in the eastern United States and elsewhere around the world. Due to the repetitive and basic design, it is safe to say that this is the lowest cost per sqft. of temples built in the last 10 or so years. Medium sized temples (those newly constructed in the Mormon corridor) are constructed of much more expensive materials than the small temples in the east and internationally.

[488] https://en.wikipedia.org/wiki/Washington_D.C._Temple, retrieved 20 Sept 2015.

[489] http://articles.latimes.com/1993-01-04/news/mn-912_1_san-diego-temple, retrieved 20 Sept 2015.

church were acceptable to God at a much lower price tag in former years, why would they not be acceptable to him today, particularly when the difference could be used to help the poor? Second, given the tenuous historical support for post-martyrdom temple worship, the many modifications to Brigham's ordinances, and the lack of any revelation from God commanding any post-Nauvoo temple to be built, can any new construction at all be justified?

These feelings seem to be echoed in prophetic scripture. It is easy for modern Mormons to condemn wicked King Noah. However, in doing so they unwittingly condemn themselves. When stripped of the defense of "the Lord wants us to build ornate temples," it becomes apparent that modern Mormons also

> ...buil[d] many elegant and spacious buildings...ornament[ing] them with fine work of wood, and of all manner of precious things, of gold, and of silver, and of iron, and of brass, and of ziff, and of copper...caus[ing] that his workmen should work all manner of fine work within the walls of the temple, of fine wood, and of copper, and of brass. (Mosiah 11:8, 10.)

Of course, we also ornament our temples with gold leaf, exquisite furnishings, highest end carpet, Chinese granite, and African wood. Moroni's words undoubtedly apply to today's temple-building Mormons:

> For behold, ye do love money, and your substance, and your fine apparel, and the adorning of your churches, more than ye love the poor and the needy, the sick and the afflicted. O ye pollutions, ye hypocrites, ye teachers, who sell yourselves for that which will canker, why have ye polluted the holy church of God? Why are ye ashamed to take upon you the name of Christ?...Why do ye adorn yourselves with that which hath no life, and yet suffer the hungry, and the needy, and the naked, and the sick and the afflicted to pass by you, and notice them not?...Behold, the sword of vengeance hangeth over you; and the time soon cometh that he avengeth the blood of the saints upon you, for he will not suffer their cries any longer. (Mormon 8:37-41.)

The Temple as a Symbol of God's Approval

Some consider the presence of modern temples to be a sign of divine approval. Elder Oaks recently said, "There are now more than 140 operating temples, just one fruit of the restored gospel and of our prophetic leadership."[490] Yet, does the number of temples,[491] or the fact that we have operating temples, signify divine approval? God said, through Jeremiah,

---

[490] Boise, Idaho, June 17, 2105.

Don't be fooled by those who promise you safety simply because the LORD's Temple is here. They chant, 'The LORD's Temple is here! The LORD's Temple is here! (New Living Translation, Jeremiah 7:4.)

Were there historic peoples who were inciting the wrath of God and still had temples? In the Book of Mormon, King Noah had a temple, yet was in an apostate state. The Old Testament contains countless examples of people who not only were apostate despite having a temple, but who actually summoned his wrath *because* of their temples. In Jeremiah we read:

Trust ye not in lying words, saying, The temple of the Lord, The temple of the Lord, The temple of the Lord, are these....Will ye steal, murder, and commit adultery, and swear falsely, and burn incense unto Baal, and walk after other gods whom ye know not; Don't fool yourselves! My temple is here in Jerusalem, but that doesn't mean I will protect you...You steal and murder; you lie in court and are unfaithful in marriage. You worship idols and offer incense to Baal, when these gods have never done anything for you. And then you come into my temple and worship me! Do you think I will protect you so that you can go on sinning? You are thieves, and you have made my temple your hideout. But I've seen everything you have done...While you have been sinning, I have been trying to talk to you, but you refuse to listen. Don't think this temple will protect you. Long ago I told your ancestors to build it and worship me here, but now I have decided to tear it down, just as I destroyed Shiloh. And as for you, people of Judah, I'm going to send you away from my land, just as I sent away the people of Ephraim and the other northern tribes. Jeremiah, don't pray for these people! I, the Lord, would refuse to listen. (Jeremiah 7:4,9,10,13-16.)

Temple worship in and of itself is not necessarily pleasing to the Lord. When we do not hearken to the ordinances God has given us, but

---

[491]"Israel is an empty vine, he bringeth forth fruit unto himself: according to the multitude of his fruit he hath increased the altars; according to the goodness of his land they have made goodly images. Their heart is divided; now shall they be found faulty: he shall break down their altars, he shall spoil their images." (Hosea 10:1-2) "Because Ephraim hath made many altars to sin, altars shall be unto him to sin. I have written to him the great things of my law, but they were counted as a strange thing. They sacrifice flesh for the sacrifices of mine offerings, and eat it; but the Lord accepteth them not; now will he remember their iniquity, and visit their sins: they shall return to Egypt. For Israel hath forgotten his Maker, and buildeth temples; and Judah hath multiplied fenced cities: but I will send a fire upon his cities, and it shall devour the palaces thereof." (Hosea 8:11-14)

replace them with the commandments of men, and build temples up to ourselves without God's commandments, we anger God.

> I hate, I despise your feast days, and I will not smell in your solemn assemblies. Though ye offer me burnt offerings and your meat offerings, I will not accept them: neither will I regard the peace offerings of your fat beasts. Take thou away from me the noise of thy songs; for I will not hear the melody of thy viols. But let judgment run down as waters, and righteousness as a mighty stream. Have ye offered unto me sacrifices and offerings in the wilderness forty years, O house of Israel? But ye have borne the tabernacle of your Moloch and Chiun your images, the star of your god, which ye made to yourselves. (Amos 5:21-26.)

As we learn with King Noah, leaders who disobey God can cause the temple to become polluted:

> Woe to her that is filthy and polluted, to the oppressing city! She obeyed not the voice; she received not correction; she trusted not in the Lord; she drew not near to her God. Her princes within her are roaring lions; her judges are evening wolves; they gnaw not the bones till the morrow. Her prophets are light and treacherous persons: her priests have polluted the sanctuary, they have done violence to the law. (Zephaniah 3:1-4.)

God said that Israel's "sins are making my holy temple unfit as a place to worship me." (Ezekiel 8:6, CEV.) The people in Jerusalem, including the leaders of the church, could not see that their acts of worship in the temple were an abomination before God. Perhaps this was because they were investing so much time, energy, and money in the effort of worship that they were blind to the fact that the worship had not originated from God but consisted of the innovations of man. What was God's reaction to the abomination? He commanded angels to slay all men, women, and children except those who were "truly upset and sad about the disgusting things" being done in the temple (Ezekiel 9:4, CEV). God will unleash the same judgment on those who similarly defile buildings allegedly built to be his house in our day, and he will only spare those who are "truly upset and sad about the disgusting things" being done in the temple.

Follow the Prophet

Joseph taught that we should not follow a man or assume what he has to say is true because of his priesthood position.

> And none are required to tamely and blindly submit to a man because he has a portion of the priesthood. We have heard men who hold the priesthood remark, that they would do anything they were told to do by those who presided over them, if they knew it was wrong; but such obedience as this is worse than folly to us; it is slavery in the extreme; and the man who would thus willingly degrade himself should not claim a rank among intelligent beings, until he turns from his folly. A man of God... would despise the idea. Others, in the extreme exercise of their almighty authority have taught that such obedience was necessary, and that no matter what the saints were told to do by their presidents, they should do it without asking any questions. When Elders of Israel will so far indulge in these extreme notions of obedience as to teach them to the people, it is generally because they have it in their minds to do wrong themselves. (Joseph Smith Millennial Star, 14:38, pp. 593-95.)

Brigham Young taught the same message on multiple occasions. He said that members had to vet everything he said with the Holy Ghost.

> As you have been told hundreds of times, how easy it would be for your leaders to lead you to destruction, unless you actually know the mind and will of the Spirit yourselves. (JD 4:368.)

> I do not wish any Latter-day Saint in this world, nor in heaven, to be satisfied with anything I do, unless the Spirit of the Lord Jesus Christ, the spirit of revelation, makes them satisfied...Suppose that the people were heedless, that they manifested no concern with regard to the things of the kingdom of God, but threw the whole burden upon the leaders of the people, saying, 'If the brethren who take charge of matters are satisfied, we are,' this is not pleasing in the sight of the Lord. (JD 3:45.)

Since then, church leaders' teachings on the subject have consistently shifted to trusting leaders no matter what they say or why they say it, a concept called "follow the prophet":

Those who listen to and follow the counsel of living prophets and apostles will not go astray. (Preach My Gospel, 2004, 75.)

Whatever comes from the voices of those who hold that authority is scripture, no matter of what they may speak. (J. Reuben Clark, Jr., Conference Report, April 1944, 112.)

Follow your leaders who have been duly ordained and have been publicly sustained, and you will not be led astray. (Boyd K. Packer, "To Be Learned Is Good I...", Ensign, November 1992, 73.)

You need the strength that comes from trusting the Lord's prophets. (Elder Neil A. Anderson, April 2014 General Conference).

Surely one of the crowning blessings of membership in this Church is the blessing of being led by living prophets of God....Trusting in and following the prophets is more than a blessing and a privilege. President Ezra Taft Benson declared that "our [very] salvation hangs on following the prophet....We can choose to follow the prophet, or we can look to the arm of flesh. May we have the wisdom to trust in and follow the counsel of the living prophets and apostles." (Elder Duncan, October 2010 General Conference.)

You can always trust the living prophets. (True to the Faith, 2004, 129.)

As we look to the prophets for guidance, we can be confident that they will not lead us astray. (L. Aldin Porter, "Search the Prophets," Ensign, April 2002, 31.)

To modern Mormons, "follow the prophet" is synonymous with "follow God." To them, the words of the president of the church and other LDS leaders are one and the same with the words of God. This characterization applies to their words no matter the topic,[492] and whether or not the words they speak actually came from God.[493]

There are significant doctrinal problems with these assertions. Joseph said, "a prophet [is] a prophet only when he [is] acting as such" (HC 5:265).[494]

---

[492] "Whatever comes from the voices of those who hold that authority is scripture, no matter of what they may speak." (J. Reuben Clark, Jr., Conference Report, April 1944, 112.)

[493] "The prophet does not have to say "Thus saith the Lord" to give us scripture." (Ezra Taft Benson, "Fourteen Fundamentals of Following the Prophet," BYU Speeches, 26 Feb. 1980.)

[494] Joseph Smith was the only man I am aware of whose word's God said we should head as if from his own mouth: "For his word ye shall receive, as if from mine own mouth, in all patience and faith." (D&C 21:5.) Yet, Joseph told the people not to assume everything he said was right or from God. "the people should each one stand

God's word is only God's word when it is God who said it. Someone who holds the office of prophet does not have license to invent God's word. Any portion of their words that is not repeated from what they heard from God is no different than anyone else's word. There is a great difference between: "I say what God says to me" and "what I say is God's word, whether he said it to me or not." It turns out that we shouldn't assume church leaders words are true, even in the rare event when they do claim to be speaking God's word:

> President Wilford Woodruff is a man of wisdom and experience, and we respect him, but we do not believe his personal views or utterances are revelations from God; and when 'Thus saith the Lord,' comes from him, the saints investigate it: they do not shut their eyes and take it down like a pill. (Apostle Charles W. Penrose, Millennial Star, v. 54, p. 191.)

Some claim that the ordination of leaders elevates their words to equality with God's words.[495] If ordination implied correct doctrine, no previous dispensation could have apostatized. Both the ancient Israelites and the Catholic church were founded on legal ordinations. Yet, their leaders were able to lead them astray.

Because any man, no matter his calling, is capable of preaching false doctrine, we should not assume that the words of any man, no matter his calling, are God's words. Doing so is putting our trust in the arm of flesh.

> ...cursed is he that putteth his trust in man or maketh flesh his arm. (2 Nephi 4:34.)

> Thus saith the Lord; Cursed be the man that trusteth in man, and maketh flesh his arm... (Jeremiah 17:5.)

> Cursed is he that putteth his trust in man, or maketh flesh his arm, or shall hearken unto the precepts of men, save their precepts shall be given by the power of the Holy Ghost. (2 Nephi 28:31.)

---

for himself, and depend on no man or men in that state of corruption of the Jewish church—that righteous persons could only deliver their own souls—applied it to the present state [1842] of the Church of Jesus Christ of Latter-day Saints—said if the people departed from the Lord, they must fall—that they were depending on the Prophet, hence were darkened in their minds, in consequence of neglecting the duties devolving upon themselves..." (Teachings of the Prophet Joseph Smith p. 238.) If this is the case for Joseph, how much more for those whose words God has *not* said are his?

[495] "Follow your leaders who have been duly ordained and have been publicly sustained, and you will not be led astray." (Boyd K. Packer, "To Be Learned Is Good I...", Ensign, November 1992, 73.)

Nephi said it is only when "their precepts [are] given by the power of the Holy Ghost" that we should "hearken unto the precepts of men." We are under no obligation to accept something said by a church leader as true,[496] until and unless the Holy Spirit testifies it is true. We have to ask God if it is true every time:

> I am more afraid that this people have so much confidence in their leaders that they will not inquire for themselves of God whether they are led by him. I am fearful they settle down in a state of blind self-security, trusting their eternal destiny in the hands of their leaders with a reckless confidence that in itself would thwart the purposes of God in their salvation. Let every man and woman know by the whispering of the Spirit of God to themselves, whether their leaders are walking in the path the Lord dictates or not. (Brigham Young, JD 9:150.)

When faced with the contradiction of "follow the prophet" and "do not trust in the arm of flesh," modern Mormons unfortunately side with the former tradition instead of the latter commandment of God. In order to reconcile the two, they conclude that somehow church leaders are excluded from the arm of flesh, perhaps because they suppose that everything a church leader says is what God himself would say if he were present.

Church leaders are not infallible. They "often" speak without inspiration,[497] and are capable of teaching damningly false doctrine. It turns out that exclusion of church leaders from "the arm of the flesh" is a modern construct. Early church leaders taught members to avoid trusting in leaders, and said that to do so was to trust in the arm of the flesh.

> Do not, brethren, put your trust in man though he be a Bishop, an apostle or a president; if you do, they will fail you at some time or place; they will do wrong or seem to, and your support will be gone; but if we lean on God, He will never fail us. When men and women depend upon God alone and trust in him alone, their faith will not be shaken if the highest in the Church should step aside. (George Q. Cannon, DW 43:322 [Mar 7, 1891]).

---

[496] "Not every statement made by a Church leader, past or present, necessarily constitutes doctrine. A single statement made by a single leader on a single occasion often represents a personal, though well-considered, opinion, but is not meant to be officially binding for the whole Church." (Official Statement, The Church of Jesus Christ of Latter-day Saints, "Approaching Mormon Doctrine" May 4, 2007.)

[497] According to Bruce R. McConkie England letter, previously cited. Nephi tells us that we should disregard the precepts of leaders as often as they speak without inspiration (2 Nephi 28:31).

Our testimony does not depend upon Joseph Smith; it does not depend upon Brigham Young; it does not depend upon John Taylor, or upon the council of the Twelve Apostles, which is now the presiding quorum in the Church. I pin my faith to no man's sleeve; I am a believer in the Scripture which says, 'Cursed be the man that trusteth in man, and maketh flesh his arm.' (Charles Penrose, August 17, 1879. Journal of Discourses 20:295.)

Those that heed every word of church leaders—whether they are from the Holy Ghost or not—are described in D&C 76 as telestial spirits.

And the glory of the telestial is one...For these are they who are of Paul, and of Apollos, and of Cephas. These are they who say they are some of one and some of another—some of Christ and some of John, and some of Moses, and some of Elias, and some of Esaias, and some of Isaiah, and some of Enoch; But received not the gospel, neither the testimony of Jesus, neither the prophets, neither the everlasting covenant. Last of all, these all are they who will not be gathered with the saints, to be caught up unto the church of the Firstborn, and received into the cloud. These are they who are liars, and sorcerers, and adulterers, and whoremongers, and whosoever loves and makes a lie. These are they who suffer the wrath of God on earth. These are they who suffer the vengeance of eternal fire. These are they who are cast down to hell and suffer the wrath of Almighty God, until the fulness of times, when Christ shall have subdued all enemies under his feet, and shall have perfected his work; (D&C 76:98-106.)

Those who follow a leader instead of the Holy Ghost are accounted no better than liars, adulterers, and whoremongers. There is a difference between being "of" a messenger and receiving the gospel, the testimony of Jesus, the prophets, and the everlasting covenant. The former just means you listened to and trust a person. The latter means that you've taken the Spirit to be your guide. If one idolizes the messenger, or follows them as a person instead of seeking God's word, they will not realize whether he is a true or false prophet, because they will not ask whether or not each of his messages contain God's word. Following God's word leads to eternal life. On the other hand, if a person focuses on a man instead of searching for God's word, they will be damned to the telestial kingdom. This doctrine was understood in the past.

Now those men, or those women, who know no more about the power of God, and the influences of the Holy Spirit, than to be led entirely by another person, suspending their own understanding, and pinning their faith upon another's sleeve, will never be capable of entering into the celestial glory, to be crowned as they anticipate; they will never be capable of becoming Gods...They never can become Gods, nor be crowned as rulers with glory, immortality, and eternal lives. They never can hold scepters of glory, majesty, and power in the celestial kingdom. Who will? Those who are valiant and inspired with the true independence of heaven, who will go forth boldly in the service of their God, leaving others to do as they please, determined to do right, though all mankind besides should take the opposite course. (Brigham Young, JD 1:312.)

We are charged by God to validate the truthfulness of what church leaders say. The Holy Ghost is the only source of truth that will never lead us astray.[498]

And I said unto them that it was the word of God; and whoso would hearken unto the word of God, and would hold fast unto it, they would never perish; neither could the temptations and the fiery darts of the adversary overpower them unto blindness, to lead them away to destruction. (1 Nephi 15:24.)

If we deny the Holy Ghost and instead trust in the arm of the flesh in the face of a multitude of examples of false doctrine taught by leaders throughout history, we make a tremendous mistake.

What a pity it would be, if we were led by one man to utter destruction! Are you afraid of this? I am more afraid that this people have so much confidence in their leaders that they will not inquire for themselves of God whether they are led by him. I am fearful they settle down in a state of blind self-security, trusting their eternal destiny in the hands of their leaders with a reckless confidence that in itself would thwart the purposes of God in their salvation, and weaken the influence they could give to their leaders, did they know for themselves, by the revelations of Jesus, that they are led in the right way. Let every man and woman know, themselves, whether their leaders are walking in the path the Lord dictates, or not. This has been my exhortation continually. (Brigham Young, JD 9:150.)

Members of the church hear a constant stream of claims that the Lord will not allow church leaders to lead the church astray.[499] This claim has

---

[498] "The First Presidency have of right a great influence over this people; and if we should get out of the way and lead this people to destruction, what a pity it would be! How can you know whether we lead you correctly or not? Can you know by any other power than that of the Holy Ghost? I have uniformly exhorted the people to obtain this living witness, each for themselves; then no man on earth can lead them astray." (Brigham Young, JD 6:100)

been applied to the church President, the First Presidency, and the Quorum of the Twelve. [500] The claim seems to have originated with Wilford Woodruff.[501]

When a principle states that something can never happen, showing that it happened just once is sufficient to prove the principle false. Though the modern discussion on the topic has been one sided, history provides for many contrary examples.

A modern example is found in Adam God doctrine. Brigham Young taught that Adam is Heavenly Father.[502] Adam God was taught at the veil in the endowment ceremony previous to the 1920s changes.[503] In October 1976 General Conference, Spencer W. Kimball said that the Adam God doctrine

---

[499] "Keep your eyes riveted n the First Presidency and the Quorum of the Twelve Apostles. We will not lead you astray. We cannot." (M. Russell Ballard, October 2014 General Conference) "Let me remind you to stay in the course chartered by the Church. It is the Lord's Church, and he will not permit it to be led astray. If we take the counsel that comes from the prophets and seers, we will pursue the course that is pleasing to the Lord." (Bruce R. McConkie, "Our Relationship With the Lord," BYU Devotional March 2, 1982.) "Keep your eye on the Prophet, for the Lord will never permit his Prophet to lead this Church astray." (Ezra Taft Benson, Conference Report, October 1966, 123.)

[500] "There is one thing which we should have exceedingly clear in our minds. Neither the President of the Church, nor the First Presidency, nor the united voice of the First Presidency and the Twelve will ever lead the Saints astray…" (Joseph Fielding Smith, Apr. 1972 General Conference.)

[501] "I say to Israel, the Lord will never permit me or any other man who stands as President of this Church to lead you astray. It is not in the program. It is not in the mind of God." (Teachings of Presidents of the Church: Wilford Woodruff, p. 199.)

[502] See Manuscript Addresses of Brigham Young, Oct. 8, 1861; Deseret News, June 18, 1873; Journal of Discourses 5:331-332; JD 1:50-51; Millennial Star, Vol. 48, Cover. For example, "How much unbelief exists in the minds of the Latter-day Saints in regard to one particular doctrine which is revealed to them, and which God revealed to me—namely that Adam is our father and God." (Sermon delivered on June 8, 1873. Printed in the Deseret Weekly News, June 18, 1873.) Some claim that because Adam God doctrine was never voted on as a church, it cannot be considered official doctrine. Yet, official doctrine that has been voted on, such as the 1835 Doctrine and Covenants or the Lectures on Faith, were subsequently changed (D&C) or removed (LoF) without a vote by membership. Similarly, many other doctrines in the church have never been voted on, including polygamy, Heavenly Mother, Jesus being Jehovah and Heavenly Father being Elohim, Jesus being the first spirit child of the Father, that God was once a man, any bit of the temple ceremonies, or that Jesus and Satan are spirit brothers. With so many doctrines never voted on, one can hardly establish this as a test.

[503] The Journal of L. John Nuttall contains a synopsis of the content under the February 7, 1877 entry.

was an example of "false doctrine." Bruce R. McConkie used this as an example of how the Lord permits false doctrine to be taught in the church:

> Yes, President Young did teach that Adam was the father of our spirits....[Brigham Young] expressed views that are out of harmony with the gospel....I do not know all of the providences of the Lord, but I do know that he permits false doctrine to be taught in and out of the Church... (Bruce R. McConkie, Eugene England Letter, p. 6.)

He went on:

> If we believe false doctrine, we will be condemned. If that belief is on basic and fundamental things, it will lead us astray and we will lose our souls. (Bruce R. McConkie, Eugene England Letter, p. 6.)

The foregoing quote makes two interesting points. First, like President Kimball, Elder McConkie believed both that it was possible for a church president to teach false doctrine and that Brigham Young's Adam God doctrine was one such example. Second, Elder McConkie taught that one can be condemned for believing church-taught false doctrine. He said that it can lead a member astray and cause them to lose their soul.

God not only allows false doctrine to be taught by church leaders, he allows them to teach doctrines that are so false that they will prevent those who believe them from obtaining salvation. This should not be shocking, as it is a pattern present in every previous dispensation. Jesus taught that some of the doctrine taught by leaders in his day would prevent those who believed it from entering the kingdom of heaven:

> But woe unto you, scribes and Pharisees, hypocrites! for ye shut up the kingdom of heaven against men: for ye neither go in yourselves, neither suffer ye them that are entering to go in....Woe unto you, scribes and Pharisees, hypocrites! for ye compass sea and land to make one proselyte, and when he is made, ye make him twofold more the child of hell than yourselves. (Matthew 23:13,15.)

The Pharisees, according to Jesus, had reached a critical mass of apostasy: the false doctrines they taught were so poisonous that they overwhelmed any good the true doctrines they taught might cause.[504] Their "traditions"—or those commandments they taught which were actually from men but passed off as if from God—were sufficient to cut off those who obeyed them from a connection from God. The commandments of men caused them to break the

---

[504] Modern Mormons consider apostasy a binary event: you are either completely for God or completely against him. Scripture and experience suggest otherwise. Any deviation from God's word is apostasy. It is a condition of degrees, with as many degrees as there are words of God to deviate from.

commandments of God, which repelled the Holy Ghost and any chance they had to return to God's presence.

> Why do thy disciples transgress the tradition of the elders? for they wash not their hands when they eat bread. But he answered and said unto them, Why do ye also transgress the commandment of God by your tradition? (Matthew 15:2-3.)

It was not just ancient church leaders who were capable of leading people astray. Ancient prophets were also known to do so. For instance, the LDS heading of 1 Kings 13 reads, "Jeroboam is smitten and then healed by a prophet from Judah—The prophet delivers his message, is led astray by a prophet from Bethel, and is slain by a lion for his disobedience..." It should be no surprise that a modern prophet, just like an ancient one, can say things that are incorrect. After all, in many instances, they speak according to their own opinions and prejudices without inspiration:

> With all their inspiration and greatness, prophets are yet mortal men with imperfections common to mankind in general. They have their opinions and prejudices and are left to work out their own problems without inspiration in many instances. (Bruce R. McConkie quoted in Dallin H. Oaks, "Teaching and Learning by the Spirit," Ensign, March 1997.)

In addition to being taught to trust in church leaders' teachings whether or not they actually come from God, leaders have also taught that we should follow their teachings whether or not they are right. Marion G. Romney told the following story, which has been repeated on several occasions, including in the June 1981 First Presidency Message and in a recent Priesthood/Relief Society manual:

> I remember years ago when I was a Bishop I had President [Heber J.] Grant talk to our ward. After the meeting I drove him home...Standing by me, he put his arm over my shoulder and said: 'My boy, you always keep your eye on the President of the Church, and if he ever tells you to do anything, and it is wrong, and you do it, the Lord will bless you for it.' Then with a twinkle in his eye, he said, 'But you don't need to worry. The Lord will never let his mouthpiece lead the people astray.' (Conference Report, October 1960, p. 78.)

This passage is most certainly false doctrine. How can one hide behind the excuse of "following the prophet" when God has amply told them explicitly not to trust in men, and instead only heed what is taught by the Holy Ghost? The Holy Ghost will never lead you astray, but church leaders have taught, are teaching, and will teach false doctrine. Joseph Smith publicly preached against this pernicious doctrine, which apparently was already taught in his time:

> We have heard men who hold the priesthood remark that they would do anything they were told to do by those who preside over them (even) if they knew it was wrong; but such obedience as this is worse than folly to us; it is slavery in the extreme; and the man who would thus willingly degrade himself, should not claim a rank among intelligent beings, until he turns from his folly. A man of God would despise the idea. Others, in the extreme exercise of their almighty authority have taught that such obedience was necessary, and that no matter what the saints were told to do by their presidents, they should do it without any questions. When the Elders of Israel will so far indulge in these extreme notions of obedience as to teach them to the people, it is generally because they have it in their hearts to do wrong themselves. (Joseph Smith, Millennial Star, 14:38, pp.593-595.)

A man is not saved through his allegiance to imperfect men, but through his seeking and following the Holy Ghost. True messengers will always act in ways to increase the connection between an individual and God, not in ways that inflate their role or make them a middleman in the process. True messengers do not seek for men to worship them instead of God. They do not consider themselves more holy than those they are called to serve and do not ask for special treatment.[505]

One way false prophets encourage idolatry is by calling themselves "prophets" absent of any transmission of God's word. This causes men to venerate the leader instead of God himself, because they are supplanting God's word with man's word. A recent conference featured a perfect example of this, when Elder William Walker encouraged us all to try to be more like President Monson so that we could be more like Jesus. "As we follow President Monson and try to be more like him, we will inevitably succeed in being more faithful disciples of the Lord Jesus Christ." (William R. Walker, "Follow the Prophet," April 2014.) Why not just encourage people to be more like Jesus directly? Are we to believe that somehow being like President Monson is a necessary waypoint in our journey to become like Christ? Contrast this with the following:

> I know of but One in all the world who can be taken as the first and only perfect standard for us to follow, and he is the Only Begotten Son of God. I would feel sorry indeed, if I had a friend or an associate in this life who would turn away from the plan of life and salvation because I might stumble or make a failure of my life. I want

---

[505] "for thus saith the Lord: 'Ye shall not esteem one flesh above another, or one man shall not think himself above another." (Mosiah 23:7.)

no man to lean upon me nor to follow me, only so far as I am a consistent follower in the footsteps of the Master. (Joseph F. Smith, Gospel Doctrine, Pg.4. See also the Juvenile Instructor, 1915, Vol. 50, pp. 738, 739.)

We are told that as we adore the president of the church, we are experiencing the adoration the Lord has for him:

That is far more than hero worship or the feelings we sometimes have of admiring heroic figures. It is a gift from God. With it you will receive more easily the gift of confirming revelation when he speaks in his office as the Lord's prophet. The love you feel is the love the Lord has for whoever is His spokesman. (President Henry B. Eyring, "Continuing Revelation," October 2014 General Conference.)

There isn't a single scripture advocating admiration, love, or reverence for church leaders. Idolatry means extreme admiration, love, or reverence for something or someone other than God. When we idolize the president of the church or any other of the brethren, we are idolizing them. Modern Mormons throw lavish birthday celebrations for their idols. They stand when their idols enter the room.[506] They call their idols "beloved." They give "oath like indication[s] that [they] recognize" the words of leaders to be "legitimate and binding upon [them]."[507] We care more about the man occupying an office than we do the presence or absence of God's word in what they say.

In modern Mormonism, pointing out the errors of leaders is an offense that can result in the revocation of temple access, release from callings, and even excommunication. For example, Elder Oaks has said, "It's wrong to criticize leaders of the church, even if the criticism is true." Some fear that questioning teachings of church leaders is risking losing their connection to salvation. To such, the word of God provides reassurance in the face of fearful false claims that one's salvation depends on unquestioning acceptance of the precepts of men:

O then, my beloved brethren, come unto the Lord, the Holy One. Remember that his paths are righteous. Behold, the way for man is narrow, but it lieth in a straight course before him, and the keeper of the gate is the Holy One of Israel; and he employeth no servant

---

[506] "And he said unto them, The kings of the Gentiles exercise lordship over them; and they that exercise authority upon them are called benefactors. But ye shall not be so: but he that is greatest among you, let him be as the younger; and he that is chief, as he that doth serve. For whether is greater, he that sitteth at meat, or he that serveth? is not he that sitteth at meat? but I am among you as he that serveth." (Luke 22:25-27)

[507] Elder Russell M. Nelson, October 2014 General Conference.

there; and there is none other way save it be by the gate; for he cannot be deceived, for the Lord God is his name. (2 Nephi 9:41.)

Without evaluating the doctrines leaders espouse, you cannot truly search for truth because questioning anything that leaders say or do causes an emotionally charged mental block. Vacuous refusal to think is equivalent to blindly following whatever they say, and is equivalent to trusting in the arm of the flesh.

Those who believe that questioning leaders is a sinful offence sometimes cite Joseph Smith as the source of the principle. They quote him as saying:

> I will give you one of the Keys of the mysteries of the Kingdom. It is an eternal principle, that has existed with God from all eternity: That man who rises up to condemn others, finding fault with the Church, saying that they are out of the way, while he himself is righteous, then know assuredly, that that man is in the high road to apostasy; and if he does not repent, will apostatize, as God lives. (Joseph Smith, History of the Church, 3:385)[508]

What is lost in the removal of context is that this sermon was not directed to members—it was directed to the apostles in light of those from that quorum who had recently left the church. Joseph charged them:

> do not betray heaven, that you do not betray Jesus Christ, that you do not betray your Brethren, & that you do not betray the revelations of God whether in the bible, Book of Mormon, or Doctrine & Covenants or any of the word of God. Yea in all your kicking, & floundering see to it that you do not this thing lest innocent blood be found in your skirts & you go down to hell. We may ever know by this sign that there is danger of our being led to a fall & aposticy. (Wilford Woodruff's Diary, July 2, 1839.)

Ironically, this quote used to teach unfailing and unquestioning support of the brethren, was given by Joseph not to teach members to trust the brethren, but to warn the brethren of their tendency to rebel against God and the gospel as provided in the standard works.

Joseph's teachings, in combination with the standard works, provide a unified argument that no leader is above reproach, that all members are subject to be called to repentance, and that the standard of measurement is God's word found in the scriptures.

---

[508] The reprinted quote in the church's "Teachings of the Presidents: Joseph Smith" incorrectly states that this quote was "reported by Wilford Woodruff and Willard Richards." The two accounts are mutually exclusive, and only Richards' account contains the quote.

In his own life, Joseph actually invited criticism and rebuke. He was always willing to be taught. After being falsely accused publicly by his brother William, Joseph wrote,

> I desire, Brother William, that you will humble yourself. I freely forgive you, and you know my unshaken and unchangeable disposition; I know in whom I trust; I stand upon the rock; the floods cannot, no, they shall not, overthrow me. You know the doctrine I teach is true; you know that God has blessed me. I brought salvation to my father's house, as an instrument in the hands of God when they were in a miserable situation. You know that it is my duty to admonish you, when you do wrong. This liberty I shall always take, and you shall have the same privilege. I take the liberty to admonish you, because of my birthright; and I grant you the privilege, because it is my duty to be humble, and receive rebuke and instruction from a brother, or a friend. (Joseph Smith in letter to his brother, DHC 2:343.)

We should feel humbled to know that the prophet of the restoration—a man who knew God better than any of his contemporaries or successors—would openly invite rebuke. Given his willingness to be censured despite his accolades, what should we make of anyone who commands unquestioning servility?

Joseph was not alone. Brigham Young taught that regular members had every right to correct errors in their leaders:

> Now when I was an Elder I was as willing to correct an error in the Brethren as I am now. But the people do not see it so. Now if you should be with the Twelve or anybody, you would have right to correct an error as well as with a member... (Brigham Young quoted in Wilford Woodruff's Journal, p. 56.)

The pattern extends backwards in time. Paul exercised his right to correct error in Peter, who was his senior in the apostleship:

> And when James, Cephas, and John, who seemed to be pillars, perceived the grace that was given unto me, they gave to me and Barnabas the right hands of fellowship; that we should go unto the heathen, and they unto the circumcision. Only they would that we should remember the poor; the same which I also was forward to do. But when Peter was come to Antioch, I withstood him to the face, because he was to be blamed. For before that certain came from James, he did eat with the Gentiles: but when they were come, he withdrew and separated himself, fearing them which were of the circumcision. And the other Jews dissembled likewise with him; insomuch that Barnabas also was carried away with their

dissimulation. But when I saw that they walked not uprightly according to the truth of the gospel, I said unto Peter before them all, If thou, being a Jew, livest after the manner of Gentiles, and not as do the Jews, why compellest thou the Gentiles to live as do the Jews? (Galatians 2:9-14.)

We do not have to rely on Joseph, Brigham, or Paul for this principle. The Lord himself taught it plainly. He said that the inhabitants of Zion will judge the apostles and prophets to see who are liars and hypocrites:

> For it shall come to pass that the inhabitants of Zion shall judge all things pertaining to Zion. And liars and hypocrites shall be proved by them, and they who are not apostles and prophets shall be known. And even the bishop, who is a judge, and his counselors, if they are not faithful in their stewardships shall be condemned, and others shall be planted in their stead. (D&C 64:38-40.)

How will the inhabitants of Zion judge apostles and prophets if apostles and prophets are above reproach? Clearly, the Lord intends for members of the church to watch over the conduct of leaders. "The inhabitants of Zion" does not imply that this task is to be conducted only by members with special callings. That this responsibility is borne by normal members[509] is underscored by the instructions the Lord provided for trying the president of the church for transgression:

> And inasmuch as a President of the High Priesthood shall transgress, he shall be had in remembrance before the common council of the church, who shall be assisted by twelve counselors of the High Priesthood; And their decision upon his head shall be an end of controversy concerning him. Thus, none shall be exempted from the justice and the laws of God, that all things may be done in order and in solemnity before him, according to truth and righteousness. (D&C 107:82-84.)

The Lord put into the hands of normal members the ability to discipline the leadership of the church, a responsibility that necessarily

---

[509] A follow-on revelation given at this time specifies that "the common council of the church" is just that—a council of nine common members of the church, three per member of the first presidency. "Thus saith the Lord, let the first presidency of my Church, be held in full fellowship in Zion and in all her stakes, until they shall be found transgressors, by such a high council as is named in the above alluded section, in Zion by three witnesses standing against each member of said presidency...The presidency of my church may be tried by the voice of the whole body of the church in Zion, and the voice of a majority of all her stakes." (Book of Law of Lord, 12 January 1838.)

requires the membership of the church to watch over the leaders and evaluate their conduct to ascertain whether it is in line with God's will. Why would God give instructions on how normal members could remove a sitting church president for transgression if a) the president of the church cannot lead members astray and b) members are not meant to judge his execution of his office? Empowerment of normal members provides a both a check on the power of church leaders to stray from God's will as well as an undeniable witness that they can stray from God's will.

Though this concept is very far from the modern traditions that leaders are above reproach, it fits quite well into the seamless scriptural theme of the need for individuals to seek after and follow the Holy Ghost instead of relying upon men. For example,

> And at that day, when I shall come in my glory, shall the parable be fulfilled which I spake concerning the ten virgins. For they that are wise and have received the truth, and have taken the Holy Spirit for their guide, and have not been deceived—verily I say unto you, they shall not be hewn down and cast into the fire, but shall abide the day. (D&C 45:56-57.)

Common non-scriptural innovations in modern Mormonism such as "don't criticize leaders, even if it is true" and "follow the prophet" are mutually exclusive from the revealed principle of "judge your leaders and their teachings." In this light, which should be retained?

While there is nothing wrong with treasuring any revelation from God vindicated by the Holy Ghost that might come through a church leader, this is a far cry from hero worship or idolatry. "No servant can serve two masters: for either he will hate the one, and love the other; or else he will hold to the one, and despise the other." (Luke 16:13.) Those who "follow the prophet" do not take the Holy Spirit to be their guide and will not surpass the telestial kingdom.[510]

---

[510] For they that are wise and have received the truth, and have taken the Holy Spirit for their guide, and have not been deceived—verily I say unto you, they shall not be hewn down and cast into the fire, but shall abide the day. (D&C 45:57)

Witnesses

Witnesses are a supremely important factor in the gospel of Christ. Joseph Smith begins the first Lecture on Faith by explaining that it was by the testimony of those who knew God that the residue of men were inspired to seek after him, and made familiar with how to do so:

> The reason why we have been thus particular on this part of our subject is that this class may see by what means it was that God became an object of faith among men after the fall, and what it was that stirred up the faith of multitudes to feel after him - to search after a knowledge of his character, perfections, and attributes, until they became extensively acquainted with him; and not only commune with him, and behold his glory, but be partakers of his power, and stand in his presence. Let this class mark particularly that the testimony which these men had of the existence of a God, was the testimony of man. For previous to the time that any of Adam's posterity had obtained a manifestation of God to themselves, Adam, their common father, had testified unto them of the existence of God, and of his eternal power and Godhead. For instance, Abel, before he received the assurance from heaven that his offerings were acceptable unto God, had received the important information of his father that such a being did exist, who had created, and who did uphold all things. Neither can there be a doubt existing on the mind of any person, that Adam was the first who did communicate the knowledge of the existence of a God to his posterity; and that the whole faith of the world, from that time down to the present, is in a certain degree dependent on the knowledge first communicated to them by their common progenitor. And it has been handed down to the day and generation in which we live, as we shall show from the face of the sacred records. (Lectures on Faith 1:34-36.)

Paul echoes the same description of the pattern of divine witnesses, describing how before a man has faith, he has to become acquainted with the report of one who has already obtained the promised blessing:

> How then shall they call on him in whom they have not believed? and how shall they believe in him of whom they have not heard? and how shall they hear without a preacher? And how shall they preach,

except they be sent? as it is written, How beautiful are the feet of them that preach the gospel of peace, and bring glad tidings of good things! But they have not all obeyed the gospel. For Esaias saith, Lord, who hath believed our report? So then faith cometh by hearing, and hearing by the word of God. (Romans 1:14-17.)

Moroni also taught about the pattern of witnesses:

And because he hath done this, my beloved brethren, have miracles ceased? Behold I say unto you, Nay; neither have angels ceased to minister unto the children of men. For behold, they are subject unto him, to minister according to the word of his command, showing themselves unto them of strong faith and a firm mind in every form of godliness. And the office of their ministry is to call men unto repentance, and to fulfil and to do the work of the covenants of the Father, which he hath made unto the children of men, to prepare the way among the children of men, by declaring the word of Christ unto the chosen vessels of the Lord, that they may bear testimony of him. And by so doing, the Lord God prepareth the way that the residue of men may have faith in Christ, that the Holy Ghost may have place in their hearts, according to the power thereof; and after this manner bringeth to pass the Father, the covenants which he hath made unto the children of men. (Moroni 7:29-32.)

Angels come to those who have risen to a level of righteousness that allows their ministry. The purpose of an angelic visit is to enable the recipient to teach those revealed truths to "the residue" who cannot receive angels because they do not yet have sufficient faith in Christ. By heeding the witness of those who have received angels, the residue of men can give place to the Holy Ghost and become the kind of person to whom God sends angels.

Being the foundation of how the gospel is preached, the concept of witnesses is sacred. The testimony of two witnesses was considered sufficient evidence for conviction of even the most serious sins under the Law of Moses. It is not surprising, then, that the Ten Commandments include the command not to bear a false witness. The penalty of breaking this commandment was death.

It is to the true witnesses in scriptures that we owe all that we believe about God beyond our own experience. For example, from these witnesses, we believe that Christ lives, even if we have not yet seen him with our own eyes. Perhaps more importantly, because of the witnesses of men who have obtained blessings we have not yet obtained, we can both have faith that we ourselves can obtain them, and know the path to obtain them.

A false witness can lead us to exert much effort in a fruitless path, distracting us from pushing forward on the path to eternal life by luring us onto a dead end deviation. "A true witness delivereth souls: but a deceitful witness speaketh lies." (Proverbs 14:25.)

The danger of false witnesses is that they can lure the unsuspecting into practicing fruitless false religion under the guise of the real thing. These people are usually both the farthest from God and the least likely to realize it since their religious practices occupy such a great portion of their lives. There is no room for them to consider any alternatives. Isaiah and Nephi quoted the Lord as saying about these,

> Forasmuch as this people draw near unto me with their mouth, and with their lips do honor me, but have removed their hearts far from me, and their fear towards me is taught by the precepts of men— (2 Nephi 27:25.)

When men's precepts take the place of eye-witness accounts of God, they are sure to both prevent people from interacting with God and prevent them from accepting course corrections from true messengers. This is why Jesus gave such scathing rebukes to the Pharisees. Jesus explained that the fruitless paths that they witnessed of were responsible for preventing many from obtaining greater interactions with God:

> Woe unto you, lawyers! for ye have taken away the key of knowledge: ye entered not in yourselves, and them that were entering in ye hindered. (Luke 11:52.)

Nephi taught that this was not a condition unique to the past. He prophesied of our day when

> They wear stiff necks and high heads; yea, and because of pride, and wickedness, and abominations, and whoredoms, they have all gone astray save it be a few, who are the humble followers of Christ; nevertheless, they are led, that in many instances they do err because they are taught by the precepts of men. (2 Nephi 28:14.)

Teaching by the precept of men is what occurs when men accept as their teachers those who do not have experience with God. Such false witnesses teach the same precepts their predecessors taught instead of witnessing of their own experiences with God. They cite their authority of their office instead of a divine source of their message. Although they may be well meaning, the consequence of heading modern false witnesses is the same as heading ancient ones.

False witnesses are not always obvious. If a wolf were not wearing sheep's clothing, he wouldn't fool anyone.[511] If the Lord will eventually cast

---

[511] "Beware of false prophets, which come to you in sheep's clothing, but inwardly they are ravening wolves." (Matthew 7:15.)

out even the imposters who did mighty miracles,[512] what of those who sit in the chief seats but offer no signs of their divine appointment? And why will they be cast out? Because they do not actually know the Lord. Knowing the Lord is the duty of every disciple of Christ, as it is the requirement for eternal life. But one group of members has a special responsibility to know the Lord face to face: Apostles.

Apostles represent a special witness because they are, by definition, eyewitnesses to the resurrected Christ. In all of scripture and church history, we only have two occasions where the qualification for being an apostle was given. The first is in the book of Acts where Peter specifies that Judas' replacement not only had to be among the over 500 who had seen the risen Christ, but also have had an eyewitness of his mortal ministry (Acts 1:21-22). This eyewitness allowed the apostles to bear powerful testimony, such as the following:

> That which was from the beginning, which we have heard, which we have seen with our eyes, which we have looked upon, and our hands have handled, of the Word of life....That which we have seen and heard declare we unto you, that ye also may have fellowship with us: and truly our fellowship is with the Father, and with his Son Jesus Christ. (1 John 1:1,3.)

The second occasion was when Oliver Cowdery, ordained of God to search out the first group of twelve in this dispensation, gave to that group. He said,

> It is necessary that you receive a testimony from heaven to yourselves; so that you can bear testimony to the truth of the Book of Mormon, and that you have seen the face of God. That is more than the testimony of an angel. When the proper time arrives, you shall be able to bear this testimony to the world. When you bear testimony that you have seen God, this testimony God will never suffer to fall, but will bear you out; although many will not give heed, yet others will. You will therefore see the necessity of getting this testimony from heaven. Never cease striving until you have seen God face to face. Strengthen your faith; cast off your doubts, your sins, and all your unbelief; and nothing can prevent you from coming to God. Your ordination is not full and complete till God has laid his

---

[512] "Not every one that saith unto me, Lord, Lord, shall enter into the kingdom of heaven; but he that doeth the will of my Father which is in heaven. Many will say to me in that day, Lord, Lord, have we not prophesied in thy name? and in thy name have cast out devils? and in thy name done many wonderful works? And then will I profess unto them, I never knew you: depart from me, ye that work iniquity. (Matthew 7:21-23.)

hand upon you. We require as much to qualify us as did those who have gone before us; God is the same. If the Savior in former days laid his hands upon his disciples, why not in latter days?....The time is coming when you will be perfectly familiar with the things of God....You have our best wishes, you have our most fervent prayers, that you may be able to bear this testimony, that you have seen the face of God. Therefore call upon him in faith in mighty prayer till you prevail, for it is your duty and your privilege to bear such a testimony for yourselves. (Oliver Cowdery, History of the Church, 2:192-98.)

Without an eyewitness, the testimony of an apostle ceases to be any more special than any other person who has received a spiritual witness of the Savior. This witness is certainly important. It can be sufficient to bring a newcomer to the gate of the gospel. However, without an eyewitness, a disciple's ability to increase faith in Jesus Christ is limited. Specifically, the disciple cannot really say that they know it is possible for a man to stand in the presence of God in this life. They also cannot say with a surety that they know that Jesus lives. Nephi gives us an example of the power that comes with a true apostolic witness:

And now I, Nephi, write more of the words of Isaiah, for my soul delighteth in his words. For I will liken his words unto my people, and I will send them forth unto all my children, for he verily saw my Redeemer, even as I have seen him. And my brother, Jacob, also has seen him as I have seen him; wherefore, I will send their words forth unto my children to prove unto them that my words are true. Wherefore, by the words of three, God hath said, I will establish my word. Nevertheless, God sendeth more witnesses, and he proveth all his words. (2 Nephi 11:2-3.)

The only way someone who has not seen God can achieve such a powerful witness is by saying things that are intentionally misleading to create the false impression that an eyewitness has been achieved. Unfortunately, such a tactic is subject to cross-examination, and when unwound will surely take with it the credibility of anything else the false witness taught or testified of.

Some would attempt to minimize Cowdery's charge without citing revelation. However, Joseph himself reaffirmed this principle several times. For example, he told the apostles,

We have work to do, that no other man can do. You must proclaim the Gospel in its simplicity and purity. and we commend you to God and the word of his grace. You have our best wishes, you have our most fervent prayers, that you may be able to bear this testimony, that you have seen the face of God. Therefore, call upon him in faith and mighty prayer, till you prevail, for it <is> your duty and your privelege to bear such testimony for yourselves. We now exhort you to be faithful to fulfil your calling, there must be no lack here. You must fulfil in all things, and permit is us to repeat, all nations have a claim on you. You are bound together as the three witnesses were. You, notwithstanding can part & meet & meet and part again till your heads are silvered o[v]er with age. (Joseph Smith Papers, Minute Book 1, 12 Feb. 1834, pp. 27–29, as written.)

The understanding that seeing Jesus was a requirement for the apostleship was present for some time after the death of Joseph. For example, in 1883 Zebedee Coltrin recounted his eyewitness of the Father and the Son, which had occurred during the school of the Prophets in Kirtland. Coltrin recounted that

the Prophet Joseph said: Brethren, now you are prepared to be the apostles of Jesus Christ, for you have seen both the Father and the Son and know that they exist and that they are two separate personages. (Minutes, Salt Lake City School of the Prophets, October 3, 1883.)

Likewise, the minutes recording the ordination of new apostles echo Cowdery's charge until around the turn of the century.[513]

Modern apostles minimize the effect of obtaining an eyewitness of Christ. For example, when Elder Oaks was recently asked "Have you seen him and witnessed His baptism, His teaching, His healing the sick and lame, the mock trial, His Crucifixion, His Resurrection, and His Ascension," he replied, "Where do you find that kind of 'witness' defined or even mentioned in the scriptures?"[514] On another occasion, Elder Oaks was confronted with the claim that:

…current apostles have no right to run the affairs of the church since they do not meet the New Testament standard of apostles because they do not testify of having seen Christ.

He responded by saying:

The first answer to this claim is that modern apostles are called to be witnesses of the name of Christ in all the world, Doctrine and Covenants 107:23. This is not to witness of a personal manifestation. To witness of the name is to witness of the plan, the work, or mission such as the atonement and the authority or priesthood of the Lord Jesus Christ, which an apostle who holds the keys is uniquely

---

[513] D. Michael Quinn, "Mormon Heirarchy: Extensions of Power," pp. 2-3.

[514] http://peace-in-paradise.blogspot.com/2015/06/prophets-dallin-h-oaks-response-to-my.html retrieved 21 Jun 2015.

responsible to do. (Elder Dallin H. Oaks, Boise, Idaho, June 17, 2105.)

It may be unthinkable to the typical member of the church to consider that the apostles' definition of "special witness" is merely an assignment independent of an actual experience with Christ. Early apostles would certainly agree. Heber J. Grant's reported anxiety of not having seen Christ shows that, at least at that time, an eye-witness of Christ was expected.

> I can truthfully say that from October, 1882, until February, 1883, [an evil spirit] followed me day and night, telling me that I was unworthy to be an apostle of the Church, and that I ought to resign. When I would testify of my knowledge that Jesus is the Christ, the Son of the living God, the Redeemer of mankind, it seemed at though a voice would say to me: 'You lie! You lie! You have never seen Him.' (Heber J. Grant, "Opening Conference Message," General Conference, 4 April 1941)[515]

As late as the turn of the century, official church sermons still featured apostles who testified of fulfilling the charge in both the New Testament and current dispensation to be an eyewitness of Christ. For example, Elder George Q. Cannon testified, "I know that Jesus lives; for I have seen Him."[516] On another occasion he said,

> I have been greatly favored of the Lord. My mind has been rapt in vision and have saw the beauties and Glory of God. I have saw and conversed with the Savior face to face. God will bestow this upon you.[517]

---

[515] Grant's conscience was soothed not by actually obtaining an eye witness, but by having a feeling on one occasion that Joseph Smith had something to do with his call to the apostleship: "I was one day riding alone and thinking of my unworthiness, when the Spirit impressed me just as though a voice had spoken, 'You were not worthy but the Prophet Joseph to whom you will belong in the next world, and your father, have interceded for you that you might be called, and now it remains for you to prove yourself worthy.'" (Abraham H. Cannon Journals, 2 April 1891.) Whether this impression occurred or not (it is a second hand account given much after the fact), being called as apostle does not qualify one to give an eye witness of Jesus Christ. As explained in Cowdery's original charge, to prove oneself worthy of the call requires obtaining an eye witness manifestation of Jesus Christ.

[516] George Q. Cannon, "Supporting Church Leaders," 6 October 1896, reported in The Deseret Weekly 53:610, 31 October 1896; reproduced in Stuy, Collected Discourses 5:225.

[517] George Q Cannon, Collected Discourses, 3:285, citing Francis Asbury Hammond, Journal, 20 April 1893.

Such an eyewitness increases the hearer's faith that Jesus not only exists, but that the hearer too can obtain an audience with the Savior in this life.

With the appointment of Elder Smoot, things changed. He was regarded as "reliable in business, but has little or no faith."[518] Instead of the charge to obtain the face of God, he was instead instructed to receive "the light of the Holy Ghost" from which to testify. At the same time, there was a clear schism in the quorum of the twelve between those who had obtained an eyewitness and those who had not. Heber J. Grant reported that during his first span of time as an apostle he was overcome with guilt because he had not obtained this witness. He said it haunted him every time he testified of the Savior. Another quorum member told him that he was a failure as an apostle until and unless he obtained an eyewitness, providing further pressure. Just two years prior to his death, President Joseph F. Smith wrote,

> Your brethren, who are called to the apostleship, and to minister in the midst of the house of Israel...are supposed to be eye and ear witnesses of the divine mission of Jesus Christ....That is their mission, and their duty; and that is the doctrine and the truth, that is their duty to preach to the world, and see that it is preached to the world. (Joseph F. Smith, Millennial Star, Vol. LXXVII, 1914, p. 336.)

With President Joseph F. Smith's death came the end of an era. The excommunication of Elders Cawley and Taylor helped Heber J. Grant overcome his cognitive dissonance. He reasoned in his diary, "I have never prayed to see the Savior. I know of men—Apostles—who have seen the Savior more than once. I have prayed to the Lord for the inspiration of His Spirit to guide me, and I have told Him that I have seen so many men fall because of some great manifestation to them, they felt their importance, their greatness." (The Diaries of Heber J. Grant, p. 468.) He told a tabernacle meeting in 1942 "I never prayed to see the Savior." (Heber J. Grant Journal, Oct. 4, 1942.)

If the appointment of Elder Smoot marked the beginning of the abandonment of the ancient and modern apostolic charge, the tenure of Heber J. Grant institutionalized the deviation. Before, these men were charged that they were not really special witnesses until they had obtained an eyewitness of the Savior. Now, they were criminalized for having one, and publicly bragged about never seeking for it. President Heber J. Grant's effort to ease his guilty conscience did not end there. A sister wrote him asking about eyewitnesses of Christ. He replied, "I know of no instance where the Lord has appeared to an individual since His appearance to the Prophet

---

[518] See D. Michael Quinn, "Mormon Hierarchy: Extensions of Power," p. 2.

Joseph Smith."[519] Since President Grant was not only in attendance when his fellow apostles had made those admissions prior to 1900, but also knew these men intimately, this statement was either an unbelievable omission, or a flat out lie with the intent to change history to fit the new standard.

Subsequent apostles continued the new standard (or lack thereof) for being an apostle. The new doctrine was that receiving an impression that Jesus was real was a stronger witness than actually seeing him and speaking with him. Somehow knowing *of* him superseded in importance *actually* knowing him. Joseph Fielding Smith wrote about apostles:

> It is their privilege to see him if occasion requires, but the Lord has taught that there is a stronger witness than seeing a personage, even of seeing the Son of God in a vision. Impressions on the soul that come from the Holy Ghost are far more significant than a vision. When Spirit speaks to spirit, the imprint upon the soul is far more difficult to erase. Every member of the Church should have impressions that Jesus is the Son of God indelibly pictured on his soul through the witness of the Holy Ghost. (Joseph Fielding Smith, "The First Presidency and the Council of the Twelve," Improvement Era, Nov. 1966, p. 979.)

On another occasion, he provided the position of the modern brethren clearly: a witness of Christ need not by visual or include his visitation at all—that the Holy Ghost was a superior witness:

> Every member of the Council of the Twelve Apostles should have, and I feel sure have had, the knowledge of the resurrection of Jesus Christ. This does not have to come by direct visitation of the Savior, but it does come by the testimony of the Holy Ghost....The testimony of the Holy Ghost is the strongest witness that can be given. It is better than a personal visit. (Doctrines of Salvation 3:153.)

President Joseph Fielding Smith on more than one occasion reiterated the displacement of the ancient and modern requirement to see the Lord. He taught that the brethren had no duty to seek the face of the Lord. Instead, they would only see him "if occasion requires." He wrote to his son after being an apostle for 38 years:

> I did not live in the days of our Savior; he has not come to me in person. I have not beheld him. His Father and he have not felt it necessary to grant me such a great blessing as this. But it is not necessary. I have felt his presence. I know that the Holy Spirit has enlightened my mind and revealed him unto me, so that I do love my

---

[519] Heber J. Grant, letter to Mrs. Claud Peery, April 13, 1926, typescript in Lester Bush papers, University of Utah Archives.

Redeemer, I hope, and feel it is true, better than everything else in this life. I would not have it otherwise.[520]

The brethren actively changed the definition of what made their witness "special." It was their calling, they were told, that made their witness greater than anyone else who had an impression that Jesus was real.

Once changed, this new doctrine was spoken about as if it had always been that way. President Harold B. Lee reported that when he was sustained as a member of the Twelve, he was told, "Now you understand that you are now to be a special witness of that great event, meaning the resurrection of the Lord." President Lee felt that since he had read the scriptures and felt that these people had actually lived, his witness was just as strong as Paul's, who had seen and conversed with the Lord. He said this was because his impression was actually greater than what Paul had seen:

> ...a witness more perfect than sight is the witness which the Holy Ghost bears to one's soul so that he knows these things are true. I witness to you with all my soul that I know, as the Spirit has born witness to my soul, that the Savior lives.[521]

Elder McConkie taught that

> It is true that the witness of the Holy Ghost is sure and absolute and that a man can know with a perfect knowledge, by the power of the Holy Ghost, that Jesus Christ is the Son of the living God who was crucified for the sins of the world. This unshakeable certainty can rest in his soul even though he has not seen the face of his Lord. (The Promised Messiah, p. 592.)

The idea that a spiritual witness is stronger than an eyewitness allows modern Mormon leaders to say things that imply that they have seen Jesus without, in their minds, being deceitful. In Bruce R. McConkie's case, the foregoing quote seriously detracts from the impact of his widely lauded last testimony, where he said

> I am one of his witnesses, and in a coming day I shall feel the nail marks in his hands and in his feet and shall wet his feet with my tears. But I shall not know any better then than I know now that he is God's Almighty Son, that he is our Savior and Redeemer, and that

---

[520] Joseph Fielding Smith Jr. and John J. Stewart, The Life of Joseph Fielding Smith (1972), 387–88; This letter was reprinted in the recent Priesthood and Relief Society lesson manual.

[521] Quoted in Bruce E. Dana, "The Apostleship" [Springville, UT: Cedar Fort, 2006], 176-77; see pp. 177-79 for additional references. Similar statements from Lee are found in Teachings of Presidents of the Church: Harold B. Lee, chapter 5.

salvation comes in and through his atoning blood and in no other way. (Bruce McConkie, "The Purifying Power of Gethsamane," April 1985 General Conference).

Knowing better than he knew then, according to Elder McConkie, would be impossible since he already had a spiritual witness, which—according to him—was stronger than an eyewitness.

We read in the scriptures that the Nephites, Paul, and others who had the privilege of touching the resurrected Christ had a transformative experience. They could witness that they indeed knew, not merely believed, that Jesus was resurrected. Today's apostles apparently believe that there is nothing special gained from an eyewitness. President Uchtdorf said, "You do not need to see the Savior, as the Apostles did, to experience the same transformation."[522] A recent conference presenter said "Our own testimonies of the Savior are framed by the testimony and teachings of the Prophet Joseph Smith."[523] However, Joseph Smith taught that,

> Reading the experience of others, or the revelations given to them, can never give us a comprehensive view of our condition and true relation to God. Knowledge of these things can only be obtained by experience in these things, through the ordinance of God set forth for that purpose. (Joseph Smith, Times and Seasons Record, October 9, 1843.)

Elder Carlos Godoy said,

> We do not need to see an angel to obtain understanding. We have the scriptures, the temple, living prophets, our patriarchal blessings, inspired leaders, and, above all, the right to receive personal revelation to guide our decisions. (Elder Carlos A. Godoy, "The Lord Has a Plan for Us," October 2014 General Conference.)

Yet, are we not clearly taught what it means when angels cease to minister to men?

> Or have angels ceased to appear unto the children of men? Or has he withheld the power of the Holy Ghost from them? Or will he, so long as time shall last, or the earth shall stand, or there shall be one man upon the face thereof to be saved? Behold I say unto you, Nay; for it is by faith that miracles are wrought; and it is by faith that angels appear and minister unto men; wherefore, if these things have ceased wo be unto the children of men, for it is because of unbelief, and all is vain. For no man can be saved, according to the words of

---

[522] President Uchtdorf, April, 2014 General Conference.
[523] Elder Dennis B. Neuenschwander, Joseph Smith: An Apostle of Jesus Christ, Jan. 2009.

Christ, save they shall have faith in his name; wherefore, if these things have ceased, then has faith ceased also; and awful is the state of man, for they are as though there had been no redemption made. (Moroni 7:36-38.)[524]

If an absence of visible angelic visitation indicates such gross lack of faith, what of a lack of visible visitations of Jesus Christ?

The fact is that we have a total lack of witnesses of Christ in modern Mormonism. Not one apostle has testified of a physical audience with Christ in over 114 years. The last public testimony of visually seeing Christ was in the 1800s. The last public testimony of seeing Christ from an apostle in a non-awake state was Elder David Haight in 1989.[525] There isn't a single member living who has heard an apostle bear an eyewitness of Christ. Since the majority of the church joined or reached adulthood after 1989, most have not heard any apostle testify of seeing Christ at all—even in a dream.

The leadership for decades has engaged in all sorts of verbal gymnastics to explain this failure to fulfill their apostolic duty. Though their "testimonies" are carefully worded to give the impression that they have seen Jesus, they would still be technically correct if this were not the case. Of course, intentionally leading people on to think something that is not correct is bearing a false witness, a crime worthy of death under the law of Moses that also becomes coupled with using the Lord's name in vain if such a "testimony" is closed in the name of the Savior.

It is important to note that the brethren do not have any problem with members believing they have seen Jesus, even if that is not the case. Elder Oaks has said, "Lying is sinful, as it has always been....Lying is simply outside the range of permitted or condoned conduct by Latter-day Saints— members or leaders." Yet, immediately after in the same talk, he claims that lying only means "asserting something that is untrue" and that this is "very different" than "not telling everything one knows." Says Elder Oaks, "the obligation to tell the truth does not require one to tell everything he or she knows." He continues, "Indeed, we may have a positive duty to keep many things secret or confidential. But this principle does not condone violating the ninth commandment, 'Thou shalt not bear false witness' (Ex. 20:16)." (BYU Speech, September 12, 1993.) Therefore, in the view of Elder Oaks and possibly church leaders, purposefully misleading members into thinking they have seen the Savior is not lying, as long as they don't explicitly say that they have when they have not. They are simply withholding that their witness is no

---

[524] Perhaps aware of the tendency of modern Mormons to speculate that angels are ministering to them, albiet invisibly, Moroni made special note to write that this incrimination applies when angels cease to appear, not visit.

[525] "The Sacrament—and the Sacrifice" (Oct 1989 General Conference). Elder Haight was in a coma at the time of his vision.

more than the witness any other member has, because they believe members are unable to appreciate the "specialness" of their witness which derives wholly from their calling, and not some exceptional experience beyond what normal members have.

To the modern leaders, what makes their witness special is the fact that they hold office in the church when bearing it. To them, there is no difference in how they received that spiritual witness as compared to any other member of the church. In an unusually direct disclosure, President Boyd K. Packer described it this way:

> President McKay explained that one of the responsibilities of an Assistant to the Twelve was to stand with the Quorum of the Twelve Apostles as a special witness and to bear testimony that Jesus is the Christ. What he said next overwhelmed me: "Before we proceed to set you apart, I ask you to bear your testimony to us. We want to know if you have that witness." I did the best I could. I bore my testimony the same as I might have in a fast and testimony meeting in my ward. To my surprise, the Brethren of the Presidency seemed pleased and proceeded to confer the office upon me. That puzzled me greatly, for I had supposed that someone called to such an office would have an unusual, different, and greatly enlarged testimony and spiritual power. It puzzled me for a long time until finally I could see that I already had what was required: an abiding testimony in my heart of the Restoration of the fulness of the gospel through the Prophet Joseph Smith, that we have a Heavenly Father, and that Jesus Christ is our Redeemer....Some years ago, I was with President Marion G. Romney....He told them that 50 years before, as a missionary boy in Australia, late one afternoon he had gone to a library to study. When he walked out, it was night. He looked up into the starry sky, and it happened. The Spirit touched him, and a certain witness was born in his soul. He told those mission presidents that he did not know any more surely then as a member of the First Presidency that God the Father lives; that Jesus is the Christ, the Son of God, the Only Begotten of the Father; and that the fulness of the gospel had been restored than he did as a missionary boy 50 years before in Australia. He said that his testimony had changed in that it was much easier to get an answer from the Lord. The Lord's presence was nearer, and he knew the Lord much better than he had 50 years before. There is the natural tendency to look at those who are sustained to presiding positions, to consider them to be higher and of more value in the Church or to their families than an ordinary member. Somehow we feel they are worth more to the Lord than are we. It just does not work that way! ("The Weak and the Simple of the Church," Oct. 2007 General Conference.)

President Packer frequently says that part of his special witness is that he knows the Lord. Yet, he has admitted that instead of from a face-to-face audience (or even vocal exchange), the way he got to know him is through feeling the cleansing effect of his sacrifice.

> I claim, with my Brethren the Apostles, to be a special witness of the Lord Jesus Christ. That witness is reaffirmed each time I feel within myself or in others the cleansing effect of His sacred sacrifice. My witness, and that of my Brethren, is true. We know the Lord. He is no stranger to His prophets, seers, and revelators. (CES Devotional, 6 November 2011.)

On another occasion, President Packer explained how, when called to be an apostle, he was surprised that he did not possess "an unusual, different, and greatly enlarged testimony and spiritual power."[526] Contrast what is implied in the following statements with what they actually mean, keeping in mind that when President Packer speaks of his "special" witness, he is testifying of the same experiences had by any member of the church who knows through the power of the Holy Ghost that Jesus is real:

> Of all that I have read and taught and learned, the one most precious and sacred truth that I have to offer is my special witness of Jesus Christ. He lives. I know He lives. I am His witness. And of Him I can testify. He is our Savior, our Redeemer. Of this I am certain. ("These Things I Know," Ensign, May 2013.)

> I want our family to know that they have heard grandpa bear his testimony. I know that Jesus is the Christ, that He lives, that the gospel is true, and that I know Him when I see Him, and I know His voice when I hear Him. I want you little ones to remember that you heard your grandfather bear a special witness of the Lord Jesus Christ and of the gift of the Holy Ghost. (Church News, Week Ending December 25th, 2010, p. 12.)

> I am a witness to the truth that Jesus is the Christ, the Son of God, the Only Begotten of the Father; that He has a body of flesh and bone; that He knows those who are His servants here and that He is known of them. (Ensign, May 1980, p. 62.)

> Now, I wonder with you why one such as I should be called to the holy apostleship. There are so many qualifications that I lack. There is so much in my effort to serve that is wanting. As I have pondered on it, I have come to only one single thing, one qualification in which there may be cause, and that is, I have that witness. I declare to you

---

[526] "The Weak and the Simple of the Church," Ensign Oct, 2007.

that I know that Jesus is the Christ. I know that he lives. He was born in the meridian of time. He taught his gospel, was tried, was crucified. He rose on the third day. He was the first fruits of the resurrection. He has a body of flesh and bone. Of this I bear testimony. Of him I am a witness. In the name of Jesus Christ. Amen. (Ensign, June 1971, p. 87.)

Most of the brethren do not focus on the details of their special witness. Why? I suspect that they are worried that no one will consider their witness to be very special if, like President Packer, they admit that it is no different than any witness of the Spirit. However, we are told that the reason why they do not share details that it is too sacred a thing to talk about; that somehow you can be a witness without witnessing of anything.

Elder Dallin H Oaks has said,

> Why don't our talks in general conference and local meetings say more about the miracles we have seen? Most of the miracles we experience are not to be shared. Consistent with the teachings of the scriptures, we hold them sacred and share them only when the Spirit prompts us to do so...In bearing testimonies and in our public addresses we rarely mention our most miraculous experiences, and we rarely rely on signs that the gospel is true. We usually just affirm our testimony of the truthfulness of the restored gospel and give few details on how we obtained it. ("Miracles," Ensign, June 2001.)

President Packer goes so far as to claim that God has given a commandment that his special witnesses should not witness of what makes their witness special:

> We do not talk of those sacred interviews that qualify the servants of the Lord to bear a special witness of Him, for we have been commanded not to do so. ("Tribute to the Rank and File," General Conference, April 1980.)

On another occasion he said, "Why cannot it be said in plainer words? Why aren't they more explicit and more descriptive. Cannot the Apostles say more?" He claimed that this was "for a witness to be given in some new and dramatic and different way."[527] Yet, it would only be different from the neutered testimonies of post-1900 Mormonism, since testimonies of Christ from Adam until 1900 always contained a description of a visual and tactile experience with him.

Apostle Marion G. Romney said,

---

[527] President Boyd K. Packer, "The Spirit Beareth Record," General Conference, April 1971.

> I don't know just how to answer people when they ask the question, 'Have you seen the Lord?' I think that the witness that I have and the witness that each of us [apostles] has, and the details of how it came, are too sacred to tell. I have never told anybody some of the experiences I have had, not even my wife. I know that God lives. I not only know that he lives, but I know him. (Marion G. Romney, cited in F. Burton Howard, Marion G. Romney: His Life and Faith (Salt Lake City, Utah: Bookcraft, 1988), p. 222.)

One would think that the answer to that question would be very simple to know: yes. It is quite odd that the modern brethren would think that something that was the expectation before 1900 is somehow now too sacred to share, and this without any revelatory change in the definition of what an apostle is and is to do. The current principles of "a witness of the Holy Ghost is more special than an eye witness" and "a visual witness is too sacred to share" add up to making it impossible for a member to know whether an apostle has seen Jesus or not, making his witness no different than any other member's, and not special in any way.

The entire cannon of scripture is full of men who readily spoke about their experiences with Christ. How much less precious would the scriptures be without their words? How much less faith would we have in Christ if Thomas did not tell us he touched him? How much less powerful would be the Nephite account if they thought it was too sacred to share the fact that they were visited? How much less would we know about the Savior if we were not told that he took the time to touch each of the over 2,000 present in Bountiful? How much less powerful would the Book of Ether be if it did not contain the account of the Brother of Jared piercing the veil? And so on.

The principle of a true witness requires that you actually say what you have seen, that others might have faith, and tell how you obtained it, that others might do the same. How can anyone attain a visual witness of Christ if they do not believe it can happen? And why should they believe it can happen if the apostles--men whose very calling is to have obtained such a witness--do not claim to have seen Christ?

The scriptures are replete with declarations that God does not work in darkness. For example, Nephi tells us "that the Lord God worketh not in darkness." (2 Nephi 26:23.) Isaiah gives us the word of the Lord speaking disparagingly about the wise men of the people "who contrive to hide their schemes from Jehovah! They work in the dark, thinking, Who will see us? Who will know?" (Isaiah 29, Gileadi Translation.) But the Lord does not work in a corner. He works his miracles in the open in order to increase faith:

> ...he manifesteth himself unto all those who believe in him, by the power of the Holy Ghost; yea, unto every nation, kindred, tongue,

and people, working mighty miracles, signs, and wonders, among the children of men according to their faith. (2 Nephi 26:12-13.)

Those who have seen must, according to the principle of witnesses, testify of that which they have seen. Otherwise, no one would have faith that the experience can happen, nor know how to obtain it. In 3 Nephi ch. 12, the Lord tells us exactly what we are to do after we see Him:

> And again, more blessed are they who shall believe in your words because that ye shall testify that ye have seen me, and that ye know that I am. Yea, blessed are they who shall believe in your words, and come down into the depths of humility and be baptized, for they shall be visited with fire and with the Holy Ghost, and shall receive a remission of their sins. (3 Nephi 12:2.)

If the brethren have not seen Jesus, members have a right to know. The doctrine of Christ promises that those who repent sufficiently to receive the Holy Ghost after baptism will, if they continue to follow God's voice, encounter Christ face to face.

> Behold, this is the doctrine of Christ, and there will be no more doctrine given until after he shall manifest himself unto you in the flesh. And when he shall manifest himself unto you in the flesh, the things which he shall say unto you shall ye observe to do. (2 Nephi 32:6)

What does it say if we follow men who purportedly teach us the gospel, but have not yet attained the end of the gospel? Is that not like going through great sacrifice to attend a GED course where the teacher has not yet obtained their diploma? Could there be any more literal fulfillment of the Savior's parable, "Can the blind lead the blind? shall they not both fall into the ditch?" (Luke 6:39.) Jesus taught plainly that "this is life eternal, that they might know thee the only true God, and Jesus Christ, whom thou hast sent." (John 17:3.) That this experience is to occur in this life for the heirs of salvation is made plain:

> But if ye receive me in the world, then shall ye know me, and shall receive your exaltation; that where I am ye shall be also. This is eternal lives—to know the only wise and true God, and Jesus Christ, whom he hath sent. I am he. Receive ye, therefore, my law. (D&C 132:23-24.)

Why would you receive teachers claiming to lead you in the way of life and salvation, who had not obtained it themselves?

Whether the brethren have seen Christ or not is beyond our ability to say, since they have not said so themselves.[528] However, the fact that they do not declare that they have means that either they have not, or they are negligent in their duty to testify as a witness of Christ. If the brethren do not know Christ, they do not have eternal life. Why should anyone belief that following them will lead to a different end than they themselves have obtained? If their "special witness" consists of nothing but an ordination, and that ordination itself has been insufficient to bring them back into the presence of Christ, what hope can their followers have that their authority alone will be sufficient to bring them back into the presence of Christ? As the Savior said to the blind leaders in his day:

> But woe unto you, scribes and Pharisees, hypocrites! for ye shut up the kingdom of heaven against men: for ye neither go in yourselves, neither suffer ye them that are entering to go in. (Matthew 23:13.)

A similar question is possed in the Book of Mormon:

> O ye wicked and ye perverse generation; ye hardened and ye stiffnecked people, how long will ye suppose that the Lord will suffer you? Yea, how long will ye suffer yourselves to be led by foolish and blind guides? Yea, how long will ye choose darkness rather than light? (Helaman 13:29.)

One unfortunate side effect of the inflation of the witness of the brethren is that they disbelieve others' accounts of having seen the Savior. In their minds, if Jesus doesn't come to them, being the most righteous among us, why would he come to anyone else?

> The fool hath said in his heart, There is no man that hath seen God. Because he showeth himself not unto us....Behold, they are corrupt; they have done abominable works, and none of them doeth good. For the Lord looked down from heaven upon the children of men, to see if there are any that do understand God. And he opened his mouth unto the Lord, and said, Behold, all these who say they are thine. The Lord answered and said, They are all gone aside, they are together become filthy, thou canst behold none of them that are doing good, no, not one. All they have for their teachers are workers of iniquity, and there is no knowledge in them. They are they who eat

---

[528] Several now-deceased brethren have said plainly that they have never seen Jesus. For example: "I did not live in the days of our Savior; he has not come to me in person. I have not beheld him. His Father and he have not felt it necessary to grant me such a great blessing as this. But it is not necessary." (Teachings of the Presidents of the Church: Joseph Fielding Smith, p. 49.) However, the current brethren have not said so, to my knowledge.

up my people. They eat bread and call not upon the Lord. (Psalm 14:1-4, JST.)

This position is one of the many fulfillments of Nephi's description of our time:

...if they shall say there is a miracle wrought by the hand of the Lord, believe it not; for this day he is not a God of miracles; he hath done his work. (2 Nephi 28:6.)

The next logical step, of course, is for the brethren to caution members against seeking an audience with the Lord, despite the fact that such is required for salvation (see "The Gospel of Christ.")

Of course, all of the righteous desire to see the face of our Savior, but the suggestions that this must happen in mortality is a familiar tactic of the adversary. To identify a worthy goal, such as to achieve exaltation, and then to use the desirability of that goal and people's enthusiasm for it to obscure the new means the adversary suggests to achieve it. (Elder Dallin H. Oaks, Boise, Idaho, June 17, 2105.)

False witnesses are not just a problem in modern Mormonism leadership, but also within the body of members. The most prominent opportunity for false witness comes in testimony meeting.

Testimony is not a thing to be taken lightly. Alma reported that the Zoramites "did pervert the ways of the Lord in very many instances; therefore, for this cause, Alma and his brethren went into the land to preach the word unto them." (Alma 31:11.) What was their grievous crime? It was the way the content and conduct of their church meetings! This is what they said:

Holy, holy God; we believe that thou art God, and we believe that thou art holy, and that thou wast a spirit, and that thou art a spirit, and that thou wilt be a spirit forever. Holy God, we believe that thou hast separated us from our brethren; and we do not believe in the tradition of our brethren, which was handed down to them by the childishness of their fathers; but we believe that thou hast elected us to be thy holy children; and also thou hast made it known unto us that there shall be no Christ. But thou art the same yesterday, today, and forever; and thou hast elected us that we shall be saved, whilst all around us are elected to be cast by thy wrath down to hell; for the which holiness, O God, we thank thee; and we also thank thee that thou hast elected us, that we may not be led away after the foolish traditions of our brethren, which doth bind them down to a belief of Christ, which doth lead their hearts to wander far from thee, our God. And again we thank thee, O God, that we are a chosen and a holy people. Amen. Now it came to pass that after Alma and his brethren and his sons had heard these prayers, they were astonished beyond all measure. For behold, every man did go forth and offer up these same prayers. Now the place was called by them Rameumptom, which, being interpreted, is the holy stand. Now, from this stand they did offer up, every man, the selfsame prayer unto God, thanking their God that they were chosen of him, and that he did not lead them away after the tradition of their brethren, and that their hearts were not stolen away to believe in things to come, which they knew nothing about. (Alma 31:15-25.)

Modern Mormons utter their own Zoramite prayer: "I know the church is true. I know President <current president> is a prophet. In the name of Jesus Christ, amen." Children and adults alike ascend LDS Rameumtoms to offer up this selfsame prayer without even thinking about what they are saying.

How many members could present a case of *how* they know that the church is true, or *what* they mean when they say that? How many could point to a prophecy by the <current president> that shows that they are a prophet? When members testify that they know something, but they don't actually have any evidence of what they are saying, they are bearing false witness. This happens all the time in fast and testimony meeting. For every principle that is testified of, the member ought to have a very good answer if someone were to ask, "how do you know?" There are certain phrases like "the church is true" that are far too ill-defined to be possible to know. If you say that you know something is true, you better have been told explicitly by God that such was the case, or at least have some anecdotal evidence. One cannot simply say that they know something just because they wish it were true, or because they trust someone else who says that they know. Mindless parroting is a false witness.

Far too often in the church, members cave to social pressure and a desire to belong, and bear a false witness. The following is an excerpt of a talk given by Russell Hancock, a counselor in the Menlo Park stake presidency, given 6 May 2012:

We're...taught that the manifestation of the spirit will be the Holy Ghost revealing truth to us....Now here's the true confession: I've never had it. This has never come to me....So as that crucial milestone came in my life where I had to decide whether to go on a mission...and yet when I was honest with myself I had to confess I didn't actually know for myself that the Church was true. I was following my parents' religion and way of life, and the testimony of family, friends, and ward members....I began to speak more loudly and in a voice that was more shrill, and I would actually testify. I would stand up in church meetings and say things that I had no right to say, that I didn't yet know for my own self. But I thought that in the act of saying them--and saying them more loudly--the testimony would come....I served a mission. You could say I caved. But I wanted to serve, and I think I had righteous reasons, but I should also tell you I felt like it was an important rite of passage. I felt all of the pressure that you feel to serve a mission, knew the opportunities I would be foreclosing if I didn't, so I submitted my papers and received a call. So I get into the mission field, where it started to trouble me that I was saying things to investigators I thought were true but didn't know were true....I decided I would wager my life that the church is everything it claims it is and live out my life accordingly. So that is what I've done and what I continue to do....Now here's what's striking. Every time I share these experiences I am assailed by people who tell me 'that's my feeling, that's my experience too.'

Modern Mormons—rank and file and leaders alike—ought to invest the significant effort required to obtain revelation from God on a subject. Until they obtain God's word, they ought to resist the temptation to lie in order to fit in, and simply remain quiet until they have something to testify of in truth.

The Lord's Chosen People

God has always offered salvation to any individual or group who is willing to seek him. Through all generations of time, select few have accepted the invitation. In a show of godly mercy, God allows the righteousness of those few individuals with whom he has made covenant to cause a cascading of blessings to their less righteous peers and posterity. Without exception, the descendants of covenant fathers such as Abraham, Isaac, Jacob, the Nephites who witnessed the resurrected Christ, etc., gradually chip away at God's patient blessings by progressively apostatizing from the covenant made to their fathers until they are ripe in iniquity.

Unfortunately, the apostate descendants of covenant fathers always seem to consider themselves equally as righteous as their forebears. They are lifted in haughty pride and call themselves chosen, though God has said no such thing.

Throughout history, the ancestors of those who achieved a connection with God considered themselves a chosen people. The false sense of security brought by the erroneous idea that God could never abandon them despite their sins fostered a degree of wickedness that usually exceeded that of their Godless peers.

Perhaps the easiest to recognize example of this phenomenon is the children of Israel between the time of Moses and Jesus. Israel was a chosen people during this time. Yet, they were in an apostate state. The evidence of their chosen status was expressed in the invitation they had received to come up to the presence of Christ. This invitation—originally made through Moses—was still available to them through the generations, as evidenced by those individuals who obtained it.

A chosen status is therefore not a measurement of acceptance by the Lord or righteousness of the people: Israel's kings were almost without exception beyond wicked, and their people were no different.

Paul distinguished between the invitation provided and the fruits obtained by accepting it:

> Not as though the word of God hath taken none effect. For they are not all Israel, which are of Israel: Neither, because they are the seed of Abraham, are they all children: but, In Isaac shall thy seed be called. That is, They which are the children of the flesh, these are not

the children of God: but the children of the promise are counted for the seed. (Romans 9:6-8.)

As he explained to the group of Gentiles he was addressing, there was a distinction between those who obtained the promise (that is, the promise of eternal life from Christ to an individual) and those who were of a "chosen" lineage. Paul argued that the same invitations available to the Israelites by lineage were available to the Gentiles—and that neither would prove of any use without the righteousness of the acceptor.

Nephi explained the same concept. A covenant people is a people with whom God has made the covenant of eternal life. Unlike other covenants, such as that God made with Aaron, the covenant of eternal life is not transmitted by virtue of descent. The individuals' relationships with God are what caused the covenant to be offered:

> For behold, I say unto you that as many of the Gentiles as will repent are the covenant people of the Lord; and as many of the Jews as will not repent shall be cast off; for the Lord covenanteth with none save it be with them that repent and believe in his Son, who is the Holy One of Israel. (2 Nephi 30:2.)

With the Israelites, God offered the covenant, but it was not accepted. Through Moses he gave to them a set of laws that would bring them to Christ, both spiritually and literally. To them the invitation to obtain was extended. Did this make them special? The invitation was and always is unto all. The distinction was not in the lack or presence of the invitation, but in the presence of an expectation and an increase in the means to obtain it. The Israelites had a dispensation of gospel knowledge. They had the righteous example of Moses and other prophets who had obtained the presence of God. This is what made them different.

Being a chosen people simply means that there is an expectation and a means provided to rise to the fulfillment of the expectation. Being a chosen people does *not* mean that you are more righteous than anyone else. Consequently, it does not mean you are any closer to divinity than anyone else. A chosen people is not more righteous than others. They are merely expected to be.

The Israelites were chosen and also generally wicked. At times, the Lord said very sharp things about them. For example, he stated they were as wicked as those who were not chosen people:

> Behold, the days come, saith the Lord, that I will punish all them which are circumcised with the uncircumcised; Egypt, and Judah, and Edom, and the children of Ammon, and Moab, and all that are in the utmost corners, that dwell in the wilderness: for all these nations are

uncircumcised, and all the house of Israel are uncircumcised in the heart. (Jeremiah 9:25-26.)

Although they were generally wicked, and were not a covenant people, the Israelites still had interaction with God at times. Their daily participation in religion *did not* create a covenant relationship with God. A people can be wholly devoted to religion and still not approach God.

In the Book of Mormon, we see the Nephites—who were the chosen people—utterly destroyed by the Lamanites. The wickedness of the Nephites was truly great: not only did their sins exceed those of the Lamanites in absolute terms, but they committed them against greater light and truth, having been taught the correct way and turned away from it.[529]

From the above points we see that:

1. A chosen people do not have greater blessings with God. They simply have an invitation from him to obtain such with an expectation to do so.

2. A group can only become a covenant people if God actually makes a promise of eternal life to them as individuals. Covenants cannot be inherited from organizational ancestors.

3. Where much is given, much is required. If a group has access to a greater portion of God's teachings, they are judged to a higher standard.

These principles stand at odds to what is commonly understood in modern Mormonism.[530] That is, that the LDS are entitled to special blessings from God, and ever will be until Christ comes again.

---

[529] "For of him unto whom much is given much is required; and he who sins against the greater light shall receive the greater condemnation. (D&C 82:3.)

[530] "I ask you to teach that nothing—not anything, not anyone, not any influence—will keep this Church from fulfilling its mission and realizing its destiny set from before the foundation of the world. Ours is that fail-safe, inexorable, indestructible dispensation of the fulness of the gospel. Our youth have no need to be afraid or tentative about themselves or about their future. Unlike every other era before us, this dispensation will not experience an institutional apostasy; it will not see a loss of priesthood keys; it will not suffer a cessation of revelation from the voice of Almighty God. Individuals will apostatize, they may turn a deaf ear to heaven, but never again will the dispensation collectively do so. What a secure thought that is! What a day in which to live! What a way to cut through fear or faintheartedness....we are the favored people that God has made choice of to bring about the Latter-day glory....ours is the dispensation God has favored. We are the ones to bring about this "Latter-day glory" spoken of. So much rests on our shoulders, but it will be a glorious and successful experience. If any of your students are unsettled, or if you are unsettled, reassure one and all that the victory in this final contest has already been declared. The victory is already in the record books...the scriptures! We know for certain that if and when everything else in the latter days is down or dying; if

Spiritual Gifts

Jesus taught that signs will follow those that believe. He reaffirmed this promise in Joseph's day on at least two occasions.

> For I am God, and mine arm is not shortened; and I will show miracles, signs, and wonders, unto all those who believe on my name. And whoso shall ask it in my name in faith, they shall cast out devils; they shall heal the sick; they shall cause the blind to receive their sight, and the deaf to hear, and the dumb to speak, and the lame to walk. (D&C 35:8-9.)

> Therefore, as I said unto mine apostles I say unto you again, that every soul who believeth on your words, and is baptized by water for the remission of sins, shall receive the Holy Ghost. And these signs shall follow them that believe—In my name they shall do many wonderful works; In my name they shall cast out devils; In my name they shall heal the sick; In my name they shall open the eyes of the blind, and unstop the ears of the deaf; And the tongue of the dumb shall speak; And if any man shall administer poison unto them it shall not hurt them; And the poison of a serpent shall not have power to harm them. (D&C 84:64-72.)

In Joseph's day, members were expected to possess spiritual gifts: dramatic, undeniable external evidences of the power of God. The receipt of the Holy Ghost was taught to always bring spiritual gifts. Apostle Orson Pratt taught:

> Whenever the Holy Ghost takes up its residence in a person, it not only cleanses, sanctifies, and purifies him, in. proportion as he yields himself to its influence, but also imparts to him some gift, intended for the benefit of himself and others. No one who has been born of the Spirit, and who remains sufficiently faithful, is left destitute of a Spiritual Gift. A person who is without a Spiritual Gift, has not the Spirit of God dwelling in him, in a sufficient degree, to save him; he cannot be called a Saint, or a child of God ; for all Saints who constitute the Church of Christ, are baptized into the same Spirit ;

---

governments, economies, industries, and institutions crumble; if societies and cultures become a quagmire of chaos and insecurity, nevertheless, through it all the gospel of Jesus Christ and The Church of Jesus Christ of Latter-day Saints that bears that gospel to the world will stand triumphant. It will stand undefiled in God's hand until the very Son of God Himself comes to rule and reign as Lord of lords and King of kings. Nothing is more certain in this world. Nothing is more sure. Nothing could be more of an antidote to anxiety." (Elder Holland, CES Fireside Church Educational System Speech, February 6, 2015.)

and .each one, without any exception, is made a partaker of some Spiritual Gift. (Orson Pratt, Masterful Discourses, pp. 539–41.)

If the miracles of gifts of the Spirit were always present in Joseph's day, have they continued to be in our day? In modern Mormonism, we hear testimonies of questionable miracles, such as someone with a priesthood blessing gradually recovering, or a missionary learning Spanish through months of instruction at the missionary training center. Yet, Jesus' list did not include subtle miracles. We do not see examples of the Lord's explicitly listed undeniable miracles: healing the sick, causing the blind to see, the deaf to hear, the dumb to speak, the lame to walk, and invulnerability to poison.

God is not a changing God. If the manifestations of believers have changed from the time of Joseph, it can only be because the content of the gospel has changed since the time of Joseph.

As modified as the endowment has become, some of the teachings on how true messengers are manifested have been preserved. True messengers always bring with them signs to identify God's approval of their message. Echoing what we are taught in the modern endowment, Joseph Smith taught that true messengers bring with them the miracles the Savior promised:

> If you will obey the Gospel with honest hearts, I promise you, in the name of the Lord, that the gifts as promised by our Saviour will follow you, and by this you may prove me to be a true servant of God. (Quoted in Hyrum Andrus, "Joseph Smith's Idea of the Gospel".)

Just as the presence of spiritual gifts is a witness of God's approbation of the teachings offered, the lack of spiritual gifts is a sign of God's disapproval of what is offered. At a minimum, one would expect these signs among the leadership of the church. Though we sustain leaders as prophets, seers, and revelators, they do not manifest any of these gifts, and haven't since the death of Joseph (see "Prophet: Title or Description?") Sidney Rigdon taught:

> There is no society of which we have an account in the revelations of God, that he acknowledged as his own, except they had visions among them, and that as long as they continued to walk according to the directions of the Holy Spirit....We readily admit that a corrupt religion can exist, and false prophecies exist, and sectarian dogmas abound; men-made worshipers increase, and the world abound in a religion that the Lord was not the author of, and yet no visions be among them; but wherever the truth of heaven abounds, there will visions abound also; for it is a part of heaven's scheme to save men, and without it, we are not authorized to say there is salvation. (Sidney

Rigdon, "Faith of the Church," Latter Day Saints' Messenger and Advocate, 1:9, p. 133.)

If the promised miraculous signs do not attend a religion, it means that the believers in said religion do not have the truth, and do not have salvation.

First, miraculous signs should be claimed in all ages by the believers in the Gospel, because Jesus promised them, and has never intimated any repeal of that promise. All Gospel promises should be claimed by Gospel believers, until divine revelation repeals them. For instance, in the same verses, where Jesus promises these signs, he also promises salvation. As both of these Gospel blessings are promised, both should be claimed. None have the right to hope for the promised Salvation who have not the promised Signs. Indeed, those who have not the Signs, are not believers ; and, therefore, instead of having a right to Salvation, Jesus says expressly, that all such 'shall be damned.' (Orson Pratt, "Necessity of Miracles.")

The lack of spiritual gifts shows a lack of faith. This is a shock to those who do not possess miracles yet consider themselves to have faith. They think they are exercising faith in God, but in reality their faith is in the false traditions of men.[531]

Because faith is wanting, the fruits are. No man since the world was had faith without having something along with it. The ancients quenched the violence of fire, escaped the edge of the sword, women received their dead, etc. By faith the worlds were made. A man who has none of the gifts has no faith; and he deceives himself, if he supposes he has. Faith has been wanting, not only among the heathen, but in professed Christendom also, so that tongues, healings, prophecy, and prophets and apostles, and all the gifts and blessings have been wanting. (Joseph Smith, TPJS, p. 270.)

As Moroni explained, if you are not witnessing the miracles of visible ministration of angels, healings, tongues, visions, prophecy, etc., you are not in possession of the gospel of salvation:

And now, my beloved brethren, if this be the case that these things are true which I have spoken unto you, and God will show unto you, with power and great glory at the last day, that they are true, and if they are true has the day of miracles ceased? Or have angels ceased to appear unto the children of men? Or has he withheld the power of

---

[531] As explained in the chapter "The Gospel of Christ," you cannot have real faith in a false principle.

the Holy Ghost from them? Or will he, so long as time shall last, or the earth shall stand, or there shall be one man upon the face thereof to be saved? Behold I say unto you, Nay; for it is by faith that miracles are wrought; and it is by faith that angels appear and minister unto men; wherefore, if these things have ceased wo be unto the children of men, for it is because of unbelief, and all is vain. For no man can be saved, according to the words of Christ, save they shall have faith in his name; wherefore, if these things have ceased, then has faith ceased also; and awful is the state of man, for they are as though there had been no redemption made. (Moroni 7:35-38.)

The opposite of faith is unbelief. Unbelief means refusing to believe, but in what? Many in our day deny that God has a reason to perform miracles, or that he wills to perform only subtle miracles.[532] Yet, the unbelief of modern

---

[532] "Behold, hearken ye unto my precept; if they shall say there is a miracle wrought by the hand of the Lord, believe it not; for this day he is not a God of miracles; he hath done his work." (2 Nephi 28:6.) "This has come in our day. Yet we find, even among those who have embraced the Gospel, hearts of unbelief. How many of you, my brethren and sisters, are seeking for these gifts that God has promised to bestow? How many of you, when you bow before your Heavenly Father in your family circle or in your secret places, contend for these gifts to be bestowed upon you? How many of you ask the Father, in the name of Jesus, to manifest Himself to you through these powers and these gifts? Or do you go along day by day like a door turning on its hinges, without having any feeling upon the subject, without exercising any faith whatever; content to be baptized and be members of the Church, and to rest there, thinking that your salvation is secure because you have done this? I say to you, in the name of the Lord, as one of His servants, that you have need to repent of this. You have need to repent of your hardness of heart, of your indifference, and of your carelessness. There is not that diligence, there is not that faith, there is not that seeking for the power of God that there should be among a people who have received the precious promises we have. Instead of the sick being healed, why, it is as much as you can do to get faith to believe that the administration of an elder will be attended with effect. There is not that seeking for the gift of healing and for the gift to be healed that there ought to be among the Saints. And so with other gifts and graces that God has placed in His Church for His people. I say to you that it is our duty to avail ourselves of the privileges which God has placed within our reach. If we have done wrong, repent of our wrong and feel after God, and not be satisfied till we have found Him, and He hears and answers us, and He speaks by His divine power in our hearts, bearing testimony to us in such a manner as cannot be doubted that He hears us, that He is near to us, and that He is watching over us and ready to bestow upon us all the blessings that are necessary for our happiness here and hereafter....God is the same today as He was yesterday; that God is willing to bestow these gifts upon His children. I know that God is willing to heal the sick, that He is willing to bestow the gift of discerning of spirits, the gift of wisdom, of knowledge and of prophecy, and other gifts that may be needed....Let us seek for these gifts....bear in mind that these gifts are for us; and let us seek for them with all our

Mormonism is more substantial. In our day, unbelief is ignorance of or rejection of what God restored through Joseph Smith (see "The Preeminence of Joseph Smith's Teachings.")

Faced with the implications of the lack of these promised gifts, modern Mormons have come up with three rationalizations. First, they claim that these gifts are had, but those who have them don't speak of them.[533] The issue with this rationalization is that—beyond the fact that it allows everyone to assume they are the minority in not having these experiences—it shifts the signs from an individual witness to a communal one. The presence of signs is a witness meant for each individual, not a group. Second, they claim that while these gifts may not be had among the lay membership, the brethren experience them.

> This failure to realize all the blessings and powers of the Priesthood does not apply to the elders and lesser Priesthood only; but it applies to the higher quorums, and comes home to ourselves, who are Apostles of Jesus Christ. We are presented before the Church, and sustained as prophets, seers and revelators, and we have received oftentimes the gift of prophecy and revelation, and have received many great and glorious gifts. But have we received the fullness of the blessings to which we are entitled? No, we have not. Who, among the Apostles have become seers, and enjoy all the gifts and powers pertaining to that calling? (Orson Pratt, JD 25:145.)

Third, they conclude that, since modern Mormons are the chosen people, though their experiences don't match the descriptions in scripture, the definition of the words in scripture must have changed. They conclude that when God says "heal the sick," he means leave the sick to be healed by a doctor or natural, slow means; that when he says "gift of tongues," he means to learn languages like any other student learns;[534] and that when he refers to

---

might, mind and strength." (Elder George Q Cannon, Millennial Star, April 1894, pp. 260–61.)

[533] For example, "Perhaps more often than any other, the question is repeated today, 'Why aren't there as many spiritual outpourings today as there were in the first generation?' This is a very revealing question, because there are. But those who ask seem to assume that their lack of experience applies to everyone." (Truman G. Madsen, "Christ and the Inner Life," Bookcraft [Salt Lake City], 1978, p. 31.)

[534] This explaining away started quite soon after Joseph's death. In 1852, John Taylor preached: "It is good for the Elders to become acquainted with the languages, for they may have to go abroad, and should be able to talk to the people, and not look like fools. I care not how much intelligence you have got, if you cannot exhibit it you look like an ignoramus. Suppose a Frenchman should come upon this stand to deliver a lecture upon Botany, Astronomy, or any other science, and could not speak a word of English, how much wiser would you be? You may say, I thought the Lord would

the healing of the deaf, the dumb, the blind, and the raising of the dead, he wasn't serious. Instead of comparing the scriptures to their experience, they force their experience onto what the scriptures say.

Who are the Gentiles?

Most accept the idea that the Gentiles spoken of in the Book of Mormon are the inhabitants of the United States. There are many passages that state as much.[535] For example,

> The Gentiles shall be blessed upon the land. And this land shall be a land of liberty unto the Gentiles, and there shall be no kings upon the land, who shall raise up unto the Gentiles. And [the Lord] will fortify this land against all other nations. (2 Nephi 10:10-12.)

What is less understood is that the Book of Mormon authors also considered members of the Church of Jesus Christ of Latter Day Saints as Gentiles. This fact should be evident from the start of the Book, as the Title Page states that the Book of Mormon should "come forth by way of the Gentile." Of course, the book came forth through Joseph Smith. Moroni said, "O ye Gentiles, it is wisdom in God that these things should be shown unto you" (Ether 8:8). Non-LDS Americans do not read the Book of Mormon. Therefore, it can be said that the only group to whom these things are shown are those who are LDS. Moroni was speaking to the readers of the Book of Mormon, which means that his appellation is used interchangeably with "members of the LDS church."

Some would contend that Joseph Smith and other members of the church cannot be referred to as Gentiles because once someone joins the LDS church, they become part of the house of Israel. For example,

> For behold, I say unto you that as many of the Gentiles as will repent are the covenant people of the Lord; and as many of the Jews as will not repent shall be cast off; for the Lord covenanteth with none save it be with them that repent and believe in his Son, who is the Holy One of Israel. (2 Nephi 30:2.)

Interestingly, however, Nephi still calls those who repent Gentiles. And, as previously stated, the Title Page calls Joseph Smith a Gentile. Joseph Smith even stated,

> Now these words, O Lord, we have spoken before thee, concerning the revelations and commandments which thou hast given unto us, who are identified with the Gentiles. (D&C 109:60.)

---

give us the gift of tongues. He won't if we are too indolent to study them. I never ask the Lord to do a thing I could do for myself." (John Taylor JD 1:27.)
[535] See also 3 Nephi 16:7-10, Mormon 5:19-22, and Ether 8:22-23.

The identity of Joseph Smith shows how church members can be both of the house of Ephraim and still Gentiles. The Book of Mormon tells us that Joseph is a descendent of Ephraim. Ephraim was the son of Joseph of Egypt, but also the son of an Egyptian woman. Therefore, Ephraim was both an Israelite and a Gentile. The Book of Mormon calls Joseph a Gentile even though it identifies him as a descendent of Ephraim. Mormons should consider themselves Gentiles and Israelites.

This labeling is exceedingly important. When Mormons understand that they are Gentiles, they can associate the warnings and descriptions of the Gentiles in the Book of Mormon with themselves instead of deflecting them to non-LDS Americans.

How Zion will be established: Not by a church

During the life of Joseph Smith, everything in the church aimed at one goal: establishing Zion, a tangible city of men and women who lived the Terrestrial law, a place where there are no poor[536] and where everyone keeps all of God's commandments.[537] After Joseph's life, successive changes shifted the goal posts: the commandments were modified, eradication of poverty was replaced with a program to regularly treat its symptoms,[538] and physical gathering was abandoned.

The question today is: as an institution, are we progressing closer to Zion, or are we moving further away? Early leaders who lived through both eras juxtaposed the church under Joseph and the church after his death. George Q. Cannon, who arrived in Nauvoo as a British convert at the age of 15 and lived two years in close proximity to church leadership (his lived with his uncle, John Taylor), said the following:

> The feeling has grown upon me, and is growing upon me every day, that as a people we do not live up to our privileges. We do not have the knowledge of the things of God that we should have. There is not that amount of revelation enjoyed by us which there should be. The gifts of the spirit are not manifest to the extent they should be. Is there revelation? Yes, I know that and can testify of it. Are there gifts, are there blessings enjoyed by the people? Yes, I am convinced

---

[536] See Moses 7:18. There are two reasons why there will be no poor in Zion. First, the rich will consecrate their goods to the benefit of the poor. Second, the poor will learn how to be wise stewards over their time and talents.

[537] "And the bow shall be in the cloud; and I will look upon it, that I may remember the everlasting covenant, which I made unto thy father Enoch; that, when men should keep all my commandments, Zion should again come on the earth, the city of Enoch which I have caught up unto myself." (JST Genesis 9:21.)

[538] See the chapter "No Poor Among Them." The fast offering program can never be a sufficient substitute for the law of consecration, which cannot be implemented except in cases of physical gathering.

of it. Are there manifestations of the goodness and the power of God among this people? I am satisfied that there are manifestations of this kind. The sick are healed. The mind and will of the Lord is communicated to the people, but it is not to that extent, that it should be considering our circumstances, and considering the length of time the Church has been organized. Who is there that is not conscious of this. (George Q. Cannon, JD 22:103.)

Orson Pratt felt the same way. He noted that the trajectory of the Saints in Utah was not headed towards Zion.

> There must be a reformation. There will be a reformation among this people, but He will plead with the stronger ones of Zion, He will plead with this people, He will plead with those in high places, He will plead with the priesthood of this church, until Zion shall become clean before him. I do not know but what it would be an utter impossibility to commence and carry out some principles pertaining to Zion right in the midst of this people. They have strayed so far that to get a people who would conform to heavenly laws it may be needful to lead some from the midst of this people and commence anew in the regions round about in these mountains. (Orson Pratt, JD 15:360.)

Apostle (later president) Joseph Fielding Smith wrote of his concerns both about how far from Joseph's teachings the church had drifted in the preceding 20 years, and how far the church would continue to drift:

> It is a very apparent fact that we have traveled far and wide in the past 20 years. What the future will bring I do not know. But if we drift as far afield from fundamental things in the next 20 years, what will be left of the foundation laid by the Prophet Joseph Smith? It is easy for one who observes to see how the apostasy came about in the primitive church of Christ. Are we not traveling the same road? (Joseph Fielding Smith Journal, 28 December 1938.)

Members during Brigham Young's tenure believed that they were only in Utah for a season, and that one day they would return to Jackson County to build Zion. Over time, this belief eroded into what modern Mormons believe: that Zion is not a physical city at all, but that we gather to Zion as we join and remain in the church in congregations around the world.

In reality, both views are incorrect. The truth contained in the scriptures, and understood by some few early leaders, is that the church of Jesus Christ of Latter-day Saints never had the charge to build Zion, and will not build Zion. Instead, Zion will be built by the Lamanites—a remnant of Joseph:

What says the Book of Mormon in relation to the building up of the New Jerusalem on this continent one of the most splendid cities that ever was or ever will be built on this land? Does not that book say that the Lamanites are to be the principal operators in that important work, and that those who embrace the Gospel from among the Gentiles are to have the privilege of assisting the Lamanites to build up the city called the New Jerusalem? This remnant of Joseph, who are now degraded, will then be filled with the wisdom of God; and by that wisdom they will build that city; by the aid of the Priesthood already given, and by the aid of Prophets that God will raise up in their midst, they will beautify and ornament its dwellings; and we have the privilege of being numbered with them, instead of their being numbered with us. It is a great privilege indeed (and we are indebted to their fathers for it,) that we enjoy of being associated with them in the accomplishment of so great a work. (Elder Orson Pratt, JD 9:178.)

Third Nephi 21 is worthy of a significant study beyond the scope of this book. Suffice it to say that it directly challenges many traditions in modern Mormonism, including the ideas that the LDS church will establish Zion, that the "marvelous work and a wonder" is something that has already occurred, that the United States will still exist as a country at the coming of Christ, and that the gathering of Israel has commenced.

Therefore, when these works and the works which shall be wrought among you hereafter shall come forth from the Gentiles, unto your seed which shall dwindle in unbelief because of iniquity; For thus it behooveth the Father that it should come forth from the Gentiles, that he may show forth his power unto the Gentiles, for this cause that the Gentiles, if they will not harden their hearts, that they may repent and come unto me and be baptized in my name and know of the true points of my doctrine, that they may be numbered among my people, O house of Israel....For in that day, for my sake shall the Father work a work, which shall be a great and a marvelous work among them; and there shall be among them those who will not believe it, although a man shall declare it unto them. But behold, the life of my servant shall be in my hand; therefore they shall not hurt him, although he shall be marred because of them. Yet I will heal him, for I will show unto them that my wisdom is greater than the cunning of the devil. Therefore it shall come to pass that whosoever will not believe in my words, who am Jesus Christ, which the Father shall cause him to bring forth unto the Gentiles, and shall give unto him power that he shall bring them forth unto the Gentiles, (it shall be done even as Moses said) they shall be cut off from among my

370

people who are of the covenant. And my people who are a remnant of Jacob shall be among the Gentiles, yea, in the midst of them as a lion among the beasts of the forest, as a young lion among the flocks of sheep, who, if he go through both treadeth down and teareth in pieces, and none can deliver. Their hand shall be lifted up upon their adversaries, and all their enemies shall be cut off. Yea, wo be unto the Gentiles except they repent; for it shall come to pass in that day, saith the Father, that I will cut off thy horses out of the midst of thee, and I will destroy thy chariots; And I will cut off the cities of thy land, and throw down all thy strongholds; And I will cut off witchcrafts out of thy land, and thou shalt have no more soothsayers; Thy graven images I will also cut off, and thy standing images out of the midst of thee, and thou shalt no more worship the works of thy hands; And I will pluck up thy groves out of the midst of thee; so will I destroy thy cities. And it shall come to pass that all lyings, and deceivings, and envyings, and strifes, and priestcrafts, and whoredoms, shall be done away. For it shall come to pass, saith the Father, that at that day whosoever will not repent and come unto my Beloved Son, them will I cut off from among my people, O house of Israel; And I will execute vengeance and fury upon them, even as upon the heathen, such as they have not heard. But if they will repent and hearken unto my words, and harden not their hearts, I will establish my church among them, and they shall come in unto the covenant and be numbered among this the remnant of Jacob, unto whom I have given this land for their inheritance; And they shall assist my people, the remnant of Jacob, and also as many of the house of Israel as shall come, that they may build a city, which shall be called the New Jerusalem. And then shall they assist my people that they may be gathered in, who are scattered upon all the face of the land, in unto the New Jerusalem. And then shall the power of heaven come down among them; and I also will be in the midst. And then shall the work of the Father commence at that day, even when this gospel shall be preached among the remnant of this people. Verily I say unto you, at that day shall the work of the Father commence among all the dispersed of my people, yea, even the tribes which have been lost, which the Father hath led away out of Jerusalem. Yea, the work shall commence among all the dispersed of my people, with the Father to prepare the way whereby they may come unto me, that they may call on the Father in my name. Yea, and then shall the work commence, with the Father among all nations in preparing the way whereby his people may be gathered home to the land of their inheritance. And they shall go out from all nations; and they shall not go out in haste, nor go by flight, for I will go before them, saith the Father, and I will be their rearward. (3 Nephi 21:5-6,9-29.)

Orson Pratt summed up this chapter this way:

There are four major events to take place in the Last Days with regards to these people. First, a remnant will be converted; second, Zion will be redeemed and all among the Gentiles who believe will assist this remnant of Jacob in building the New Jerusalem; third, missionaries will be sent...to gather all...His people unto the New Jerusalem; fourth, the power of heaven will be made manifest in the midst of this people, and the Lord also will be in their midst. (Orson Pratt, JD 17:302.)

None of these items on Elder Pratt's list has yet occurred.

Some minority of the Latter-day Saints will repent from their false traditions, receive a covenant, and be numbered among the remnant of Jacob (see 3 Nephi 16:10-16), but most will be destroyed in the calamites the Lord has promised to bring at the conclusion of the space allotted for the Gentiles to repent:

Verily, verily, I say unto you, darkness covereth the earth, and gross darkness the minds of the people, and all flesh has become corrupt before my face. Behold, vengeance cometh speedily upon the inhabitants of the earth, a day of wrath, a day of burning, a day of desolation, of weeping, of mourning, and of lamentation; and as a whirlwind it shall come upon all the face of the earth, saith the Lord. And upon my house shall it begin, and from my house shall it go forth, saith the Lord; First among those among you, saith the Lord, who have professed to know my name and have not known me, and have blasphemed against me in the midst of my house, saith the Lord. (D&C 112:23-26.)

Those who profess to know God's name but do not really known Him[539] and who have blasphemed against him in the midst of his house[540] are those upon whom this judgment will fall.

---

[539] Interestingly, the brethren have, in recent years, spoken much on how their "special witness" is of the name of Christ, and how they do not need to see him to have this special witness. See "Witnesses" chapter.

[540] "My house" can have many meanings, such as those who believe in God, or such as the temple. Blaspheming against God in the midst of his house could refer to the abomination of desolation, which occurs when something abominable happens in the temple that causes God to make desolate the people who have committed the offense. The abomination of desolation is an act that happened in ancient times and is prophesied to happen again in our day.

While modern Mormons consider themselves the Lord's chosen people, the scriptures suggest they are little more than a group doomed to failure whose singular achievement will be having preserved the Book of Mormon for the Lamanites to later accept.

What God has Said About the LDS Church

We don't have to guess how the Lord feels about the church. He has spoken about it several times in what we regard as scripture.

In 1831, the Lord said:

> Wherefore, let all men beware how they take my name in their lips— For behold, verily I say, that many there be who are under this condemnation, who use the name of the Lord, and use it in vain, having not authority. Wherefore, let the church repent of their sins, and I, the Lord, will own them; otherwise they shall be cut off. Remember that that which cometh from above is sacred, and must be spoken with care, and by constraint of the Spirit; and in this there is no condemnation, and ye receive the Spirit through prayer; wherefore, without this there remaineth condemnation. (D&C 63:61-64.)

The Lord said that there were people in the church attributing things to him that he had not said, and doing things in his name he had not commanded. He said that the church needed to repent or else they would be cut off. He said that those who claim their own words are God's words, when the Spirit has not spoken to them, are condemned.

The Lord spoke again about the church in 1832. He said:

> And whoso receiveth not my voice is not acquainted with my voice, and is not of me. And by this you may know the righteous from the wicked, and that the whole world groaneth under sin and darkness even now. And your minds in times past have been darkened because of unbelief, and because you have treated lightly the things you have received—Which vanity and unbelief have brought the whole church under condemnation. And this condemnation resteth upon the children of Zion, even all. And they shall remain under this condemnation until they repent and remember the new covenant, even the Book of Mormon and the former commandments which I have given them, not only to say, but to do according to that which I have written— That they may bring forth fruit meet for their Father's kingdom; otherwise there remaineth a scourge and judgment to be poured out upon the children of Zion. (D&C 84, 1832.)

Here, the Lord said that those who do not receive revelation are not of him. He said that the church had taken the revelations that Joseph Smith received lightly, and for this reason were under condemnation. He said that this condemnation applied to every member of the church, and would stand until they repented and obeyed the Book of Mormon and other commandments from God through Joseph Smith. Do we as a people obey the Book of Mormon and other commandments from God through Joseph Smith more than those in 1832? This question is discussed in the chapter entitled "The Preeminence of Joseph Smith's Teachings."

In 1841, the Lord spoke about the church for the last time as recorded in our scriptures. He said,

> ...build a house to my name, for the Most High to dwell therein. For there is not a place found on earth that he may come to and restore again that which was lost unto you, or which he hath taken away, even the fulness of the priesthood....But I command you, all ye my saints, to build a house unto me; and I grant unto you a sufficient time to build a house unto me; and during this time your baptisms shall be acceptable unto me. But behold, at the end of this appointment your baptisms for your dead shall not be acceptable unto me; and if you do not these things at the end of the appointment ye shall be rejected as a church, with your dead, saith the Lord your God. For verily I say unto you, that after you have had sufficient time to build a house to me, wherein the ordinance of baptizing for the dead belongeth, and for which the same was instituted from before the foundation of the world, your baptisms for your dead cannot be acceptable unto me; For therein are the keys of the holy priesthood ordained, that you may receive honor and glory. (D&C 124:27-34.)

Here, the Lord did not say the condemnation placed upon the church in 1832 had been lifted. Instead, he stated that the fullness of the priesthood had been taken away from the church.[541] He charged the church to build the Nauvoo

---

[541] The Lord himself prophesied that this would occur: "And thus commandeth the Father that I should say unto you: At that day when the Gentiles shall sin against my gospel, and shall reject the fullness of my gospel, and shall be lifted up in the pride of their hearts above all nations, and above all the people of the whole earth, and shall be filled with all manner of lyings, and of deceits, and of mischiefs, and all manner of hypocrisy, and murders, and priestcrafts, and whoredoms, and of secret abominations; and if they shall do all those things, and shall reject the fullness of my gospel, behold, saith the Father, I will bring the fullness of my gospel from among them." (3 Nephi 16:10, emphasis added.) Students of history know that, as antithetical as these descriptions seem to modern Mormons, they are an apt description for the actions of a surprising number of members of the church in the 1830s and 1840s. Danites were pillaging the countryside under secret oaths, priestcrafts abounded, an astounding number of brethren and sisters were

temple, and stated that if the task was not completed in a certain time, the church would be rejected with its dead. The Saints did not build the Nauvoo temple, spending their money on lavish brick homes and a Masonic temple instead of the Lord's house.[542] The Saints fled Nauvoo before the temple was completed. God never came to the temple, and he never restored anything in it. [543] Additionally, the promised penalties fell upon them prior to the

---

committing adultery, money was being embezzled, and financial speculation was out of control.

[542] "I never shall forget the words he spoke on the first Sunday after I came to Nauvoo. The temple was built a few feet above the ground. While preaching he pointed towards it and said, 'The Lord has commanded us to build that temple. We want to build it, but we have not the means. There are people in this city who have the means, but they will not let us have them. What shall we do with such people? I say damn them!' and then he sat down." (recollection of Elder William E. Jones.)

[543] Joseph taught that Elijah would come to the Nauvoo temple and restore all things ever revealed, including a priesthood which holds the priesthood by right from the Eternal Gods and not by descent, the administration of the Levites in the temple, including animal sacrifice, and the covenants made to the fathers (the patriarchs, not our ancestors). Though the modern Mormonism claims all these rights (other than animal sacrifice, which they teach will not be practiced again), they must answer where they obtained them, as Joseph preached until his death that they had not yet been restored, and that they would not be restored until the Nauvoo temple was completed. This never happened. For the reader's benefit, some of the passages of Joseph's sermons where he lays out these points are reprinted below (spelling preserved as recorded):

"it is generally supposed that Sacrifice was entirely done away when the great sacrifice was offered up—and that there will be no necessity for the ordinance of Sacrifice in future, but those who assert this, are certainly not acquainted with the duties, privileges and authority of the priesthood. or with the prophets The offering of Sacrifice has ever been connected and forms a part of the duties of the priesthood. It began with the priesthood and will be continued until after the coming of Christ from generation to generation—We frequently have mention made of the offering of Sacrifice by the servants of the most high in ancient days prior to the law of moses, which ordinances will be continued when the priesthood is restored with all its authority power and blessings. Elijah was the last prophet that held the keys of this priesthood, and who will, before the last dispensation, restore the authority and delive[r] the Keys of this priesthood in order that all the ordinances may be attended to in righteousness." ("Words of Joseph Smith", 5 Oct 1840) "the offring of Sacrifice which also shall be continued at the last time, for all the ordinances and duties that ever have been required by the priesthood under the direction and commandments of the Almighty in the last dispensation at the end thereof in any of the dispensations, shall all be had in the last dispensation. Therefore all things had under the Authority of the Priesthood at any former period shall be had again—bringing to pass the restoration spoken of by the mouth of all the Holy Prophets." (Words of Joseph Smith) "It will be necessary here to make a few observations on the doctrine, set forth in the above quotation, As it is generally supposed that Sacrifice was entirely

completion of the building, demonstrating that the temple was not completed in time to fulfill God's commandment.

Joseph repeatedly warned that there was a time given by the Lord for them to build the temple, and, as the Lord said in D&C 124, if the Saints didn't fulfill the commission in time, they would lose the opportunity to gain the promised blessings.

> I will now ask this assembly and all the Saints if you will now build this house and receive the ordinances and blessings which God has in store for you; or will you not build unto the Lord this house, and let

---

done away when the great sacrife was offered up—and that there will be no necessity for the ordinance of Sacrifice in future, but those who assert this, are certainly not aquainted with the duties, privileges and authority of the priesthood. or with the prophets The offering of Sacrifice has ever been connected and forms a part of the duties of the priesthood. It began with the prieshood and will be continued untill after the coming of Christ from generation to generation—We freequently have mention made of the offering of Sacrifice by the servants of the most high in antient days prior to the law of moses, See which ordinances will be continued when the priesthood is restored with all its authority power and blessings. Elijah was the last prophet that held the keys of this priesthood, and who will, before the last dispensation, restore the authority and delive[r] the Keys of this priesthood in order that all the ordinances may be attended to in righteousness." (Words of Joseph Smith, 5 Oct 1840) "Elijah was the last Prophet that held the keys of the Priesthood, and who will, before the last dispensation, restore the authority and deliver the keys of the Priesthood, in order that all ordinances may be attended to in righteousness...'And I will send Elijah the Prophet before the great and terrible day of the Lord,' etc., etc. Why send Elijah? Because he holds the keys of the authority to administer in all the ordinances of the Priesthood; and without the authority is given, the ordinances could not be administered in righteousness." (HC 4:207-212) "...it is generally supposed that sacrifice was entirely done away when the Great Sacrifice the sacrifice of the Lord Jesus was offered up...but those who assert this are certainly not acquainted with the duties, privileges and authority of the Priesthood, or with the Prophets. .... These sacrifices, as well as every ordinance belonging to the Priesthood, will, when the Temple of the Lord shall be built, and the sons of Levi be purified, be fully restored and attended to in all their powers, ramifications, and blessings....else how can the restitution of all things spoken of by the Holy Prophets be brought to pass[?]" "how shall god come to the rescue of this generation. he shall send Elijah law revealed to Moses in Horeb—never was revealed to the C. of Israel and he shall reveal the covenants to seal the hearts of the fathers to the children and the children to the fathers.—anointing & sealing—called elected and made sure without father &c. a priesthood which holds the priesthood by right from the Eternal Gods.—and not by descent from father and mother" (Words of Joseph Smith, 27 Aug 1843) "The world is reserved unto burning in the last days—he shall send Elijah the prophet. and he shall reveal the covenants of the fathers in relation to the children.—and the children and the covenants of the children in relation to the fathers." (WoJS 13 Aug 1843.)

Him pass by and bestow these blessings upon another people? I pause for a reply. (June 11, 1843, DHC 5:423-427.)

In April 1842, the Prophet said:

The Church is not fully organized, in its proper order, and cannot be, until the Temple is completed, where places will be provided for the administration of the ordinances of the Priesthood. (History of the Church, 4:603; from a discourse given by Joseph Smith on Apr. 28, 1842, in Nauvoo, Illinois; reported by Eliza R. Snow.)

This did not occur.

The three times God spoke on the subject, he indicated that the church needed to repent, that they were under condemnation, and that they were rejected with their dead. If any claims that the LDS church is the Lord's church, they have the obligation of pointing out where he has reversed his position as clearly defined in the Doctrine and Covenants on three occasions.

Can God Withdraw from the LDS Church?

Modern Mormons claim that God could never turn away from the LDS church. For example, Elder Holland recently wrote:

The gospel of Jesus Christ is the most certain, the most secure, the most reliable, and the most rewarding truth on earth and in heaven, in time and in eternity. Nothing—not anything, not anyone, not any influence—will keep this Church from fulfilling its mission and realizing its destiny declared from before the foundation of the world. Ours is that fail-safe, inexorable, indestructible dispensation of the fulness of the gospel. There is no need to be afraid or tentative about the future.Unlike every other era before us, this dispensation will not experience an institutional apostasy; it will not see a loss of priesthood keys; it will not suffer a cessation of revelation from the voice of Almighty God. Individuals will apostatize or turn a deaf ear to heaven, but never again will the dispensation collectively do so. What a secure thought! What a day in which to live! (Elder Jeffery R. Holland, Facebook, May 27th, 2015.)

The scriptures and words of early LDS leaders disagree.

There are innumerable examples in the Old Testament of God rejecting his covenant people through their iniquity (see, for example, Jeremiah 12:7-17, Jeremiah 18:5-10, Isaiah 1:21-23, Hosea 1:8-9, Hosea 4, Ezekiel 18, Ezekiel 22:17-18, and Zephaniah 3:11). Modern Mormons do not dispute that when ancient people deviated from God after he established a covenant with them, they were cut off. They dispute that God would ever have a reason to cut the LDS off. They believe that the Lord has promised that the LDS church will continue in his graces until Christ comes again, a position that ignores that, by 1841, the Lord had already told the church that it was in sin, under condemnation, and rejected.

Early leaders understood that the Lord could cut off the church. They hastened to finish the Nauvoo temple after the death of Joseph for fear that they would be cut off for disobeying God's command. Orson Hyde stated:

> If we moved forward and finished this house we should be received and accepted as a church with our dead, but if not we should be rejected with our dead. These things have inspired and stimulated us to action in the finishing of it which through the blessing of God we have been enabled to accomplish and prepared it for dedication. In doing this we have only been saved as it were by the skin of our teeth. (Wilford Woodruff Journal, May 8, 1846.)

Heber C. Kimball taught that God could take the priesthood from the Saints through disobedience:

> We receive the priesthood and power and authority. If we make a bad use of the priesthood, so you not see that the day will come when God will reckon with us, and he will take it from us and give it to those who will make better use of it? (JD 6: 125.)

George A. Smith said the Lord could abandon the Saints in favor of another people,

> God has set his hand at the present time to establish his kingdom. But unless the Saints will so live and so exert themselves that they can preserve the purity of the holy Priesthood among them, the work will be left to other people. (JD 6: 161.)

There are many additional witnesses that the church can be cut off. The Lord said in D&C 63: "let the church repent of their sins, and I, the Lord, will own them; otherwise they shall be cut off." (D&C 63.) If it was the inalterable destiny of the LDS church to usher in the second coming of Christ, why would Christ himself tell them it was possible for them to be cut off? If it was not possible for the church to sin sufficiently to be cut off, why would God say that it was possible? If it were not possible for the Lord to choose another people, why did Joseph threaten the Saints who were sluggish in responding to the commandment to build the Nauvoo temple:

> I will now ask this assembly and all the Saints if you will now build this house and receive the ordinances and blessings which God has in store for you; or will you not build unto the Lord this house, and let Him pass by and bestow these blessings upon another people? I pause for a reply. (June 11, 1843, DHC 5:423-427.)

If, once given, God cannot remove the keys because of disobedience or ordinances changed contrary to his word, why did Joseph Smith say:

> The power, glory, and blessings of the priesthood could not continue with those who received ordination only as their righteousness continued, 11 for Cain also being authorized to offer sacrifice but not offering it in righteousness, therefore he was cursed. It signifies then, that the ordinances must be kept in the very way God has appointed, otherwise their priesthood will prove a cursing instead of a blessing. (Joseph Smith, 5 Oct 1840, Robert B. Thompson record.)

In order to believe that God cannot cut off the LDS, one would have to disbelieve each of these statements from Joseph Smith and God himself. They are too plain to be misunderstood, and therefore must be somehow directly ignored.

Perhaps one reason why there is such resistance to the idea to God cannot cut off the LDS is a misunderstanding of Daniel's prophecy of the stone cut without hands rolling forth until the second coming.

> From thence shall the gospel roll forth unto the ends of the earth, as the stone which is cut out of the mountain without hands shall roll forth, until it has filled the whole earth. (D&C 65:2.)

The gospel was revealed through Joseph Smith. The kingdom was revealed by Joseph Smith. The gospel is not the church, and the kingdom is not the church. Neither the gospel nor the kingdom are the exclusive property of the LDS church. To the degree that the church turns away from the gospel as revealed through Joseph Smith, they turn away from the kingdom. Or, as the Lord said,

> I am the true vine, and my Father is the husbandman. Every branch in me that beareth not fruit he taketh away: and every branch that beareth fruit, he purgeth it, that it may bring forth more fruit. (John 15:1-2.)

If the church ceases to bear fruit, he will cut it off and burn it (see Jacob 5), and turn to another people.

The prophecies state that God will do a great and marvelous work involving the Lamanites, and that the LDS church will not preside over this work, but will be cut off as a result of their turning away from the commandments and ordinances revealed through Joseph, modern Mormons who repent of the traditions of the fathers and accept the Lord's teachings from Joseph will remain members of the kingdom. In fact, the priesthood and everything else restored by Joseph can and will remain on the earth independent of the success or failure of the LDS church. The destiny of the LDS church was never to establish Zion, but to act as a seed pod of sorts to preserve the Book of Mormon, the teachings of Joseph, and the priesthood[544] for a time to deliver it to another people who would honor and appreciate them. As the Lord prophesied:

> But if they [the Gentiles] will not turn unto me, and hearken unto my voice, I will suffer them, yea, I will suffer my people, O house of Israel, that they shall go through among them, and shall tread them down, and they shall be as salt that hath lost its savor, which is thenceforth good for nothing but to be cast out, and to be trodden under foot of my people, O house of Israel. (3 Nephi 16:15.)

Those Gentiles who are trodden down "shall be as salt that hath lost its savor." In the Doctrine and Covenants we are given a clear definition of what this means.

> When men are called unto mine everlasting gospel, and covenant with an everlasting covenant, they are accounted as the salt of the earth and the savor of men; They are called to be the savor of men; therefore, if that salt of the earth lose its savor, behold, it is thenceforth good for nothing only to be cast out and trodden under the feet of men. (D&C 101:39-40.)

These Gentiles are the LDS: the only ones in the last days who have been called unto the everlasting gospel and have made an everlasting covenant with God. According to these scriptures, these covenant people will reject the fulness of the gospel that will be taken away and given to the house of Israel. When read in context, it is difficult to interpret these scriptures any other way.

Conclusion

Some modern Mormons would contend that God could not have cut off the LDS church, because if he had they would not have the benefits they enjoy as members of the church. They are ignorant of scripture, which voluminously attests to the general failure of people who have been cut off to notice.

Isaiah speaks of a people who are "weighed down by sin," "forsaken Jehovah," and "lapsed into apostasy," yet they make "abundant sacrifices" in the temple, has "meetings at the New Month and on the Sabbath," and "spread[s] forth [their] hands" in temple ordinances (Isaiah 1:4,11,14-15, Gileadi Translation.) They "importune me daily, eager to learn my ways, like a nation practicing righteousness and not forsaking the precepts of its God." (Isaiah 58:2, Gileadi Translation.)

---

[544] "God will preserve a portion of the meek and the humble of this people to bear off the Kingdom to the inhabitants of the earth, and will defend His Priesthood; for it is the last time, the last gathering time; and He will not suffer the Priesthood to be again driven from the earth." (Brigham Young, JD 2: 184.)

In 3 Nephi, chapter 27, the Lord gives the criteria by which we can determine that an organization is His church. First it must be called by His name. Second, it must be built on His gospel. Third, it must demonstrate the works of God (examples in 3 Ne. 26:11). While the LDS church fulfills the first requirement, its institutional neglect and active abandonment of the gospel as revealed through Joseph Smith suggests that the second criteria is not met. A Mormon from 1842 would not recognize the church today if he were teleported to our day. What about the third criteria? Does the church and its members bear the fruits of the gospel? On Sept 13th, 2015 Elder Ballard praised the Utah South area. These are the accomplishments he lauded them for:

- A nationwide polling service found Utah to be the most religious state.
- Three missions.
- Six temples with two under construction.
- The largest religious university in America.
- Vibrant institutes of religion programs associated with the great colleges and universities in the area.
- An expanding Missionary Training Center in Provo.
- Numerous ward, stake, and seminary buildings.

Where are the fruits? All of these items—all of them—are a result of how much money a people has. As demonstrated by the Israelites and by King Noah's people, all of these characteristics can be demonstrated while being in complete apostasy from God. How many members of the church have been baptized by fire? How many prophesy? How many miraculously heal the sick, the blind, or the deaf? How many have seen angels? How many have seen God? Instead of being known for these fruits, Utah leads the nation in suicides per capita, porn use, and prescription antidepressants.

So many times, modern Mormons contest "But this is the Lord's church, therefore whatever it does must be sanctioned by God." Wouldn't it be nice if we could point to the church's actions and say, "these match God's word, therefore this is God's church" rather than using the claim that it is God's church (a claim God himself hasn't made since before 1832 when he said this church was under condemnation) to justify actions that are contrary to God's revealed word?

Modern Mormons truly are dripping in pride about their supposed exalted status. Yet, the Lord has explicitly rejected them. Though their failure as an institution is sealed, the fate of each individual member is still at stake. Chuck Baldwin once said,

> What happens when an institution becomes more important than the cause for which the institution was formed? How long should people who believe in the cause remain loyal to such an institution? And at

what point does loyalty to such an institution comprise an abandonment of the cause itself?

As the church continues to turn away in greater and greater degrees from the restored gospel of Jesus Christ, members must choose: will they align their actions and beliefs to God's word as revealed in scripture, or will they join the church in drifting further and further away from God?

> They wear stiff necks and high heads; yea, and because of pride, and wickedness, and abominations, and whoredoms, they have all gone astray save it be a few, who are the humble followers of Christ; nevertheless, they are led, that in many instances they do err because they are taught by the precepts of men. (2 Nephi 28:14.)

Only those few true followers of Jesus will be able to escape the calamity that is about to fall on the Gentiles, and be numbered among the remnant of Jacob.

Where Do We Go from Here?

The Book of Mormon is full of descriptions of our day, with the warning that

> ...when ye shall see these things come among you that ye shall awake to a sense of your awful situation (Ether 8:24).

The judgment to come upon the Gentiles is sealed and is coming fast. However, there is still time for individuals to repent and escape the calamities ordained for the collective whole. No matter how entrenched you were in the false traditions of men, you can be forgiven instantaneously if you will only seek God and seek to do his will:

> But if the wicked will turn from all his sins that he hath committed, and keep all my statutes, and do that which is lawful and right, he shall surely live, he shall not die. All his transgressions that he hath committed, they shall not be mentioned unto him: in his righteousness that he hath done he shall live. (Ezekiel 18:21-22.)

This entire book is filled with instructions on what to do in context of what not to do, but for the sake of leaving on a constructive note, let us recap.

Stop listening to men.[545] They don't control your eternal salvation. Only God does that. Your task is to find and obey God's word, not man's

---

[545] The Lord told me to say: You prophets and priests think so little of me, the Lord, that you even sin in my own temple! Now I will punish you with disaster, and you will slip and fall in the darkness. I, the Lord, have spoken. The prophets in Samaria...led my people astray. And you prophets in Jerusalem are even worse. You're unfaithful in marriage and never tell the truth. You even lead others to sin instead of helping them turn back to me. You and the people of Jerusalem are evil like Sodom and Gomorrah. You prophets in Jerusalem have spread evil everywhere. That's why I, the Lord, promise to give you bitter poison to eat and drink. The Lord said: Don't listen to the lies of these false prophets, you people of Judah! The message they preach is something they imagined; it did not come from me, the Lord All-Powerful. These prophets go to people who refuse to respect me and who are stubborn and do whatever they want. The prophets tell them, "The Lord has promised everything will be fine." But I, the Lord, tell you that these prophets have never attended a meeting of my council in heaven or heard me speak. They are evil! So in my anger I will strike them like a violent storm. I won't calm down, until I have finished what I have decided to do. Someday you will understand exactly what I mean. I did not send these

word. The distinction is of utmost importance, and something that you need to take the responsibility for, because you will be held accountable.

Give heed to what Joseph restored. Read the Book of Mormon. Pay attention to what it actually says, and try to forget what you've been told it says. Study what Joseph wrote and spoke. Find it online. Find it in "Words of Joseph Smith" or "The Joseph Smith Papers Project." Study the other scriptures. Don't forget the Old Testament. So much of what those prophets taught applies today.[546]

---

prophets or speak to them, but they ran to find you and to preach their message. If they had been in a meeting of my council in heaven, they would have told you people of Judah to give up your sins and come back to me....These unfaithful prophets claim that I have given them a dream or a vision, and then they tell lies in my name. But everything they say comes from their own twisted minds. How long can this go on? They tell each other their dreams and try to get my people to reject me, just as their ancestors left me and worshiped Baal. Their dreams and my truth are as different as straw and wheat. But when prophets speak for me, they must say only what I have told them. My words are a powerful fire; they are a hammer that shatters rocks. These unfaithful prophets claim I give them their dreams, but it isn't true. I didn't choose them to be my prophets, and yet they babble on and on, speaking in my name, while stealing words from each other. And when my people hear these liars, they are led astray instead of being helped. So I warn you that I am now the enemy of these prophets. I, the Lord, have spoken. (Jeremiah 23:,11-22,25-32 , CEV.)

[546] For example: "And the word of the Lord came unto me, saying, Son of man, prophesy against the shepherds of Israel, prophesy, and say unto them, Thus saith the Lord God unto the shepherds; Woe be to the shepherds of Israel that do feed themselves! should not the shepherds feed the flocks? Ye eat the fat, and ye clothe you with the wool, ye kill them that are fed: but ye feed not the flock. The diseased have ye not strengthened, neither have ye healed that which was sick, neither have ye bound up that which was broken, neither have ye brought again that which was driven away, neither have ye sought that which was lost; but with force and with cruelty have ye ruled them. And they were scattered, because there is no shepherd: and they became meat to all the beasts of the field, when they were scattered. My sheep wandered through all the mountains, and upon every high hill: yea, my flock was scattered upon all the face of the earth, and none did search or seek after them. Therefore, ye shepherds, hear the word of the Lord; As I live, saith the Lord God, surely because my flock became a prey, and my flock became meat to every beast of the field, because there was no shepherd, neither did my shepherds search for my flock, but the shepherds fed themselves, and fed not my flock; Therefore, O ye shepherds, hear the word of the Lord; Thus saith the Lord God; Behold, I am against the shepherds; and I will require my flock at their hand, and cause them to cease from feeding the flock; neither shall the shepherds feed themselves any more; for I will deliver my flock from their mouth, that they may not be meat for them. For thus saith the Lord God; Behold, I, *even* I, will both search my sheep, and seek them out. As a shepherd seeketh out his flock in the day that he is among his sheep that are scattered; so will I seek out my sheep, and will deliver them out of all places where they have been scattered in the cloudy and dark day. And I will bring them out from

We have a limited amount of time before the Lord returns, and significant desolation has to occur even before then. Use your time for the weightier matters. Only very few will be spared.

> But if a man be just, and do that which is lawful and right, And hath not eaten upon the mountains, neither hath lifted up his eyes to the idols of the house of Israel, neither hath defiled his neighbour's wife, neither hath come near to a menstruous woman, And hath not oppressed any, but hath restored to the debtor his pledge, hath spoiled none by violence, hath given his bread to the hungry, and

---

the people, and gather them from the countries, and will bring them to their own land, and feed them upon the mountains of Israel by the rivers, and in all the inhabited places of the country. I will feed them in a good pasture, and upon the high mountains of Israel shall their fold be: there shall they lie in a good fold, and in a fat pasture shall they feed upon the mountains of Israel. I will feed my flock, and I will cause them to lie down, saith the Lord God. I will seek that which was lost, and bring again that which was driven away, and will bind up that which was broken, and will strengthen that which was sick: but I will destroy the fat and the strong; I will feed them with judgment. And as for you, O my flock, thus saith the Lord God; Behold, I judge between cattle and cattle, between the rams and the he goats. Seemeth it a small thing unto you to have eaten up the good pasture, but ye must tread down with your feet the residue of your pastures? and to have drunk of the deep waters, but ye must foul the residue with your feet? And as for my flock, they eat that which ye have trodden with your feet; and they drink that which ye have fouled with your feet. Therefore thus saith the Lord God unto them; Behold, I, even I, will judge between the fat cattle and between the lean cattle. Because ye have thrust with side and with shoulder, and pushed all the diseased with your horns, till ye have scattered them abroad; Therefore will I save my flock, and they shall no more be a prey; and I will judge between cattle and cattle. And I will set up one shepherd over them, and he shall feed them, even my servant David; he shall feed them, and he shall be their shepherd. And I the Lord will be their God, and my servant David a prince among them; I the Lord have spoken it. And I will make with them a covenant of peace, and will cause the evil beasts to cease out of the land: and they shall dwell safely in the wilderness, and sleep in the woods. And I will make them and the places round about my hill a blessing; and I will cause the shower to come down in his season; there shall be showers of blessing. And the tree of the field shall yield her fruit, and the earth shall yield her increase, and they shall be safe in their land, and shall know that I am the Lord, when I have broken the bands of their yoke, and delivered them out of the hand of those that served themselves of them. And they shall no more be a prey to the heathen, neither shall the beast of the land devour them; but they shall dwell safely, and none shall make them afraid. And I will raise up for them a plant of renown, and they shall be no more consumed with hunger in the land, neither bear the shame of the heathen any more. Thus shall they know that I the Lord their God am with them, and that they, even the house of Israel, are my people, saith the Lord God. And ye my flock, the flock of my pasture, are men, and I am your God, saith the Lord God." (Ezekiel 34:1-31.)

hath covered the naked with a garment; He that hath not given forth upon usury, neither hath taken any increase, that hath withdrawn his hand from iniquity, hath executed true judgment between man and man, Hath walked in my statutes, and hath kept my judgments, to deal truly; he is just, he shall surely live, saith the Lord God. (Ezekiel 18:5-9.)

Seek for the experiences you have not yet received, such as baptism by fire, an audience with Christ, and the promise of eternal life. Getting there will require a focus on yourself, your family, and your neighbors instead of outward checklists. Stop wasting time in the hamster wheel of temple ordinances,[547] family history, and church callings.

It is of extreme importance that you do whatever you can to help the oppressed, wherever they are found.[548] Seek out and help the poor.

Thus speaketh the Lord of hosts, saying, Execute true judgment, and shew mercy and compassions every man to his brother: And oppress not the widow, nor the fatherless, the stranger, nor the poor; and let none of you imagine evil against his brother in your heart. But they refused to hearken, and pulled away the shoulder, and stopped their ears, that they should not hear. Yea, they made their hearts as an adamant stone, lest they should hear the law, and the words which the Lord of hosts hath sent in his spirit by the former prophets: therefore came a great wrath from the Lord of hosts. (Zechariah 7:9-12.)

Paying tithing as the Lord has revealed will provide sufficient funds for everyone to help the poor more than they currently are.[549]

---

[547] "Wherewith shall I come before the Lord, and bow myself before the high God? shall I come before him with burnt offerings, with calves of a year old? Will the Lord be pleased with thousands of rams, or with ten thousands of rivers of oil? shall I give my firstborn for my transgression, the fruit of my body for the sin of my soul? He hath shewed thee, O man, what is good; and what doth the Lord require of thee, but to do justly, and to love mercy, and to walk humbly with thy God? (Micah 6:6-8) Get a parachute yourself before you worry about sealing your ancestors to you. They cannot be saved until you are, and you cannot be saved by sealing yourselves to them if they have not been saved.

[548] "Thus saith the Lord; Execute ye judgment and righteousness, and deliver the spoiled out of the hand of the oppressor: and do no wrong..." (Jeremiah 22:3.)

[549] "But in aiding and blessing the poor I do not believe in allowing my charities to go through the hands of a set of robbers who pocket nine-tenths themselves, and give one-tenth to the poor." (BY, Journal of Discourses, 18:357) Outsourcing your charity to the church guarantees that less than 100% of your donation will be spent on the purposes you intend (see "No Poor Among Them").

Wash yourselves clean: remove your wicked deeds from before my eyes; cease to do evil. Learn to do good: demand justice, stand up for the oppressed; plead the cause of the fatherless, appeal on behalf of the widow. (Isaiah 1:16-17.)

Help others break out of the bondage of false traditions. In speaking of what to be done to qualify for Zion, Zechariah was told: "These are the things that ye shall do; Speak ye every man the truth to his neighbor..." (Zechariah 8:16) As you have been awakened, take efforts to wake up others. Though time is short, be patient and long-suffering. Use wisdom and tact to teach others on their level to give them the greatest chance of listening.

To summarize it all: "Respect and obey God! That is what life is all about." (Eccl. 12:13, CEV.) May God bless all of us to flee from false traditions, whatever they may be. Let us not exercise the fruitless religion of our fathers that brings:

> Knowledge of speech, but not of silence;
> Knowledge of words, and ignorance of the Word.
> All our knowledge brings us nearer to our ignorance,
> All our ignorance brings us nearer to death,
> But nearness to death no nearer to GOD. (TS Eliot)

AMEN.

28601051R00218

Made in the USA
San Bernardino, CA
02 January 2016